A Global Perspective on the European Economic Crisis

T0298873

The financial and economic crisis in Europe is not over, and the radically opposing strategies on how to proceed has only increased the complexity of problems in the region, revealing the shortcomings of the EU's architecture. The European Union, perhaps for the first time in its history of more than seventy years, is being perceived as a threat to the financial and monetary stability of the world.

A Global Perspective on the European Economic Crisis explores the connection between internal EU actions and institutions and the external factors that influence the ongoing response to the European crisis. With a unique collection of international and interdisciplinary essays, this book considers the complex macroeconomic and challenging political landscape of Europe, looking at how and why the European Union is untenable in its current state. The chapters outline what should be done to make the common currency area more resilient, and explain why external events are particularly problematic for the EU, ultimately offering suggestions for what Europeans should do in order to avoid harmful internal consequences.

This volume confronts the causes of the crisis' persistence, its economic and political consequences, and the impact of more recent events and policy decisions. It will be of interest to researchers and policy-makers keen to understand the EU relations and the influence of international organizations in the European economic crisis.

Bruno Dallago is Professor of Economics and Director of the Research Unit on Local Development at the University of Trento, Italy.

Gert Guri is External Lecturer of two International Master Programs at the University of Trento and Link Campus University of Rome, Italy.

John McGowan is a Professor of English and Comparative Literature at the University of North Carolina, USA.

Routledge Studies in the European Economy

A Global Perspective on the European Economic Crisis

Edited by
Bruno Dallago, Gert Guri
and John McGowan

LONDON AND NEW YORK

First published 2016
by Routledge
2 Park Square, Milton Park, Abingdon, Oxon OX14 4RN

and by Routledge
52 Vanderbilt Avenue, New York, NY 10017

First issued in paperback 2020

Routledge is an imprint of the Taylor & Francis Group, an informa business

British Library Cataloguing in Publication Data
A catalogue record for this book is available from the British Library

Library of Congress Cataloging in Publication Data
Names: Dallago, Bruno, 1950- editor. | Guri, Gert, editor.
Title: A global perspective on the European economic crisis / edited by Bruno Dallago, Gert Guri and John McGowan.
Description: New York : Routledge, 2016.
Identifiers: LCCN 2015044454| ISBN 9781138189089 (hardback) | ISBN 9781315641829 (ebook)Subjects: LCSH: Financial crises--European Union countries. | Eurozone. | Monetary policy--European Union countries. | Europe--Economic integration. | European Union countries--Politics and government--21st century.
Classification: LCC HB3782 .G567 2016 | DDC 330.94--dc23
LC record available at http://lccn.loc.gov/2015044454

ISBN 13: 978-0-367-66841-9 (pbk)
ISBN 13: 978-1-138-18908-9 (hbk)

Typeset in Times New Roman
by HWA Text and Data Management, London

Contents

Figures

Tables

Contributors

Nicola Acocella was Professor Emeritus of Economic Policy at the University of Rome 'Sapienza' from 1984 to 2011.

Eric Brunat is Professor of Economics at the University Savoie Mont Blanc, France. He holds honorary doctorates from the State Universities of Sochi (2010) and Irkutsk (2012), Russia. Previously he was senior economist for UNDP in Russia, Belarus and Moldova, he is also an associate member of the Savoie Academy of Arts, Sciences and Literature.

László Csaba is Distinguished Professor of International Political Economy at the Central European University and Corvinus University of Budapest, as well as a Member of the Hungarian Academy of Sciences.

Bruno Dallago is Professor of Economics and Director of the Research Unit on Local Development at the University of Trento, Italy.

Scott Greer, a political scientist, is Associate Professor of Health Management and Policy at the University of Michigan School of Public Health, USA and Senior Expert Advisor on Health Governance for the European Observatory on Health Systems and Policies, Brussels. He researches the politics of health policies, with a special focus on the politics and policies of the European Union and the impact of federalism on health care.

Klaus Gretschmann is a former Director-General in the EU Council of Ministers in Brussels, Belgium and was involved in preparing the EU summits for 10 years. Previously, he served as Director-General for Economics in the German Chancellor's Office. He studied economics at the Universities of Cologne, Vienna and Rome, and taught public finance and international political economy at several universities worldwide. He is the author of numerous publications. Currently, he works as an independent adviser and as the President of CATE: www.kgr-consilium.eu.

Gert Guri is External Lecturer of two international master programs at th University of Trento and Link Campus University of Rome, Italy.

Holly Jarman is Assistant Professor of Health Management and Policy at th University of Michigan School of Public Health, USA. Her work focuse on the politics of crossborder trade, with special interest in patient mobility tobacco control, and information.

Jacob Kipp holds a PhD from Penn State University, and taught Russian militar; history at Kansas state University, Miami University and the University o Kansas. He served as Director of the US Army Foreign Military Studies Offic and Deputy Director of the US Army School of Advanced Military Studies.

Paul Marer is Professor of Business at the Business School of the Centra European University, Budapest, Hungary. Previously, he was Professor o International Business at the Kelley School of Indiana University. For most o his career, his research has focused on the economies of Central and Easter Europe.

John McGowan is a Professor of English and Comparative Literature at th University of North Carolina, USA.

Joachim Möller is full Professor in the Department of Economics at th University of Regensburg, Germany, and is the Director of the Federal Labou Office's Institute of Employment Research (IAB), Nuremberg. His researcl interests include regional and labour economics, empirical macroeconomic: and applied econometrics as well as East–West economic relationships.

Paolo Pasimeni is an Economist at the European Commission, Directorat General for Employment, Social Affairs and Inclusion, where he has beer working on cohesion policy, research and innovation, employment and socia affairs.

Simona Piattoni is Professor of Political Science at the University of Trento Italy, where she teaches comparative politics, European politics and loca government. She has previously taught at the University of Tromsø, Norway and University of Innsbruck, Austria. She has been visiting scholar at th European University Institute, Florence, Italy, and the University of California Berkeley.

John Pickles is the Earl N. Phillips Distinguished Professor of Internationa Studies in the Department of Geography at the University of North Carolina Chapel Hill, USA. He is a Fellow of the Institute for Arts and Humanities anc of the Center for Urban and Regions Studies, and serves on the advisory board: for the Center for European Studies, the Carolina Asia Center, the Center fo

Muslim and Middle Eastern Civilizations, the Office of Study Abroad, and the University Program in Cultural Studies. His research currently focuses on global production networks, European economic and social spaces, particularly post-socialist transformations in central Europe and Euro-Med neighborhood policies in southern Europe.

Steven Rosefielde received an AM degree in soviet regional studies (1967) and PhD in economics from Harvard University (1972). His special areas were Soviet economy and comparative systems theory including Asian economic systems, labor managed firms and international trade. He is Professor of Economics at the University of North Carolina, USA, and has served simultaneously as Adjunct Professor at various universities including the U.S. Naval Postgraduate School, Monterey.

Herman Mark Schwartz is Professor of Politics in the Department of Politics at the University of Virginia, USA.

Preface

This book deals with the connection between internal EU actions and institutions and the external factors that influence the ongoing response to the European crisis. The collected essays highlight the nature and relationship between challenges and opportunities deriving from this crisis. This book is a follow-up to the recent Routledge publication on the European crises edited by Bruno Dallago and John McGowan (*Crises in Europe in the Transatlantic Context: Economic and Political Appraisals*, 2015).

After more than seven years, the financial and economic crisis in Europe is not over. The persistence of the crisis, particularly in the Eurozone, reveals the shortcomings of the EU architecture. Indeed, these shortcomings are the dominant reason for the ailing economic performance and persistent financial instability. In consideration of this fact, the book highlights the deep nature of the European crisis and its many sides, but with an emphasis on the relation between internal factors and the international context.

Two issues receive particular attention in the book, issues that, taken together, highlight the structural and systemic nature of the European crisis:

1   the complex European macroeconomic and political landscape and challenges, with particular reference to the Eurozone; and
2   the interaction of the European Union with the external context, which is presenting growing challenges.

The Eurozone's apparently intractable problems have important institutional and economic causes. These include the incomplete European institutions and the lack of a common government of the economy. There is also the political weaknesses that derive from the fundamental lack of trust among the Eurozone countries, a situation that generated the insistence that national economies be balanced in the short-run through austerity policies. Successful but uncoordinated national reforms, such as the reform of the German labour market, may add further internal tensions and make the overall situation of the Eurozone more difficult. Mounting external tensions, such as those coming from the Ukrainian crisis and the tense relations with Russia, threaten to further increase the clashes of interests within the European Union. Clearly, at this point only a political agreement, or at least a compromise among the member countries, can make the crisis and institutional reforms manageable, particularly in the Eurozone.

The main themes of the book address both internal and external issues to the European Union and their interaction:

- the main causes of the institutional, economic and financial fragility of the EU and the policy and strategic instruments for strengthening its internal cooperation and coordination;
- the political and social dimensions of the institutional build-up of the European Union, which are placing potentially serious obstacles to the management of the economic and financial crises; and
- the external dimension of the crisis, that increases the distress of the EU. This is a dimension that is independent from the will of the EU, but that the EU has not managed well. The external dimension also includes the negative reading of the Eurozone situation by external partners and international organizations.

This new book complements the previous one in a variety of ways. While the former book was primarily focused on the origin of the crisis and the consequential transatlantic relations, the present one deals with the causes of the crisis's persistence, its economic and political consequences, and the impact of more recent events and policy decisions. Like the previous book, the present one follows an interdisciplinary approach (in particular, economics and political sciences) and includes a group of authors from different countries.

While the presence of the two editors of the previous book ensures a harmonized and further developed investigation of the European crises, the novelties in the analytical framework have called for a new set of contributors. The authors have developed their input starting from short drafts of papers initially presented in an international conference (Chapel Hill, 17–19 September 2014). This conference followed the conference held at the University of Trento on 7–9 November 2013. Thanks to the feedback provided by the discussants in the conference and the book editors, authors have revised and coordinated their drafts after the conference. To address components of the analysis missing in the conference program, the editors have solicited the input of two internationally renowned scholars (Gretschmann and Marer), who were not present at the conference.

Several people contributed to the organization of the conference and the elaboration of the present book. Without pretending completeness, we would like to thank the directors of the involved departments and centres for their support of the initiative. These are in particular the Center for European Studies, the Institute for the Arts and Humanities and the Departments of Economic and Political Science at UNC in Chapel Hill, the Department of Sociology and Social Research and the Research Unit on Local Development and Global Governance in Trento. Various people in the administration of both the Center for European Studies and the Institute for the Arts and Humanities contributed to the administrative requirements of the conference.

Several institutions supported the conference in various ways. The Institute for the Arts and Humanities in Chapel Hill and the Research Unit on Local Development and Global Governance in Trento co-sponsored the conference. The Center for European Studies and the Institute for the Arts and Humanities in Chapel Hill organized and hosted the conference. Crucial financial support was received from the Global Studies and the College of Arts and Sciences at UNC.

In addition, the initial phase, the conference in September 2014, of this project was supported by the European Union. The contents of this book are the sole responsibility of the individual authors and can in no way be taken to reflect the views of the European Union.

The contents of this book were developed under grant P015A140119 from the US Department of Education. However, these contents do not necessarily represent the policy of the US Department of Education, and you should not assume endorsement by the Federal Government.

Special thanks also go to the participants for their active and valuable contribution to a lively debate and for their collaborative cooperation in preparing this book. We would also like to thank Michael Ritter for his highly professional editing of the manuscript and Routledge (in particular Lisa Thomson) for collaboration and support in its preparation.

Bruno Dallago, Gert Guri and John McGowan

Introduction

Where is Europe headed?

Bruno Dallago, Gert Guri and John McGowan

The recent European drama over Greece, with radically opposing views and strategies on how to proceed, has raised alarm and suspicion in countries around the world. The European Union, perhaps for the first time in its peaceful and constructive history of more than 70 years, is being perceived as a threat to the financial and monetary stability of the world, a dead weight over economic expansion, and increasingly as a political risk. Particularly impressive were the appeals and the not-so-hidden diplomatic actions by the US administration and the governments of China and Russia, supporting a sustainable solution of the Greek crisis based on a viable compromise. The IMF, which has been an important partner of the EU and the European Central Bank in supporting the economy of Greece and other European countries whose finances and economies were in distress, became openly critical of the EU's attitude and behaviour.

During the fateful days of the "compromise" over Greece in June and July 2015, US President Obama repeatedly telephoned European leaders and pressed for a fast and fair solution that would keep the need for growth high on the agenda while addressing the unsustainable Greek debt. The US Treasury Secretary, Jacob J. Lew, toured Europe in the days following the Greek agreement to press for more flexible, pro-growth European policies. The IMF published, while the meeting for finding a solution was going on, a previously classified report on the unsustainability of the Greek debt and the likely necessity to remit part of the debt (IMF 2015b). This publication was generally, and correctly, perceived as a move to contrast German rigour.

Perhaps more worrying from a European perspective was the fading appeal of the European project among Europeans. Fault lines along national identities, until then mostly hidden and implicit, became increasingly evident. An external scholar of the EU situation observes and asks:

> That experiment cannot survive if supported only by economic rigour and rules. What can continue to justify a political entity after the urgent realities and convictions that drove its establishment have faded to the pages of history and civics books or, at best, are the subject of grandparents' stories?
>
> (Slaughter 2015)

Finding a persuasive and effective answer to this question is of the utmost importance to the EU and, given its international economic and political importance, to the rest of the world.

This book intends to offer a global perspective on the European crisis, a perspective that involves the US assessment and action together with the European one. The US and the EU represent the world's two largest economies, particularly strongly intertwined through financial, monetary, and real links, so that what happens in the United States strongly influences the EU and vice versa. The US perspective is also especially important, since it was this country which took the initiative to try to lead the EU to a settlement that would be favourable to the EU and its member countries, but that would also keep in consideration the expectations of the rest of the world. This book aims to offer a broad view of the international meaning of the EU crisis, attending to the breeding grounds of the crisis around the EU, and considering the ongoing problem of the EU's relations to Russia and Ukraine.

The crisis and Europe

The global crisis started in the United States (US) at the end of 2007 and caught Europe unprepared. In the US the reliance on unregulated markets greatly expanded the financialization of the economy. Policies favouring business and finance to the disadvantage of labour fostered excess and risky credit, financial and real bubbles, and financial disequilibria. Once the financial crisis broke out in 2008, the American administration adopted massive government intervention to support financial institutions in trouble. In spite of these attempts, the crisis soon spread to the real economy and generated a "great contraction" (Reinhart and Rogoff 2009; Stiglitz 2010).

The European Union (EU) in general, and the Eurozone in particular, were for some time affected by illusions about their strengths and merits. Along with the virtue and strength of the common currency, the European Union was considered safer also thanks to the benefits of integration, prudent financial regulation, and the sturdy features of continental European capitalism. The latter include lower financial depth and integration, conservative financial regulation, and the prudent attitude of financial institutions. The only exception appeared to be macroeconomically unbalanced small economies: some external deeply integrated economies (Iceland), other non-Eurozone member economies (Hungary and Great Britain), and Eurozone economies (Greece and Ireland), where the crisis was evident already in 2008.

Various transatlantic linkages caused and reinforced the spread of the crisis to the Eurozone. These included financial, real, policy, political, and psychological linkages in what is often understood as a contagion process.[1] The money market's sudden arrest; the fact that European financial institutions held a large share of US mortgage-based assets, thus sharing in the losses that arose once the US housing bubble burst; and the sequence of falls in the stock market led to a substantial shrinking of bank credit. Export to the US market, which accounted for 23.2 per cent of total EU exports in 2006, decreased at an annual average rate of 5.1 per cent starting in 2007 and up to 2009. The strong real appreciation of the euro before 2008 significantly hampered export. At the same time, the increasing volatility of other currencies and of the price of commodities has had an adverse impact on the European economy. The economic slowdown activated automatic stabilizers, increasing social spending and decreasing, at the same time, governments' fiscal revenues. The road to growing fiscal deficits and increasing sovereign debts was paved.

Along with the US influence in the unfolding of the crisis in the Eurozone, the asymmetric presence of domestic imbalances and other forms of structural and policy vulnerability in different countries; the obstacles to signalling such imbalances at the Eurozone level (see Chapter 2) and the interconnection of these aspects with institutional idiosyncrasies and policy failures both at the national and at the European level were specific factors within Europe exacerbating the crisis. Structural and policy vulnerabilities included public and private debt, market rigidity, unemployment structure, demography, inequalities, fiscal policies, and the diverse domestic effect of the common monetary policy. These factors played an important role in explaining the differential vulnerability and resilience, and hence performance, of distinct European countries.

Although some of the problems are common to the entire European Union, it is within the Eurozone that they appear in their full significance. Indeed, the common currency takes monetary policy out of the hands of national governments and the Stability and Growth Pact (SGP) strongly limits their fiscal policies. These constraints to policy-making create what was named the "impossible trinity"[2] and exacerbate the effects of shocks to the disadvantage of economies in vulnerable positions. With no sovereign monetary policy and strictly constrained fiscal policy, governments cannot counteract external shocks. Given the lack of complementary common institutions providing common support – through a lender of last resort, a common budget, and financial transfers, or the mutualization of debts – a symmetric external shock, such as the US crisis, inevitably causes a set of asymmetric negative consequences for the member countries of the Eurozone, given their different economic and financial situations. Economically and financially unbalanced countries thus become vulnerable to the external shock since they lack policy instruments to withstand or recover from the effects of such shocks. The confidence of financial markets in the solvency of those countries may thus be shaken.

According to ECB data, the Residential Property Price Index of the Eurozone, which refers to new and existing dwellings, doubled between 1994 and 2008. This growth was the outcome of different national situations. According to the house price indices published by *The Economist*, house prices in Spain, Ireland, Great Britain, Iceland, Estonia, and Lithuania were steadily and sharply growing from the end of the 1990s to 2006. Between 2004 and 2005 the prices of the houses grew at a rate of 9 per cent or more in Italy, Belgium, Denmark, and Sweden, reaching in Spain and France annual growth rates of over 15 per cent. This is a much faster pace than those in the rest of Europe and in the USA.

However, in Germany house prices had steadily declined between 1997 and 2010.

Banks in the EZ-core have massively invested in the periphery countries. Large German current account surpluses vis-à-vis current account deficits of the so-called PIGS countries (Portugal, Ireland, Greece and Spain), together with low interest rates in the latter countries thanks to the common currency, led to strict interconnectedness in the Eurozone (Baldwin and Gros 2010). Interconnectedness, in turn, increased the vulnerability of the Eurozone banking system, as became evident during the three rounds of refinancing the liquidity and solvency crisis in Greece; in spite of the modest size of the Greek economy (less than 2 per cent of the Eurozone GDP), the way to a systemic crisis of the Eurozone was opened.

Along with being strictly interconnected, European banks were also assertively expanding lending – particularly in the Eastern European markets – and were overleveraged. The Irish, French, Spanish, and Italian banks in particular increased their exposure at an unprecedented pace,[3] and German banks were also massively exposed towards PIGS markets. It was primarily through the bank channel that the default in the US derivatives market threatened the stability of the Eurozone as well as the credibility and stability of the common currency. This is what actually happened in 2009–2010.

Noteworthy are also the outstanding leverage ratios (shareholder equity to total assets) of Eurozone banks (Gros and Micossi 2008). The thirteen largest European banks average leverage ratio was 35 compared to an average of 20 in the US. However, the European average covers wide national differences: French, German, and British banks were more exposed than Italian and Spanish ones, which were subject to a more prudential domestic regulation. Moreover, different governments responded differently and to a dissimilar extent to the problem of toxic assets, and in general to the difficulties of the banking sector, thus further highlighting the lack of coordinated banking policy within the Eurozone.[4] This contributed to the financial vulnerability of the largest economies (Baldwin and Gros 2010).

Many Eurozone banks were in a fragile state when faced with the risk of a sudden financial arrest (Caballero 2010). Financial instability in the Eurozone was thus largely a consequence of the failure of financial and banking regulation, which caused the fragility of the financial system. Basel II favoured the undercapitalization of banks and contributed to the financial crisis through low capital coefficients, admission of hybrid capital, lax criteria for risk evaluation, and wide possibilities for circumventing the rules (Spaventa 2010).

Important differences also exist in other indicators. Uneven inflation rates within the Eurozone led to different real interest rates, in spite of the common monetary policy. This outcome had important consequences for borrowing-based investments in housing and for financing sovereign debts. In Eastern and Southern European countries this might have encouraged a substantial surge in private and foreign debts experienced before the crisis onset. Germany shows a different trend, with declining private debt.

It is interesting to note that the European Commission report on the first ten years of the Economic and Monetary Union (EMU) (EC 2008) stressed that disregarding non-fiscal dimensions, such as competitiveness, credit booms, and current-account deficits, was a mistake. Another fundamental issue is the participation of Eurozone countries in the evolving international labour division and global value chains (see Chapter 10). However, financial issues have dominated debates and policy-making, and efforts have concentrated on the need to strengthen the financial architecture and practice of the Union and its member countries. Lately, much debate has taken place on the behaviour of individual countries and their actual (lack of) respect for the commonly devised rules of behaviour (see Chapter 3). Such critical issues as diverging productivity within the Eurozone, the sudden reversal of capital flows between the north and the south of the Eurozone, or the divergence of real exchange rates and their consequences for the integration and sustainability of the Eurozone are mostly confined to academic debate with scant appearance in European governments' concerns (Dallago 2015).[5]

It is by now clear that concentrating on financial issues is a one-sided approach that cannot solve European problems. The present financial risks and difficulties of various EU member countries inhibit their possibility to grow and create jobs and new dangers may be on the horizon (Sinn 2014). Financial problems have a preemptive nature only in view of the present incomplete institutional architecture of the Union, with particular concern for the Eurozone. First, the incompleteness of the financial and monetary architecture reflects the fundamental lack of trust among member countries, which they try to overcome by means of financial discipline (see Chapter 4). If we take a broader, longer, and deeper perspective, it appears that the present financial and monetary crisis of the Union is rooted in the real economy (see Chapters 5, 7 and 8). Second, concentrating on a fiscal and monetary solution to the crisis by means of restrictive policies is likely to be untenable in the medium-to-long run because of its depressive effects on the real economy, the negative effect on sovereign debt, as well as heavy social costs and political destabilization (see Chapter 1).

This sequence of events in the Eurozone corresponds to what Reinhart and Rogoff (2010) found in more than 70 countries over two centuries: private debt increase, fuelled by the growth of both domestic banking credit and external borrowing, is a recurrent antecedent to domestic banking crises, which, in turn, tend to precede or accompany sovereign debt crises. What is peculiar to the Eurozone is the difference among member countries and the lack of compensating mechanisms and instruments. For instance, in the Eurozone as a whole household debt increased from 52 per cent to 70 per cent of GDP from 1999 to 2007, while financial institutions increased their debt from less than 200 per cent of GDP to more than 250 per cent (De Grauwe 2010). However, in the so-called Eurozone-core (EZ-core) (Germany, France, Austria, Belgium and the Netherlands) households have been fiscally rather solid, while in the so-called periphery households' debt increased at a much higher pace.

The conclusion is straightforward: the Eurozone crisis came from across the Atlantic only in part, and not in its major effects. The conditions were ripe for an autonomous Eurozone crisis. The American shock gave the initial push, but the crisis would have come anyway, probably somewhat later and perhaps in a slightly milder form and over a longer period.

The consequences of the incomplete monetary union

The deep economic and financial asymmetries among countries in an economic and monetary union may have perverse consequences when common institutions are incomplete or ineffective. In normal times the internal divergence among member countries tends to increase, but in the absence of traumatic events the process can go on for a long period of time. In fact, countries have different devices to accommodate the negative effects of divergence, including the political will to be part of the union. However, things change when external circumstances become adverse, which typically happens when there is an external shock.

Divergence of productivity growth among the member economies of a monetary union represents a particularly serious problem. The negative consequences of productivity differentials can be attenuated in different ways and therefore they do not translate automatically into an unsustainable economic situation in weaker countries. An institutionally complete union, similar to a national government, has various instruments to this end, including: a common government of the economy able to directly transfer resources to the advantage of the weaker economies (fiscal sharing or a transfer union); a lender of last resort, typically a common central bank; and socialization of debt through common bonds. In all these cases the weaker economy can remain part of the monetary union while enjoying a level of income similar to that of the stronger countries. While economic performance in a weaker economy is lagging behind, incomes and investment may remain high, thanks to the use of resources produced elsewhere in the union. In exchange, the weaker part consumes a higher quantity of goods and services produced in the stronger part and perhaps deposits or invests savings and capital in organizations of the stronger part. Common instruments allocate resources from one part of the monetary union (one country or group of countries) to another one, similarly to what happens with regions in a country. Thus, there is a need for a strong agreement among the members of the union, strong commitment and full mutual trust, which dramatically prolong the time horizon of cooperation. This comes usually in the form of a common government of the economy and political unification.

If, for whatever reason, a monetary union does not have a full institutional architecture, national governments still have other instruments that can serve the purpose of improving the country's competitiveness and reduce external account imbalances that burden the weak economies. In order for competitiveness to improve, productivity must increase. This can be done by shedding workers and decreasing labour costs.

There are various ways through which unit labour costs in weaker countries can improve and converge with those of their trade competitors. Unfortunately, some of them require a long time, social consensus, and participation. In a monetary union the internal depreciation of the currency is rejected by definition. External depreciation of the common currency against third country currencies would ease the situation of weak union countries but would have moderate advantages due to their deep economic integration with stronger countries. Prolonging the working time for the same wage would be another technically rather simple solution, yet politically and socially difficult, and would probably exacerbate unemployment. This in itself does not solve the problems if it is not accompanied by other measures that improve the productive capacity of the economy. Indeed, weak Eurozone economies, such as Greece and Portugal, already have the longest working times within the OECD.[6]

Sounder ways to decrease the unit labour costs are investments that improve and strengthen the production capacity of the country, improving the effectiveness and efficiency of economic organizations and the public administration, as well as decreasing transaction costs and the relative weight of rents to the disadvantage of profits and wages. Unfortunately, investments require substantial financial resources and sufficient human capital, which may be scarce in the weak economies, and it takes time before they come to maturity. A decrease in the transaction costs and the relative weight of rents require serious reforms of the economic and administrative organization. Reforms may be cheap, but they inevitably provoke social and political opposition and the action of disadvantaged interests groups, and reach maturity and effectiveness, presumably after a rather lengthy time. Therefore, reforms require political determination and social support.

Under the pressure of events and, even more so, of the Eurozone authorities and the strong countries, economically weak countries had to resort to internal devaluation policies. Internal devaluation is usually meant as a set of policies used to regain competitiveness in order to adjust current account costs and disequilibria by directly decreasing public budget prices in a situation that does not allow the use of currency depreciation – i.e. in monetary unions and currency boards. In order to decrease prices production costs must fall, which requires the cutting of wages and other costs (welfare costs and transaction costs, mostly those of an administrative and political nature) and implementing institutional and structural reforms in order to increase productivity. In a market economy the government can hardly limit the sovereignty of firms, which largely depends upon the market sector – particularly after the sweeping privatization policies of the 1980s and 1990s.

Therefore, the easier way to implement internal devaluation is through deflationary policies. Given the weak control that a government has over prices, this is usually pursued through an increase in the value added tax (VAT) and the reduction of payroll taxes and social security benefits paid by the employer in order to decrease the cost of labour. The second important way is through cutting wages and decreasing the government expenditure for welfare and social benefits. Typically, the purpose is to push down those private sector prices that are fundamental for the labour cost in the tradable sector, although these prices are out of the government's direct competence. A further means toward deflation implemented in the public sector is to make the state less costly. This in turn should allow a decrease in taxes on economic activities. If the manoeuvre succeeds, resources are freed to be invested in the private tradable sector and, if wages decrease, employment should increase if all the remaining conditions continue to be equal.

These policies unfortunately have serious drawbacks that go well beyond the social and political opposition that they inevitably are confronted with and the lengthy time they require for transmitting the effect of lower wages to prices. Given the tense situation of public finances in weak economies, it is difficult to reform the tax system as would be required. Therefore, internal devaluation policies have been typically implemented through public expenditure cuts and downward pressure on wages. While this may have improved external competitiveness in the short run, typically more important has been the depressive effect on the internal market. This happens both directly, when most consumers become poorer and more pessimistic and thus reluctant and unable to spend, and indirectly because, with imperfect competition, wage and tax cuts are passed to consumers with a delay and only partially. Moreover, the overall effect is positive for the economy only if the external market is more important than the domestic one, which is not usually the case for the vulnerable countries of the Eurozone, except Ireland.

A serious negative effect of internal devaluation policies is the increase of internal inequality. This is due to the fact that wage cuts tend to hit some groups of mostly low-wage workers – typically employed in the public sector – more than others. Politically strong groups of workers in both the public and the private sector, employees with scarce competences and self-employed people who can fix their remuneration – including managers in the financial sector – lose less or may even gain. When inequalities increase, fairness as well as social and professional mobility suffer as a consequence. A particularly negative consequence of increasing inequalities is the effect on human capital. Many families have insufficient resources for supporting the education of their children, governments decrease scholarships and support to educational institutions and perhaps increase taxation, and educational institutions may react by increasing the price of education for families in order to recover resources or worsening the quality of their supply (e.g. reducing scholarships or cutting teaching programs).

When internal devaluation is successful in reducing inflation, there may be dangerous and financially destabilizing consequences for debts, both public and private. Such consequences are particularly serious if the internal devaluation causes deflation. Under these conditions the real value of debt is increased and the ratio of debt over GDP may also increase due to a typically high value of fiscal multipliers in economic recessions (Blanchard and Leigh 2013; Nuti 2013). Refinancing the debt may become difficult and the country may lose the confidence of markets and find it more difficult to finance investments.

In a monetary union the common monetary policy cannot deal with the effects of asymmetric shocks in individual parts of the monetary union. Equally important is the fact that the larger the internal variety of the monetary union, the greater the probability for the unique monetary policy to have asymmetric effects. First, economic, social, and institutional features of regions or countries within a monetary union may differ substantially. For instance, their labour markets may be structured and work differently, the price elasticity of their exports may be different, their import energy intensity may vary, the industrial structure and the size of enterprises could be different, and the role of the state and the size of the public debt may be different. Second, financial structures may differ from one region or country of a monetary union to another, and the nature and size of asymmetric shocks and the transmission mechanism of the monetary policy may differ consequently. For instance, the features and structure of financial markets (financial depth) and the ability of enterprises to get credit may vary.

Since the currency reputation and its exchange rate typically depend on stronger regions or countries of the union, the common monetary policy is likely to favour economically and politically strong members of the union and disfavour the weak and vulnerable ones. It is therefore of the utmost importance for the common currency to be accompanied by compensating factors that counteract the asymmetric effects of the common monetary policy. These include independent (regional or national) budget policies and the transfer of resources among regions or countries by means of government actions or through private insurance mechanisms. A common central bank that acts as a lender of last resort can ease asymmetries and tensions. A bank union and supervision can implement an inter-regional or inter-country transfer of financial resources.

Considering that the external shocks tend to randomly hit activities and countries, it is in the interest of the countries that form a currency union to activate a sort of mutual insurance mechanism by transferring resources to the advantage of the members of the union that are hit by the external shock. Inter-country fiscal transfers have the advantage of alleviating the recession in the country hit by the shock and mitigating the expansion in others. Such a solution can be implemented through the common fiscal capacity (a common budget) that acts as a mechanism of shock absorption and risk sharing. The question remains open whether such a transfer mechanism should be based in a common institution, such as a common government of the economy, or rely on inter-governmental agreements. A common central bank acting as a lender of last resort could also effectively intervene to alleviate the consequences of the shock.

The role of the common economic government and the central bank is a critical one in an optimal currency area (OCA) and, to be effective, requires the policy preferences of the member countries to be homogeneous. This is technically and politically important, since policy responses to shocks typically have distributive consequences that may create winners and losers within the currency union. Since this is inevitable, and since policy preferences in different countries are often different, the union is viable only if losers are compensated or if the advantages of being members of a currency union are perceived to be greater than the cost of policies (see Rosefielde's introduction to Part I of this book). Although such a guarantee may be important, a currency union needs to be supported by the member countries' common vision of the future, their international role and the internal support the union affords to the wellbeing of the population. These sentiments help the union to foster mutual solidarity that can temper tensions, especially during times of crisis, and prolong the time horizon of all involved actors.

Fiscal policies could be used in a monetary union as insurance mechanisms against asymmetric shocks. The mechanism works differently depending on the institutional features of budgets. If there is a centralized common budget under a common government of the economy, this can work as a public insurance system by allowing automatic transfers between countries within the monetary union. This mechanism can offset asymmetric shocks as happens in an independent country with automatic stabilizers. However, this is not the situation of the European Union or the Eurozone, also due to the tiny size of the common budget (around 1 per cent of the EU GDP).

An alternative is the existence of flexible national budgets. Centralized budgets with automatic stabilizers and discretionary intervention exist in each individual member country. In this case the disadvantaged country can allow deficits to accumulate in order to support demand. If capital markets are integrated, as typically is the case of a monetary union, capital markets can redistribute income in order to finance the deficit. However, this mechanism causes automatic transfers between generations within the same country and may create problems of debt accumulation and sustainability. Moreover, if national budgets can intervene, either automatically or discretionarily, without any constraint, this can create problems of moral hazard within the monetary union. The European Union has agreed on the Maastricht criteria and the Stability and Growth Pact to avoid such consequences.

Integrated capital markets offer an alternative mechanism that can be compared to a private insurance system. With integrated capital markets, the mobility of capital allows automatic insurance against shocks if capital flows to where it is more needed (i.e. to deficit countries). However, there are two problems with this private mechanism. First, the insurance works if the deficit country is rich enough to pay higher returns in the form of a positive spread over benchmark return rates in strong economies. Poor countries are usually unable to do so or, if they do, they may be further impoverished. Second, if capital markets perceive the deficit country to be particularly risky as a destination for investment, the capital may abstain from flowing to the country. Even worse, when risk is perceived as high, domestic capital can leave the deficit country. Therefore, differential risk may hamper the working of integrated capital markets as insurance systems.

In the Eurozone, the private insurance mechanism worked rather smoothly before the crisis. The surplus countries' capital, particularly Germany's, financed deficit countries, including Italy and Spain, where interest rates were slightly higher and the risk of default was considered to be virtually non-existent thanks to the economic and monetary union. However, when the crisis hit vulnerable countries, and the common umbrella proved to be non-existent, German capital flew out of these countries in spite of higher returns, and the vulnerable countries' domestic capital, too, flew to strong surplus countries.[7]

To summarize, when external shocks are asymmetric, a monetary union causes costs that would not arise in the situation of monetary independence. The common central bank cannot deal with these asymmetries. In this case it would be wise to leave fiscal policies in the domain of national governments, as the European Union did for years. Independent fiscal policies could thus be used to adapt countries to asymmetric shocks or the asymmetric effects of external symmetric shocks. Unfortunately, unless countries have compatible economic situations (particularly if they have similar economic systems, comparable competitiveness and the same public budget constraint) or engage in reforms to that end, it will sooner or later be necessary to restrict the national use of financial policies in order to safeguard the common currency. This is exactly what happened with the Maastricht criteria and the SGP, a development that opened the delicate issue of the fiscal architecture of the Eurozone (see Chapter 6).

The European crisis and the external context

After more than seven years, the international economic crisis is not over. The European crisis is still intertwined with the US crisis (see Chapter 11). In spite of important episodes of recovery, particularly in the United States, growth rates at world level are decelerating. This time it is primarily emerging countries – including China and India and even more so Russia and Brazil – that are undergoing decreasing (albeit in the former two countries still quite positive) or negative (as with the two latter countries) growth rates. The ailing performance of the rich countries, such as Japan, but not the United States, is one of the fundamental reasons for the deceleration in the emerging countries that showed a remarkable resilience during the first years of the crisis. Yet they also are under the negative influence of domestic and idiosyncratic effects (e.g. the excessive dependence upon the export of raw materials and the falling world price of oil in the case of Russia). The perspective of a secular stagnation, caused by negative demographic, economic, and financial events in the most developed countries and increasingly also in emerging economies, is openly debated as a likely outcome (IMF 2014; Summers 2014; Teulings and Baldwin 2014). The European Union appears to be the economy most vulnerable to secular stagnation.

Within this rather gloomy general picture, the situation of the member countries of the European Union, which adopted the euro as their common currency, the Eurozone, appears particularly negative and worrying. This conclusion follows from the comparison between the EU member countries from Central and Eastern Europe, only some of whom adopted the euro (see Chapter 9). Given the economic importance of the Eurozone countries in the world economy, their economic and financial situation is one of the important causes, perhaps the most important individual cause, of the inability of the world economy to exit this long and deep economic and financial crisis. Admittedly, the Eurozone crisis has been influenced by the international crisis and the US crisis that caused it. Yet the Eurozone has been accumulating domestic factors for crises that presently are certainly the dominant reason for their ailing performance and financial instability.

The Eurozone crisis reveals serious institutional and macroeconomic troubles. Yet many of these have microeconomic origins, in particular in the countries in greater economic and financial difficulty. An already difficult situation became even more difficult and perhaps threatening due to unfavourable external events independent from the will of the Eurozone as well as from mismanagement within the Eurozone .The crisis with Russia is the most prominent and potentially dangerous, both politically and economically for the Eurozone (see Chapters 12 and 13), and combines an external event with European policies that contributed to its severity. In a different, potentially positive direction, are other events, the most prominent being the potential treaty for a Transatlantic Trade and Investment Partnership (TTIP) between the European Union and the United States. The treaty has important potential advantages, although it also includes dangers and drawbacks, particularly for the economically and financially weaker countries.

There are two endogenous issues that are particularly important for the evolution of the Eurozone crisis. The political dimension of the crisis is becoming increasingly important and is presenting potentially serious obstacles to the management of the economic and financial crises. It is clear that without a political agreement, or at least a compromise among the Eurozone countries, the management of the crisis and the necessary institutional reform of the Eurozone are hardly manageable. Finally, the Eurozone crisis is having serious and presumably permanent consequences for the economic and social structure of the Eurozone countries. Particularly important are the processes going on in the labour market (see Chapters 7, 8 and 10), which are one of the important reasons behind the dramatically increasing inequalities in nearly all Eurozone countries and the growing divergence between northern and southern Europe.

In the following we review these fundamental issues and introduce the chapters dealing with each of them.

Fundamental issues on the European Union and its institutional architecture

There is no shared analysis of the causes of the Eurozone crisis and even less analysis of the present situation. The two competing explanations are that the crisis is due to (a) financial mismanagement, with particular reference to public deficits and debts, and (b) austerity policies. A more convincing analysis is one that also considers the weakness of real economies and the negative consequences of the institutional incompleteness of the economic and monetary union (EMU).

Divergence of analyses and opinions is even greater concerning the policies necessary to overcome the present difficulties. Competing explanations so far have been (a) a mainstream explanation seeing austerity policies and financial discipline as necessary steps to discipline free-riding member countries and as preconditions for growth, and (b) post-Keynesian explanations supporting the necessity of public spending. Lately a more complex view has been evolving, which sees also the necessity of implementing institutional and structural reforms, particularly in vulnerable countries, as preconditions for policies to be effective. The ECB has been a particularly strong supporter of this view, with its accent placed on the ineffectiveness of the transmission mechanism and the necessity to reform economies in order to reactivate the transmission mechanism of monetary policy. Reforms are increasingly seen as a precondition for mildly expansionary financial policies – which the European Commission and the Eurogroup are also considering – to be effective.

Overall, opinions are still divided on the perspectives of the euro and the Eurozone and its viability and, among those who see a positive although difficult outcome, there is disagreement on the path to consolidation. This book includes various contributions on this subject that differ in their approach and their policy consequences.

The first part of the book deals with the European Union seen from inside that is moving from the crisis to a future that still looks blurred. This part includes chapters dealing with some general problems and others dealing with more particular, yet fundamental issues (plus Rosefield's introduction).

Klaus Gretschmann (Chapter 1) provides a general account of where the EU stands today. In his view, the EU project stands at a crucial crossroads. Certainly, the starry-eyed optimists who believed Europe was moving steadily to increasing integration have proved wrong. The "beginning", the development of common European institutions and the common currency, is now over. At stake now is whether those institutions and the currency can succeed in dealing with the unexpected difficulties the crisis has revealed – or whether the whole project will be abandoned. Gretschmann thinks the European Union can be saved, but only if there is strong, coordinated action to address its current deficiencies.

Nicola Acocella (Chapter 2) offers a detailed analysis of the EMU, focusing on why it proved so vulnerable to crisis. In particular, he considers the extent to which constraints established in Brussels could actually generate needed reforms in member countries, while also arguing that the information flows ("signals") between the different economies in the EMU were far from perfect. The pre-existing economic imbalances between the member countries were, to some extent, exacerbated by their currency union, while the moral hazards centralization introduced provided temptations that various countries did not resist. While not discounting other causes and consequences of the crisis, Acocella wants us to understand the impact of signalling imbalances, both on augmenting the crisis and in thinking about adequate responses to it.

László Csaba (Chapter 3) provides perhaps the most optimistic paper in this volume. He argues that the architecture of the EMU is basically sound and that its benefits for member countries outweigh its disadvantages. Crucial to the EMU's success going forward is more strict adherence to its rules by the various participating nations. Because the advantages of membership are substantial in Csaba's view, there exists adequate incentive to play by those rules.

Simona Piattoni (Chapter 4) contests the prevalence of cost-benefits analysis in evaluations of the EU's desirability and viability. An instrumental calculation that focuses only on whether membership in the union is advantageous misses the fact that the Union can only work on a basis of trust. Such trust, paradoxically, must pre-exist the rationalist's calculation, even as the benefits of union are only possible if that trust is present. Piattoni argues forcefully that mere utility can never underwrite a successful European project. Rather, only a set of democratically established and supported values such as rule of law, solidarity, and non-domination can create the kind of common commitment and mutual trust that make a supranational European Union possible.

Paolo Pasimeni (Chapter 5), an economist working for the European Commission, considers various assessment tools that can be used to ascertain Europe's progress toward the goals established in the Commission's 2020 strategy. Crucial to the success of that strategy is a transparency that provides information that allows the Commission to gauge the progress of member nations. Complicating such assessment is the need to consider both formal and informal institutions. Along with "hard" measurements of wealth and growth, Pasimeni argues forcefully that less quantitative factors such as good governance and social capital are crucial indicators. He proposes various ways to assess these harder to measure qualities.

Scott Greer and Holly Jarman (Chapter 6) offer what is perhaps the most pessimistic assessment of the EU in this volume. In their view, the EU is a regulatory state that attempts to shape the economic and political behaviour of the member nations through a set of rules. They contrast this kind of rule-based sovereignty to one based on expenditure, which carries out policies by financing their implementation. The crisis has seen the EU respond in a characteristic way; it has created new rules and has attempted to find ways to enforce them. But, especially when member countries are under economic stress, the incentives to follow those regulations are diminished while allegiance to the union wanes. There seems little reason or desire for member nations to continue to pay attention to Brussels.

Bruno Dallago (Chapter 7) also considers an issue that seems to place nationalistic sentiments at the front of member nations' concerns: migration. Resistance to in-migration by non-citizens has proved a sentiment that anti-EU political parties in the various member nations have been able to exploit. But, as Dallago forcefully shows, the popular understanding of migration as a threat completely misunderstands the economic consequences of migration. In face of aging populations and the economic asymmetries between EU member countries, labour mobility can be as economically beneficial as various kinds of fiscal transfers.

Joachim Möller (Chapter 8) offers a detailed account of the German labour market reforms of the early 2000s. Critics often complain that these reforms were deliberately deflationary in an attempt to retain Germany's status as a strong exporter nation – and that the reforms represented German capitulation to the anti-labour pressures of globalization and neoliberalism. Möller offers a more nuanced analysis, conceding that some workers' wages did decline, but arguing that the "German model" of capitalism, which provides strong protections for workers (especially in job security and job training) was preserved despite the necessary adjustments made to remain competitive in the world market.

The external context and the European Union

This second part of our volume looks at the contact area between the Union and key international actors, be it through exchange rates, production and global value chains, or neighbouring nations. After chapters that address the EMU's relation to the Eastern European countries that have still not joined the euro, the EU's member countries' participation in global value chains, and the ongoing relations of economic entanglement between the EU and the US, we turn to the Ukraine crisis. The relation with Russia and the Ukrainian crisis have a particularly important bearing for the EU, for both geo-political and economic reasons. Politically, the Ukrainian crisis has introduced a new fault line between the European Union and Russia. Rising political tensions have diverted the attention of governments and increased political, and consequently economic, uncertainty. A potentially important disagreement between much of the European Union and the United States over the management of the crisis may still be latent. The current sanctions are not necessarily in the present or long run interests of most European countries. Disagreement over how to address the Ukraine crisis introduced new cracks among EU member countries, including between Great Britain and Germany. In addition, the crisis has moved Russian interest away from Europe and increasingly towards China, with unpredictable long run consequences. The crisis also requires that the EU revise its Neighbourhood Policy and carefully manage the accession policy. The latter, in particular, was improperly managed and was important in fostering the Ukrainian crisis.

As to economic consequences, these span from direct to more indirect and contextual ones. The tension with Russia has been directly jeopardizing the flow of energy sources to EU member countries, many of which depend largely upon Russian sources. Western sanctions and Russian counter-sanctions are very costly to many EU member countries, particularly so in the present difficult economic situation. Another important direct economic consequence is the cost of the support to the Ukrainian economy, which for the time being is unlikely to bring returns. Important indirect consequences are the climate of uncertainty over international economic relations and the potential long-run cost to the EU member countries from decreasing integration with and opportunities offered by the Russian economy. Finally, the political and economic split between the West and Russia – and increasingly so China – weakened the possibility to find solutions for the growing instability around the European Union, particularly in North Africa and the Middle East.

Paul Marer (Chapter 9) provides a valuable overview of the economic and political calculations that underlie the stance adopted toward the common currency by twelve Eastern European countries. The ongoing crisis has halted what was supposed to be the steady progression toward adoption of the euro by the Eastern European nations. Instead, each nation is now considering the costs and benefits of the euro – and the policies they adopt will go a long way toward determining the future of European integration. Marer offers a careful country-by-country account of the specific local factors that figure into the thinking of these twelve states.

John Pickles (Chapter 10) is interested in how changes in global production patterns impact European labour markets specifically and the European economy more generally. As the production of commodities is globalized, specific goods are often produced in various countries. Successful twenty-first century economies do not necessarily specialize in the production of a particular commodity, but instead find a way to contribute partially to the production of a commodity that is assembled out of work done in multiple locales. Pickles traces the consequences of this new mode of production for labourers, considering the ways that worker safety, environmental protections, and labour standards might evolve in relation to this increased international interdependency. Also at stake is the EU's ability to discover particular niches that allow its participation in these productive processes.

Herman Schwartz (Chapter 11) argues that the EU is dangerously dependent on and linked to the US economy. Not only was the EU crisis precipitated by the American financial crisis, but the EU is also overly reliant on American consumers to support EU growth and prosperity. Thus, Europe's financial sector is overly integrated with US financial institutions that remain risky and under-regulated, while Europe's economic well-being is overly dependent on US prosperity. Finally, the fact that the EMU is not an optimal currency area means that the Eurozone has a limited ability to respond to economic downturns. This situation, which has not changed since 2008, makes Europe extremely vulnerable.

Both Eric Brunat (Chapter 12) and Jake Kipp (Chapter 13) address the growing rift between the EU and Russia. Both authors recognize that the association process through which the EU forged economic ties with the former Soviet republics of Ukraine, Moldova and Georgia alienated Russia and played a role in precipitating the ongoing Ukraine crisis. Russia, which in Kipp's view was open to cooperation with the EU and the US even as recently as 2006, has been pushed to create its own economic and political alliances with neighbouring states such as Belarus and Kazakhstan, and has had to look at creating more extensive cooperation with China. Thus, the creation of a Eurasian bloc, created to counter the European one, is now a possibility – with obviously difficult consequences for the EU. Brunat provides a detailed account of the development of the Russian economy over the past fifteen years – an account that goes a long way toward explaining the complex situations of Putin's Russia. Kipp, on the other hand, focuses on the unfolding of the Ukraine crisis, and pessimistically concludes that, after a series of missed opportunities, there are no obvious ways out of the current impasse of a low-level, but unstoppable, civil war in eastern Ukraine.

Notes

1 No shared definition has yet been reached in the literature on the controversial notion of contagion, which encounters serious problems across theory and empirical work. It is useful to briefly recall the fundamental distinction, upheld by most of the literature on financial contagion (Reinhart and Calvo 1996; Kaminsky and Reinhart 2000; Eichengreen et al. 1996), between (a) the development of synchronized shocks in different countries, which are due to similar structural vulnerabilities rather than to the presence of channels of contagion, and (b) the cross-country transmission of shocks.

As to the latter, this literature further distinguishes between fundamentals-based contagion, which occurs when the infected country is linked to others via trade or finance, and true contagion which takes place when common shocks and all channels of potential interconnection are absent (Reinhart and Calvo 1996).

2 The impossible trinity at the core of the Eurozone vulnerability consists of strict prohibition of monetary financing, lack of co-responsibility for public debt and bank-sovereign interdependence (Pisani-Ferry 2012). The first and second components derive from the institutional architecture of the union, as defined in the European treaties. The third component is a pragmatic, yet dangerous adaptation to the former two elements.

3 In total, bank assets as a percentage of GDP rose from 360 per cent in 2001 to 705 per cent in 2007, in France from 229 per cent to 373 per cent, in Spain from 177 per cent to 280 per cent and in Italy from 148 per cent to 220 per cent (Baldwin and Gros 2010).

4 Overall, public support (by the government and the central bank) to banks was particularly strong in Germany, Ireland, and the Netherlands – and even more in the UK. Public support was mild in France and negligible in Spain and Italy.

5 However, the international organizations (IMF 2013; OECD 2014) and the American administration has occasionally addressed the crucial issues that were ignored by European policymakers: "Within the euro area, countries with large and persistent surpluses need to take action to boost domestic demand growth and shrink their surpluses. Germany has maintained a large current account surplus throughout the euro area financial crisis, and in 2012, Germany's nominal current account surplus was larger than that of China. Germany's anemic pace of domestic demand growth and dependence on exports have hampered rebalancing at a time when many other euro-area countries have been under severe pressure to curb demand and compress imports in order to promote adjustment. The net result has been a deflationary bias for the euro area, as well as for the world economy" (USDT 2013: 3).

6 See http://stats.oecd.org/index.aspx?DataSetCode=ANHRS.

7 According to the IMF (2012: 27), capital outflows from vulnerable to strong countries took place at a pace typically associated with currency crises, and they were considerable. In the 12 months prior to June 2012 Spain lost €296 billion (27 per cent of its 2011 GDP) and Italy €235 billion (15 per cent of the GDP). There were structural differences of capital flight in the two countries. In Italy a large share of outflows originated in foreign investors retreating from the country's bond market. In Spain, the outflows were broader-based and corporate bonds accounted for a significant part.

References

Baldwin, R. and D. Gros. 2010. "Introduction: The Euro in Crisis – What to Do?" In *Completing the Eurozone Rescue: What More Needs to Be Done?*, edited by R. Baldwin, D. Gros and L. Laeven, pp. 1–24. Washington, DC: CEPR and VoxEU.org.

Blanchard, O. J. and D. Leigh. 2013. *Growth Forecast Errors and Fiscal Multipliers.* Working paper WP/13/1, January. Washington, DC: International Monetary Fund.

Caballero, R. J. 2010. "Sudden Financial Arrest." *IMF Economic Review.* Available at http://dspace.mit.edu/handle/1721.1/64707.

Dallago, B. 2015. *One Currency, Two Europes.* Singapore: World Scientific.

De Grauwe, P. 2010. "Fighting the Wrong Enemy." 19 May. Available at www.voxeu.org/article/europe-s-private-versus-public-debt-problem-fighting-wrong-enemy.

EC. 2008. *EMU@10 – Successes and Challenges after Ten Years of Economic and Monetary Union.* Brussels: European Commission, DG Economic and Financial Affairs. Available at http://ec.europa.eu/economy_finance/publications/publication12682_en.pdf.

Eichengreen, B., A. K. Rose and C. Wyplosz. 1996. *Contagious Currency Crises.* Working Paper N° 5681. Cambridge, MA: National Bureau of Economic Research. Available at www.nber.org/papers/w5681.pdf?new_window=1.

Gros, D. and S. Micossi. 2008. *The Beginning of the End Game.* Commentary/18, September. Brussels: Centre for European Policy Studies. Available at http://aei.pitt.edu/11581/1/1712[1].pdf.

IMF. 2012. *Global Financial Stability Report: Restoring Confidence and Progressing on Reforms.* October. Washington, DC: International Monetary Fund.

IMF. 2013. *Reassessing the Role and Modalities of Fiscal Policy in Advanced Economies.* IMF Policy Paper. September. Washington, DC: International Monetary Fund. Available at www.imf.org/external/np/pp/eng/2013/072113.pdf.

IMF. 2014. *World Economic Outlook: Legacies, Clouds, Uncertainties.* October. Washington, DC: International Monetary Fund.

IMF. 2015a. *World Economic Outlook: Uneven Growth. Short- and Long-Term Factors.* April. Washington, DC: International Monetary Fund.

IMF. 2015b. *Greece: Preliminary Draft Debt Sustainability Analysis.* IMF Country Report no. 15/165, 26 June. Washington, DC: International Monetary Fund. Available at www.imf.org/external/pubs/ft/scr/2015/cr15165.pdf .

Kaminsky, G. L. and C. M. Reinhart. 2000. "On Crises, Contagion, and Confusion." *Journal of International Economics* 51(1): 145–168.

Nuti, D. M. 2013. *Perverse Fiscal Consolidation.* Paper presented at the international conference on Economic and Political Crises in Europe and the United States: Prospects for Policy Cooperation, Trento, 7–9 November. Available at http://web.unitn.it/files/download/31972/nuti_trento_perversefc.pdf.

OECD. 2014. *Economic Challenges and Policy Recommendations for the Euro Area.* Better Policies Series, February. Paris: OECD. Available at www.oecd.org/eu/Euro_Area_Brochure_EN.pdf.

Pisani-Ferry, J. 2012. *The Euro Crisis and the New Impossible Trinity.* Bruegel Policy Contribution N° 2012/01. Brussels: Bruegel. Available at www.econstor.eu/bitstream/10419/72121/1/683140442.pdf.

Reinhart, C. M. and S. Calvo. 1996. "Capital Flows to Latin America: Is There Evidence of Contagion Effects?" In *Private Capital Flows to Emerging Markets After the Mexican Crisis,* edited by G. A. Calvo, M. Goldstein and E. Hochreiter, pp. 151–171. Washington, DC: Peterson Institute for International Economics.

Reinhart, C. M. and K. S. Rogoff. 2009. *This Time Is Different: Eight Centuries of Financial Folly.* Princeton, NJ: Princeton University Press.

Reinhart, C. M. and K. S. Rogoff. 2010. *Debt and Growth Revisited.* MPRA Paper no. 24376. Munich: Munich Personal RePEc Archive. Available at http://mpra.ub.uni-muenchen.de/24376/1/MPRA_paper_24376.pdf.

Sinn, H.-W. 2014. "Europe's Next Moral Hazard." 24 April. Available at www.project-syndicate.org/commentary/hans-werner-sinn-laments-the-renewed-run-up-in-public-debt-in-key-eurozone-economies.

Slaughter, A.-M. 2015. "Europe's Civil War." 21 July. Available at www.project-syndicate.org/print/greek-crisis-future-of-europe-by-anne-marie-slaughter-2015-07.

Spaventa, L. 2010. "How to Prevent Excessive Current Account Imbalances." 30 September. Available at www.eurointelligence.com/news-details/article/how-to-prevent-excessive-current-account-imbalances.html?cHash=13c2b4eb6c8a8efab5fc5f147f960318.

Stiglitz, J. E. 2010. *Freefall: America, Free Markets, and the Sinking of the World Economy.* New York: W. W. Norton.

Summers, L. H. 2014. "US Economic Prospects: Secular Stagnation, Hysteresis, and the Zero Lower Bound." *Business Economics* 49(2): 65–73.

Teulings, C. and R. Baldwin (eds). 2014. *Secular Stagnation: Facts, Causes, and Cures.* London: CEPR Press.

USDT. 2013. *Report to Congress on International Economic and Exchange Rate Policies.* 30 October. Washington, DC: US Department of the Treasury, Office of International Affairs. Available at www.treasury.gov/resource-center/international/exchange-rate-policies/Documents/2013-10-30_FULL%20FX%20REPORT_FINAL.pdf

Part I
The European project
Moving forward with dry eyes

Steven Rosefielde

Introduction

Klaus Gretschmann contends that the economics and politics of the EU Project are on life support.[1] Will the project survive? The answer is yes, even with Grexit and Brexit (Greek ejection from the Eurozone/British de-accession from the EU) because EU supranationality is legislatively embedded, immensely difficult to dissolve, and has as its mission subject to perpetual rationalization.[2] However, should Europe cling to its current supranational project? This is the right question.

The answer depends on opportunity costs and context, not on visionary wishful thinking. If as a practical matter, independent European nations can outperform the EU in the emerging post-global partnership epoch, transnationality and welfare-impairing programs should be abandoned, preserving as much of supranationality's benefits as possible through bi and multilateral agreements. If not, EU supranationality should be preserved. The ideal possibilities of perfect markets, perfect plans, and perfect governance, often the centrepieces of net assessments, are subsidiary because satisficing, power-seeking, unscrupulousness, wilfulness and anti-competitiveness excluded from rationalist models often critically determine real outcomes (Rosefielde and Pfouts 2014). Rational actor theories shed some light, but mostly conceal fundamental factors determining EU behaviour. The substantive issue therefore isn't what might be if people were comprehensively upright, rational actors, but what actually can be achieved by European nations independently or within the EU framework.

This is an elusive problem because the comparative merit of EU and national arrangements cannot be laboratory tested under controlled conditions. Nonetheless, some insight into the matter can be gleaned by examining contemporary sources of dysfunction and vulnerability. Let us consider three issues among a multitude of possibilities:

1 Is the EU violating its credo by evolving toward hegemonic supranationality?
2 Does Putin's great power restoration campaign challenge the EU's identity?
3 Is supranationality contributing to EU growth retardation?

Hegemonic supranationality

The European project is a vision, framework, and strategy for constructing a post-war united Europe.[3] The vision is rational, ideal, democratic, and harmonist. It postulates a two-tiered supranational (transnational) governance regime where matters of common concern are amicably managed in Brussels;[4] and a space reserved for national authorities, often with shared jurisdiction for local and joint activities (Razin and Rosefielde 2012a, 2012b; Rosefielde and Pfouts 2014; Kaiser and Starie 2009; Baldwin and Wyplosz 2012). This division of responsibility doesn't preclude discord, but facilitates conflict resolution through administrative, judicial, democratic, and consensus building methods. Some of these mechanisms have coercive aspects. Supranational administrations including the European Central Bank (ECB) are supposed to compel without being authoritarian, operating under the rule of law with democratic consent, buttressed by cooperative consensus.

The European Union's founders conceived EU supranationality as a unique system of democratic governance that enabled members to preserve their autonomy and culture while simultaneously reaping the benefits of the collective management of a common market with shared values, standards, and regulations under the rule of law. Diversity and universality were to flourish where they should in their respective spheres, requiring supranational governors to restrain themselves from circumscribing national and local liberties.

Advocates understood that these principles occasionally might be violated, but claimed that transgressions would be minor because members shared the same vision and were committed to mutual support, without carefully considering the possibility of hegemonic capture. If a single powerful member, or cabal at the supranational level finds ways to coerce and dominate, then the EU can be transformed from a democratic into an authoritarian regime without altering its formal structures. Supranationalism is an organizational form, not a guarantee of harmonious diversity and universality. It can be co-opted in the twinkling of the eye.

The danger can be appreciated by pondering Germany's hidden agenda in the recent fracas over Grexit: usurping control of Greece's public finances by coercive means (putatively for Athens's own good; see Schäuble 2015). German Chancellor Angela Merkel and Finance Minister Wolfgang Schäuble worried that Greece had adopted a too-big-to-fail strategy in the hopes of never having to repay its debts. They feared that this disease might become contagious (De Grauwe and Ji 2013); that other highly indebted states (GIIPS: Greece, Ireland, Italy, Portugal, and Spain) might follow Greece's bad example, and sought a structural solution that forced Athens to accumulate the budgetary surpluses needed to pay down its obligations (Cline 2014). The appropriate recourse in a democratic supranational union should have been to work out a collective program for debt resolution and abide by it,[5] even if this compelled Germany to bear some losses.[6] Merkel and Schäuble, however, decided to bully Athens instead by using Germany's control over the ECB to deny Greek banks the euros needed to avert bankruptcy.[7] They demanded that Greece relinquish substantive control over its public finances to assure debt repayment,[8] or face the consequences,[9] effectively imposing new hegemonic rules of the game on what was supposed to be a democratic resolution process.

Greece was brought to its knees by "supranational" capital flight, an exotic form of capital flight associated with otherwise independent nations using a common currency.[10] Greeks and foreign depositors began withdrawing unsustainable amounts of euro deposits from private banks because they correctly feared that the ECB might cut off currency supplies in an attempt to jawbone Greek Prime Minister Alexis Tsipras into accepting public finance structural reforms. Capital flight traditionally has been equated with hot money fleeing currencies ripe for devaluation. The Greek case was different.[11] Euro devaluation wasn't an issue. Depositors fled Greek banks because they wanted to retain access to the euro, not because they feared euro devaluation.[12] They recognized that the ECB might curtail euro access and that Greek banks might collapse if a run-for-the-liquid-euro couldn't be accommodated because banks assets were illiquid.[13]

This vulnerability and the difficulty of quickly re-adopting the drachma were invisible as long as supranational cooperation and consensus were mandatory.[14] Shutting the ECB spigot was unimaginable, Cyprus being viewed as a special case (Economist 2013).[15] Compassion and the mishandling of Germany's debt after World War I were supposed to have precluded a draconian debt settlement (Mankiw 2015; Keynes 1920), but didn't (Marks 2013). Now that the genie is out of the bottle, however, it can be assumed that Germany will exert hegemonic power again whenever there is a looming threat of supranational capital flight. The right of EU member nations to autonomously manage their public finances, unless sanctioned by supranational consensus, has been infringed, and may herald a more comprehensive thrust of powerful members to impose their authority on the weak (Tirole 2015).[16]

Coping With Russia

The EU's identity is tied to the claim that its supranationality is superior to the competition of nations and a model for the world. EU leaders have sought to spread their gospel through the Eastern Partnership Project and beyond as a paradigm for virtuous globalization.[17] The EU successfully championed Enlightenment-based universal rights of man, humanism, democracy, competitive markets, liberalization, traditional social democratic entitlements, affirmative action, internal and external egalitarianism, free migration, convergence, and the international rule of law in a world without potent opposition until Russia annexed Crimea. Suddenly, the glue binding EU identity is being seriously challenged by Russian President Vladimir Putin, who seeks to restore Russian great power, thus thwarting EU expansion and rolling back some past gains (Rosefielde 2016). EU leaders and the community more generally therefore can no longer be confident that the future is theirs, or even that member solidarity is secure. Some countries are sympathetic with Putin's brand of authoritarianism, providing fertile ground for mischief. This means that supranational rules and policies are going to chaff more in the future at the regional, national, and local levels than they did before March 2014,[18] with unpredictable consequences. Supranational authorities may choose to turn a blind eye to the bickering, or follow Germany's hegemonic gambit against Greece in novel forms. Whatever the specific reverberations, the harmony and solidarity that purportedly epitomized the EU project are unlikely to prevail, calling into question whether the gains from the EU supranationality outweigh transnationality's costs. EU supranationality isn't the free ride advocates claimed and seems to be strewn with snares.

European Union growth retardation

European economic growth has fallen persistently since 1975, after postwar catch-up possibilities petered out. The European project didn't prevent this loss of vitality and there are sound grounds for believing that superfluous supranational regulation contributed to the dyspepsia. Klaus Gretschmann reminds us that the EU supranational structures for a multiplicity of reasons relentlessly expand their regulatory reach without adequate justification.[19] Over-regulation is wasteful by definition and often impedes growth by warping and dis-incentivizing innovation, technological progress, entrepreneurship, and investment. Over-regulation devitalizes national economies; supranational over-regulation compounds the problem by adding an additional level of obstruction and waste.

European Union woes

Hegemony, Putin's great power restoration campaign, and secular economic stagnation cannot be blamed on supranationality or the EU project's intent. Germany might well have pressed its claims against Greece as an independent nation state (Eaton and Gersovitz 1981).[20] Putin's gripe is with America and Europe poaching on Russia's pre-war spheres of influence, and the micro and macroeconomic causes of Europe's impaired growth are attributable to policies that may have been adopted anyway had members remained independent. Nonetheless, EU supranationality doesn't seem to have added much value in coping with these challenges, despite its immense expense.

The EU project as originally conceived has secured the peace in Europe and this virtue is likely to endure, but it hasn't been a ringing economic and political success as the chapters in Part I make plain. Nor is it poised to recover its lost lustre anytime soon because its credo-driven policies are counterproductive. Its supranational institutional structure is vulnerable to capture by special interest groups and hasn't provided the miraculous benefits promised. It is premature to predict the ultimate outcome, but the time is at hand for policymakers and economic theorists alike to take dry-eyed stock of the EU dream in order to better address tomorrow's challenges unencumbered by idealist blinders (Obstfeld 2015).[21]

Notes

1 See Chapter 1, this volume: "Both in economic and political terms, the EU is on life support. Its former attractiveness as an economic powerhouse, a political "soft power" and a much appreciated social model seems to be waning in the face of the Eurozone troubles and the political and military challenges at its borders."

2 See Chapter 6, this volume: "the whole apparatus of fiscal governance and conditional lending ... is entrenched in law, treaties, and member state constitutions, and in theory subjects member states to a broad, deep, and automatic mechanism that shapes their fiscal and therefore public policies."

3 There are currently 28 members of the European Union. Bulgaria, Croatia, Czech Republic, Denmark, Hungary, Poland, Romania, Sweden and the United Kingdom have their own currencies and do not participate in the Eurozone. The Maastricht Treaty established the European Union in its present form in 1993. There are 19 members of the Eurozone: Austria, Belgium, Cyprus, Estonia, Finland, France, Germany, Greece, Ireland, Italy, Latvia, Lithuania, Luxembourg, Malta, Netherlands, Portugal, Slovakia, Slovenia, and Spain. It is officially called the euro area, and is an economic and monetary union (EMU). Other EU states are obliged to join once they qualify, except the United Kingdom and Denmark. Members cannot secede or be expelled in principle. Monetary policy is the responsibility of the European Central Bank (ECB). Monaco, San Marino, and Vatican City have concluded formal agreements with the EU to use the euro. Andorra did so on July 1, 2013. Kosovo and Montenegro have unilaterally adopted the euro, but are not EU members.

4 The governing bodies of the EU's supranational governance tier are the European Parliament, Council of the European Union, European Commission, the European Council, European Central Bank, Court of Justice of the European Union, and European Court of Auditors. Supranational bodies have exclusive competence over: (1) the "customs union," (2) competition policy, (3) Eurozone (EZ) monetary power, (4) a common fisheries policy, (5) a common commercial policy, (6) conclusion of certain international agreements. They also have the right to shared competence in (7) the internal market, (8) social policy for aspects defined in the treaty, (9) agriculture and fisheries, excluding the conservation of marine biological resources, (10) environment, (11) consumer protection, (12) transport, (13) trans-European networks, (14) energy, (15) the area of freedom, security, and justice, (16) common safety concerns in public health aspects defined in the treaty, (17) research, development, technology, and space, (18) development, cooperation, and humanitarian aid, (19) coordination of economic and social policies, (20) common security and defence policies. Additionally, supranational bodies enjoy supporting competence in (21) protection and improvement of human health, (22) industry, (23) culture, (24) tourism, (25) education, youth sport, and vocational training, (26) civil protection (disaster prevention), and (27) administration.

5 Every country has laws that regulate default and bankruptcy in the private sector to protect debtors from rapacious creditors. Germany's threat to destroy Greece's banks is tantamount to Germany's Chancellor dictating intra-EU default and bankruptcy law to Greece instead of developing more flexible solutions. A Euro monetary system with no fiscal union or ability to politically agree on debt mutualization is the main cause behind the Greek debt crisis. In June 2012, the European Council launched the movement of the euro area toward banking union. In December 2012, it adopted a three-step process to achieve this goal (Veron 2013). The first step is the concentration of supervision and regulation in an SSM under the aegis of the ECB. The second step is the adoption of legislation set forth in two proposals of the European Commission: Bank Recovery and Resolution Directive (of June 2012) and the Deposit Guarantee Schemes (DGS) Directive (of July 2010). The third step is the creation of a Single Resolution Mechanism once the BRR and DGS legislation is in place. Véron (2013)

26 *Steven Rosefielde*

and Veron and Wolff (2014) identify the need for a fourth step: to go beyond the Single Resolution Mechanism in the areas of insolvency, resolution, and deposit insurance. There was a brief moment in mid-2012 when it appeared that direct ESM (bank bailout institution) recapitalization of banks could alleviate a debt burden otherwise borne by the government in Spain (and even in Ireland retroactively), but Germany, Finland, and the Netherlands promptly rejected that possibility by ruling out ESM direct recapitalization for "legacy" assets. Subsequently the scope for ESM bank recapitalization was limited to €60 billion, so in any event the scope for its preventing meaningful additions to sovereign debt will be modest. More broadly, the hope is that banking union will sever the doom loop because unified supervision will set the stage for mutualized responsibility (see Cline 2014).

6 Bulow and Rogoff (2015b): "That said, now is not the time for debt relief. The only leverage creditors have over Greece is, in a sense, precisely that the country continues to be in financial dire straits. Instead of forgiveness, what the Eurozone countries could offer is flexibility. They could draw up a list of conditions 'worth' more than $95 billion, and assign points to different reform measures. Greece can then exercise autonomy and adjust to changing political and economic circumstances by picking and choosing from that list."

7 Schäuble (2015) denies the contention.

8 The theory literature on debt repayment is divisible into two branches (see Bulow and Rogoff 2015b). The first is the "reputation approach" pioneered by Eaton and Gersovitz (1981). Their view is that countries value access to international capital markets because it allows them to smooth consumption in the face of volatile output and/or fluctuating investment opportunities. They can be trusted to repay loans in good times because they know some day bad times could return, and they don't want to lose their reputation as reliable debtors. This approach is not applicable to the Greek crisis because it does not account for the "economic war" between the Eurozone creditors and Greece. The second approach is the Bulow–Rogoff punishment approach. In the case of Greece, their theory is similar in spirit to an "economic war" between creditors and the debtor as a way to resolve the debt conflict. See note 16 for the distinction between punitive measures and economic war.

9 Bulow and Rogoff (2015b): "To address those concerns, the eurozone countries, led by Germany and Finland, have produced a set of conditions Greece needs to meet to receive more money. They range from budget deficit goals to structural reforms. The goal of these conditions is to ensure that Greece can meet its obligations and that it will ultimately be able to stand on its own feet while remaining in the currency union." See Fischer (2015): "Greece could either exit or accept a program that effectively makes it a European protectorate, without any hope of economic improvement. Greece is now subject to a cure – further austerity – that has not worked in the past and that was prescribed solely to address Germany's domestic political needs."

10 Supranational capital flight should be distinguished from bank runs in dollarized economies like Argentina and Russia during the 1990s. In the supranational case, countries facing capital flight have some influence over the transnational central bank. By contrast Argentina and Russia merely used dollars with no possibility of receiving assistance from the Treasury or Federal Reserve Bank. Argentina, like Greece, was confronted with a conundrum. It sought to restore access to the international capital market (sovereign debt problem) by raising taxes and cutting public expenditures to pay down its indebtedness. But, in doing so it risked making repayment more difficult by plunging the economy into deep depression. Kiguel (2011) argues that Argentina's budget cutting had precisely this adverse effect, and cautions the EU accordingly. His preferred solution is to hold the line on deficit spending insofar as possible, and promote productivity and competition with non-deflationary tactics. Another complementary approach that he fails to consider is steamrolling vested political interests, streamlining government

services and earmarking savings for debt repayment. The structural similarities between Argentina and Greece that guide Kiguel's recommendation are: (1) loss of devaluation option (currency board and dollarization in the Argentinian case; replacement of the drachma with the euro in the Greek case), (2) loss of access to the international capital market (excess sovereign debt), (3) and loss of monetary options due to dollar/euro-ization. On the policy front, both Argentina and Greece tried to acquire external assistance and ultimately failed to obtain enough. They also resorted to deflation to spur competitiveness, but here too were unsuccessful. The only thing that really links Russia's 1998 financial crisis to Greece is duplicity. Yeltsin officials, after scamming their own people innumerable times as in the infamous 1996 "Loan for Shares" swindle of the millennium, began a massive issue of GKO (*gosudarstvennoye kratsrochoye obyazatel'stvo*; government short-term obligations) designed to entice foreign hot money by paying 150 per cent interest, at a time when it could not cover its budgetary expenses with tax revenues hopelessly in arrears. Yeltsin insiders knew that the obligations couldn't be met, but also saw opportunities for self-enrichment and played the situation that way. They secured a 22.6 billion IMF rescue package on 13 July, swapping GKOs for long-term Eurobonds to string the process out, before finally repudiating their GKO and Euro-denominated obligations, and abruptly devaluing on 17 August 1998. In the Asian case, foreign capital fled because private sector risks had increased. By contrast, in the Russian case it fled because carry traders realized that the Russian government was intent on ripping them off. The only question was when, not if, the Kremlin would strike (Razin and Rosefielde 2012c, 2012d, 2012e).

11 The Cyprus case also can be classified as supranational capital flight, but of a different sort. It was basically an old-fashioned bank insolvency crisis, with the novel feature of large offshore bank participation complicated by the ECB's capacity to repay depositors out of the vast pool of EU funds. It wasn't a public finance deficit spending crisis. The debt crisis in Greece conditioned the banking crisis, not vice versa, and the deep issue at stake is Germany's control over Athens's public finance as the driver for capital flight.

12 However, if the euros received from capital flight were used to purchase dollars, investors would have made handsome capital gains. There was precedence for this in the Cyprus banking crisis of 2012–2013.

13 One basic mechanism outlined in recent currency crisis models (see Razin 2015) is where unhedged foreign currency liabilities play the key role in causing and transmitting crises. One of the first models to capture this joint problem was presented in Krugman (1999). In his model, firms suffer from a currency mismatch between their assets and liabilities: their assets are denominated in domestic goods, and their liabilities are denominated in foreign goods. Then, real exchange rate depreciation increases the value of liabilities relative to assets, leading to deterioration in firms' balance sheets (see also Schneider and Tornell 2004; Holmstrom and Tirole 1997; Krugman 1998, 1999; Calvo 1998; Chang and Velasco 2001; Caballero and Krishnamurthy 2001).

Chang and Velasco (2001) model the vicious circle between bank runs and speculative attacks on the currency. On the one hand, the expected collapse of the currency worsens banks' prospects, as they have foreign liabilities and domestic assets, and thus generates bank runs. On the other hand, the collapse of the banks leads to capital outflows that deplete the reserves of the government, encouraging speculative attacks against the currency. Accounting for the circular relationship between currency crises and banking crises complicates policy analysis. For example, a lender-of-last-resort policy or other expansionary policy during a banking crisis might backfire as it depletes the reserves available to the government, making a currency crisis more likely, which in turn might further hurt the banking sector that is exposed to a currency mismatch. See De Grauwe and Ji (2013) for the lender-of-last-resort role.

28 *Steven Rosefielde*

14 Bulow and Rogoff (2015a) write: "It is true that a major early motivation for the EU to lend to Greece was to subsidize its banks, but it is not true that Greece's creditors were taking money out of the country, at least until the Greeks chose to postpone or stop meeting the terms of its second bailout deal in the second half of 2014. Europe continued to provide cash inflows to Greece until that time, on top of the banking system support it still provides, and arguably does not really expect to be a net receiver of very much if any money over the next few years (at the very least). The bailout deals negotiated with Greece were meant to provide it with the cash needed to ease the transition from running primary deficits in its heavy borrowing years and to help keep its banks running and its private creditors at bay. The problems that Greece faces are due to a loss of confidence in the state, not only by foreign private investors but also by Greece's own citizens. Indeed, the latter have withdrawn over a hundred billion euros from the banking system since the onset of the crisis in early 2010. While Europe has replaced much of this money through Target2 loans (now primarily 'Emergency Liquidity Assistance') the Greek banks have also been weakened by the 33.5 per cent of their private loans that are non-performing, reducing their capacity to take on new risky loans. It is partly for this reason, as well as because of the losses Greek banks suffered in 2012 on their holdings of Greek Government Bonds, that a significant part of the new money that Greece received over the past five years had to be used to recapitalize Greek banks. Whereas the EU has actually been a net provider of funds to Greece since the beginning of the crisis, this is not to say that its motivation has been entirely charitable. Greece has been able to combine the threat of default (which would create an unknown and potentially massive risk for the EU), a promised commitment to economic reforms that would put it on the road to self-sufficiency, and its 'too small to fail' status to gain extraordinary financial support. Over time, the risks of 'Grexit' – Greece leaving the euro – while still unknown, appear to have lessened for most observers. At the same time, the Greeks have recently elected a party seemingly intent on rolling back some of the country's hard-won economic reforms, negotiations have become harder [*sic*]. Nevertheless it seems unlikely that in any deal Greece would be asked to pay back as much cash as it receives in net subsidies from the EU, at least for a long time to come."

15 The Cyprus crisis focused on the potential insolvency of banks operating with euros, rather than the larger Greek issue of excessive public debt. Its resolution differs too because Greek depositors have not yet been subjected to haircuts. The Cyprus crisis was caused by offshore bank over-leveraging in the wake of a land speculation boom fuelled in significant part by Russian overseas investors. These banks held €22 billion of Greek private-sector debt, more than 90 per cent of Cyprus's GDP. Bank deposits, half of which were from Russia, exceeded $120 billion. Russian oligarch Dmitry Rybolovlev owned a 10 per cent share in the Bank of Cyprus. The mismatch between Cyprus's obligations and its ability to repay gradually induced bank deposit holders to withdraw their funds and transfer them abroad. This transformed and expanded the debt issue into a banking crisis as the pace of withdrawals from overseas investors fleeing the country with their money accelerated. The problem was resolved by compelling Cyprus to close its second-largest bank, the Cyprus Popular Bank (also known as Laiki Bank), imposing a one-time bank deposit levy on all uninsured deposits, and a 48 per cent levy on uninsured deposits in the Bank of Cyprus (the island's largest commercial bank) held largely by wealthy citizens of other countries (many of them from Russia) who were using Cyprus as a tax haven. Non-insured deposits of €100,000 or less were spared, but local Cypriots still suffered large losses to pay for the speculative excesses of others. The Greek crisis differs from Cyprus's because it is rooted in public sector overspending, rather than overseas financial speculation. The solution too is different because the ECB didn't seize control over Cyprus's public fiscal sector. Moreover, there was no evidence that Brussels was manoeuvring to expel Cyprus from the EU, as has been alleged in the Greek case.

16 Tirole analyses the determinants of international solidarity and their impact on institutions and sovereign borrowing in a principal agent framework where the equilibrium is on the efficiency frontier up to the point that there are spillovers (externalities) that are part of the equilibrium. If there are large negative externalities the equilibrium may be value-destroying, but the result is unintentional. This paper stresses an alternative possibility where Berlin deliberately threatens to harm Athens to gain control over Greece's fiscal policy. Germany's behaviour is a form of economic war. Tirole's framework relies on rational risk sharing in a cooperative environment, which excludes economic warfare. He distinguishes between two forms of solidarity: ex post (spontaneous) and ex ante (contractual). Ex post, the impacted countries may stand by the troubled country because they want to avoid the externality or collateral damage inflicted by the latter's default: Where does this quote end? "Ex ante, they may commit to support levels beyond what they would spontaneously offer ex post, through joint-and-several liability or alternative risk-sharing mechanisms. Spontaneous and contractual bailouts are not equivalent. They correspond roughly to the European approach to date and to the various Eurobond proposals. First, joint-and-several liability redistributes resources from healthy countries to fragile ones as the latter have no means to compensate the former for the resulting insurance (they would have to borrow even more to do that). Second, even in the absence of initial asymmetries, joint liability affects the countries' borrowing capability and probability of default. A failure to stand by a failing country implies a cost of own default on top of the collateral damage incurred when the failing country defaults. Joint liability therefore may create domino effects and increase default costs if the guarantor does not have deep pockets. Conversely, it reduces the occurrence of default if debt levels are moderate enough so as to allow the guarantor to stand by its promise to cover the other country's debt if needed. The paper investigates when countries are willing to extend solidarity by entering ex ante risk-sharing arrangements. It looks at optimal contracts in two environments. In the asymmetric case, a risky country (the "agent") under laissez-faire borrows from the market; when defaulting, it exerts an externality on some other country (the "principal"), which has deep pockets. Tirole concludes first that solidarity is driven by the fear that spillovers from the distressed country's default negatively affect the rescuer, and second that once the veil of ignorance is lifted (as is currently the case in the eurozone), healthy countries have no incentive to accept obligations beyond the implicit ones that arise from spillover externalities.

17 The European Commission controls the Eastern Partnership (EaP). It is an initiative of the European Union governing its relationship with the post-Soviet states of Armenia, Azerbaijan, Belarus, Georgia, Moldova, and Ukraine, and was intended to provide a venue for discussions of trade, economic strategy, travel agreements, and other issues between the EU and its eastern neighbours. The project was initiated by Poland and a subsequent proposal was prepared in co-operation with Sweden. It was presented by the foreign minister of Poland and Sweden at the EU's General Affairs and External Relations Council in Brussels on 26 May 2008.The Eastern Partnership was inaugurated by the European Union in Prague on 7 May 2009. The Eastern Partnership consists of the post-Soviet states: Armenia, Azerbaijan, Belarus, Georgia, Moldova, Ukraine, and the European Union. See de Waal and Youngs (2015).

18 After the Federation Council approved upon the final reading of the treaty of accession of the Crimea to the Russian Federation, Vladimir Putin ratified the inclusion of two new areas into the Russian Federation: the Republic of Crimea and the City of Federal Importance of Sevastopol.

19 See Chapter 1, this volume: "The EU has turned into a legislative machine trying to interpret her fields of competence ever more widely. Ceaselessly, the Commission is working on weaving an ever closer web of harmonized European laws and regulations – the result thereof, the 'acquis communautaire', is presently estimated to comprise some 100,000 printed pages."

20 This is a slippery proposition. Sovereign states frequently repudiate their obligations, leaving creditors little practical recourse. If Greece wasn't a Eurozone member Germany probably couldn't collect (cf. Bulow and Rogoff 1989, 2015b). The Greek crisis is a hybrid of an international debt crisis and an "economic war" (a currency crisis of a "sudden stop" variety (see Calvo 1998; cf. Bulow and Rogoff 1998). The literature on the international debt features that contracts under limited enforcement provides doesn't adequately illuminate the Greek debt crisis. A benchmark for the literature is that with access to complete international credit markets, an economy would be able to borrow to finance a stable level of consumption and investment. However, in reality, countries often experience capital outflows in very low-income periods. Eaton and Gersovitz (1981) pioneered the stream of literature dealing with incomplete international credit markets and the risk of debt repudiation. International lenders cannot fully seize collateral from another country when it refuses to honour its debt obligations. Inter-temporal sanctions arise because of a threat of cut-off from future borrowing if a country defaults. As shown by Eaton and Gersovitz (1981), the level of debt is the minimum of the economy's credit demands and the constraints on credit imposed by the lenders. Borrowing occurs in periods of relatively low income and must be fully repaid in the following period. Failure to repay prevents borrowing in a subsequent period. Note that the "incentive compatibility" constraint is most likely to be hit in a period where, in order to maintain the borrower's reputation, she is called upon to make an exceptionally large repayment; an empirically irrelevant feature. Bulow and Rogoff (1989) model the debt crisis differently. They assume that International lending must be supported by the direct sanctions available to creditors and cannot be supported by a country's "reputation for repayment. Aguiar and Gopinath (2006) demonstrate how countries default in bad times to smooth consumption. Building on the inter-temporal approach, Bulow and Rogoff invoke the premise that countries that default do not suffer from a substantially higher cost of borrowing after the debt crisis. They regain access to the international credit markets soon after they default on their debt. A new study by Cruces and Trebesch (2013), which extends the work of Sturzenegger and Zettelmeyer (2006), finds that default episodes with large "haircuts" to creditors are associated with (1) high future sovereign spreads and (2) long periods of market exclusion. But this literature so far is unable fully to account for why sovereign default does occur and why international lenders extend credit to bad borrowers as much as they do. The theoretical literature on international debt often makes strong assumptions about creditor behaviour.

21 Obstfeld proposes a new policy trilemma for currency unions such as the Eurozone: A country cannot simultaneously maintain all three of (1) full cross-border financial integration, (2) financial stability and (3) national fiscal independence. Supposing that countries forgo the options of financial repression and capital controls (goal 1), they cannot credibly stabilize their financial systems (goal 2). If the single-currency area has reached a sufficient degree of financial integration, these countries cannot achieve financial stability without external fiscal support either directly (from partner country treasuries) or indirectly (through monetary financing from the union-wide central bank), thus sacrificing goal 3. Alternatively, a country that is reliant mainly on its own fiscal resources (goal 3) will likely sacrifice financial integration in order to achieve financial stability, as is true in the euro area today, because markets will then assess financial risks along national lines. Alternatively, voluntary withdrawal from the single financial market might allow a country with limited fiscal space to control and insulate its financial sector enough to minimize its fragility.

References

Aguiar, M. and G. Gopinath. 2006. "Defaultable Debt, Interest Rates and the Current Account." *Journal of International Economics* 69(1): 64–83.

Baldwin, R. and C. Wyplosz. 2012. *The Economics of European Integration*, 4th edn. New York: McGraw-Hill.

Bulow, J. and K. Rogoff 1989. "Sovereign Debt: Is to Forgive or Forget?" *American Economic Review* 79(1): 43–50.

Bulow, J. and K. Rogoff 2015a. "The Modern Greek Tragedy." *CEPR Vox* (10 June). Available at www.voxeu.org/article/modern-greek-tragedy.

Bulow, J. and K. Rogoff. 2015b. "Why Sovereigns Repay Debts to External Creditors and Why It Matters." *CEPR Vox* (10 June). Available at www.voxeu.org/article/why-sovereigns-repay-debts-external-creditors-and-why-it-matters.

Caballero, R. and A. Krishnamurthy. 2001. "International and Domestic Collateral Constraints in a Model of Emerging Market Crises." *Journal of Monetary Economics* 48: 513–548.

Calvo, G. 1998. "Capital Flows and Capital-Market Crises: The Simple Economics of Sudden Stops." *Journal of Applied Economics* 1: 35–54.

Chang, R. and A. Velasco. 2001. "A Model of Financial Crises in Emerging Markets." *Quarterly Journal of Economics* 116: 489–517.

Cline, W. 2014. *Managing the Euro Area Debt Crisis*. Washington, DC: Peterson Institute for International Economics.

Cruces, J. J. and C. Trebesch. 2013. "Sovereign Defaults: The Price of Haircuts." *American Economic Journal: Macroeconomics* 5(3): 1–34.

De Grauwe, P. and Y. Ji. 2013. "Self Fulfilling Crises in the Eurozone: An Empirical Test," *Journal of International Money and Finance* 34 (April): 15–36.

De Grauwe, P. 2010. "The Greek Crisis and the Future of the Eurozone: The Structural Problem in the Eurozone is Created by the Fact that the Monetary Union is Not Embedded in a Political Union." *Eurointelligence* (November), p. 5.

De Grauwe, P. 2000. *Economics of Monetary Union*. New York: Oxford University Press.

de Waal, T. and R. Youngs. 2015. "Reform as Resilience: An Agenda for the Eastern Partnership." May 14. Available at http://carnegieendowment.org/2015/05/14/reform-as-resilience-agenda-for-eastern-partnership/i8k4?mkt_tok=3RkMMJWWfF9wsRoju aTIZKXonjHpfsX56OsvXqGg38431UFwdcjKPmjr1YcIRct0aPyQAgobGp5I5FEIQ7 XYTLB2t60MWA%3D%3D.

Eaton, J. and M. Gersovitz. 1981. "Debt with Potential Repudiation: Theoretical and Empirical Analysis." *Review of Economic Studies* 48 (2): 289–309.

Economist 2013. "What Happened in Cyprus?" *The Economist* (28 March). Available at www.economist.com/blogs/freeexchange/2013/03/interview-athanasios-orphanides.

Fischer, J. 2015. "The Return of the Ugly German." *Project Syndicate* (July 23). Available at www.project-syndicate.org/commentary/return-of-the-ugly-german-by-joschka-fischer-2015-07.

Holmstrom, B. and J. Tirole. 1997. "Financial Intermediation, Loanable Funds, and the Real Sector." *Quarterly Journal of Economics* 112: 663–691.

Kaiser, W. and P. Starie, eds. 2009. *Transnational European Union: Towards a Common Political Space*. London: Routledge.

Keynes, J. M. 1920. *The Economic Consequences of the Peace*. New York: Harcourt, Brace and Howe.

Kiguel, M. 2011. "Argentina and Greece: More Similarities than Differences in the Initial Conditions." *Vox* (August 16). Available at www.voxeu.org/article/argentine-lessons-europe-sovereign-debt-and-banking-crises.

Krugman, P. 1998. *It's Baaack! Japan's Slump and the Return of the Liquidity Trap.* Brookings Papers on Economic Activity 2. Washington, DC: Brookings Institution.

Krugman, P. 1999. "Balance Sheets, the Transfer Problem, and Financial Crises." *International Tax and Public Finance* 6: 459–472.

Mankiw, G. 2015. "History Echoes Through Greek Debt Crisis." *New York Times* (July 19), p. 4.

Marks, S. 2013. "Mistakes and Myths: The Allies, Germany, and the Versailles Treaty, 1918–1921." *The Journal of Modern History* 85(3): 632–659.

Obstfeld, M. 2015. *Trilemmas and Trade-Offs: Living with Financial Globalisation.* BIS Working Papers 480, January. Basel: Bank for International Settlements. Available at www.bis.org/publ/work480.pdf.

Razin, A. and S. Rosefielde. 2012a. "A Tale of a Politically-Failing Single-Currency Area." *Israel Economic Review* 10(1): 125–138.

Razin, A. and S. Rosefielde. 2012b. "What Really Ails the Eurozone? Faulty Supranational Architecture." *Contemporary Economics* 6(4) (December): 10–18.

Razin, A. and S. Rosefielde. 2012c. "Asian Currency and Financial Crises in the 1990s." In *Prevention and Crisis Management: Lessons for Asia from the 2008 Crisis*, edited by S. Rosefielde, M. Kuboniwa and S. Mizobata. Singapore: World Scientific, p. 16.

Razin, A. and S. Rosefielde. 2012d. "The 2008-09 Global Crisis." In *Prevention and Crisis Management: Lessons for Asia from the 2008 Crisis*, edited by S. Rosefielde, M. Kuboniwa and S. Mizobata. Singapore: World Scientific, p. 28.

Razin, A. and S. Rosefielde. 2012e. "PIIGS." In *Prevention and Crisis Management: Lessons for Asia from the 2008 Crisis*, edited by S. Rosefielde, M. Kuboniwa and S. Mizobata. Singapore: World Scientific, p. 88.

Rosefielde, S. 2016. *The Kremlin Strikes Back: Russia and the West after Crimea's Annexation.* Cambridge: Cambridge University Press.

Rosefielde, S. and R. W. Pfouts. 2014. *Inclusive Economic Theory.* Singapore: World Scientific Publishers.

Schauble, W. 2015. "There Is No German Dominance." *Spiegel* (July 17). Available at www.spiegel.de/international/germany/interview-with-german-finance-minister-wolfgang-schaeuble-a-1044233.html.

Schneider, M. and A. Tornell. 2004. "Balance Sheet Effects, Bailout Guarantees and Financial Crises." *Review of Economic Studies* 71: 883–913.

Sturzenegger, F. and J. Zettelmeyer. 2006. *Debt Defaults and Lessons from a Decade of Crises.* Cambridge, MA: MIT Press.

Tirole, J. 2015. "Country Solidarity in Sovereign Crises." *American Economic Review* 105(8): 2333–2363.

Veron, N. 2013. "A Realistic Bridge Towards European Banking Union." Policy Brief 13–17, 26 June. Available at http://bruegel.org/2013/06/a-realistic-bridge-towards-european-banking-union.

Véron, N. and G. B. Wolff. 2013. *From Supervision to Resolution: Next Steps on the Road to European Banking Union.* Bruegel Policy Contribution 2013/04 (February). Brussels: Bruegel.

1 The European Union in stormy seas

Beginning of the end or end of the beginning

Klaus Gretschmann

The future has many names:
for the weak it is the unreachable
for the fearsome it is the unknown
for the courageous it is an opportunity.

Victor Hugo

The report of my death was an exaggeration.

Mark Twain

Introduction

There is a fact which is widely known but of which we are rarely aware: European integration from its very beginning has always been a unique social, economic, and political experiment. Integration, communication, coordination, and cooperation between nation states on the basis of common rules and institutions and an ever-closer interlocking of powers between which there had been much friction and conflict over centuries, was the magic incantation. Johan Olsen's dictum holds true, according to which far-reaching tectonic shifts have been created in Europe over the past five decades, which contain a high degree of irreversibility, a kind of locked-in effect ascertaining that no falling away from what the EU has created, occurred. However, just this alleged irreversibility is today very much in doubt.

Both in economic and political terms, the EU is on life support. Its former attractiveness as an economic powerhouse, a political "soft power" and a much appreciated social model seems to be waning in the face of the Eurozone troubles, the political and military challenges at its borders, and its internal bickering and conflicts of interest. Far away from traditional integrationist thinking, which claims that the EU has always been on an irreversible trend towards an ever-closer union, some observers even hold that the end is near; that the Union is losing its internal coherence, its historical significance, and economic usefulness. Today, we witness disintegration and the *beginning of the end*! Other students of the EU integration argue that the EU has always fluctuated like the swing of a pendulum: periods of integration and disintegration have alternated. What we go through today is the *end of the beginning*, through the crises towards a new powerful

Europe, admittedly with still blurred outlines. This chapter will analyse what new deficiencies and qualities the crises have laid bare, what the odds are that these will be overcome, and which measures are required to arrive at the bright side.

The re-emergence of dormant yet fundamental problems

For many decades EU politicians have followed the guiding star of an ever-closer union. However, recent crises, notably debt and financial problems, political legitimacy, and over-bureaucratic machinery in Brussels have effected a sharp drop in the Union's attractiveness.

Political systems fray and decay Europe-wide. An increasing number of Member States from Spain to Greece are afraid that they may face "ungovernability" with dramatic consequences for the social and political glue holding the Union together.

Indeed, these are the most testing and taxing times for the EU. Geopolitical tensions are at historic levels, growth is stalling widely and citizens' dissatisfaction throughout the Union is growing. Public disenfranchisement with Brussels politics has become the focus of the crises. Reasons for growing Euroscepticism abound. At its very heart seems to be the perception (right or wrong) by the people in the streets that an elitist power cartel of pro-European agents with disregard for the real problems citizens all over the Union are facing has developed and has started a "power grab" from national governments beyond what is established in the Treaties. They feel disempowered, alienated, and subject to forces they cannot control.

Although Brussels is often the scapegoat for perceived aberrations rather than genuinely at fault, public antagonism has reached unprecedented levels that put the pro-integration proclivity and sentiment to a serious test. This may derail the EU project faster than we expect. Eurosceptic parties are advancing everywhere, and while their direct effects in elections are still modest, their way to shape the public discourse can be felt in many policy areas. Referring to a new state of fragility in the EU, Mark Leonard pinpoints "the root of Europe's political crisis: the necessity and impossibility of integration" (Leonard 2011: 1). It is without question that only if *Europe in its entirety* can be put back on the track of economic success is she able to remain a realm of peace, liberty, security, and welfare. Unfortunately, today Europe (with few exceptions) is rather a realm of recession, deflation, unemployment, and a lack of social and political stability. Before the financial and economic crisis of 2008 the belief prevailed that the European economy was in a state of "great moderation."[1] Today, it rather appears as if we were in an era of great volatility and instability. The ongoing nationalist revival in Western and Eastern Europe is caused by the confluence of several factors: It is the emergence of major new and pressing problems accompanied by placating and dispiriting remarks of politicians that rule the day, problems which may entail serious disintegration (Eppler and Scheller 2014) and furthermore:

•   The persistent crisis of the Eurozone and the "Grexit" problem;
•   serious disputes over migration and asylum issues;

- energy and climate policies;
- Russia and the revival of geopolitics; and
- technocratic and bureaucratic governance in the Union.

Before going into some of these problems in closer detail below, I do think it is useful if not outright indispensable to recall some theoretical foundations which can pinpoint the interest structure, and the behaviour of nation states in international settings.

The EU and her nation states – a most complex and complicated relationship

Analytical groundwork

Fundamentally, states seek to increase their power in international (economic) relations in order to create conditions that minimize the costs of pursuing their domestic priorities in an interdependent world. Their policy choices are conditioned by the constraints and opportunities they face in the international environment.

EU interdependence provides both costs and opportunities for all actors involved. The main benefit of interdependence is the welfare gain that results from a more efficient allocation of resources. The foremost price of interdependence is a relative loss in national decision-making autonomy. Under the conditions of interdependence the ability of a government to pursue its own domestic priorities is constrained by external forces over which it has little or no control. Governments can control domestic conditions only if they can influence the decisions taken in other countries. Thus, states want to avoid or constrain negative externalities of other governments' pursuits of domestic (economic) priorities.

Up until 2008/2009, it seemed to be a kind of generic law in integration that whenever a nation's ability to control its economy was constrained by either market forces, the most prominent of which is international capital mobility, or by spillover from economic policy measures abroad, integration provided a tool for regaining control and material sovereignty at a supra-national level, through the pooling of resources, co-operative governance, and institutionalization of rules for policy-making.

Against this backdrop, it is necessary to reconcile conflicting national preferences, perceptions, interests, and "beliefs." This is particularly relevant since the EU policymaking is only rarely built upon a shared, consistent, and coherent concept of policymaking for Europe as a whole.[2]

What the present crises have exposed is that many aspects that arise because of European Union integration have impacted severely on factors such as:

- *Sovereignty:* Governments are increasingly often unwilling to limit or constrain sovereign decision-making, for example by accepting binding rules or international monitoring of their own compliance with agreements.

- *Heterogeneous preferences:* Governments often have divergent interests and priorities as regards specific solutions, even where they share general long-term goals. Energy policy or CO_2 reduction policies may impact differently on individual EU Member States.
- *The "weakest link" problem:* Some desirable results can only be achieved when every government fully complies with a common approach. Success can be eroded by a single act of non-compliance, sometimes due to a country that cannot – at a reasonable cost – carry the burden.

However, there seems to be a waning will to coordinate policy in Europe. While Article 121 of the *Treaty on the Functioning of the European Union* requires Member States to consider their economic policies as a matter of common interest, the reality is that agreement on joint policymaking is rather thin. Whereas *"Euroland"* is characterized by a single currency and a single monetary authority, fiscal policy, incomes policies, and social policies in Europe are still the domain of national governments. This raises questions of policy consistency, compatibility of decisions, and instruments as well as the timing and extent of policy changes. The problem, however, is that there is as yet no clear vision of where we are heading.

Indeed, co-ordination is particularly difficult if policymakers do not agree on the "true model" (i.e. an accurate characterization of how the economy functions). What are required are common perceptions and interpretations of what elements can and should be influenced as well as a sufficient degree of homogeneity among the relevant actors. Unfortunately, as analysed in the literature on policy coordination in the late 1980s, difficulties can be attributed to four main factors:

- There are different national constraints on the policy instruments available (*limited domain*).
- There is disagreement about the effects (both of their scale and nature) of specific policy changes on policy targets (*differences in beliefs*).
- There are cross-country differences in the degree of (inter-)dependence (*differences in spill-over effects*).
- There are different models of how national economies and the EU economy work (*model uncertainties*).

Feldstein (1988) and Frenkel and Rockett (1988) have proven conclusively that if policymakers do not agree on the "true model", policies may well entail welfare losses. In any international setting like the EU, the probability that there is model certainty and consensus is pretty low – notably in the wake of the crises. The above argument about model uncertainties and disparate beliefs demonstrates that in fact (economic and monetary) integration has not yet sufficiently overcome national interests and is still embedded in and constrained by disparate (economic) beliefs and ideas of what kind of Europe we should envisage. Against this backdrop, there is a need to reconcile conflicting national preferences, perceptions, interests, and "beliefs."

The crisis of the Eurozone

The troubles facing the euro area are many and substantial. However, most of the problems that have materialized over the past years have already fuelled the literature at the time when the introduction of a common currency was discussed:

- EMU was designed as a profoundly different policy regime, albeit sold to the public as a re-birth of the German monetary system.
- The probability of asymmetric shocks, which had been analyzed as a danger to a unified monetary policy regime, was ignored or outright denied.
- The one-size fits all problem of a single interest rate for the Union as a whole was defined as "manageable."
- The European Central Bank (ECB) was sold as a Bundesbank clone both in its structure, independence, and policy style.
- The Stability and Growth Pact (SGP) was a poor substitute for a lacking common or at least co-ordinated fiscal policy among Member States.
- No system of fiscal equalization was considered even though it would have been badly needed to balance out the different welfare and income levels among Member States.
- The loss of the exchange rate mechanics in a monetary union was widely underestimated.
- The fact that a unified low interest rate at the German level which enabled the high interest countries to lower their debt burden and trigger new capital inflows at low costs was ignored.
- It was assumed that the monetary unification would entail political integration in its own right; however national interests and political rivalries lasted.
- Institutional and legal rules and regulations were thought to hold water but were never watertight; rather, they were subject to political gusts of wind influenced by the powers that be.

(Gretschmann 1993)

However, those who dared to speak up about the flaws and downsides of the EMU were either ignored or side-lined (Geppert 2014). Indeed, while for more than a decade the introduction of the Euro could be viewed as a success story, today the Euro has uncovered its political downside: it has become an explosive charge, a divisive device which contains the main ingredients for setting individual Member States of the Union apart. However, the argument that the very existence of a single currency has brought misery to many parts of Europe and has severely damaged the European project goes too far. Yet admittedly, being locked in a currency union makes it on the one hand easier for deficit countries to build large imbalances through tapping the "savings and capital pools" of the rich countries at very low costs (i.e. interest rates) and makes it – at the same time – impossible to find an easy escape route and adjust their economies in difficult times.

Today, the Eurozone faces the prospect of ongoing deep recessions in individual Member States and concomitantly strong support for populist parties. It is possible but not probable that Eurozone governments will bite the bullet and agree to a fiscal union including a degree of risk mutualisation and transfers between participating economies. Rather, we observe today a reverse thrust away from an ever-closer Union. Weak public finances in a group of countries, persistent imbalances, slow productivity growth, unemployment, etc. became increasingly overt and distinct in the wake of the global financial crisis. And there is no denial: the Eurozone and its governments have repeatedly broken the legal provisions and limitations which they have committed the Member States to respect at all costs in the Maastricht Treaty. The running excuse as spelled out by then-French Finance Minister Christine Lagarde, viz. that politicians have violated the Treaty repeatedly only in order to save Europe, sounds hollow and apologetic. The same applies to the many decisions of the ECB, which appear to trespass into areas that are explicitly forbidden by the Treaties.[3] Consequently, a wave of scepticism has ensued both in the general public and in professional circles.

The "Greece Problem" between gimmickry, tragedy, and sound economics

Sometimes the impression prevails that politicians (ab)use economics like drunkards use a streetlight: they are in search of a foothold not of light or even enlightenment. This proposition seems to be strongly supported by the discussion on Greece and Grexit. Indeed, the *Greece problem* is only partly about sound economics; rather, it displays all the ingredients of political gimmickry: both creditors and debtors play all kinds of tricks on each other – stalling for time, refusing to compromise, threatening to defect, setting incentives, etc. This confirms the theoretical analysis above: there is no trust and solidarity, no convergence of beliefs and models, but rather a lot of national self-interest as well as more deals than ideals on all sides of the negotiation table.

Let us backtrack for a moment. Ever since the beginning of the sovereign debt crisis in Europe 2009/2010 (in the wake of the Lehman collapse), Greece has played a major role. Due to its very shaky economy and its over-indebtedness, capital markets decided to test the euro by dropping Greece bonds, making Greece debts impossible to finance. Greece was left with no chance but to apply for outside help and both the EU and IMF promised a rescue package, which proved to imply a heavy social and economic burden: cut-backs in public spending, sacking civil servants, increasing taxes, and cutting wages and pensions accompanied by privatizations in exchange for massive bail-out money. More than 5 years and many emergency summits and stimulus packages later, it is again Greece which may mark, as some pundits maintain, the end of the Eurozone and possibly even the EU as we have known it. Indeed, we have entered the most critical phase that the single European currency has seen so far. In the wake of massive negative effects resulting from the – some say imposed, others indispensable – austerity measures, the Greek elections of December 2014 produced a new hard-left government to run the country. The new ruling Syriza players aimed at a reversal of the "malign" bailout reforms.

In the wake of the new government taking office, Greece and her lenders have tried to agree on a new reform program, which would enable the creditors to release 7.2 billion euros that in 2015 remained in the second rescue package. Ever since, ever newer proposals and papers have been produced and submitted by both sides – each time purportedly the very last offer – before being rejected or withdrawn and the whole process started all over again. In the meantime, economic agents and market participants were losing their last ounce of trust and confidence, capital outflows maximized, the Greek government was no longer able to pay Greece's bills, company shares were falling rapidly, and unemployment mounted to 27 per cent.

The new government was fighting hard to avoid being forced to carry on the "old" reform strategy; yet basically the choice was between two evils – either to sign up to the new austerity measures against which they had campaigned, or plunge Greece into default and the possible exit from the Eurozone.

Against this backdrop, there was only one strategy left: demanding major debt relief while rejecting reforms. Knowing that Europe would do its utmost to avoid a Grexit (less for economic and more for political reasons), the calculus was stalling for time until the very last second before full default and hope that the creditors would blink and go for a "soft" deal.

As convincingly argued by Aristides Hatzis:

> there are two conflicting narratives about the deadlock in negotiations between Greece and its Eurozone partners. (1) Greece is governed by populist radical leftists who blackmail the Eurozone by threatening to explode the financial equivalent of a suicide bomb, i.e. Grexit. (2) Greece is bullied by callous partners who are only interested in making an example of it.
>
> (Hatzis 2015: 7)

In this setting, there is also the domestic logic involved. The government cannot give in and accept a new bailout agreement based on the "old design", signaling that it would break every promise they had been elected for, viz. no more austerity. On top of this, there is a strong ideological opposition within the Syriza party to virtually any deal with creditors, consequently threatening to break up the government.

In order to break the impasse, this kind of gambling has to stop. However, in the face of the amount of money and reputation at stake, this is hardly probable. On the one hand, no party can give in without a drastic loss of domestic political support; on the other hand no side is prepared to take the blame if talks fail and a Grexit ensues.

Unfortunately, Greece's new rulers have played the game in a most inept way, alienating and feuding with the partners, trying to make them lose face and thereby making it more difficult to compromise. Athens may be "dangerously miscalculating" in the belief that Greece's creditors will, at the last minute, "blink".

Greece may count on quite a lot of external pressure on the EU to solve the Greek problem by a U-turn in their economic and political approach, viz. towards more growth stimuli and less austerity. Notably, the USA, Japan, and Canada worry about the unforeseeable consequences of a breakup of the Eurozone. They are afraid that the world economy, fragile as it is, may be hit hard and that a kind of failed state might result at the south-eastern corner of NATO. And indeed Greece is playing its bargaining chips quite skillfully: Closer cooperation with Russia, funds to ask for from China, vetoing the Russian sanctions in the European Council, etc. have been put in the midst. Moreover, both the EU and the IMF may be afraid that when it comes to a Greek default their money (in June 2015, up to 240 billion euros plus an additional €83 billion in ECB liquidity assistance) may be lost. Small wonder that under strong domestic political pressure the Greek government was playing for time, alternately refusing to submit a list of meaningful reform proposals and then coming back with new and sometimes awkward ideas, just to be rebuked again.[4] This stalling strategy enabled Prime Minister Tsipras to "silently" envisage and carry out a "referendum" on the reform proposals, viz. "obligations" that the "institutions" (i.e. ECB, IMF, COM) and the Member States wished to impose.

The final deal to unlock the more than €86 billion bailout involves laws that implement VAT hikes, cuts pensions, takes steps to ensure the independence of Greece's statistics office, and puts measures in place to automatically slash spending if Greece fails to meet its targets on primary surpluses (revenue minus expenditure excluding debt servicing costs). Moreover, Greece will have to overhaul its civil justice system, bring bank resolution laws in line with the EU rules, and will have to sell off €50 bn of Greek assets (via privatization).

Unfortunately, the ultimate deal that has been reached will be a short-term fix rather than a long-term solution, as it does not bring sufficient real debt relief.[5] What is imperative is that Greece increase growth and productivity. For this, domestic and foreign investments as well as fresh money is needed, together with a long-term, cross-party package that addresses fundamental institutional problems and is supported across Greek civil society. The creditors, on the other hand, need to back such a long-term plan, and put wise fiscal targets and promising debt relief on the table.

What stands between Greece and prosperity is not another labour reform or wage cuts to make the economy more "competitive", nor further fiscal consolidation or a pension reform to instill confidence in investors. The real issues run deeper than that. Only if Europe is able to help unlock the growth potential of Greece and do away with growth and productivity impediments,[6] will it be able to pass the litmus test of its existence. However, for this process to be implemented, we may need to reinvent an active and activist EU!

Migration and asylum: gutless procrastination rather than tough decisions

Next to the Euro's problems, recent surveys show that the EU citizens worry most about immigration and asylum polices in the Union and the Member States. Also, in spite of immigration and asylum having been named as one of the ten priority policy areas of the Juncker Commission, both EU decision-makers and Member States' politicians seem to be sitting on their hands, shying away from making courageous decisions for fear of their constituents' reaction.

Indeed, although already a running theme in the Union for many years,[7] in the more recent past Europe has been surprised and overwhelmed by the massive rise of illegal immigration and large numbers of fugitives and asylum seekers from all over the world and notably Africa, Near, and Middle East and the Balkans.

The migrant traffic and trafficking is rising for various reasons: the disintegration of North African countries such as Libya, the Shia-Sunni wars in the Near East such as in Yemen; repression in Eritrea; civil war in Sudan and South Sudan; the situation in Nigeria and last but not least wars and terrorism in Iraq and Syria. People coming to Europe are trying to find shelter, refuge, and sanctuary here. Others would simply like to escape their poor economic situation back home. The EU's general public is irritated and confused and faced with a trilemma:

1   On the one hand the European values dictate to help fugitives from outside the Union on moral grounds. Notably, rescue operations in the Mediterranean seem to be the tall order of the day, in order to prevent the Mediterranean Sea from becoming a watery mass grave.
2   On the other hand, rescue operations making the crossing of the sea less risky may well contribute to a mounting wave of migrants into Europe, as the risks will be reduced and the incentives will rise.
3   From a purely rational vantage point and leaving humanitarian aspects aside, rescue operations or even – as discussed in some circles – the opening up of large legal channels for immigration – would not serve the regulation but rather the stimulation of immigration into the Union, the reason being that this would *not* help at all in stabilizing the situation in the countries of origin.

So, Europeans are afraid that ten years from now, Europe will look completely different unless we are willing to take hard decisions and make "tough choices" on migration and asylum. Unfortunately, leaving lip service aside, leaders and politicians within the Union do not agree on the right decisions and basic philosophies and rules on this phenomenon. In addition, different Member States are affected to varying degrees by migration and asylum seekers.[8] And, while the churches and various southern European political leaders have made appeals for a shared commitment to humanitarianism, further north the migrant flood has stoked a surge of anti-immigrant sentiment.

While many citizens of Europe feel and perceive that Europe cannot absorb all the millions from Africa, the Near East, or Asia who wish to gain access in order to share western standards of living and wealth, the EU politicians are most reticent to make the decisions needed. The need to define a ceiling (at whatever high or low level) regarding the volume of the inflow has NOT so far been acknowledged by either Member States' politicians or the Union's representatives. Rather, the European Commission is in search of finding a fairer way to distribute asylum seekers and migrants in the EU.

Despite problems with some reluctant Member States, the Commission unveiled concrete proposals for the relocation and the resettlement of large numbers from outside the EU across Member States. Under the Commission's scheme, the 28 Member States would be required to accept asylum seekers in proportion to the size of their economy, unemployment rate, and population. However, such a distribution key needs to find acceptance with the populations in the respective countries and needs to be adopted by the Council, voting by qualified majority. It looks like the plan will be rejected due to exactly the national policymakers' rationales as described above.

In order to regain citizens' trust and confidence all over Europe, and to compensate for the loss of the EU attractiveness, policymakers need to act jointly and with a focus on the troublesome issue of determining the amount of migrants to accept and only as a second step to decide about the national quotas. As long as policymakers are beating around the bush, the EU's attractiveness and popularity will continue to be severely damaged. So, alongside the Euro problem, asylum and immigration issues are a second explosive charge able to bring the EU integration to an end.

Where are the citizens? Legislative overreach, bureaucratic regulation, and the lack of subsidiarity

The citizens in the EU have learned that the EU institutions – not least the European Commission – are often acting as players to grab more power and influence (Eurobarometer 2014). EU bureaucrats push their little pet projects – no matter how many more urgent and important problems are hitting the peoples of Europe. European officials engage in a multitude of rather unimportant activities and legislative initiatives and produce legislative overreach. Any attempt to slow down or slim down such over-activism has so far run into trouble (a) inside the Commission since Commissioners wish to gain a high public profile as political benefactors and (b) inside the European parliament where the MEPs clearly favour more legislation (no matter how sensible) over less in order to justify their own role, existence, and budgets (EurActiv France 2015).

Today, just a third of citizens in EU support the idea of ever-closer union. Support dwindles as people think integration has "gone too far" and powers should be handed back. In a survey of 7,000 people from seven European countries by polling firm Opinium Research, just 35 per cent said they supported closer union (Groves 2015). Moreover, across Europe citizens' trust in the EU has plummeted to around 35 per cent – compared with over 50 per cent only a decade ago. This despite the EU institutions gaining more powers. The only feasible way to regain people's trust seems to be to bring back decisions closer to home – "European localism and subsidiarity" is the tall order of the day.

Examples of "power grab" and fighting for more centralization among EU institutions and Member States abound. Notably, interferences from and intermeddling by the EU Commission in matters such as Eurozone decision-making, migration crisis, environment, social policy, or energy policies where

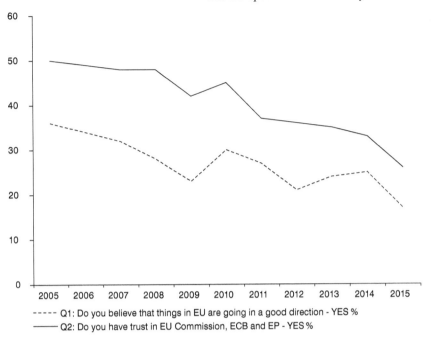

Figure 1.1 Trust in the European Union

Source: Standard Eurobarometer, various issues

the Treaty of the Functioning of the EU (TFEU) gives them only very limited competences, are matters of continuous rivalry. Article 114 TFEU, laying down rules for the approximation of the provisions in Member States, which may affect the functioning of the internal market, has always been used to justify EU action (Herzog 2014: 91).

Indeed, over-activism has characterized the EU legislative process and procedures: in 2014, the EU issued 2304 regulations and provisions. Rather than focusing on the grand issues as outlined above and on correcting the framework conditions of national policy-making, the EU has lost her grand thinking and has slipped into regulating the "small things of everyday life" For this aberration Roman Herzog (2014: 85) has coined the term "norms based hypertrophy". Is it really the principal task of the Union to determine and decide which fuel we fill into our tanks, which kinds of chocolate we eat, which light bulbs we buy, how much water we flush down our toilettes, or what type of ladder we are allowed to climb?

For the normal citizen, this smells of undue prohibition, intervention into our private lives, bureaucratic paternalism, and an erroneous sense of mission by those in the distant Brussels. The political and social value added of an ever-closer Union thus dissolves into thin air! Integration is losing its legitimacy, while paternalism prevails. The impression is created that the EU strives for imposing rules by decree from above.[9]

Indeed, under its traditional governance structure, the EU has turned into a legislative machine trying to interpret her fields of competence ever more widely (Eppink 2007). The Commission is ceaselessly working on weaving an ever-closer web of harmonized European laws and regulations – the result thereof, the *acquis communautaire*, is presently estimated to comprise some 100,000 printed pages.

The model of an "ever-closer union" seems to have reached its limits. And the crises have laid bare the deficiencies and insufficiencies that the EU has developed over the past decades. Today, to many observers the model looks degenerated and misplaced. It certainly does not appear up to solving the real problems in the years ahead. There are many reasons for the EU to rethink its project, should we intend to preserve the basic value of a unified Europe. However, only one thing is worse: not to even acknowledge the trouble Europe faces.[10]

Either we stop Europe's self-deceit and over-ambition, acknowledge unpleasant truths, ready ourselves for tough choices, get our act together and exit our "fools' paradise" or we will end up as a footnote in the future textbooks of history!

By way of conclusion: how to avoid the "beginning of the end" and to turn it into "the end of the beginning"

"The European idea", once hailed as a model for the world, is about to lose its attractiveness due to misperceptions, arrogance, ambition, and insufficient self-criticism. Today we are confronted with the depletion of an ideal.

Over the past 60 years or so, scholars of the European integration have convincingly argued that the process of integration is path-dependent and, therefore, more or less irreversible. And indeed, despite the fact that the EU is often considered an "unfinished union on the way to an unknown destination" (Weiler 1999), and in spite of being criticized as a "soft power", (Cooper 2004; and critical analysis in Witney 2014), it is moving ahead steadily. While undergoing major changes over the last 50 years – from six Member States in 1959 to twenty-eight today, and from a "trade-driven" (Customs Union) via a "factor-driven" (Single Market) and a money-driven (EMU) to an "innovation-driven" undertaking – the EU has acquired both political and economic influence and reputation. Its model of regional integration, which promised until recently unprecedented socio-economic progress, badly needs overhaul and redesign. So, the question arises: does the "irreversibility theorem" still hold today or has it been overcome by recent crises, tectonic social shifts, and new political framework conditions. Or is the EU falling victim to Paul Kennedy's "the rise and fall of great powers" (1987), even before it managed to be one?

In a globally interwoven setting "externalities" are changing the boundaries between domestic and international politics and are eroding the traditional modes of governance. National decision-makers must focus on international and intra-EU cooperation; new "extra-national" institutional arrangements have gained in significance; existing organizations adapt their working methods; and economic policy coordination is badly needed. At the same time, however, the citizens of the Union being used to trust primarily their national representatives mistrust such developments in which they are not involved and which they cannot control. This comes under the magic formula of "subsidiarity" (Gretschmann 1991). The former President of the European Council, Herman Van Rompuy, tried to capture this by pointing out that the EU of the past may have devoted too much effort and attention to "space" while ignoring "place":

> With Europe, the focus has always been on space. From the very start, the typical action was to remove borders, for goods, workers, investment, to let people and companies move, take initiatives, seize opportunities. Even today – on fields as diverse as energy, telecom or the digital economy – it is still about bringing down borders, creating this big common "space". But we've never really thought of Europe as a home, a shelter, and today we pay a price for it. Europe, the great 'opener' of opportunities is now perceived by many as an unwelcome 'intruder', the friend of freedom and space is seen as a threat to protection and to "place".[11]

Economic crises not only involve costs in terms of money and capital, but also in terms of trust and confidence in the competence and integrity of political and economic elites. Loss of confidence paired with poor reasoning and weak persuasiveness of the leaders give rise to social instability and disillusion on the part of the citizens.

In order to avoid the notion that the end of the European integration is getting nearer and to rather make sure that the present crises are just the end of the beginning (in historic terms) of a new powerful and united Europe, Europe today needs a refreshed rationale and a new vision for the future. Its representatives must assure the citizens that they intend to preserve variety and national peculiarities, a broad variety of choices and lifestyles, and at the same time reinvigorate a genuine European spirit. This needs to go hand in hand with "benign" measures to transform and modernize the European economy in order to create more jobs, growth, and welfare. Unless Europe can come up with convincing and compelling answers, the EU is bound to further lose credibility, confidence, and trust. One thing is certain: integration, without a firm foundation in the will of the peoples of Europe, is bound to fail!

Notes

1   "Great Moderation" refers to a reduction in the volatility of business cycle fluctuations starting in the mid-1980s, believed to have been caused by institutional and structural changes in developed nations in the later part of the twentieth century; this was the view of Ben Bernanke in a speech at the 2004 meetings of the Eastern Economic Association.
2   Essentially, there are two major forces at work: deals and ideals. As we know from economic psychology, ideals tend to dominate in periods of economic well-being, high growth rates, and stable political situations, in which certainty and security prevail; whereas interests and deals become the predominant force in situations of

instability, economic slow-down, unemployment crises, etc. When it comes to deals and interests playing the major role, there seems to be less leeway for visions: only if there is interest mediation and positive gains for those involved, will agents stick to treaties and contracts. If interests cannot be made compatible, agents will start to defect. It seems to be quite obvious that due to the many elements of instability and uncertainty currently arising, interests may dominate over ideals.

3   Notably, in 2014 and 2015 the ECB has been on the verge of overstretching her competences by buying government bonds with new money to sure up national economies in trouble, which can be interpreted as funding bankrupt governments through money printing and swamping the world with liquidity. This triggered a bitter dispute about quantitative easing and whether the ECB has stepped beyond its remit.

4   However, thanks largely to the ECB, the Greek government appears able to secure a favourable outcome in the end – including increased financial assistance and reduced reform requirements. Basically, Greek citizens take out loans from local banks, funded largely by the Greek central bank, which acquires funds through the European Central Bank's emergency liquidity assistance (ELA) scheme. They then transfer the money to other countries to purchase foreign assets (or redeem their debts), draining liquidity from their country's banks. The big black hole caused through capital outflows in the Greek banks' balance sheets is thus filled by the ECB. Cf. Sinn (2015).

5   Still, by the end of July, the IMF declared itself unwilling to join any bailout scheme until debt relief demands are met.

6   For an excellent overview see Petrakos et al. (2007).

7   See Communication from the Commission to the European Parliament and the Council—5th Annual Report on Immigration and Asylum (2013) (COM(2014) 288 final) accompanied by the Commission staff working document (SWD(2014) 165 final.

8   Four or five countries currently receive around 70 per cent of the EU's migrants/refugees. Until mid-2015, Italy has received two-thirds of the irregular immigrants who arrive in Europe and is the third (most popular) country after Germany and Sweden for the number of requests for political asylum.

9   In this situation, the often heard arguments that the proponents of EU integration should focus on public relations and marketing the achievements of the Union, communicate the benefits from the EU, and get the citizens better informed will fail. The old saying that "personal experience beats indoctrination and instruction" prevails today more than ever! Only a focus on policy delivery may be able to tackle the problem of a fraying and collapsing Union.

10 "Futurologist" Jeremy Rifkin (2004), whose book sales seem undented by a record of consistent mis-prognostication, claims emphatically that the post-post-modern era is characterized by the EU model of pooled sovereignty, peaceful cooperation, soft power and social justice. Europe is "the new superpower to come" and will run the twenty-first century. Reading this against the backdrop of the recent crises and the rise of Euroscepticism, I do think he is wholly incorrect.

11 Speech by President Herman Van Rompuy upon receiving the International Charlemagne Prize, Aachen, 29 May 2014 (European Council President EUCO 120/14 PRESSE 321 PR PCE 110).

References

Cooper, R. 2004. "Hard Power, Soft Power and the Goals of Diplomacy." In *American Power in the 21st Century*, edited by D. Held and M. Koenig-Archibugi, pp. 167–180. Cambridge: Polity Press.

Eppink, D.-J. 2007. *Life of a European Mandarin*. Brussels: Lannoo.

Eppler, A., and H. Scheller (eds). 2014. *Zur Konzeptualisierung europäischer Desintegration*. Baden-Baden: Nomos.

EurActiv France 2015. "Worries Mount as the European Parliament Sits Idle." 30 April. Available at www.euractiv.com/sections/eu-priorities-2020/worries-mount-european-parliament-sits-idle-314261.

Eurobarometer. 2014. "Data Annex, T42." *Standard Eurobarometer* 82. Available at http://ec.europa.eu/public_opinion/archives/eb/eb82/eb82_en.htm.

Feldstein, M. 1988. *International Economic Cooperation.* Chicago, IL: Chicago University Press.

Frenkel, J. A. and R. E. Rockett. 1988. "International Macroeconomic Policy Co-ordination when Policymakers Do Not Agree on the True Model." *American Economic Review* 78(3): 318–340.

Geppert, D. 2013. *Ein Europa das es nicht gibt* [*A Europe that does not exist*], Berlin: Europa-Verlag.

Gretschmann, K. 1993. *Economic and Monetary Union – Implications for Policy-makers,* Maastricht: EIPA.

Gretschmann, K. 1991. "Le Principe de subsidiarité: Quelles responsabilités à quelle niveau de pouvoir dans un Europe intégré?". In European Institute for Public Administration (EIPA) (ed.) *Subsidiarité: défi du changement,* pp. 49–70. Maastricht: European Institute for Public Administration (EIPA).

Groves, J. 2015. "Just a Third of Citizens in EU Support Idea of Ever Closer Union: Support Dwindles as People Think Integration has 'Gone Too Far' and Powers Should Be Handed Back." *The Daily Mail* (13 August). Available at www.dailymail.co.uk/news/article-3195754/Just-citizens-EU-support-idea-closer-union.html.

Hatzis, A. 2015. A Split Verdict on the Blackmail and Bullying over Greece." *Financial Times* (11 June): 7.

Herzog, R. 2014. *Europa neu erfinden* (*Re-inventing Europe*). Munich: Siedler Verlag.

Kennedy, P. 1987. *The Rise and Fall of Great Powers.* New York: Vintage Books.

Leonard, M. 2011. "Four Scenarios for the Reinvention of Europe." *ECFR* 43. Available at www.ecfr.eu/publications/summary/four_scenarios_for_the_reinvention_of_europe36149

Petrakos, G., P. Arvanitidis and S. Pavleas. 2007. *Determinants of Economic Growth: The Experts' View.* Dynreg Working Paper 20/2007. Brussels: EU.

Rifkin, J. 2004. *The European Dream: How Europe's Vision of the Future Is Quietly Eclipsing the American Dream.* New York: Polity.

Sinn, H.-W. 2015. "Varoufakis's Great Game." Available at www.project-syndicate.org/commentary/varoufakis-ecb-grexit-threat-by-hans-werner-sinn-2015-05#tFCuRaMWwUQqx1XM.99.

Weiler, J. 1999. *The Constitution of Europe.* Cambridge: Cambridge University Press.

Witney, N. 2014. "Hard Truths about Europe's Soft Power." Available at http://europesworld.org/2014/02/24/hard-truths-about-europes-soft-power/.

2 Signalling imbalances in the Economic and Monetary Union

Nicola Acocella

Introduction

Expectations from the Economic and Monetary Union (EMU) were high and appeared to be realized to a large extent up until 2008, but then the Union precipitated into a deep crisis. Before the EMU, the existence of asymmetries and imbalances within the Union was recognized, but they were thought to be irrelevant, as the EMU institutions – in essence, the common currency and free movements of factors and goods – were able to eliminate them. Proper signals would give an incentive to private and public decision-makers in order to cope with them. The transformation of the financial crisis in private markets into a sovereign debtor crisis and its prolongation beyond the time it lasted in the United States needs an explanation. The explanation must take account of the specificities of the EMU as a(n imperfect) currency union, very different from the United States. The suspect is that the roots of this crisis were in the previous performance of the Union. Going even further back, the institutional architecture and policies of the Union should have been lacking (Acocella 2014, 2015) and forecasts of their ability to cope with the different structural conditions of the participating countries and the existing asymmetries and imbalances should have been "greatly exaggerated".

This chapter studies some specific aspects of the following issues:

- The influence of external constraints and contractionary monetary and fiscal policies on the adoption of suitable reforms in higher-inflation countries.
- The possibility that the late manifestation of crisis can be due to signals coming out of market trends, which are noisy, for a number of reasons.
- Whether wrong signals might have induced moral hazard and adverse selection of public and private decision-makers.

Many contributions have been published on these topics, but most of them need further discussion, especially with regard to the interaction between the different factors of the crisis underlined by the different contributions.

The chapter is organized as follows. The next section deals with the imbalances in the Union, both those pre-existing to its creation and those that loomed later;

it compares expectations as to their permanence to realizations, ending with the private and public debt crisis in more recent years. I then deal with the effects of the monetary and fiscal discipline imposed by the European institutions and policies. Following that is a section that focuses on the incentives arising before and after the institution of the EMU, due to the change in the perspectives, the incoming budget constraint and the different signals. The penultimate section discusses the interconnection between signals, moral hazard and the adverse selection of politicians. Finally I present a model of signalling imbalances in the EMU.

Imbalances in the EMU

Expectations from the Union

Expectations for the possible accomplishments of the Economic and Monetary Union were high (e.g. Commission of the European Communities 1990, 1991). Only a few critiques were raised against the project of a monetary union that was deprived of some essential pre-conditions for its proper functioning and aimed almost exclusively at achieving monetary stability while not being complemented by other institutional pillars tending to cope with imbalances and stimulating growth in an uneven environment.[1]

From the point of view of each participating country, the loss of one instrument (monetary policy) in favour of a centralized authority might not imply a parallel loss in the ability to control the economy, as entering in the monetary union would also imply a parallel drop in one target, that of the balance of payments equilibrium.[2] Some authors had drastically claimed that the effects of "asymmetrical shocks would be eliminated under a monetary union with perfect capital mobility and currency substitution" (Weber 1991: 204), even if, according to a few others (see the previous footnote), this was more problematic.

From the point of view of the Union as an integrating area, there were imbalances among the different countries. These were due to inertial, behavioural and structural factors in some countries (which stemmed, on the one hand, from diffuse inefficiencies and, on the others, the Balassa-Samuelson effect), showing themselves in their public accounts as well as in other features of their economies, such as higher-inflation rates. These imbalances had been reduced, but not eliminated, in the transition to the EMU (Allsopp and Vines 1998) and also afterwards (Lane 2006). With this tendency persisting, together with, possibly, the artificially high level of domestic demand deriving from the high public spending, the current account of the balance of payments would tend to be negative. However, this would not have raised any concern for two reasons. First, because any imbalances in the current account would be cleared by free movements of capital (Blanchard and Giavazzi 2002: 43), who conclude that, "although benign neglect may not be optimal, it appears to be a reasonable course of action"). Second, in the process, the common currency as well as integration of markets and limits to public deficits and debts would induce policymakers and other agents to change their conduct and introduce needed reforms, with the result of eliminating public accounts imbalances, reducing public debt, rising competitiveness, and reducing risk prospects (see, for example, Commission of the European Communities 1990, 1991; Jahjah 2000; Papademos 2001; see also references in Fernandez-Villaverde et al. 2013), not only in higher-inflation countries, but also in other countries such as France, which suffered from other kinds of imbalances.

This change in the conduct of public and private agents in higher-inflation countries was an implicit assumption behind the institutional design of the EMU. Specifically, a beneficial impulse for re-balancing would derive from:

- The impossibility of governments to maintain unemployment any longer below its natural rate by expansionary demand policies; this would be the effect of the Stability and Growth Pact (SGP) and a conservative central bank, which would force governments to change their conduct; reduced public imbalances would contribute to lower demand and put a curb on excess inflation, with positive effects on current account imbalances.
- The impossibility of private decision-makers to rely on competitive exchange-rate devaluations as a kind of soft budget constraint (i.e. in order to regain the competitiveness lost due to inefficiencies, rent-seeking and wrong conduct, workers, unions and firms in higher-inflation countries could no longer earn "monopoly" rents, and would thus change their conduct in order to bring back inflation in those countries in line with that of more stable countries, with beneficial current account imbalances).
- The wider effects on context and opportunities for comparisons and choice (especially for asset returns, once these were cleared of the currency risk component), which would induce public and private agents to adopt more cautionary policies; higher transparency and the possibility to compare prices across the EMU countries would also imply that even in non-tradable sectors beneficial changes in the conduct of agents could come, thanks to a higher pressure from consumers and the government or competition from foreign direct investment (Commission of the European Communities 1990, 1991; Dyson and Featherstone 1996).

Realizations

The expectations appeared to be confirmed before the crisis struck. In 2007, the average unemployment rate in the EMU-17 had dropped to 7.5 per cent, starting from levels higher than 9 per cent at the beginning of the decade, with a very low dispersion.[3] Poverty rates had reached their lowest point in 2009 and families at risk of poverty or social exclusion were 21.3 per cent of the total.

Nevertheless, optimism was out of place. The initial favourable expectations mentioned in the previous section contained a contradiction. After entering into the EMU, governments were certainly relieved of the balance of payments constraint/target, but, pending structural imbalances and current account deficits this could only happen if there were lasting capital inflows. However, reduction in domestic interest rates due to the elimination of the country risk and capital inflows, even if beneficial for the governments and private agents, could have softened their budget constraint.

This contradiction materialized for the worse under the effects of the financial crisis that began in 2007–2008. Unemployment rates soared to 12.0 per cent in 2013 showing a much higher dispersion, while people at risk of poverty in 2012 had increased by 2 percentage points.[4] Imbalances in the current account and government budget as well as other structural imbalances causing them had remained un-tackled for too long, were compensated by capital inflows into the peripheral countries for too long, and were finally transformed into a sovereign debt problem (Acocella 2015). The signals were perceived only by a limited number of people (see Fernandez-Villaverde et al. 2013) and were evident only rather late, as a consequence of the burst of the bubble itself and, to some extent, also thanks to the emergence of new theoretical insights (Acocella 2014).

More specifically, real interest rate changes and expected future rates acted on international transactions quicker than changes in goods prices. As stated, the latter tended to rise more in some countries for structural reasons. With practically equalized nominal interest rates across the EMU, due to the common currency, high-inflation countries had an incentive to borrow and direct funds to speculative operations in the real estate and stock markets (De Grauwe 2010a), while low-inflation countries had an incentive to lend abroad. Thus, capital inflows and external financing of banks made construction booms possible, leading to soaring financial asset prices and easy lending to the public sector (Lane and McQuade 2013). The effects of a deteriorating current account induced by structural imbalances were slower to act, as usual (EEAG 2011).

The implication (again EEAG 2011: ch. 2) was that the policymakers in high-inflation countries indulged in the illusion that everything went for the best and didn't do their homework (i.e. they did not reduce public deficits and debts and appropriately supervise and regulate financial intermediaries; nor did they implement structural changes to make their economies more competitive).[5] On the other hand, private agents could also finance their consumption or investment activity more easily, in particular in speculative activities. Even when they finally realized they had arrived at the edge of the precipice, both policymakers and private agents (in particular, banks) did not care and in some cases relied on other countries' bailout (moral hazard). This is certainly a part of the explanation. More precisely, it is true that there was an "illusion" of the soundness of the situation. But "illusion" is an elusive term. In "Incentives and signals" below we will explore if there was more than that.

According to some authors (e.g. Fernandez-Villaverde et al. 2013), capital inflows propelled into higher-inflation countries caused high rates of growth, which have raised incentive problems, as they softened or cancelled the necessary reactions and favoured adverse selections of politicians and other decision-makers. Thus, the high real growth, according to Fernandez-Villaverde et al. (2013), made the signals coming out of imbalances noisy, not only for policymakers but also for ordinary citizens. Expectations of high real growth acted similarly, which convinced people of the debt's sustainability (EEAG 2011). This argument will be dealt with extensively below. In the next section we explore the effects on reforms for efficiency and equity, first by introducing the new common institutions devised for the EMU and, in addition, by adopting tight monetary and fiscal policies, without reference to the existence of proper signals of imbalances.

The effects of the EMU institutions and monetary and fiscal discipline

The EMU as an external tie

Three issues arise both in retrospect and in prospect with reference to the EMU crisis:

1   What reforms were and are necessary in a currency union such as the EMU?
2   Were these reforms possible within the rules adopted by the Union and suggested in the literature?
3   Were the respective roles of the EMU institutions and that of the national governments and agents clear enough?

Milone (2014) largely covers the first issue, mainly by reviewing a vast literature, predominantly originated by public organizations such as the IMF and OECD. Milone refers specifically to reforms that appear necessary to implement after the crisis, but these are largely the same as those needed before it. Necessary reforms differ among the various countries, but should aim at increasing both static and dynamic efficiency, reducing excessive income inequality, and reforming political institutions. Monastiriotis and Zartaloudis (2010) deal only with those reforms referred to labour markets, in particular with flexibility. They argue that theoretical and empirical considerations show the existence of a variety of degrees and directions for (de)regulation of labour markets and the agenda is open for an active exploration of the most appropriate policy options. The latter should have been discussed and disciplined even before the crisis, which has simply accentuated the underlying issues, having to do with the essential features of the "European model" (rules versus discretion, the role of free markets, of fiscal policy, the relative weights of price stability, and employment in the welfare function of the policymakers).The variety of policies needed to address inefficiencies and inequality is important, because it is apparently consistent with the existence of different institutions at various levels of the EMU governance and also impinges on the latter two issues listed at the beginning of this section, which are the focus of our analysis.

Notwithstanding the variety of institutions, both the founding fathers of the Union and the literature *before* the establishment of the EMU practically delegated most of the burden for integration, alignment, reforms, etc. to the institutions at the Union's levels in a wide sense. The most important common institution is obviously the common currency, but much trust was put in markets too, in a practical vacuum of other common institutions and with specific limitations to national action in the fiscal field, through the SGP. Many economists and politicians saw this institutional architecture as imposing a strong network of ties on the conduct of the agents, both public and private, in the countries with higher inefficiencies. These ties should – almost naturally – compel them to change their conduct and enact the needed reforms.

A number of theoretical considerations and catchphrases were advanced to explain the virtues of these external ties and their capability to foster the necessary changes of conduct by local public and private agents. First, the role of the European Monetary System (EMS) and later the EMU in imposing the necessary changes was asserted in various forms, such as the *vincolo esterno*, or external empowerment (Carli 1993: 406; Dyson and Featherstone 1999), the "tying one's hands" or "scapegoat" mechanism (Giavazzi and Pagano 1988; Begg 2002), the "back against the wall" (Alesina et al. 2006) and "there is no alternative" (Bean 1998) theses.[6] As Featherstone (2001: 1) pointed out, this argument has been used differently within different institutional settings, as either a strategic lever for reform or a stimulus to shift norms and beliefs affecting policy. Higher inflation countries used this argument as a lever for reforms. Lower inflation countries used the same argument for successfully changing their norms, as in the case of Germany in the early 2000s. Legitimization of reforms at the local level was thus largely devolved upon the EMU institutions, including markets' operations.

However, as McNamera (1998) put it, the argument and the option of the *vincolo esterno* were mainly a fruit of a consensus among élites redefining the role of the state. Penetration among most sections of the population lagged or was entirely lacking. We can also add that the consensus was fragile in many cases, each of the various sections of the élites hoping to shift the burden of adjustment to the others. The consensus and reliance on the virtues of markets and the common currency as well as the SGP on the one side, deprived national governments' policies of much content, or reduced their effective range of action and, on the other, convinced the public of the possibility that everything was about to be settled automatically, simply as an effect of participating in the Union. Public opinion did not really put much emphasis on the need for structural reforms. The nature of the adjustment needed[7] – with the possible exception of reducing the public debt – and the possibility of being exposed to shocks and crises were not clear. A similar effect of reducing the expectations of adjustment at the national level derived from the consideration that much of the necessary convergence of the higher-inflation countries had been obtained as an effect of complying with the Maastricht rules for admission. Admission was thus considered by many as the final act in the series of painful measures to be adopted by these countries. Further, comparisons with the state of Germany in the first years of the Union tended to confirm this orientation and induced optimism.[8]

Even those who were conscious of the necessity of reforms and did not trust national governments or private agents concerning the will and ability to undertake them somehow relied on the European action. However, as stated, the

EMU and other existing common institutions were not empowered with most of the required competences.

Bean (1998) presented a rather balanced view of economic and political considerations favouring or being an obstacle to structural reforms at the national level. His economic arguments in favour – notably the "there is no alternative" (TINA) argument (or a variant of it), and in particular the incentive to render the local environment more attractive for business, the increasing decentralization of labour bargaining – seem to prevail over those against. This is mainly the argument that the incentive for reforms is lower in a monetary union from the point of view of time inconsistency, and absence of rules for debt consolidation lowers incentives. All in all, the arguments sustaining their political feasibility were less favourable to the adoption of reforms. A decisive obstacle to reforms are the short-run costs that they would impose on a rather wide group of people. Their opposition could be easily overcome in a growing environment, but this is difficult to obtain at the Union level, as reforms are a prevailing issue for a subset of countries and are not considered to be a common issue.

In Italy the *vincolo esterno* argument was rather diffuse. An independent external monetary authority could enhance separation of the Italian central bank from the government and its "whip". Together with the passage to a common currency it could make markets and foreign competition to work and ensure efficiency: the external constraints would be capable of forcing politicians, businessmen, and trade unions to a more efficient conduct in due time (Dyson and Featherstone 1999: ch. 10, 11).

Begg (2002) presented a balanced view and in substance advocates participation of social partners too in the process of reforms to avoid disruptive results. Participation was seen as necessary, since, "if guidelines are issued by 'Brussels' that call for unpopular or controversial reforms, they risk being seen as unacceptable (Chassard 2001: 318). A risk in this regard was that the EU could be used as a scapegoat. Indeed it might be argued that this could provide part of the motivation for the Europeanization of governments keen to push through unpopular measures such as agreeing to pension reforms at the European level in order to circumvent a lack of domestic support.' (Begg 2002: 14–15). Another risk was that different levels of governance had roles that should be complementary, but in practice could be subject to competitive overlapping, originating confusion (the "too many cooks" syndrome), rather than the ideal *fusion* of the kind suggested by Wessels (1997), which is necessary for the establishment of a single policy system. In particular, heterogeneity of employment and employment policy in the EMU called for the clarification of a model towards which change should be directed as well as of the agents that would push toward it at the various levels (see Begg 2002).

Recent reflections by Heinemann and Grigoriadis on the ways to harmonize different agent's expectations and conduct can be useful:

On the general level, the theoretical reasoning and the empirical jointly suggest that a theory of reform resistance is severely flawed if it is simply based on the view of reform-resistance driven by narrow self-interest. The micro-evidence, in particular, underlines the role of (procedural) fairness considerations. Voters need a minimum confidence into their democratic institutions in order to accept the uncertainties involved in far-reaching institutional change. Interestingly, trust in European institutions can to some extent be a substitute for trust in national institutions.

(Heinemann and Grigoriadis 2013: 38)

Trust in Europe was in effect high and this could compensate for the lack of trust in the national governments in many EMU countries. However, Europe was not empowered with the appropriate policy instruments needed to reform labour markets, business structure and conduct, or public administration.

We must be clear about the reasons why the EMU would represent an external tie as well as the agents that would have been constrained by the Union's institutions. These reasons can refer to: adoption of contractionary monetary and fiscal policies, the existence of a more fierce competition in product and labour markets, and limits to public deficits and debts. In the next subsection we deal with national policymakers' attitudes towards reforms simply as a consequence of contractionary monetary and fiscal policies. The issue of signals and incentives to both policymakers and private agents deriving from strict monetary and fiscal discipline and market constraints before and after admission to the Union is the object of subsequent sections.

Policymakers' attitudes towards reforms with contractionary monetary and fiscal policies

Adoption of a regime of fiscal and monetary discipline would generate mixed effects according to Coricelli et al. (2006) and Acemoglu et al. (2008). A regime of discipline was enforced both in the way to the common currency (at least in the higher-inflation countries, for which fulfilling the Maastricht requirements was more problematic) and afterwards (as the ECB had to establish a reputation and the SGP was in effect).

Acemoglu et al. (2008) have presented a model where reforms of the kind advocated in other contexts by the Washington Consensus (basically, restrictive fiscal and monetary policy, reforms that are supposed to be efficiency-enhancing such as market liberalization, privatization, etc.) can be detrimental. In their opinion such reforms induce politicians to adopt other instruments for furthering their redistributive action, patronage, etc., thus originating a kind of "see-saw" effect.

In Coricelli et al. (2006), as well as Dalmazzo (forthcoming), a stricter *monetary policy* has positive effects on both inflation and unemployment, as it imposes a discipline on trade unions. However, according to Dalmazzo, "commitment to price-stability may allow governments to persist in "bad" fiscal policies and tolerance for low competition", as governments can trade part of the social gains deriving from it for distortionary taxation, redistribution, patronage, and the like" (Dalmazzo forthcoming: 4). Hence a more conservative central bank tends to raise the tax rate, thus questioning the desirability of this type of monetary authority claimed by Coricelli et al. (2006).[9] In addition, monetary discipline reduces market deregulation. This result casts doubt on the validity of the argument in favour of resorting to an external constraint under the form of a conservative central bank in order to reform countries characterized by lax fiscal policies and scarcely competitive goods markets.[10] However, these implications can be accepted only after careful analysis. Not only because models such as in Dalmazzo (forthcoming) are used, admitting no trade-off between inflation and unemployment (at least in the short-run). In addition, they do not consider that, notwithstanding the similarities in the two periods insofar as adoption of stricter monetary and fiscal discipline is concerned, as stated, these have other features, which can justify apparently different behaviour of public and private agents in the transition period and after membership has been gained. Thus the conclusion reached by using the models under consideration do not fully take into account the incentives of policymakers and private agents before and after the admission to the EMU. In the next two sections we discuss precisely these issues.

Incentives and signals

Incentives during the transition to the EMU and after

The "transition" to the EMU of the various countries, in particular of the peripheral countries that were not part of the EMS, implied a number of effects on incentives. Some of them pertain to the adoption of a stricter regime of monetary and fiscal discipline. As stated above, this has featured not only the proper transition period before admission to EMU, but also transition period of the following full participation in the Union. However, each of these two periods has specific features, as we explain now.

The former also implied some kind of mitigation in the effects of contractionary policies deriving from both reduced real interest rates due to disappearance of the country currency risk, and the prospect of a future "prize" attached to the admission to the Union (for this effect see also IMF 2004: 114). This prospect of a prize certainly affected the conduct of some agents, notably the government, big firms, and trade unions (at least those with some degree of centralization), which were conscious of the stricter relation between their conduct and the possibility to earn the prize (on this see Acocella et al. 2009). More questionable is the likelihood of a similar conduct by small- and medium-size enterprises, due to their likely free-rider attitude.

By contrast, after the EMU admission, there was no apparent prospect of a future prize tied to restructuring, eliminating inefficiencies, and unsustainable budgets, as the effects of contractionary policies at the EMU level were mitigated by some kind of soft budget constraint.[11] Strictness of the regime in existence after admission to the EMU can in fact be – and has been – questioned, as credit availability increased in peripheral countries. This is really an effect that began to loom – along with reduction in real interest rates in these countries – during the transition period. However, it could take momentum only after some time and especially after the signal of formal admission of peripheral countries to the EMU, which was commonly perceived as crossing the finishing line. Capital inflows to higher-inflation countries from abroad, mainly from Germany, raised credit availability, especially to private agents, and created a bubble. Absence of a (further) prize related to the EMU participation coupled with a soft-budget constraint could thus have reduced incentives to enact structural reforms in higher-inflation countries. In terms of Dalmazzo's model, this would correspond to an exogenous rise in the weight put on redistribution of rents; differently, however, from his model, this rise in the weight would derive from having reached the target of being admitted to the Union.

Then, on top of a common issue (i.e. contractionary monetary and fiscal policies at the EMU level), the two periods could imply different outcomes for both public and private agents. What certainly makes the two periods differ is that an issue of reduced incentives for a "correct" conduct of public and private agents was more likely to arise after the prize of the admission to the Union had been cashed and no future prize was in sight. In addition, the influence of the changed budget constraint deriving from low interest rates and credit availability also induced optimistic or "distorted" beliefs and expectations of future prospects. We deal with the implications deriving from the changed budget constraint in the next subsection.

The budget constraint and incentives

According to Baskaran and Hessami (2013), the EMU did not imply a harder budget constraint of the kind advocated by the supporters of the argument of the external tie induced by fixed exchange rates. Instead, in accordance with the literature since Wildasin (1997), they find empirical support for the idea that the EMU itself created a soft budget constraint.[12] In their opinion, this would derive from the failure of the European Council to sanction France and Germany in 2003, which – in addition to Portugal – had violated the SGP. According to them, this failure reduced public and private agents' incentives for reforms in other countries. This explanation might be insufficient, as the effect would have acted only after that date.[13] The additional issue arising from it is why the soft budget constraint, first inaugurated by France and Germany, operated in some countries only (those with a higher inflation), not in others in the following years. Nor it would explain why the violation of the SGP induced a "virtuous conduct by Germany, but not by Portugal.

A different explanation would be that the signal of a soft budget constraint could have come from the way the EMU was conceived and worked since its first years of existence, as the bubbles generated in the peripheral countries by capital inflows gave the impression that everything was right there (Fernandez-Villaverde et al. 2013). Fernandez-Villaverde and colleagues basically suggest two reasons for the existence of a soft budget constraint:

- The public decision process can be assimilated to a war of attrition (Alesina and Drazen 1991); this implies that free capital movements and capital inflows, like aid, have the effect of delaying reforms (Casella and Eichengreen 1996) by relaxing budget constraints.
- Independently from that, it is difficult for "principals"[14] to extract good signals with bubbles and booms. Easy borrowing leads to low long-run growth, as it multiplies future engagements for wrong or low-productive investment, thus wasting resources. Among a number of implications, it causes a variant of the Dutch disease, leading to misallocation of resources away from the tradable sector, as well as a deterioration in policy and institutions, which are reduced to resorting to debt and postponing reforms.[15]

This explanation – which would also clarify why the decision of the European Council not to sanction France and Germany in 2003 would have acted only on higher-inflation countries in the following years – emphasizes the interaction between bubbles and policies. Bubbles induced public and private agents to choose "soft" policies (i.e. they gave the politicians an incentive to raise deficits and private agents to increase their leverage). Lane and McQuade (2013) in fact find a positive correlation between net capital inflows and domestic credit. This made it easier for the government and the private sector to borrow, thus reducing their incentive to adopt "sound" policies. Reduced interest rates in the period preceding the EMU membership didn't have similar effects, especially on politicians, as their conduct should have been "virtuous", pending admission. In addition, capital outflows from "core" countries had not yet materialized.

By contrast, Germany, as a country with very low inflation rates, exported capital abroad and suffered from a kind of hard budget constraint, also as an effect of the policies following unification with the former Eastern Germany.

Looking at figures, the government's debt (as a percentage of GDP) lowered for some higher-inflation countries (Portugal and Greece, up to 1999–2000) and then increased; for other countries, the reduction lasted (but at a slower rate than in the period up to 2000) until 2004 (in Italy) or 2007 (Spain, Ireland).

More uniform in all higher-inflation countries was the growth performance, which was strong or very strong until 1999 or 2000. It was slightly lower since, up to the financial crisis in 2007–2008,[16] with the exception of the service sector and constructions. By contrast, growth was rather high in Germany until 2001, which reflected also on a current account deficit until 2002–2003, but drastically dropped afterwards. Thus, with the only exception of Greece, there was no boom in higher-inflation countries after their inception into the EMU, as claimed by Fernandez-Villaverde et al. (2013) and EEAG (2011). However, the soaring asset prices certainly relaxed credit and budget constraints in high inflation countries, even if this was not to such an extent as to propel a boom, at least in comparison with the pre-EMU period, with the exception of Greece (Eurostat, no date). Some constraints deriving from the new institutions, such as a monetary policy that was contractionary at least until mid-2001, might have broken a possible boom. More than total GDP growth, growth in specific sectors, such as construction and the financial sector, is important as an indicator of growing asset prices and wealth. This was of the utmost importance for growth of consumption[17] and is likely to have generated some misperception or a false assessment of fundamentals. This was "corrected" only when the crisis erupted in Greece in the second half of 2009.[18]

All in all, however, bubbles certainly existed. They supported an otherwise very low growth in the whole economy, as an effect of a rather contractionary monetary policy and limits to budget deficits introduced by the SGP. This would suggest an explanation of the evolution of policies and the performance of higher-inflation countries based on the absence of proper signals for the need of a change. We deal with this in the next subsection.

Why wrong signals can arise

After accession, the important signals of the balance of payments and the exchange rate were lost. Relaxation of the external constraint due to free capital movements implied not only a rather high growth rate in that course of action, but also the loss of proper signals, at least for the government, of the reduction in the country's competitiveness, which in due time could have a negative influence on growth and the very possibility of continuing to extract rents. The balance of payments, the current account as well as some indicators of competitiveness could still be calculated, but the idea that any current account deficit could be balanced by capital inflows, with no negative impact on the (nominal) exchange rate, together with the moderately high rate of growth, were reassuring for policymakers. For private agents, the contemporaneous fall or reduction in aggregate demand abroad and at least partial substitution of the domestic to the foreign market (made possible to some extent by the looming bubble) also meant that signals of a loss of competitiveness were noisy. Finally, reliance on temporary jobs as well as on relocation abroad of some industrial production lines implied that many firms could cope with reduced demand abroad, the impossibility to resort to nominal currency devaluation, inefficiencies, and rents without suffering a substantive loss in their competiveness, at least in the short or medium run.

More generally, the ability of private and public agents to perceive the right market signals can be debated. From this point of view, two issues emerge:

- Can markets send the right signals to policymakers and agents and, in the affirmative, under what conditions? Symmetrically, what are the difficulties of signal extraction in market economies?
- Do markets send correct signals in a monetary union and, more specifically, in the case of EMU?

Why do difficulties of signal extraction arise in a market economy?

There are a number of reasons for the existence of difficulties in signal extraction from market trends. Some refer to markets and political institutions in general.

First, signals coming out of market trends can be noisy, depending on the existence of multiple equilibria. In addition, even if there was a unique equilibrium, mention should be made of short-sightedness, of people and policymakers and the role of political institutions, populism, and national specificities. Short-sightedness is particularly acute in financial markets and certainly acted in the EMU (De Grauwe and Yi 2013). Moreover, the procedure followed by public and private agents for extracting the right signals is imperfect, as they do not know the right model.[19] In the end there might be a few people able to apply correct methods of signal extraction. Most private agents perceive signals and adapt their expectations mainly on the basis of the specific market where they operate. Their ability to perceive imbalances looming elsewhere and ultimately having a reflection on the market where they operate is often scanty. Even when this is not so and some agents look at the generality of markets, they may ignore signals from other related markets, being specifically interested in the evolution of their own, as either this is more pressing or interrelations between markets are difficult to assess.

This phenomenon has induced some authors to suggest alternative ways to cope with excessive capital inflows and current account imbalances. The former can be regulated by proper direct control or taxes. In the case of a current account imbalance due to competitiveness, wages should be lowered or raised according to the nature of the imbalance, also by means of income policies. Imbalances in the current account not due to competitiveness should be faced by boosting or contracting aggregate demand. There are, however, two opposing considerations especially addressed to the use of direct policy instruments: one is theoretical; the other is practical. The former asserts that, "we find such proposals naive and dangerous, because, by attempting to mimic through controls the outcome of market discipline, they are bound to confuse symptoms with causes and direct the attention to policy tools that are entirely inappropriate as remedies against long-term structural deficiencies of market economies" (EEAG 2011: 82). The latter has to do with the Union's institutional architecture, which rules out capital controls and emphasizes market self-adjustment, practically banning other forms of common policy intervention.

Both these considerations are debatable. As to the former, it is true that causes rather than pure symptoms should be removed. However, this requires time, as the causes are difficult to tackle, the more so when this must be done at the country level, in the absence of suitable common labour and industrial policies. Arguments against the position expressed by the EEAG also derive from the critique of the theoretical foundations of the EMU institutions and the need to reform them (see Acocella 2014).

Signals to policymaketers and agens

Apart from these considerations, another question arises: do markets in a monetary union send the right signals to policymakers and agents? And can they operate in such a way as to overcome them? The answer to both questions could be conditionally in the affirmative. As for the current account imbalances, correctness and effectiveness of signals depend not only on the size of imbalances and imperfections in the product markets, but also on the degree of wage flexibility and labour mobility, as labour markets are often characterized by more rigidities and tend to react to the signals with a longer delay. As to capital markets, they can send signals, if policymakers correctly interpret them. However, they are plagued by issues such as beauty contests and, as seen, can overreact and create bubbles. Issues can then be complicated by the different speed of adjustment as between the different markets.

Is a monetary union conceivable without free capital mobility? Possibly not, but in this case common policies – financial regulation, in particular of banks, industrial and labour policy, appropriate monetary and fiscal policies – should be added to avoid imbalances in different areas. The very way of operating a monetary union with structural differences among the different countries and free capital movements would expose (and has exposed) it to a risk of break up in the absence of other common policies, low labour mobility, a lack of fiscal union, and no lender of last resort for governments (Krugman 2013).

Incentives, moral hazard and adverse selection of policymakers

Signals and moral hazard

An absence of a proper system of incentives does not imply moral hazard, as this requires the existence of asymmetric information and a conduct by agents that is detrimental to the principal. Moral hazard arises because the agent does not take the full consequences and responsibilities of its actions, thus acting less carefully than it otherwise would and leaving the principal to bear some negative consequence of the actions. Absence of incentives or disincentives simply implies that some wrong signal let him think that the environment where he acts has lasting negative or positive features, which induces the agent to think that his current conduct is profitable.

Let us refer to the different markets where moral hazard might have played a role. The main markets are those for goods, labour and financial assets. There is no immediate way of devising some kind of asymmetric information relevant for our issues in the first two markets. However, the change in institutions can act on the incentives usually existing in those markets. Take the case[20] of the Hartz reforms in Germany: the situation of hard budget constraint existing there for the reasons already indicated induced the government to enact a series of reforms related to the labour market that had a positive impact on the workers' incentive to accept a job and possibly also to change the terms of wage bargaining. An even more manifested kind of moral hazard could have interested financial operators and the government, but most likely, after the insurgence of the crisis, when some kind of guarantees were expected in certain contingencies.

Bubbles, the entry of politicians as a pre-selection process and adverse selection

Bubbles can act not only on incentives of agents in general, but also on an advers selection of politicians and other agents.

Taking issues of partisanship aside, when we introduce asymmetri information, separating bad from good politicians is very difficult, as th program of future policy declared by each candidate before the election is alway incomplete and may not correspond to his real intentions and future choices. Thi is especially important after admission to the EMU. In fact, after 1999 the proces of restructuring the economy of "peripheral" countries had still to be completec but the prospects of continuing relatively high growth rates and benefits fror participation to the EMU was so diffuse. Then people were more inclined t opt for candidates – even the less able and/or those having a special non-publi interest in taking office – promising some relaxation of the restrictive polic experienced until then (Le Borgne and Lockwood 2012). Those politicians wh promised soft budget constraint to the "core" constituency were appealing whil appearing credible, influencing positively the probability of a poll success or th political survival of a ruling government (Robinson and Torvik 2009).

Let us suppose, as an example, that all the assumptions for the validity of th median voter model hold. Each constituent will vote according to his preferences under the constraint of his current and prospective budget. Let us assume also tha current incomes have all been reduced by contractionary policies. Two partie offer different prospects for their policies: one promises to continue its presen contractionary policy; the other promises to reduce taxes just as a way to prevail ii the entry stage of the political process. The latter will be chosen, as the alternativ prospect is no longer tied to the promise of a benefit like that of entering th EMU, an event thought to be fruitful of future gains. Whether this theoretica conclusion corresponds to stylized facts in "peripheral" countries is a matter o inquiry, since the median voter model not only has a number of limitations, bu there also exist different specific circumstances that operate in each country tha make non-populist politicians prevail.

Conclusions

Markets show well-known difficulties in delivering the right signals of loomin; imbalances, may underreact or overreact to them, and cannot properly correc them. Pure monetary unions, i.e. unions with no other common institutions tha the common currency and markets, add no significant system of signalling o provide an instrument for re-adjustment, at least in the short- or medium-run, an can even cause further imbalances, as free mobility of capital can create bubble which mask them. The more so if the asymmetries producing such imbalance have a structural nature, as, in this case, some markets, such as labour markets may not work in an appropriate way. In particular, the high capital mobility is no matched by a high international labour mobility and an essential condition for ;

currency union to work is thus not fulfilled. In this situation moral hazard and adverse selection easily arise, making the correction of imbalances more difficult. The system should then be helped to deliver proper signals and to correct them. The OCA theory must be made to work and appropriate non-market institutions, mainly at the union level, should be created. In particular, public common institutions should have been created in order to regulate current and capital account imbalances in addition to public finance imbalances. As to the former, a limit was only set in 2012 and this limit is asymmetric. Asymmetry, with a higher limit for surpluses and a lower one for deficit, implies no correction of the export-led policies that helped in creating large current account imbalances. Moreover, no common regulations were established that tried to limit risky accumulation of credit (and debt) positions. As for the latter, first France's and Germany's violations of the SGP and later those of Italy should not have been tolerated. These are only the signalling parts of an incomplete institutional setting that should have also included other active common institutions and policies. This incompleteness is the main determinant of the protracting crisis.

Notes

1 An extensive and penetrating ex ante critique, based on theoretical as well as empirical considerations, is in Begg (1997) and Allsopp and Vines (1998), which also show the questionable underpinnings of the EMU construction. An ex post reconstruction of the theoretical foundations of the Union and an account of the reasons for their obsolescence is in Acocella (2014). For a reconstruction of the process leading to the Maastricht Treaty and the forces conditioning it see Dyson and Featherstone (1999).

2 An implicit assumption is that the target value for inflation set by the ECB is the same as that of the country under consideration and that the former is optimal or, at least, not too low to prevent the necessary adjustment of the real wage in countries where the nominal one is rigid, which was and normally is still the case in most of the EMU countries (Krugman 2013). Otherwise, problems would arise of the kind that materialized later.

3 The standard deviation of the unemployment rates was 2.08 per cent. Among countries with higher unemployment there were still some with excess of labour in agriculture and the services, such as Spain, Portugal, and Greece. Somewhat puzzling is the fact that Germany also had an unemployment rate above the average. For a more appropriate way to take disguised unemployment into account see, for example, Howell (2005).

4 This figure undervalues the increase in poverty, as one component of the risk of poverty (the poverty rate) is calculated as a ratio of the individual household income to the median income and the latter had been lowered by the crisis. In addition, disposable income was to a large extent preserved by social transfers, whose rise negatively affected public deficit and debt, with negative long-term consequences.

5 The idea that everything went for the best was also widespread among citizens. This could be one of the reasons why they did not supervise or did not select policymakers properly, as we will see.

6 On this see also Monastiriotis and Zartaloudis (2010).

7 A number of options were open. And the adoption of one of them in one country might have been consistent with a different option chosen in another country. Take the case of the labour market. Here a number of solutions exist that can all ensure wage moderation (Monastiriotis and Zartaloudis 2010). The one adopted in Germany,

through decentralized bargaining, was not very different in principle from the solution taken by Italy of a centralized bargaining with a supplementary possibility of decentralization, which had led Italy out of the deep exchange rate crisis of 1992. Success would be ensured by adoption of complementary industrial and general policies both at the country and the EMU level.

8 With reference to Italy, Bassanetti et al. (2013: 15) confirm that Germany has been a sort of benchmark for Italy.

9 A conservative central bank, instead, generates higher social gains the lower the degree of competition in the product markets (Dalmazzo forthcoming: 11).

10 Dalmazzo also studies the effects of a higher fiscal discipline on tax rates, which are positive (i.e. the former implies a lower tax rate). This should reduce distortions and rent distribution. However, the variable he uses to indicate a higher fiscal discipline represents more the preferences of the government than the discipline. Thus, we do not take this effect into account in the text.

11 According to EEAG, "abundance of cheap funds brought a period of 'soft budget constraints' to capital-importing countries, to cite a concept that Janós Kornai once used to predict the fall of Communism ... The soft budget constraints meant that a credit-fuelled internal boom was spreading from the construction industry to the entire economy, pushing wages, prices and incomes from the provision of non-traded goods above the level sustainable in the long-run, creating the bubble that ultimately resulted in the European debt crisis. By the same token, Germany suffered from overly tight budget constraints as resources were withdrawn, entering a period of low growth rates and near stagnation under the euro, which ended abruptly when the debt crisis suddenly changed risk perceptions" (EEAG 2011: 77–78). In the next subsection we discuss the exact nature and possible determinants of a soft budget constraint.

12 This runs counter to Jahjah (2000) and the whole literature starting from the idea that the EMU would constitute a kind of external constraint for public and private decision-makers.

13 Also, other countries might have violated the SGP fiscal rules, without incurring informal infraction procedures. This was certainly the case for Italy. In the period 2001–2006 this country overshot the upper boundary of 3 per cent to net borrowing and disregarded the rule of the budget parity over the medium-run (Bassanetti et al. 2013: 15). This only emerged in 2004–2005 as a consequence of a revision of national accounts. Improper monitoring (Eurostat was empowered to monitor national statistics only with some lag) facilitated the violation.

14 Use of the term "principal" implies that, as in Fernandez-Villaverde et al. (2013), an issue of moral hazard arose. We are inclined to think that incentives can be affected even without moral hazard, as we will clarify in the section on "Signals and moral hazard" below. Then we use the term in a loose meaning.

15 It also leads to the diffusion of low quality agents and principals and a reduction in incentives of agents and tilts political–economic equilibrium against reforms. We deal with these consequences later in "Incentives, moral hazard and adverse selection of policymakers", which deals with moral hazard and adverse selection more specifically.

16 However, one must consider that in the early 2000s growth rates lowered in the whole EMU. This was the consequence not only of the contractionary effects of the common monetary policies and fiscal rules, but also of the slowing down of the growth rate in the USA, after the burst of the financial bubble created by the crisis of the "new economy" and the 2001 terrorist attack.

17 Even with reference to Italy, where the bubble was not so large as in other PIIGS countries, Bassanetti et al. (2013) assess a contribution to growth of higher asset values equal to 0.4 per cent, out of a total average growth equal to 1.6 per cent in the period 1998–2007 (an additional contribution of 0.2 per cent came from relaxation of fiscal policy due to reduction in the primary surplus).

18 Giordano et al. (2013) find evidence of a "wake-up-call contagion".

19 The theory often offers a variety of contrasting arguments, as, for example, if one compares the position of those supporting the external tie to those, such as Blanchard and Giavazzi (2002), who tend to neglect the existence of a foreign constraint in the EMU.

20 This is only an example. Institutions – and also effective reforms of them – are very specific to each country; in other countries reforms similar to those enacted in Germany could not have been effective, especially if the reproduction of German institutions were only partial.

References

Acemoglu, D., S. Johnson, P. Querubin and J. Robinson. 2008. *When Does Policy Reform Work? The Case of Central Bank Independence.* Brooking Papers on Economic Activity (Spring). Brookings Papers on Economic Activity. Washington, DC: Brookings Institution.

Acocella, N. 2014. "The Theoretical Roots of EMU Institutions and Policies During the Crisis." *Fondazione Einaudi* 2013–2014: 3–36.

Acocella, N. 2015. "A Tale of Two Cities: The Evolution of the Crisis and Exit Policies in Washington and Frankfurt." In *Crises in Europe in the Transatlantic Context Economic and Political Appraisals*, edited by B. Dallago and J. McGowan. London: Routledge, pp. 84–96.

Acocella, N., G. Di Bartolomeo and P. Tirelli. 2009. "The Macroeconomics of Social Pacts." *Journal of Economic Behavior and Organization* 72(1): 202–213.

Alesina, A. and A. Drazen. 1991. "Why are Stabilizations Delayed?" *American Economic Review* 81(5): 1170–1188.

Alesina A., S. Ardagna and F. Trebbi. 2006. *Who Adjusts and When? On the Political Economy of Reforms.* Working Paper no. 12049. Cambridge, MA: National Bureau of Economic Research.

Allsopp, C. and D. Vines. 1998. "The Assessment: Macroeconomic Policy after EMU." *Oxford Review of Economic Policy* 14(3): 1–23.

Baskaran, T. and Z. Hessami. 2013. *Monetary Integration, Soft Budget Constraints, and the EMU Sovereign Debt Crises.* Working paper Konstanz: Department of Economics, University of Konstanz.

Bassanetti, A., M. Bugamelli and S. Momigliano. 2013. *The Policy Response to Macroeconomic and Fiscal Imbalances in Italy in the Last Fifteen Years.* Occasional paper 211 (November). Rome: Bank of Italy.

Bean, C. 1998. "Monetary Policy Under EMU." *Oxford Review of Economic Policy* 14(3): 41–53.

Begg, D. K. H. 1997. *The Design of EMU.* Working paper 99 (August). Washington, DC: IMF.

Begg I. 2002. *EMU and Employment.* Working paper no. 42. Brighton: "One Europe or Several?" Programme, University of Sussex.

Blanchard, O. J. and F. Giavazzi. 2002. *Current Account Deficits in the Euro Area: The End of the Feldstein-Horioka Puzzle?* Brookings Papers on Economic Activity. Washington, DC: Brookings Institution. Available at www.brookings.edu/~/media/Files/Programs/ES/BPEA/2002_2_bpea_papers/2002b_bpea_blanchard.pdf.

Carli, G. 1993. *Cinquant'anni di Vita Italiana.* Laterza: Bari.

Casella, A. and B. Eichengreen. 1996. "Can Foreign Aid Accelerate Stabilization?" *Economic Journal* 106(436): 605–619.

Chassard, Y. 2001. "European Integration and Social Protection. From the Spaak Report to the Open Method of Co-ordination." In *Social Exclusion and European Policy*, edited by D. G. Mayes, J. Berhman and R. Salais. Edward Elgar, London, pp. 291–321.

Commission of the European Communities. 1990. "One Market, One Money: An Evaluation of the Potential Benefits and Costs of Forming an Economic and Monetary Union." *European Economy* 44 (October).

Commission of the European Communities. 1991. "The Economics of EMU." *Background Studies for European Economy* 44. "One Market, One Money." European Economy, Special edition, No 1.

Coricelli F., A. Cukierman and A. Dalmazzo. 2006. "Monetary Institutions, Monopolistic Competition, Unionized Labour Markets and Economic Performance." *Scandinavian Journal of Economics* 108(1): 39–63.

Dalmazzo, A. Forthcoming. "Monetary Discipline as a Substitute for Fiscal Reforms and Market Liberalizations." *Economic Notes*.

De Grauwe, P. 2010. *Economics of the Monetary Union*. Oxford: Oxford University Press.

De Grauwe, P. and Y. Ji. 2013. "More Evidence that Financial Markets Imposed Excessive Austerity in the Eurozone." *Ceps Commentary* (February), pp. 1–15.

Dyson K. and K. Featherstone 1996. "Italy and EMU as a 'Vincolo Esterno': Empowering the Technocrats, Transforming the State." *South European Society and Politics* 1(2): 272–299.

Dyson K. and K. Featherstone .1999. *The Road to Maastricht: Negotiating Economic and Monetary Union*. Oxford: Oxford University Press.

EEAG. 2011. *The EEAG Report on the European Economy*. Munich: Cesifo.

Featherstone, K. 2001. *The Political Dynamics of the Vincolo Esterno: The Emergence of EMU and the Challenge to the European Social Model*. Queen's Papers on Europeanization 6. Belfast: Queens University.

Fernandez-Villaverde, J., L. Garicano and T. Santos. 2013. "Political Credit Cycles: The Case of the Euro Zone." *Journal of Economic Perspectives* 27(3): 145–166.

Giavazzi F. and M. Pagano. 1988. "The Advantage of Tying One's Hands: EMS Discipline and Central Bank Credibility." *European Economic Review* 32(1): 55–75.

Giordano, R., M. Pericoli and P. Tommasino. 2013. *Pure or Wake-up-Call Contagion? Another Look at the EMU Sovereign Debt Crisis*. Working paper. Rome: Bank of Italy.

Heinemann, F. and T. Grigoriadis. 2013. *Origins of Reform Resistance and the Southern European Regime*. W. Package 104 MS20. Brussels: 7th Framework Programme, European Commission.

Howell, D. 2005. "Beyond Unemployment." *Challenge* 48(1): 5–28.

IMF. 2004. "Has Fiscal Behaviour Changed Under the European Economic and Monetary Union?" *World Economic Outlook* (September): 103–136.

Jahjah, S. 2000. *Inflation, Debt and Default in a Monetary Union*. Working paper 00/179. Washington, DC: IMF.

Krugman, P. 2013. "Revenge of the Optimum Currency Area." In *NBER Macroeconomics Annual*. Chicago, IL: University of Chicago Press, pp. 439–448.

Lane, P. R. 2006. "The Real Effects of EMU." Centre for Economic Policy Research, pp. 1–39.

Lane, P. R. and P. McQuade. 2013. *Domestic Credit Growth and International Capital Flows*. Working paper 1566 (July). Frankfurt: ECB.

Le Borgne, E. and B. Lockwood. 2002. *Candidate Entry, Screening, and the Political Budget Cycle*. Working paper 02/48. Washington, DC: IMF.

McNamera, K. 1998. *The Currency of Ideas: Monetary Politics in the European Union.* Ithaca, NY: Cornell University Press.

Milone, L. M. 2014. *Le Riforme Strutturali nell'Unione Europea Dopo la Crisi Globale: Problemi e Prospettive.* Mimeo.

Monastiriotis, V. and S. Zartaloudis. 2010. *Beyond the Crisis: EMU and Labour Market Reform Pressures in Good and Bad Times.* LEQS paper no. 23 (June). London: LSE.

Papademos, L. D. 2001. "Opening Address: The Greek Economy: Performance and Policy Challenges." In *Greece's Economic Performance and Prospects*, edited by R. C. Bryant, N. C. Garganas and G. S. Tavlas, pp. 33–39. Athens: Bank of Greece/Washington, DC: Brookings Institution.

Robinson, J. A. and R. Torvik. 2009. "A Political Economy Theory of the Soft Budget Constraint." *European Economic Review* 53: 786–798.

Weber, A. 1991. *EMU and Asymmetrical and Adjustment Problems in the EMS: Some Empirical Evidence.* 448, C.E.P.R. Discussion Papers. London: Economic Integration, Centre for Economic Policy Research. Available at https://ideas.repec.org/s/cpr/ceprdp.html

Wessels, W. 1997. "An Ever Closer Fusion? A Dynamic Macropolitical View on Integration Processes." *Journal of Common Market Studies* 35(1): 267–299.

Wildasin, D. E. 1997. *Externalities and Bailouts: Hard and Soft Budget Constraints in Intergovernmental Fiscal Relations.* Policy Research working paper no. 1843 (November). Washington, DC: World Bank.

3 On the crisis of the EMU

Failed construction, failed implementation or failed crisis management?

László Csaba

There is an overall feeling of crisis in the Economic and Monetary Union (EMU and libraries have been produced in an attempt to identify the roots of the *malaise* The three propositions, equally present in academia and in the policy discourse are to some degree mutually exclusive, and to some degree, complementary But before jumping in *medias res* in discussing each, one needs to observe tha the single currency has proven to be an *unprecedented success in its own terms* While Helmut Kohl was often ridiculed in his time for the claim that the eur is going to be "as stable as the D-Mark", this has proven to be the case. Non of the dangers feared from the very outset (i.e of *inflation* – over 3 per cent – o *deflation* –the decline of the general price level, reflected in the HICP) has actuall materialized. While for short periods both phenomena occurred, for the perio of four[1] consecutive quarters, as defined by the European Central Bank (ECB it has never happened. Annual inflation fluctuated between 0.5 and 2.6 per cen in the period between 1999 and 2014. This is above the pedantic interpretatio adopted by the ECB in 2003 of 2 per cent or less. But it is in line with practica policy needs and established financial and business standards, while avoidin; the ruinous relapse into deflation, as feared by many, especially during the grea recession of 2007–2009.[2] The external value of the euro – yet another subject o heated debate – fluctuated between 0.85 and 1.55 against the greenback, and thi flexibility has proven right. The accumulated capital and current account balanc of the Eurozone never went beyond plus or minus 1 per cent of the total, thu reflecting an ideal equilibrium position that tended to be different by the yea Thereby the major requirements set by exchange rate theory were fulfilled.[3]

But why is there such *a deep-seated dissatisfaction* in most of the countrie of the EMU? Why is the view of Martin Feldstein,[4] voiced prior to the entry int the EMU, so widely shared? As it is known, this was the first elaborate theoretica claim on the impossibility of the entire European monetary integration projec and it argued that the level of development differences as well as difference in fiscal capacity, rooted in governmental capabilities and traditions, render th entire project impossible to sustain; or if it is, only at substantial costs. The answe is multiple. The latter often equal to mixing up issues that emerge in one or mor nations with those attributable to any Community arrangement, more specificall; to the stipulations of EMU.

Inflated expectations in terms of trade and welfare growth, synchronization of the business cycle and the ensuing real convergence of per capita incomes failed to materialize and even suffered severe setbacks during the recession. The existence of the balance of payments surpluses/losses should not be seen as warning signs, since those do exist within federations and confederations, from Germany to China, none of whom constitute "optimal currency areas." Similarly, trade and capital surpluses should not be equated with gains, while deficits are equated (?) with losses, as under mercantilist theory. Deficits may well be conventional signs of faster modernization by poorer countries, and surpluses may equal the lack of local investment possibilities in richer nations. Division of labour along Ricardian lines thus may well be welfare-enhancing for both – and the history of the EU is a case in point.

It has become customary, both for politicians and economists, to blame "Brussels" and its alleged orthodox "monetarism" for basically all the mishaps in the respective national economies. Startling cases in point were the rejection of the European Constitution by the French, Dutch, and Irish electorates, basically in order to send a reminder to their respective local political elites, rather than to rectify any real or perceived mistakes in the Treaty proper. Likewise, the daunting issue of chronically high rates of unemployment, observed often prior to the crisis, but grossly exacerbated by it, tended to be blamed on the EMU architecture and/or on the workings of the *troika,* managing and often micro-managing the crisis in the defaulting countries. In reality, the EU has next to no competence on labour market issues, and it is also lacking the financial capacity to deal with it, should it have such a project or intention.[5]

The EMU has been seen – also by its proponents – as much more than a merely monetary arrangement, let alone a technique devised to secure low-cost funding for profligate governments. It was clearly understood that if the Feldsteinian propositions held, the consequences would be ruinous. Namely, if national fiscal positions tend to diverge, and furthermore, if productivity levels continue to be vastly different, and lastly, if the governmental capacity/bureaucratic ability to manage the macro-economy over and above smoothing the business cycle is lacking, the single currency leads to depression. In other words, the ability and willingness to introduce market-type reforms is the clue to the entire project.[6] *The non-reform scenario, by contrast, was seen to be a clear case of economic brinkmanship.*

But politics – the perceived need to avoid the shame of being left out – prevailed, irrespective of the foreseeable costs. Let us note: it would be hard to believe that derailments in 1999-2008 were pre-ordained, done deals, and policy-makers in the southern countries would indeed not have had any of the options, which were open, say, to their Baltic counterparts, who run much poorer and weaker countries.

The latter aspect tended to be neglected in the debates over who, when and to what degree the Maastricht nominal criteria, and its later, stricter version, the Stability of Growth Pact of 2005, was actually fulfilled. No wonder that much of the number-gazing proved ill-advised and misleading in terms of judging the actual – let alone the future – macroeconomic fragility of individual EMU states.

Doctoring the statistics, a practice that was later unmasked in several EMU states, including France and the Czech Republic, has only contributed to the ensuing disarray. The more economic analysis tended to be confined to econometric exercises while disregarding broader, qualitative, historical, structural aspects, as well as policy traditions and the like, the bigger was the ensuing chaos.

Actions taken through ignorance, political instrumentalization, and bad economics enhanced by public discourse together gave rise to the impression that Europe lags behind the USA primarily due to the switch to EMU and the related financial orthodoxy. This widespread fallacy spreads by replication rather than substantiation.[7] Empirical studies have long dismissed this claim as factually wrong. More recently van Ark et al. (2013)[8] and Péter Halmai (2014)[9] as well as the broad literature cited in both indicate that European convergence to the US had halted already four decades ago by 1973. Moreover, since 1995 (i.e four years before the EMU was launched), divergence has become pronounced and sustaining ever since. These analyses demonstrate the pivotal role of structural and institutional factors, such as low IT intensity and slow technological progress in terms of use and overregulation – not only on labour markets – among the fundamental causes. If those claims hold, easy money, provided via the monetary or the fiscal channel, or both, as actually practised since September 2012, is unlikely to cure any of the ills.

Managing the crisis has become a source of later, seemingly never-ending crises. Therefore, it can be discussed at least on two levels. On the national level, a great variety of specific answers to the challenges emerged. Some of these, as in the case of Latvia, Slovakia, Estonia, Romania and Germany, have proven to be quite effective in limiting the time span as well as the macroeconomic costs of interventions. Still, in other cases, especially in those of Greece, Italy, France, Portugal and Spain, adjustment policies have proven to be less than satisfactory, leading to procrastination. This in Greece, has translated to contractions exceeding those of the Great Depression of the 1930s. But Greece is an exception, not the rule to build a model on.[10]

At the Community level, answers tended to be improvised and politicized, following haphazard bureaucratic logic rather than any economic theory, whether Keynesian, Austrian, monetarist or otherwise. In short, the logic of "discipline for money", a rather simple, transparent, but not very efficient idea, seems to have ruled. This idea was meant to please the taxpayers of the net contributor countries, who were involved in a series of ad hoc bailouts. Given that in the vast majority of cases the roots of the crisis, including institutional rigidities, overregulation, non-targeted overspending, and lack of controls were not addressed, or only with a great delay, it is unsurprising to see that imbalances tended to reoccur.[11] Diminishing current disequilibria often took just a different form or size, rather than indicating any meaningful improvement.[12] This is reflected in an integrated fashion in the growing trend in terms of gross public debt/GDP ratios, which continued to grow also during times of "austerity." The pre-crisis (2007) level of 67 per cent grew to 93.6 per cent by 2014. This is in itself a disproof of the alleged "too much austerity" or "too much orthodoxy" claim, voiced not only in academia, but also in large parts of the European parliament as well as in national policy-making fora alike.

There has emerged no consensus, neither at the professional, let alone at the political level, whether the crisis allows for inferences concerning the *fundamental non-viability of austerity politics?* Or conversely, it calls for even more stringency. In my view, this debate, taken up by most of the policy fora on European integration, is basically flawed, if for no other reason than because it diverts attention from fundamental issues; namely, if, and to what degree, *structural reforms and good quality governance* has been introduced. For it is common wisdom that these two factors are decisive on the sustainability of any changes, even of the most radical ones. What we observe in the more successful Baltic countries, Ireland, and Slovakia, is the emphasis on those measures that ensure the lasting improvement in competitiveness. Those may include tax cuts, de-regulation, and most of the other usual suspects.[13] In other words, it is not the presence of quantitative easing or the lack of it, nor the size and scope of the fiscal stimulus – and the related number gazing – but the quality of institutions and the quality of governance/macroeconomic policies which has proven decisive for the outcomes, especially in the medium term.[14]

The double-dip crisis in Europe (the recession in 2009 was followed by yet another one in 2012) and the recurring difficulties of implementing decisions on the ground have called attention to some of the structural or constructional weaknesses of the financial architecture of the EMU. The latter have to do with a number of factors, in part related to the *political climate* that reigned at the time of its establishment, and in part owing to the *economic doctrines* along which the regulatory frame had been constructed.

At the time of launching the EMU, the idea of *voluntary rule-abiding behaviour*, also in terms of fiscal policy, sounded like common sense. The sanctioning mechanisms were considered to be of minor interest. Not only was the EU conceived as a club of gentlemen; there was also an overwhelming view of the virtue and goodness that fit the rules-abiding behaviour, in fiscal and monetary policies alike. Whenever governments, as in Germany under Oskar Lafontaine's administering of the Treasury, went astray from the practices of orthodoxy, punishment by markets was imminent. Thus the prevailing view was that EMU members will follow the EMU rules out of their own convictions and interests, and no supranational disciplinary mechanism was needed.[15] Valid on its own, the opportunistic behaviour of France and Germany in 2003–2004 *has created an atmosphere of cynicism and rule avoidance.* This was, however, not the root of fiscal profligacy in Greece as demonstrated, for instance, in an arms race with Turkey and the staging of the Olympic Games in 2004, actions that were obviously beyond the financial capabilities of any small country. Still, it created an environment under which the subsequent Greek governments could get away with regular and recurring cheating of their officially-endorsed government statistics that were regularly unmasked by Eurostat. Fiscal like-mindedness could not, and cannot, be taken for granted, as decisions on public spending and its pattern is at the heart of any democratic government (best known in the USA).

Market players have long criticized the *lack of the regulation of private finance*, more specifically of accumulating corporate indebtedness. Global financier George Soros, for example, calls it a major flaw of design in EMU.[16] And indeed, according to ECB,[17] we see that debt of non-financial corporations in the EMU approximate to that of Japan, or 105 per cent of GDP, exceeding the respective US value and public debt/GDP ratios alike. One of the perplexing lessons from the debt crisis of 2007–2009 has been the inadmissibility and impracticality of the previous custom/tradition of separating public and private debts via a Chinese wall. This did not hold, either in theory or in practice. At times of crises public money was used to bail out private banks, while private money was also used – sometimes via coercive arrangements – to bail out bankrupted governments. The two debts are thus, for any analytical purpose, two sides of the same coin.

Ongoing improvements in banking regulations, such as the formation of a banking union and joint banking resolution do not address this issue in an adequate manner, since only the largest 125 banks will be put under joint supervision, and that under the ECB, which has a very different mandate. Let us be clear: the ECB is a very peculiar construct, just as much as the European Union has been, reflecting its unfinished nature (neither a federation, nor just a free trade area). The establishment of a fully fledged central bank, with lender of last resort functions, usually does require a political union; what the EU – according to the reformed Treaty of the EU as of December, 2009 is surely not. Thus the ECB cannot be entrusted with any function at will. All the less so, since the depoliticized structure of its statute makes its decisions exempt from the type of political accountability; what any major fiscal function, especially re-distributive ones, would call for. As long as we do not pretend that it is immaterial who foots the bill at the final settlement, the ECB cannot be entrusted with any fiscal functions. For the latter is at the very heart of any democracy: who pays what and why so. Entrusting fiscal functions to a de-politicized body must be seen as arbitrary and dangerous.

Finally, the vesting of regulatory functions in what was devised as a purely monetary authority may also raise eyebrows. The regulator is a representative of public good. The public (*demos*) has yet to come about at the Union level. Bellamy[18] rightly argues that this notion may exist, for the time being, only in plural. His call for *demoicratic* controls (i.e an arrangement in which each participant has equal rights and opportunities to control outcomes) is the only viable option. This precludes further centralization, as the transformation of the ECB into a fully-fledged federal reserve would presuppose, especially if banking resolution is also vested in it. Cross-border settling of bills does require watchdogs and dispute settlement mechanisms.

The initiative to *create a fiscal union* represents perhaps an excess in the opposite direction. As it is known, during the management of a crisis a series of arrangements have been created, such as the Six Pack, the Fiscal Compact and the European Semester, which all aim at disciplining national fiscal policies. The unlimited asset purchases of the ECB since September 2012 have conferred a clear fiscal competence to an EU body, which had traditionally been de-politicized, in order to avoid mingling into its affairs by politicians. These features have further been strengthened by the outright monetary transactions programme, involving the ECB in targeted (*sic!*) purchases of bonds issued by weaker member states.[19] However, if and when the ECB is engaged in micro-managing debt obligations, with a view to relieve national budgets from its unfavourable impacts, the need for more political supervision – or less operational independence – comes immediately to the fore.[20] The more and broader tasks are assigned to an un-elected body, the broader and more meticulous the accountability mechanisms should be according to the theory and practice of public administration. Supervisory functions vested in the European parliament, where each MEP represents about 800,000 voters, with little or no professional support,[21] is a problem hardly being addressed in an appropriate manner.

As far as the more traditional items of fiscal policy are concerned, it is perhaps two innovations that are particularly harsh, given the soft, inter-governmentalist construction of the Lisbon Treaty, effective as of December, 2009. *First*, the European semester envisages ex ante coordination of major expenditure items, an idea that was seen to be naive from the very beginning. For it was hard to believe from the very outset that, for example, the French or Italian government would indeed drop a major investment project, or an election-winning distributive scheme, in order to meet the expectations of Brussels.[22] *Second*, and perhaps even more biting, is the innovation allowing for the suspension or even withdrawal of funds (cohesion funds, farming subsidies or environmental financing) should the country repeatedly be found trespassing the joint fiscal rules. The latter arrangement is certainly raising the problem of retro-activity and proportionality, *two basic principles of the rule of law* in any society. If we consider that, for example, a Hungarian farmer may suffer in his already approved projects for the eventual laxity of governmental spending, over which he has no control, the trickiness of the innovation becomes quite palpable.

One of the most challenging features of both crisis and crisis management has been *the growing gap between EMU-ins and EMU-outs*. This has practical ramifications on a number of planes, political and economic alike. Being part of EMU has a number of overwhelming advantages both politically and economically. The Eurogroup of finance ministers is the place where most decisions take place, rather than in Ecofin or even less in the Council, where enlargement has created a *complexity and intransparency to an incomprehensible degree*; incomprehensible not only to laymen, outside observers such as journalists, but the participants themselves. As a result, the outcome of complex bargains has increasingly produced results that were not really intended by anybody, at least not in its actual form and formulation.[23] Thus being an EMU-out implies, by definition, *second rank membership*, as the UK has repeatedly experienced. By contrast, being EMU-in allows even for small countries like Slovakia to exert their influence.

Being an EMU-in allows for reliance on *the new instruments of supra-national crisis management*, which emerged over the past years, without necessarily enjoying democratic legitimation,[24] as, for example, the unconstrained purchases of government bonds by the European Central Bank, as well as reliance on the newly established European Stability Mechanism. The ESM is a technocratically managed independent body, allowing for the bailout of major financial institutions, currently controlling over 750 billion euros of joint facilities. While the latter was used to bail out major Spanish, Irish, and Italian banks, the former helped overcome the second recession in 2012. EMU-outs cannot benefit from these innovations, making both their public and private finances more vulnerable to external shocks.

Being an EMU-in allows all participants to draw on the *well-known financial advantages of a currency union,* as saving on transaction costs, enhanced competition, lower prices, bigger consumer welfare and the like. One may go on at length citing examples, but the finding is rather self-explicatory. This factor is particularly important in the non-tradable sector, especially services industries, accounting for 75 per cent of the GDP of EU countries.

Being an EMU-in saves the respective country from the speculation against its national currency and the ensuing risks of *volatility, of sudden stops and capital flow reversals,* as well as of imported inflation. A temporary dispersion interest rate convergence and convergence of the yields on government bonds has returned to a common low level, as did the CDS mark-ups and spreads; the latter reflects the differential assessment of country-specific risks.[25] Contrary to expectations prevailing both among theorists and business executives, during the crisis the EMU *has failed to become a truly irreversibly uniform economic bloc, comparable to a single country,* since country-specific reactions prevailed over the common rules, both among the good guys and among the bad ones.[26] This circumstance renders any generalization about "European responses" or "European economic policies" hard to define, let alone easy to turn into empirically testable propositions.

Being an EMU-in has also *a number of drawbacks, although these tended to be over-emphasized* in the recent literature. *First,* currency union implies the giving up of the exchange rate instrument, commonly discussed in introductory textbooks. However, this is less of a sacrifice than it looks, as in more sophisticated economies the impact of devaluations is limited anyway to short periods of time. Furthermore, the transmission mechanism of exchange shocks also changed (e.g. for Hungary from 0.6 to 0.7 per cent in the early eighties to 0.1 to 0.15 per cent at time of writing), meaning that devaluations do not work either way. *Second, a* joint monetary policy does not allow differentiated crisis responses. But is it not the case say, for Sicily and Piemonte? Or Brandenburg and Bavaria? Shanghai and Uiguria? Or even Iowa and Maryland. This should not be a problem, per se. *Third,* fiscal instruments, especially discretionary ones, cannot be used at will. But the more we believe in the longer run ineffectuality of those instruments in generating growth, the less we consider this to be a sacrifice. Lacking a political union, the solution is the voluntary and forward-looking *adjustment of the expenditure pattern, rather than its size,* when managing the crisis. In the Scandinavian countries, for instance, enhancing R&D expenditures, as well as spending more on re-training people helped create what is by now commonly known as flexicurity[27] (i.e a combination of both of the goodies economists usually strive for). Unemployment rates in 2014 stand at 6.5 per cent in Denmark, 7.1 per cent in Sweden and 8.8 per cent in Finland against the 11.1 per cent of the Eurozone let alone the 24.5 per cent in Spain or 27.3 per cent in Greece.[28] True, in the overall climate of distrust the open method of coordination, to use the EU jargon, is less effective than it looked a few years ago. But experience of the past years has clearly showed that straightjackets are not a realistic solution either, especially if large players, like France and Italy, openly disobey, and the Eurosceptic discourse becomes mainstream in many countries, not only in the UK.

In any event, the big question, for theory and policy alike, remains open: how much fiscal policy can attain in matters of structural adjustment? And if the theory of optimal currency areas is no longer relevant as a point of reference, does Confederation Europe really need a huge centralized budget comparable to that of the federal American state, post-bellum? If we follow the ideas of the Nobel Lecture by Thomas Sargent in 2011,[29] barely so.

The ensuing big question – the central theme of the present volume – is, if all the experiences with sustaining and changing EMU are going to *lead, or should lead, to the fundamental restructuring, or even abolition, of the established continental European social model?* Certainly, a lot depends on what we consider to be constituting features of the model, and what counts as auxiliary, a matter of size rather than of substance. Should we follow the tradition established in the textbooks on comparative economic systems, published over the past seven or eight decades, *the milestones could not be set in exclusively or even primarily in quantitative terms*, such as the share of governmental spending in GDP, or the share of persons living under the international poverty line. In this reading the defining feature of the social market economy is its modus operandi, aiming and also attaining a fair balance between economic competitiveness and social cohesion.[30] Time and space does not allow us to stray into the country and model specific assessment of the varieties of European capitalism, as political scientists would name it. What is clear from the summary evidence presented above is a few points:

- EU level changes do not require fundamental rearrangements, let alone artificial unification/standardization of various domestic social models, rather than adherence to established basic financial principles.
- Prudent macroeconomic policies are not about austerity or the lack of it. Fiscal sustainability, however, does matter, but viability and growth is contingent upon structural measures and strategic thinking.
- The customary practice, focusing exclusively on number gazing on its own, not complemented by considering qualitative factors and contextuality, might be politically misleading. If policies revolve around magic numbers and substantive features, such as the composition of growth, the generational aspects of unemployment and the efficiency of the system of education, from kindergartens to PhD schools, or the capability and credibility of central and local administration may be pushed to the background.
- Elections, both at the national and EU level, have shown a convincing majority for forces favourable to both features of the European social model, namely to *sustaining acceptable levels of social transfers and commitment to the European project.* While media tends to over-rate euro-sceptic and radical protest movements, this has more to do with their visibility, fun, and

input into infotainment, rather than a reflection of major changes in basic societal values. Analyses of the latter, perhaps most extensively by the annual survey of attitudes through the Commission-sponsored *Eurobarometer*, but also other, competing publications, show the largely unchanged commitment of most of the population to those values. Indeed, with all diversity, the overwhelming feature is the lack of support either for the demolition of the welfare state along Thatcherite political discourse, or to national seclusion, along the lines of President Lukashenka of Belarus.

Thus, taking the long view, one may tend to agree with the eminent economic historian Iván T. Berend,[31] who in his recent analysis of European crises calls for the preservation of the European social market model as a major accomplishment of European civilization while allowing for the necessary financial and structural adjustments that are necessary for the economic sustainability and vigour of the project as a whole.

On our side we would put perhaps a somewhat different emphasis on the conclusion, while agreeing with the fundamental claim. In our reading, *most of the flaws have been coming from a politically overdetermined and economically narrow mode of crisis management,* not following any clear-cut logic of any economic or political school of thinking. Fiscal adjustment is yet to be made in many large countries in the EU. Furthermore, it is more about *its quality than its size,* more about its pattern than about its short-term quantitative attainment of jointly set reference thresholds.

While the latter do play a highly useful role in orienting decision-makers – who are, as in any democracy, generally laymen – meeting or missing these should not be the major standard for overall assessment. Rather, meeting the quantitative targets should be seen as a kind of *scope condition,* which help to understand how long a road is ahead of us and how much it is likely to cost if we are to make this way successfully. The latter is going to be judged by the respective societies themselves, who have already benefitted tremendously from sustaining the EMU also at times of crisis, rather than allowing for the siren voices to disintegrate it in the name of ad hoc political considerations.

Acknowledgements

Comments by Hermann Schwarz, Steve Rosefielde and the editors are appreciated, with the usual caveats.

Notes

1 Note that the ECB definition deviates from the customs of the USA, where a contraction of two quarters already counts as a recession. By contrast, the ECB opted for 4 quarters, both for theoretical and practical reasons; the most important among these is the relative unreliability of preliminary data, and also the need to avoid recurring interventions owing to those uncertainties. For a broad discussion of the underlying theoretical and policy considerations that have led to this option cf. O.

Issing, I. Angeloni and V. Gaspar, 2004, *Decision-Making in the European Central Bank*, 2nd revised edition, Cambridge: Cambridge University Press.
2 Sources of all data: ECB, *Statistics Pocket Book*, various issues (see www.ecb. europa.eu/pub/spb/html/index.en.html). Some analysts claim, citing the findings of the Bosworth Commission of the USA, that these headline numbers imply in reality a *deflation*, should the US standard hold with headline inflation being, on average, 1.1 points over actual, final numbers. Cf. B. Moulton, K. Moses, R. Gordon and B. Bosworth, 1997, "Addressing the Quality Change Issue in the CPI", *Brookings Papers on Economic Activity* 28(1): 305. But such corrective analyses were made for the US only, whose results should not be mechanistically transposed to Europe. Also, Eurostat is continuously improving its practices, and unless proven otherwise, data released by them should be accepted.
3 M. Obstfeld, 2012, "Does the Current Account Deficit Still Matter?", *American Economic Review* 102(3): 1–23 elaborates on these issues in more general terms.
4 M. Feldstein, 1997, "The Political Economy of the European Economic and Monetary Union: Political Success of an Economic Liability", *Journal of Economic Perspectives* 11(4): 23–42. This view is the radicalization of the older Mundell-Flemming claim on the EEC/EU not being an optimal currency area. Discussing the libraries of literature on OCA and its applications on EMU would require a different paper of much longer size.
5 The European Employment Strategy may qualify as such, but this is little more than a set of suggestions, rather than an operational policy document supported by funding. For more on this issue, see T. van Rie and I. Mary, 2012, "The European Union at Work? The European Employment Strategy from Crisis to Crisis", *Journal of Common Market Studies* 50(2): 335–356.
6 This has been particularly brutally expressed by the German conservative economists, who forecasted a major crisis, should those reforms not be forthcoming. See fine detail in D. Cassel (ed.), 1998, *Europaeische Integration als ordnungspolitische Gestaltungsaufgabe*, Berlin: Duncker und Humblot.
7 More recently in the notable public lecture by Joseph E. Stiglitz, 2014. "Can Illiberal Democracies Create Shared Prosperity?", Central European University, Budapest, 10 November.
8 B. Van Ark, M. Mcmahoney and M. Timmer, 2013, "Europe's Productivity Performance in Comparative Perspective: Trends, Causes and Perceptions", in *World Economic Performance: Past, Present and Future*, edited by D. S. Prasada Rao and B. van Ark, pp. 290–315, Cheltenham: Edward Elgar.
9 P. Halmai, 2014, *Krízis és növekedés az Európai Unióban* [Crisis and growth in the EU], Budapest: Akadémiai Kiadó.
10 A. Visvizi, 2013, "Addressing the Crisis in Greece: the Role of Fiscal Policy", in *The Aftermath of the Global Crisis in the European Union*, edited by B. Farkas, pp. 211–240, Newcastle: Cambridge Scholars Publishing.
11 V. Tanzi, 2013, *Dollars, Euros and Debt: How We Got There and How Can We Get Out of It?* New York: Palgrave.
12 An extreme example is the Polish model, where debt and deficit figures do not even remotely overlap. This is explained by the Ecofin allowing Poland to subtract pension expenditures – largely responsible for the deficit – from debt stock reporting, a practice first employed by France in 1999.
13 For the more controversial Baltic case, cf. K. Staehr, 2013, "Austerity in the Baltic States During the Global Financial Crisis", *Intereconomics* 48(5): 293–302.
14 This point is emphasized in the comparative analysis of the two ideal types of adjustment, Latvia (the success story) and Hungary, the less successful case, in D. Győrffy, 2015, "Austerity and Growth in CEE: Understanding the Link through Contrasting Crisis Management in Hungary and Latvia", *Post-Communist Economies* 27(2): 129–152.

15 For re-stating these ideas on the post-crisis landscape, cf. the eloquent argumentation in G. Kopits, 2012, "Can Fiscal Sovereignty be Reconciled with Fiscal Discipline?", *Acta Oeconomica* 62(2): 141–161.

16 G. Soros and and G. P. Schmitz, 2014, "The Future of Europe: An Interview with George Soros", *New York Review of Books* (24 April), available at http://www.nybooks.com/articles/2014/04/24/future-europe-interview-george-soros/

17 *Statistics Pocket Book* (see note 2 above).

18 R. Bellamy, 2013, "An Ever Closer Union Across the Peoples of Europe: Republican Inter-governmentalism and *Demoicratic* Representation within the EU", *Journal of European Integration* 35(5): 499–516.

19 It is hard not to see the monetary transactions programme as an open form of monetization of debt, strictly prohibited by the statutes of the ECB. It is hardly by chance that the negative ruling of Karlsruhe, the German Constitutional Court, is being appealed to the European Court of Justice, which has yet to offer an opinion at the time of finalizing the current paper. However, in terms of economic substance, the legal interpretation is of little relevance. Those fearful of deflation may even cheer the monetization option as long overdue.

20 C. Weber and B. Forschner, 2014, "ECB: Independence at Risk?", *Intereconomics* 49(1): 45–51.

21 A regular MEP has only two personal assistants, whereas the European Parliament has jurisdiction over a series of complex professional matters, from regulation of audiovisual substances via migration issues to cohesion issues.

22 The debate with both governments with the Commission became the subject of public controversy in October 2014, with both of them adopting defiant stances despite their signing the Fiscal Compact.

23 Cf. the broad account of a long-time insider and former Commission member: P. Balázs, 2014, "EU 36: The Impact of EU Enlargements on Institutions", in *A European Union with 36 Members? Perspectives and Risks*, edited by P. Balázs, pp. 227–256, Budapest: CEU Press for CENS.

24 As reflected in the clear ruling of the German Constitutional Court of Karlsruhe, declaring the unlimited bond purchases unlawful from the perspective of sovereignty transfer (*Frankfurter Allgemeine Zeitung*, 14 February 2014).

25 A. Hernandez-Sanchez, 2014, "Financial Integration in the Euro-zone: The Case of the Banking Union", MA Theses. Department of IRES, CEU, Budapest, June, 2014 provides detailed statistical evidence for this claim. The source is available online at the university library website.

26 A. Boltho and W. Carlin, 2013, "EMU's Problems: Asymmetric Shocks or Asymmetric Behavior?", *Comparative Economic Studies* 55(3): 387–403, and my own reading in L. Csaba, 2012, "Re-visiting the Crisis of the Euro-zone: Challenges and Options", *Zeitschrift für Staats- und Europawissenschaften*10(1): 53-77.

27 P. Flaschel and A. Greiner, 2012, *Flexicurity Capitalism: Foundations, Problems and Perspectives*, Oxford, New York: Oxford University Press.

28 *Statistics Pocket Book* 44 (see note 2 above).

29 T. Sargent, 2011, "United States Then, Europe Now", Nobel Lecture delivered on 8 December in Stockholm, available at www.nobelprize.org.

30 I tried to expand on this less than trivial – and most controversial – theoretical and policy issue in my recent book, L. Csaba, 2014, *Európai közgazdaságtan [Economics for Europe]*, Budapest: Akadémiai Kiadó, pp. 88–125. There I attempted to compare the German, French, and post-communist models.

31 Berend, I. T., 2013, *Europe in Crisis: Bolt Out of the Blue?* Cambridge: Cambridge University Press.

4   The European crisis

Testing the trust foundations of an economic and monetary union

Simona Piattoni

Introduction

All main theories of European integration start from the assumption that the European Union (EU) is the result of the rational calculation of sovereign states that expect to attain jointly higher benefits – commonly summarized by the phrase "peace and prosperity" – than those that they could attain on their own. Theories then diverge on the emphasis that they put on whether these same calculations can explain all subsequent steps taken towards the increasing deepening and widening of the Union – whether these too are dictated by sheer rationality and self-interest or other social, cultural, or institutional factors are at play.

The joint attainment of public goods requires a certain dose of reciprocal trust, which is paradoxically presupposed, and at the same time challenged, each time a new step towards further integration is taken by referring to the utility of the individual member states. The Economic and Monetary Union (EMU) is a glaring example of how trust must be simultaneously presupposed and carefully guarded by all those who join in this agreement on macroeconomic management and, for those member states who already belong to the euro-area, in the common currency. The euro crisis – a synthetic term by which we mean the difficulties encountered by members of the euro-area in the period 2009–2015 for reasons having to do with speculative bubbles, private overspending, and public excessive debt – laid bare the contradiction implicit in entering a long-term (possibly never-ending) contract – the single currency – founded upon what I will call "conditional and guarded trust". In times of crisis, when the short-term interest of the individual euro-area member states is at odds with their long-term commitments, not only the behaviour of the various member states is questioned but the very impartiality of the agencies (the European Central Bank and the Commission) that were entrusted with oversight over and enforcement of the contract is also called into question.

This chapter will argue that strictly rationalist arguments are insufficient to carry the euro-area or the EMU through times of crisis. More than that: the way in which the decision to join the euro-area is justified and the costs and benefits of sticking to the commitments made in Maastricht are presented to the national citizenry undermines the credibility of those commitments and shakes the trust foundations of that decision, thus weakening the legitimacy bases of EMU and the euro and injecting a potentially lethal dose of distrust in the system. It consequently also shakes the political support for what was initially hailed as a major step towards an "ever growing union". After discussing the rationalist bases of these arguments and showing how, at crucial junctures, these arguments have served to weaken the trust bases upon which the euro was founded, the chapter will then critically discuss principles other than utility which could serve as the basis for a more resilient "guarded and conditional trust", in particular "responsible responsiveness".

In a nutshell, I will argue that it is not until the political leaders of the euro-area member states decide to "tell the full story" to their citizens – that is, explain again why they (the citizens) decided to join and what costs and benefits can be realistically expected from being members of the euro-area and also, spell out which commitments were made and how they can eventually be re-discussed – that the crisis will be reasonably faced. Unfortunately, national political leaders seem more prone to keep playing the "two-level *blame* game" (cf. Putnam 1988) whereby they blame the Union (or the euro) for everything that goes wrong and take individual credit for all decisions that appear to improve the national interest.

The rationalist bases of integration

Among the many theories of European integration, those that have their roots in an interpretation of the Community/Union (henceforth simply Union or EU) as the outcome of the pursuit of the national interest of the member states are the majority. Most of these theories treat states as units of analysis, to which rational cost-benefit calculations – hence the extension or withdrawal of trust – can be applied. The early, and until now main, theories of European integration – first and foremost intergovernmentalism (in both its statist and liberal variant) but also neofunctionalism and neoinstitutionalism – are based on some rational explanation of how member states or economic interests (through national governmental representatives) try to maximize their utility through integration.

Intergovernmentalists have based their explanations on the obvious utility advantages that ensue from putting an end to reciprocal (if not necessarily equivalent) externalities (Moravcsik 1993). In his detailed analysis of the history-making decision to integrate, Moravcsik argues that negative externalities are more powerful than positive externalities in prompting states to agree on common policies. In both cases, the benefits of a behaviour or action accrue to subjects who do not bear the costs of that behaviour or action; bringing the two into line thus increases utility. However, while in the case of reciprocal negative externalities, the benefits to all parties are immediate and contextual to the agreement, and are hence sufficient to explain their occurrence, in the case of positive externalities at least one of the parties may wish to retain the status quo by withholding from the agreement and will have to be otherwise convinced.[1] The incentives for an agreement are consequently lower or more complicated in the case of positive externalities. This is the reason why in the European Union many strides forward in integration are achieved through *side-payments*, aimed at convincing the losing or not-gaining party, or through *package deals*, in which all parties to the agreement may find at least something that they like in the deal and are hence induced to accept also the other items.

The deepening of the Common Market and the EMU have been famously explained in this way (see Dinan 2012: 37, for example). In particular, the decision of Germany to give up its own currency in favour of a common currency has been explained in terms of the other European member states accepting the reunification of Germany (Risse et al. 1999). Similarly, the agreement to complete the Common Market or to adopt strict convergence criteria in order to become members of the euro-area on the part of the weaker economies, which could not expect to gain as much as the stronger economies from these measures, has been explained by pointing to the much increased expenditures through the Structural Funds and the Cohesion Fund which flowed mostly to the poorer members of the Union (Pollack 1995; Allen 2000). These kinds of agreements are inherently brittle. To begin with, long-term structural changes (e.g. merging all currencies into one) are traded for one-off redistributive advantages. Admittedly, cohesion policy has become a fixed and growing item of the EU budget at least since 1988 (when the big-bang reform of European regional development policy took place; e.g. see Brunazzo forthcoming). Moreover, it is notoriously difficult to undo past decisions, as shown by Scharpf's "joint decision trap" theorization (Scharpf 1988, 2006, 2010), but while the principles that sustain the Common Market become part of the *acquis*, the financial transfers to the EU budget for cohesion policy are bargained every five to six years (Bachtler et al. 2013). Budgetary cutbacks, in the end, are much simpler than undoing the common currency or reneging on mutual recognition.

But what is probably more damaging for the long-term sustainability of the Union than simply the lopsided nature of many package deals that have characterized the process of EU integration according to the intergovernmental view – lopsidedness that cannot be blamed in itself, as all rational actors are assumed to bargain in full knowledge of their own best interests – is the idea that short- or long-term national advantages may suffice to carry the integration project forward. To begin with, calculations may prove faulty and countries may fail to realize their expected advantage; hence, the pressure to renegotiate the agreement or to exit may become very strong. What is more troubling, however, is that given the rational and conditional justification for the agreement, all parties will expect all others to be willing to defect as soon as the expected advantages should not materialize. In fact, the expectation of free-riding on agreements that provide selective common benefits are a staple in this worldview, hence the need to create supranational institutions like the Commission, the European Court of Justice, the European Central Bank to monitor behaviour and enforce agreements. Interstate trust is conditional on systemic trust, and vice versa. In many ways, this rational expectation injects a "moral" incentive (the national interest) to free-ride on agreements and makes distrust into a self-fulfilling prophecy: if agreements are entered solely in view of reaping selective benefits, then trusting that the other parties will also stick to the agreement, when doing so might prove disadvantageous, is certainly a "moral hazard".

Also, *neofunctionalists* locate the prime mover of European integration on a rationalist vision, arguing that Europe is the level at which economic interests can best exploit economies of scale. In this approach, functional interconnections and social forces play a more central role (Sandholtz and Stone-Sweet 1998; Stone-Sweet et al. 2001). While also in the liberal version of intergovernmentalism economic interests supposedly dictate the national agenda, which governmental representatives then seek to maximize at the EU level, according to neofunctionalists economic interests are capable of mobilizing directly at the supranational level and pushing for solutions to their common problems at this level. State representatives are complementary figures in this play, and not necessarily welcome ones. To this also rational understanding of the motivations for agreements – pressures from economic interests and transnational civil society – neofunctionalists add a never fully worked-out psychological (or, again, perhaps only rational) transfer of "loyalties" towards the new political centre, that is, Brussels (Haas 1970; Schmitter 1970). This transfer of expectations – that policy solutions should be forthcoming from the supranational level – and loyalties is the real distinguishing trait between neofunctionalists and intergovernmentalists.

Whether the transfer of loyalties is interested and conditional or reflexive and unconditional, we witness a progressive suspension of rational calculations and the development of affective sentiments. This cognitive and psychological transformation, which supposedly takes place among social and economic actors, creates a reservoir of positive predispositions, which can be tapped during times of crisis. Directing expectations and loyalties towards this new supranational political entity is assumed to become "the new normal" – provided that at EU level all the channels for being heard and for exerting pressure are activated. If these expectations are disappointed, however, the withdrawal of loyalty may also ensue. State actors may be tempted to disrupt this direct dialogue between societal actors and supranational institutions by interjecting power politics into the pragmatic resolution of functional issues and by trying to act as "gate-keepers" (Hoffmann 1966). Luckily, the supranational institutions which have been created to facilitate the smooth functioning of the market and its progress towards an ever-closer union will have an institutional interest in keeping the momentum going and will counter the potentially disruptive free-riding behaviours of state actors.

Neoinstitutionalists have focused precisely on the independent effect that institutions – understood in their broader sense, both as organizations and as rules and procedures – have on the continuing progress of European integration, pinning its continuation on the sheer force of rules, procedures, standard practices, and on the institutionalization of certain tacit expectations and routines. In this case, too, the tone of the argumentation is mainly rational, in the sense that governmental and non-governmental actors know how far they can push the raw maximization of their utility and where they must instead stop, retreat, or take a more circuitous route. In other words, among the many institutionalisms (Hall and Taylor 1996; Schmidt 2008, 2010) the most practiced one has been rational choice institutionalism (Garrett 1992; Garrett and Tsebelis 1996; Pollack 2010).

This is not to say that other – sociological (Checkel 2010), historical (Pierson 1996, 2004) or constructivist (Christiansen et al. 2001) – interpretations have not been offered. Quite to the contrary, these strands of neo-institutionalism, which put a premium on historical and cognitive factors, have become predominant in EU studies since the turn of the century. Still, the rationalist approach to European integration has never disappeared and has received a new boost since the beginning of the crisis. There is nothing like a crisis that can strip bare the ultimate aims – survival and aggrandizement – supposedly lying at the heart of all human endeavour, most certainly of states and economic interests.

To conclude, in political science rationalist explanations have acquired the status of "base-line explanations" of sorts: i.e. explanations that are allegedly so fundamental and self-evident that no reference to further motives or reasons is necessary. They are parsimonious. Cultural, historical, sociological, or psychological explanations are considered of a "lower quality" because they need to summon up additional factors that are difficult to prove (or which are less in tune with the dominating scientific approach of our times). Also, the functioning of the European Union is fundamentally based on rational – that is, at the bottom, sceptical and distrustful – expectations about member states' behaviour. Again, whether the main drive is the maximization of domestic interests or the maximization of geo-political goals, the functioning of the EU has been marked by the need to create institutions which could secure that this guarded and conditional trust would not be breached or that, if that were to happen, it would be met with consequences.

Nevertheless, the need for a value-based or even sentiment-based analysis of European integration has been increasingly felt. Particularly in times of crisis, when heavy sacrifices are asked in the name of an economic and political construct that has stopped (or appears to have stopped) producing advantages for its citizens, other grounds for integration must be found. The latest development of integration theory is currently analysing the myths on which the Union may be politically based (Della Sala 2010) or the values – such as non-domination, tolerance, justice, or solidarity – on which its legitimacy may be grounded (Pettit 1997; Weiler and Wind 2003; Neyer 2010; Habermas 2013).

In this contribution, I will explore the way in which the crisis has laid bare the need to justify the creation and development of the Union in non-rationalist terms which, at the same time, would not clash with the equally fundamental need of the Union to prove its effectiveness in solving common problems and furthering mutually compatible interests. Single-minded pursuit of strict rational goals and a rationally inspired fundamental distrust in the representatives of member states' ulterior motives is not going to carry the Union very far and runs the risk of undermining the progress made so far.

Institutional provisions to sustain trust

Trust is, at the same time, a precondition and objective of the Union. The European Community was founded upon the knowledge that long-time enemies (primarily Germany and France, but also Britain, Italy, and many other European countries) had to reconstruct relationships of mutual trust that had been shattered by two world wars. Trust among sovereign nation states, however, is always "conditional and guarded". National interest conventionally understood – "power and plenty", in the fortunate and concise expression of Viner (1948) – although "morally bankrupt" after World War II, soon re-emerged and threatened to undo the commitments entered into with the signing of the Treaties of Paris (1951) and Rome (1957). The creation of such powerful supranational institutions – much more powerful than the secretariat of any other international organization – has been since the beginning the distinctive trait of the European Union. These institutions were justified precisely in terms of the need to have neutral and independent agencies capable of monitoring and enforcing agreements and facilitating further agreements and decisions, acting thus as engines of integration (Pollack 2003).

There is an ongoing debate on whether the EU supranational institutions have fulfilled this role faithfully or have rather interjected their own institutional interests (preservation, aggrandizement) in the discharging of their duties. The task of these institutions is a delicate one, which requires striking a balance between being too lenient and subservient to national interests, especially those of the larger member states, and being too proactive and too forceful in disciplining non-compliance. It is generally acknowledged that the Commission, with ups and downs due mostly to the different capacity of the various Commission presidents to steer the EU decision-making process, has managed to get the balance about right, while most criticisms have been levied against the European Court of Justice (ECJ) and the European Central Bank. But even in these cases opinions differ. The ECJ has been criticized by those who see "integration through law" – that is, using the four freedoms as justifiable legal principles with momentous consequences on the regulatory traditions which characterize the "social compact" between state and citizens in the individual member states – as an unwarranted and undemocratic attack on national welfare state traditions (Scharpf 2009, 2010). These critics have shown that the ECJ can pursue at most "negative integration" – the dismantling of socially entrenched barriers to the free circulation of goods, money, people, and services – while it is unable to stimulate "positive integration" – the creation of common regulatory regimes that can extend to all EU citizens' rights which are acceptable to all. The ECB has been criticized for being either too technocratic and insensitive to the plight of economically troubled euro-area member states or too political and exceeding the limits of its mandate.

On the one hand, the line between trying to fulfil their institutional role by signalling to the member states areas of further integration and preparing policy proposals that make this possible and, on the other, forcing the hand of reluctant national governments is very thin indeed. I will concentrate below on the role that, in particular, Commission and ECB have played in the Euro-crisis "morality play". Suffice here to say that one very strong position in the debate is that policy decisions at the EU level are possible only insofar as they are Pareto-optimum – leaving no one worse off while making some better off – which would justify subtracting responsibility for these types of decisions altogether from the political class and assigning it to technical committees of experts, "unencumbered" as it were from fastidious political pressures. Truly political decisions that cause a redistribution of resources among different constituencies would instead be impossible given that the EU lacks the necessary attributes of a national state and the underlying democratic legitimacy (Majone 1999). Those who consider this as a false dichotomy and argue that all decisions are explicitly or implicitly redistributive – even regulatory decisions that should move along a theoretical Pareto-optimum frontier – have criticized this argument.

Management of the EMU is precisely one such area, which has been presided over by a very independent agency (ECB) as well as being the object of particular surveillance by another agency (the Commission) and managed through "heightened intergovernmentalism" (Euro-group, Euro summits). To safeguard themselves against cheating, free-riding and shirking, member states have set in place rules and procedures, such as the Broad Economic Policy Guidelines (BEPGs) and the Stability and Growth Pact (SGP), right at the start of EMU, which have been later reinforced, after the crisis, through the Six-Pack and Two-Pack and the Treaty on Stability Governance and Coordination (TSGC). They have done so to secure shared and transparent knowledge of member states' macroeconomic conditions, supervisory and enforcement capacity and, if necessary, sanctioning powers of supranational agencies. Since the Union lacks competence over crucial macroeconomic areas such as fiscal, budgetary, and (until lately) banking policy and over the equally strategic areas of labour and welfare policies, the Commission can only encourage euro-area member states to try and coordinate their decisions in these areas so as not to "rock the euro boat" and, in case of external shocks, to try and absorb them as quickly and as efficiently as possible. In other words, lacking direct policymaking power, the Commission can only try and steer euro-area member states towards "coordination" (Dølvik and Martin 2014).

From a rationalist point of view, entrusting the ECB and the Commission with these tasks is only wise; from a political and normative point of view, it may backfire. On the one hand, creating too strong and independent agencies runs the risk of eliciting complaints against "technocratic rule" while strictly and inflexibly applying rules and procedures smacks of domination. On the other hand, management of the EMU and the euro in the absence of such independent agencies would have been politically impossible and a lax or flexible application of the rules would devoid them of any constraining power. Clearly, at the bottom lies the (reasonable) expectation that, particularly in times of crisis, euro-area member states would be tempted to assuage their national constituencies by relaxing their commitments vis-à-vis the other member states. One of the unwelcome consequences of such a rationalist reading of European integration and institutional growth of the Union is that they are premised on "conditional and guarded trust", which is thin and may be easily disrupted by critical events. In other words, the institutional dice are loaded against trust. Modern politics and political theory are both based on "educated distrust" (Madison's checks-and-balances, Montesquieu's division of powers, and Rosanvallon's counter-democratic theories all testify to this), but political practice and political theory are not one and the same and should not be arbitrarily superimposed.

As I will try to show below, this approach to EMU and the euro has tainted the relationship between European countries, particularly in times of crisis, and has become the single most important reason why the EMU may fail. What the development of the crisis has demonstrated, particularly since 2011, is that member states do not trust each other's political and institutional system to deliver those domestic policies and decisions which should make EMU a self-sustaining construct.

Trust as the core value of EMU

Scholars who operate from a rationalist perspective must explain what induces member states to become dependent on the loyal cooperation of other member states not so much for the attainment of immediate higher benefits but for long-term, eventual goals (such as stability and growth), and might decide to relinquish the management of monetary and exchange rate policy – two of the main macroeconomic levers of open capitalist economies – to an independent supranational agency. Economic theory (Mundell 1961) explains under which circumstances an "optimum currency area" – therefore self-evidently advantageous – can and should be established. Needing no further reasons than the sheer maximization of utility, this theory squarely belongs to the rationalist camp. As many authors pointed out right from the start (Martin and Ross 2004), the euro-area was quite clearly *not* an optimum currency area but it was nevertheless established mostly for political reasons (Dyson and Featherstone 1999).

In the case of the European Union, several explanations were advanced.Some pointed to a logical progression from a free trade area to a common market, to an economic and monetary union and, ultimately, to a political union (Balassa 2011[1961]). Others insisted on the market-enhancing effect inherent in customers and producers being able to compare prices directly across the Union, while others still indicated the underlying psychological effect of holding a single currency – normally one of the most powerful symbols of political power (Hellheiner 2002). None of these explanations is purely rational and all require reference to ulterior goals to justify the creation of a single currency. Very few explored in any depth the management problems that a single currency might create, but rather pointed to the very political choice of entrusting the governance of the new currency to a new institution, the European Central Bank, modelled on the very independent German Bundesbank (Dyson 2002).

The most common explanation in circulation, in the end, refers to a sort of natural progression of integration towards an "ever closer union", which in turn concealed the aim of finally reaching that political union which some pro-EU circles had hoped to reach for a long time. Immediate and future costs and difficulties were minimized or presented as the price that some countries had to pay in order to truly "belong to Europe" (Sbragia 2000). Britain's refusal to join the Euro was presented as a manifestation of British exceptionalism, while

Denmark's opt-out was a cause of minor concern given the limited size of the Danish economy and was interpreted as an expression of the reluctance of the Danes before any major integration step. Sweden's de facto opt-out was taken as a manifestation of the usual Swedish caution, which would be certainly overcome in due time. Meanwhile, for the other member states it was more a question of being "found worthy" of joining a club which all member state would eventually have to join. EMU provisions applied to all member states, while only the member states which belonged to the euro-area had to stick to the more stringent Stability and Growth Pact rules (please notice the sequence of words, where stability comes before growth).

Justifying the creation of a common currency became all the more difficult whenthe EMU and euro management rules started to deliver apparent and immediate *sacrifices*, which obfuscated the less apparent and more deferred *benefits* that they had promised to deliver. The balance between the two has become particularly skewed during the crisis, which revealed the financial, fiscal, and productivity differentials present in the euro-area. According to some scholars, to overcome these structural differentials would have required a major overhaul of the various European economies and societies and might probably never fully be attained (Hall 2012; Bonatti and Fracasso 2013; Pasimeni 2014); for others, overcoming these differences was the ultimate reason for the creation of the Euro (Padoa-Schioppa 2004). While the future vision of an economic and political union could initially trump these concerns, it proved insufficient to weather the crisis.

What appears to undermine the euro and the vision of a European political union, however, are values and expectations that can only be partially explained in rational terms. One of the main culprits for the current stagnation is the insistence on stability over growth contained in the SGP, which is in turn itself the consequence of the German insistence with price and monetary stability. This is attributed to the prevalence, in Germany and Austria, of the "ordoliberalism", an economic theory according to which the state has to provide the context of laws and regulations (*Ordnung*) within which economic actors have to aim at increasing levels of productivity without resorting to deficit spending (Dullien and Guérot 2012). According to this paradigm, competitiveness gains must be obtained by boosting the efficiency of the production process through continuous technological upgrades and flexibilization of labour relations. Higher profits through increased exports would then provide the means to be distributed socially among workers. This strategy, then, presupposes the existence of a specific "variety of capitalism" (Hall and Soskice 2001) – the coordinated market economies – which for historical and cultural reasons are no prevalent in the Union.

This paradigm can be stifling for two reasons: first, because there are times when deficit spending is the only way out of a crisis (Krugman 2012); second because it is not generalizable to all EU member states. In times of global crisis, advanced industrial economies cannot rely only on the demand from emerging economies, but must also create their own demand even at risk of creating some inflation (Notermans 2012). In this sense, ordoliberalism is not just the legacy of the German economics school, but it is also the historical legacy of the sequence of hyperinflation and depression which the Germans experienced in the 1920s and 1930s, which in turn led to the rise of Hitler and World War II. Since then, Germany has created the structural and social conditions to avoid that experience again. They have implemented a system of industrial relations capable of harnessing both excessive wage depression and excessive wage inflation and an educational and labour management system aimed at productivity increases capable of compensating the relatively more expensive cost of German labour vis-à-vis the rest of the world. Price stability has been the bedrock on which Germany (and other northern European economies such as Finland and the Netherlands) has built its prosperity. This macroeconomic policy recipe is equivalent to a socially orchestrated supply-side economics according to which the means for greater prosperity are "earned" through carefully orchestrated productivity increases.

Different is the situation and macroeconomic management tradition in several southern European countries characterized by different social conditions and different cultural traditions. In these countries, growth is the result of demand-side stimuli coming from state procurements, from internal catching-up between areas at different levels of income and wealth, and from successful exports of niche products to the rest of Europe and the world. The corresponding macroeconomic management tradition is not premised on state thrift and wage and price stability, but rather on loose monetary and fiscal policy and a hands-off approach to competitiveness and wage increases. Eventual imbalances have been traditionally absorbed through inflation, currency depreciation, and public debt expansion. Prosperity in the South has therefore been traditionally built upon repeated cycles of inflation and currency depreciation and on public debt growth. These are now excluded by EMU arrangements, and the economies of the European sSuth are suffering for this reason (Viesti 2015). How such diverse macroeconomic management traditions could ever be kept together under the same monetary roof is difficult to see.

Given the difference in structural macroeconomic conditions of northern and southern European countries and the opposite way in which growth and prosperity are traditionally pursued in the two areas, one and the same monetary policy could not have been equally apt for both. What is more, the fiscal and budgetary implications of the Stability and Growth Pact were bound to depress the economies of the southern euro-area member states – which traditionally rely on currency devaluation to keep up with productivity gains elsewhere and on deficit spending to keep their fractious societies under control – and elicit accusations of economic imperialism on Germany and the other northern member states. The very way in which the EMU and the common currency were achieved suggested this reading.

Chancellor Helmut Kohl secured a firm commitment for an automatic transition to the final stage of Economic and Monetary Union (EMU). He aimed to make the EMU process irreversible, forcing a commitment to a union ahead of member states [sic] readiness to join. This is the crux of the matter that we come back to again and again. The member states were obliged to work in tandem toward a go[al] for which some were more ready than others. As a consequence, the politics of the Eurozone have been "institutionalized asymmetry".

(Mazzucelli in NCAFP 2014: 77)

Should monetary management be loosened in order to help growth in the southern euro-area member states, the northern euro-area member states would feel betrayed and dragged into potentially dangerous inflationary spirals. Objective macroeconomic difficulties would quickly translate into badly damaged trust relations.

What appears to be jeopardizing the euro-area and the very progress of European integration towards a fiscal and political Union, then, is not so much the crisis in and of itself, but the weakening of the already shaky trust relations upon which the euro-area was based (Roth 2009). In turn this is the consequence of having built EMU and euro management rules upon rational distrust among member states (interstate trust). Of the four threats, and corresponding narratives, that the crisis subsumes, Nicolas Véron underscores particularly the *loss of trust in EU institutions* (systemic trust):

European institutions are becoming part of the problem because their decision-making process and commitment are inadequate. Decisions are delayed until it is too late to avoid adverse economic consequences. Not only is there a democratic deficit, with citizens not being represented properly in the decision-making process; an executive deficit that mirrors the democratic deficit is also present. *Decisions are simply not made* – irrespective of whether they are legitimate or not. The one exception is the institution that is outside of the normal political framework: the European Central Bank. But the ECB, despite its broad shoulders, cannot handle the responsibility of addressing all crises management and resolution.

(Véron in NCAFP 2014: 63–64)

Reciprocal accusations of reaping unfair advantages from the euro governance arrangements and even profiting from the difficulties of the southern euro-area member states versus not doing enough to keep within the SGP parameters and dangerously free-riding on other euro-area member states' diligence are jeopardizing the entire EMU/euro construct. Fissures in interstate trust created tensions in EU institutions, which in turn depleted the citizens' trust in the system. Yet, trust is not depleted all at once. "One question, of course, is how that evolves over time. We are talking about fundamental tenets of trust of the public in the system. The public learns from a repeat game. At the beginning of the crisis, there was high trust" (NCAFP 2014: 69). Ultimately, the slow and inadequate responses from the Union leaders did just as much to undermine public trust as the inherent flaws of EMU. The "intense inter-governmentalism" with which European leaders reacted to the crisis could not replenish citizens' declining trust in the system. "This intensive bargaining among governments is insufficient to resolve the crisis ... Bargaining among national governments is not enough to legitimize the European project in the eyes of the citizens" (Lemke in NCAFP 2014: 77).

To make things worse, actual breaches of trust did happen in the euro-area. The one episode that most angered northern European partners was the admission in 2004, on the part of the Greek left-wing government, that the national accounts had been doctored. The discovery of the necessary correction in Greek accounts, coming at the height of an international financial crisis, shook confidence in the stability of the common currency and undermined euro-area trust foundations. Admittedly, north-European member states had also benefitted from a certain "flexibility" in interpreting SGP rules, a flexibility that according to many had been politically negotiated, thus flying in the face of "strict rules". This was in part the consequence of the decision made in Maastricht to govern EMU and the euro through "heightened" or "new" intergovernmentalism (Bickerton et al. 2014) and to leave the institutional architecture of the euro-area unfinished (no European banking agency, no European securities agency, no European credit-rating agency, etc.) (F. Fabbrini et al. 2014). Moreover, Eurostat had never been empowered to compile national account statistics based on homogenous criteria. Euro-area member states had to trust each other also when providing basic information on their own public accounts, but different national accounting traditions aroused suspicions of concealing embarrassing data.

The half-way construction of a supranational institutional architecture for EMU and the euro, the significant structural imbalances among euro-area economies and the actual episodes of deceit and special treatment placed too heavy a burden on the thin, rationalist foundations of trust relations among Euro-area member states, which could be expected to crumble at the first significant shake. But what else can prop trust in a shifting and unstable macroeconomic environment? What values other than the maximization of utility could support the euro-area?

Conclusion: towards shared and responsible sovereignty

No European member state can any longer claim to be sovereign in a classical sense, and not just because they agreed to pool their sovereignty in the European Union, but because of the heightened interdependence that would characterize their economies and societies *even in the absence of the Union.* No state is any longer in control of its own economic and social destiny and, correspondingly, no European government can any longer be fully held to account for events that affect the lives of the citizens uniquely through national channels. Unfortunately, the institutional architecture of the EU and of its EMU core is still at best incomplete or contradictory (S. Fabbrini 2013), and scholars, commentators and citizens hold radically different opinions on how it should develop (Piattoni 2015a). What is most unsettling is that decisions of monetary, budgetary, and fiscal policy, which have such a heavy impact on the lives of EU citizens, are either taken in forums that are only indirectly legitimated (such as Euro-group or European Council meetings) and are, despite extensive journalistic coverage, still opaque to most common citizens or taken by agencies which are structurally unresponsive to them (such as the BCE). Accountability mechanisms at the national level appear painfully insufficient and ineffective. The sometimes heated debates that take place in national parliaments on stability measures, structural reforms, and fiscal policies all too often revolve around how to *bypass current rules* or whether to *exit the euro-area* altogether rather than about how to *change the rules* of the EMU or *reinforce the democratic temper of EMU governance*. At the European level, this deficit in accountability is intensified further by the fact that the negotiations are held in a non-directly legitimated body – the Council of the European Union or the European Council – and aggravated by the fact that they are too technical and often interpreted by the media in ways which intensify the distrust in EU citizens. Transparency and full and accessible reporting is a precondition for accountability.

What is seldom recalled is that, upon entering the Union, the governments of the member states of the European Union pledged to lend each other "loyal cooperation", a form of reciprocity aimed at creating and sustaining trust in each other and in the Union. Loyal cooperation logically implies responsibility: a commitment not to make decisions and engage in actions which could damage other member states and rather keep other member states' interests present when making domestic decisions. Without delving too deeply into the normative debate, such a commitment is equivalent to a pledge in favour of "non-domination" (Pettit 1997; Piattoni 2015b). Domination is "arbitrary interference": "an act of interference will be non-arbitrary to the extent that it is forced to track the interests and ideas of the persons suffering the interference" (Pettit 1997: 55). A pledge to loyal cooperation is then equivalent to a pledge to non-domination and to fully track the interests and ideas of all affected parties. European and national institutions, I would argue, are legitimate insofar as they help realize this value.

It is, however, possible that responsibility may more than occasionally clash with responsiveness to national citizens' preferences, in turn a fundamental component of democratic representation (Pitkin 1967). This clash persists only insofar as we consider only national constituencies as the legitimate referent of national governments. At the same time, in the "new circumstances of politics" (Weale 1999: 10), that is, in the interdependent context of the European Union, the legitimate referent of each European national government are all European citizens. We could even argue that all national governments ought to act responsibly vis-à-vis all affected parties, whether or not they are members of the national constituency. In other words, sovereignty and autonomy have changed their meaning in the interconnected and interdependent setting of the European Union (Bohman 2007).

In terms of the current crisis management, responsibility means proposing and adopting policies that do not arbitrarily interfere with the citizens of any other member state, even by appealing to apparently unassailable values such as balanced budgets and stability measures. There are no overarching principles which could not and should not be discussed, even those enshrined in the prevalent ordoliberal paradigm. In this scenario, national governments are no longer "accountable" in a traditional sense, but they are accountable in the sense that they owe their national constituents disclosure of a veritable and full picture of the economic and financial situation, the sense of responsibility vis-à-vis the national constituencies of the other euro-area partners, and proposals of measures that aim at balancing responsiveness to their national constituency with responsibility vis-à-vis common commitments. In this sense, the BEPGs and particularly the European Semester are rather daring and bold examples from a normative point of view – of this new notion of "responsible responsiveness". They invite, on the one hand, national governments to fully disclose their national accounts to each other and to discuss together the structural reforms necessary to uphold the common currency and the EMU. On the other hand, any principle regulating EMU and the euro should be subjectable to full discussion on the part of all national communities and no economic paradigm should be allowed to prevail without a full and explicit endorsement of all euro-area members. This exercise, rather than the reinforced surveillance mechanisms of the revised SGP, which smacks of "guarded and conditional trust", are the hallmarks of a legitimate Union which wants to strengthen its trust foundations.

I will conclude by quoting Habermas, but inviting the reader to read "responsibility" where Habermas writes "solidarity":

> This leads me to the final and philosophical question: What does it mean to show solidarity, and when are we entitled to appeal to solidarity? Showing solidarity is a political act and by no means a form of moral selflessness that would be misplaced in political contexts. Solidarity loses the false appearance of being unpolitical, once we learn how to distinguish obligations to show solidarity from both moral and legal obligations.
>
> (Habermas 2013: III)

While solidarity is not synonymous with justice, be it in the moral or the legal sense of the term, responsibility is. We call moral and legal norms just when they regulate practices that are in the equal interest of all those affected. Just norms secure equal freedoms for all and equal respect for everyone. Responsibility is also just.

Note

1   Examples may help clarify these situations. If two neighbours impose negative externalities onto one another (the smoke of the barbecued sausages of neighbour A fills the garden of neighbour B, while the leaves of the trees of neighbour B fall into the garden of neighbour A), both have an interest in regulating both barbecuing and leaf collection so as to attain jointly a higher level of utility. If, however, neighbour A needs the agreement of neighbour B in order to arrange the door-to-door delivery of milk, but neighbour B does not care about fresh milk as much as neighbour A, then neighbour B may withhold his consent from the door-to-door delivery of milk and will be convinced only by a side-payment (or, more unlikely, by appeals to good neighbourly spirit).

References

Allen, D. 2000. "Cohesion and Structural Adjustment." In *Policy-Making in the European Union*, pp. 209–233.Oxford: Oxford University Press.

Bachtler, J., C. Mendez and F. Wishlade. 2013. *EU Cohesion Policy and European Integration: The Dynamics of EU Budget and Regional Policy Reform*. Farnham: Ashgate.

Balassa, B. 2011[1961]. *The Economic Theory of European Integration*. New York: Routledge.

Bickerton, C., D. Hodson and U. Puetter. 2014. "The New Intergovernmentalism: European Integration in the Post-Maastricht Era." *Journal of Common Market Studies* 53(4): 703–722.

Bohman, J. 2007. *Democracy across Borders. From Dêmos to Dêmoi*. Cambridge, MA: MIT Press.

Bonatti, L. and A. Fracasso. 2012. "The German Model and the European Crisis." *Journal of Common Market Studies* 51(6): 1023–1039.

Brunazzo, M. (forthcoming). "The Origins and Development of Cohesion Policy." In *Handbook of Cohesion Policy in the EU*, edited by S. Piattoni and L. Polverari. Cheltenham: Edward Elgar.

Checkel, J. 2010. "Constructivism and EU Politics." In *Handbook of European Union Politics*, edited by K. E. Jørgensen, M. Pollack and B. Rosamond, pp. 57–75. London: Sage.

Christiansen, T., K. E. Jørgensen and A. Wiener (eds). 2001. *The Social Construction of Europe*. London: Sage.

Della Sala, V. 2010. "Political Myth, Mythology and the European Union." *Journal of Common Market Studies* 48(1): 1–19.

Dinan, D. 2012. "How Did We Get There?" In *The European Union: How Does it Work?*, edited by E. Bomberg, J. Peterson and R. Corbett, pp. 23–45. Oxford: Oxford University Press.

Dølvik, J. E. and A. Martin (eds). 2014. *European Social Models From Crisis to Crisis: Employment and Inequality in the Era of Monetary Integration*. Oxford: Oxford University Press.

Dullien, S. and U. Guérot. 2012. "The Long Shadow of Ordoliberalism: Germany's Approach to the Euro Crisis." *European Council for Foreign Relations Policy Brief* 49 (February), p. 22.

Dyson, K. 2002. *European States and the Euro: Europeanisation, Variation, and Convergence*. Oxford: Oxford University Press.

Dyson, K. and K. Featherstone. 1999. *The Road to Maastricht: Negotiating Economic and Monetary Union*. Oxford: Oxford University Press.

Fabbrini, F., E. H. Ballin and H. Somsen (eds). 2015. *What Form of Government for the European Union and the Eurozone?* Oxford: Hart Publishing.

Fabbrini, S. 2013. "Intergovernmentalism and Its Limits: Assessing the European Union's Answer to the Euro Crisis." *Comparative Political Studies*, 46(9): 1003–1029.

Garrett, G. 1992. "International Cooperation and Institutional Choice." *International Organization* 46(2): 533–560.

Garrett, G. and G. Tsebelis. 1996. "An Institutional Critique of Intergovernmentalism." *International Organization* 50(2): 269–300.

Haas, E. 1970. "The Study of Regional Integration: Reflections on the Joy and Anguish of Pre-theorizing." *International Organization* 24(4): 607–646.

Haas, E. 2001. "Does Constructivism Subsume Neofunctionalism?" In, *The Social Construction of Europe*, edited by T. Christiansen, K. E. Jørgensen and A. Wiener, pp. 22–31. London: Sage.

Habermas, J. 2013. "Democracy, Solidarity and the European Crisis." Social Europe. http://www.socialeurope.eu/2013/05/democracy-solidarity-and-the-european-crisis-2/.

Hall, P. and D. Soskice. 2001. *Varieties of Capitalism: The Institutional Foundations of Comparative Advantage*. Oxford: Oxford University Press.

Hall, P. and R. Taylor. 1996. "Political Science and the Three New Institutionalisms." *Political Studies* 44 (5): 936–957.

Helleiner, E. 2002. *The Making of National Money: Territorial Currencies in Historical Perspective*. Ithaca, NY: Cornell University Press.

Krugman, P. 2012. *End this Depression Now!* New York, NY: W.W. Norton.

Hoffmann, S. 1966. "Obstinate or Obsolete? The Fate of the Nation-State and the Case of Western Europe." *Daedalus* 95(3): 862–915.

Majone, G. 1999. "The Regulatory State and its Legitimacy Problems." *West European Politics* 22(1): 2–25.

Martin, A. and G. Ross (eds). 2004. *Euros and Europeans. Monetary Integration and the European Model of Society*. Cambridge: Cambridge University Press.

Moravcsik, A. 1993. "Preferences and Power in the European Community: A Liberal Inter-governmentalist Approach." *Journal of Common Market Studies* 31(4): 473–524.

Moravcsik, A. 1998. *The Choice for Europe: Social Purpose and State Power from Messina to Maastricht*. Ithaca, NY: Cornell University Press.

Mundell, R. 1961. "A Theory of Optimum Currency Areas." *American Economic Review* 51(4): 657–665.

NCAFP 2014. "Eurozone Crisis: Is the Union at Risk?" *American Foreign Policy Interests: The Journal of the National Committee on American Foreign Policy* 36(1): 61–83.

Neyer, J. 2010. "Justice, Not Democracy: Legitimacy in the European Union." *Journal of Common Market Studies* 48(4): 903–921.

Notermans, T. 2012. "Predatory Preferences and External Anchors: The Political Sources of European Imbalances." *Baltic Journal of European Studies* 2(2): 8–20.

Padoa-Schioppa, T. 2004. *La lunga via dell'euro*. Bologna: Il Mulino.

Pasimeni, P. 2014. "An Optimum Currency Crisis." *The European Journal of Comparative Economics*, 11(2): 173–204.

Pettit, P. 1997. *Republicanism. A Theory of Freedom and Government*. Oxford: Oxford University Press.

Piattoni, S. (ed.) 2015a. *The European Union: Democratic Principles and Institutional Architectures in Times of Crisis*. Oxford: Oxford University Press.

Piattoni, S. 2015b. "The European Union: Legitimating Values, Democratic Principles, and Institutional Architectures." In *The European Union: Democratic Principles and Institutional Architectures in Times of Crisis*, edited by S. Piattoni, pp. 3–28. Oxford: Oxford University Press.

Pierson, P. 1996. "The Path to European Integration: A Historical Institutionalist Analysis." *Comparative Political Studies* 29(2): 123–163.

Pierson, P. 2004. *Politics in Time: History, Institutions, and Social Analysis*. Princeton: Princeton University Press.

Pitkin, H. 1967. *The Concept of Representation.* Berkeley, CA: University of California Press.

Pollack, M. 1995. "Regional Actors in an Intergovernmental Play: The Making and Implementation of EC Structural Policy." In *The State of the European Union, Vol. 3,* edited by C. Rhodes and S. Mazey, pp. 361–390. London: Longman.

Pollack, M. 2003. *The Engines of European Integration: Delegation, Agency, and Agenda Setting in the EU.* Oxford: Oxford University Press.

Pollack, M. 2010. "Rational Choice and EU Politics." In *Handbook of European Union Politics,* edited by K. E. Jørgensen, M. Pollack and B. Rosamond, pp. 31–55. London: Sage.

Putnam, R. 1988. "Diplomacy and Domestic Politics: The Logic of Two-Level Games." *International Organization* 43(2): 427–460.

Risse, T. et al. 1999. "To Euro or Not to Euro? The EMU and Identity Politics in the European Union." *European Journal of International Relations* 5(2): 147–187.

Roth, F. 2009. "The Effect of the Financial Crisis on Systemic Trust." *Intereconomics* (July/August): 203–208. DOI: 10.1007/s10272-009-0296-9.

Sandholtz, W. and A. Stone-Sweet (eds). 1998. *European Integration and Supranational Governance.* Oxford: Oxford University Press.

Sbragia, A. 2000. "Italy Pays for Europe: Political Leadership, Political Choice, and Institutional Adaptation." In *Transforming Europe: Europeanization and Domestic Change,* edited by M. Green Cowles, J. Caporaso, and T. Risse, pp. 79–95. Ithaca, NY: Cornell University Press.

Scharpf, F. 1988. "The Joint Decision Trap: Lessons from German Federalism and European Integration." *Public Administration* 66(3): 239–278.

Scharpf, F. 2006. "The Joint Decision Trap Revisited." *Journal of Common Market Studies* 44(4): 845–864.

Scharpf, F. 2009. "Legitimacy in the European Multilevel Polity." *European Political Science Review* 1 (2): 173–204.

Scharpf, F. 2010. "The JDT Model. Context and Extensions." In *The EU's Decision Traps. Comparing Policies,* edited by G. Falkner, pp. 217–236. Oxford: Oxford University Press.

Schmidt, V. 2008. "Discursive Institutionalism: The Explanatory Power of Ideas and Discourse." *Annual Review of Political Science* 11 (June): 303–326.

Schmidt, V. 2010. "Taking Ideas and Discourse Seriously: Explaining Change through Discursive Institutionalism as the Fourth 'New Institutionalism.'" *European Political Science Review* 2(1): 1–25.

Schmitter, P. 1970. "A Revised Theory of Regional Integration." *International Organization* 24(4): 836–868.

Stone-Sweet, A., W. Sandholtz and N. Fligstein (eds) 2001. *The Institutionalization of Europe.* Oxford: Oxford University Press.

Tsoukalis, L. 2012. "The Political Economy of the Crisis: The End of an Era?" *Global Policy* 3 (December): 42–50.

Viesti, G. 2015. "Why Europe is in a Trap." *Stato e Mercato* 35(1): 53–84.

Viner, J. 1948. "Power Versus Plenty as Objectives of Foreign Policy in the Seventeenth and Eighteenth Centuries." *World Politics* 1 (1): 1–29.

Weale, A. 1999. *Democracy.* London: Macmillan.

Weiler, J. and M. Wind. 2003. *European Constitutionalism Beyond the State* Cambridge: Cambridge.

5 Assessing the Europe 2020 strategy

Paolo Pasimeni[1]

Introduction

The art of government is a particularly complex one. Public policies are subject to more or less scrutiny, to a higher or lower level of accountability, and to a more or less stringent need to assess their success or failure. In any case one of the main questions in public policy is how to monitor and evaluate the results. The broader the scope of the policy, the more complex the task of evaluating it.

Thanks to an unprecedented abundance of new statistics, indicators, and data, we can today move towards a better measurement and analysis of public policies. Statistics can help us concentrate the complexity of government intervention into meaningful and relevant information for policy makers and citizens.

The evaluation of public policies has become a democratic requirement to ensure the transparency and objectivity of policy making, and timely and appropriate statistics are increasingly used by citizens to evaluate political decisions and the politicians who support them. Adequate statistics are therefore indispensable.

As the conference of the Directors General of the National Statistical Institutes (DGINS) recognized in the famous Sofia Memorandum of September 2010, "there is a growing societal and political demand to measure progress, well-being and sustainable development in a more comprehensive way."

This recognition of the need for a broader approach to the monitoring and evaluation of public polices guided the conception of the main development strategy for the current decade in the European Union (EU): the Europe 2020 Strategy, launched in March 2010. It was the result of a political consensus among the governments of 27 Member States (MS) to address the main structural challenges of the EU.[2]

Three priorities were identified as main pillars of the Europe 2020 strategy to "offer a vision of Europe's social market economy for the 21st century":

- *Smart growth* – developing an economy based on knowledge and innovation.
- *Sustainable growth* – promoting a more resource efficient, greener, and more competitive economy.
- *Inclusive growth* – fostering a high-employment economy delivering economic, social, and territorial cohesion (European Commission 2010).

The key deliveries for the Europe 2020 Strategy at the national level are the so-called "National Reform Programmes" (Nrps), which are to be presented by the national governments in April of each year, along with the stability and convergence programmes. NRPs contain national targets relating to EU-wide headline targets and explain how governments intend to meet them and overcome obstacles to growth. They also set out what measures will be taken, when, by whom, and with what budget implications.

The new initiative tries to overcome one of the main weaknesses of the Lisbon Strategy: the lack of a comprehensive system of monitoring of the performance achieved by the Member States towards the common objectives (Martens 2010). Both the Lisbon and the Europe 2020 Strategies based their governance structure on a coordinated action approach, among member states (MS) and the European Institutions.

One of the main reasons why these supranational strategies may fail to reach their objectives is that some of the main policy areas they focus on fall outside the EU's legal competence. Most of the core Lisbon targets, for instance, concerned areas where the EU does not have any jurisdictional competence (Erixon 2010). Political action at the national level, then, could determine the effectiveness of the strategy.

A second reason often presented to explain why the Lisbon Strategy did not actually deliver the expected results relates to the lack of an appropriate system of monitoring and evaluation of performance, based on clear, punctual, and precise indicators. The risk for the Europe 2020 Strategy was to maintain these inherent strategic weaknesses in its architecture (Sarcinelli 2011).

In the preparation of this new strategy, therefore, there was the conviction that a verifiable progress could only be made if the related policy assessments were grounded in an indicator-based analysis. For this reason a set of eight indicators, with targets and expected results, was proposed and accepted for the Member States.

Some attempts have been made in the literature to use these indicators to study the preliminary results of the strategy. It is clear that a supranational strategy so dependent on initiatives and actions by individual governments requires a stronger monitoring mechanism and more accountability among member states.

The great complexity of this strategy is strictly linked to the very peculiar arrangements of the EU (Jachtenfuchs 2010). One of the key features of the European integration has been the dilution of national sovereignty through collective decision-making and supranational institutions. The concept of multilevel governance (Hooghe and Marks 2010) has emerged as a tool to understand the inter-relationship within and between different levels of governance and government.

The key problem, for our purposes, refers to the fact that multilevel governance risks leading to a deficit in democratic accountability (Papadopoulos 2010). Moreover, there is a problem of effectiveness for a strategy agreed upon at the supranational level, but whose main policy leverages are mainly anchored at the national level.

The role of the national governments will be decisive in determining the success or failure of the strategy. Consequently the need to enhance accountability implies a stronger effort towards the evaluation of policy actions implemented at the national level. The set of agreed indicators is fundamental to ensure that a proper monitoring system is put in place and the measurement of performance is timely.

As Martens (2010) noted, the official Europe 2020 framework

> still leaved [sic] open essential operational questions, such as the link between the evaluation of states' performance under this strategy and the monitoring done under the SGP, or the creation of more concrete mechanisms of economic governance that will complement national efforts.

The contribution that this work intends to bring goes precisely in this direction, aiming at strengthening the evaluation of member states' performances in the strategy. I develop a synthetic composite index to quantify, measure, and monitor progress achieved by countries in the strategy. I will then use this index to study which factors are more likely to determine success or failure in the progress towards the achievements of the strategy's goals.

I will also use the index to study which factors are more likely to determine success or failure in the Europe 2020 Strategy, measuring the relative importance of economic and institutional factors. The next section presents the index, develops it for ten years (2003 to 2012), and monitors the different performances of the MS. Section 3 presents the current policy context, while section 4 explains the theoretical foundations of the institutional economics hypothesis. Section 5 presents the econometric analysis and results, which are discussed in section 6. Section 7, finally, concludes.

The Europe 2020 Index

When the Europe 2020 strategy was launched, three dimensions of growth were identified as main pillars of this strategy and they were associated to a set of indicators to assess the progress towards the objectives and also for purposes of comparison. I build a specific index for each of the three main dimensions of the Europe 2020 strategy and develop a synthetic "Europe 2020 Index" to allow a quantification of the relative position of each member state towards the objectives of the strategy. This index seeks to give a concrete form to this policy initiative, in a way that accounts for the different dimensions and policy priorities, and in a manner that allows quantification and monitoring of its progress.

The eight indicators proposed by the European Commission to monitor the Europe 2020 strategy are:

- Tertiary education attainment (TEDU) (2000–2013)
- Gross domestic expenditure on R&D (GERD) (1990–2012)
- Greenhouse gas emissions (GGE) (1990–2012)

- Share of renewable energy in gross final energy consumption (RNEW) (2003–2012)
- Energy intensity of the economy (EINT) (1990–2012)
- Employment rate of the population aged 20 to 64 (EMPL) (1992–2013)
- Early leavers from education (SCHO) (1992–2012)
- Population at-risk-of-poverty or exclusion (POV) (2003–2012)

They are calculated at the national level by Eurostat and their detailed definitions and explanations are presented in Annex 1. Three thematic indices can be created by grouping these indicators, reflecting the three main pillars of the Europe 2020 strategy: the Smart Growth Index (SMGI), the Sustainable Growth Index (SUGI), and the Inclusive Growth Index (INGI), which in turn form the Europe 2020 Index. I decide to link each indicator to only one dimension of the strategy. So tertiary education attainment (TEDU) and gross expenditures on R&D (GERD) are considered the main drivers of the Smart Growth dimension; greenhouse gas emissions (GGE), the share of renewable energy (RNEW), and the energy intensity of the economy (EINT) are the components of the Sustainable Growth dimension; and employment rate (EMPL), the rate of early school leavers (SCHO) and the share of the population at risk of poverty or social exclusion (POV) determine the Inclusive Growth Index. Figure 5.1 shows the structure of the Index.

Eurostat extracts the data used and at the moment the largest common period for which all of them are available is from 2003 to 2012. The eight indicators are presented in different units and scales. The first step to make them comparable, so that they can be aggregated, is to normalize them, in a way that all the values are comprised between one and zero. For "positive" indicators, like TEDU, GERD, RNEW and EMPL, I apply:

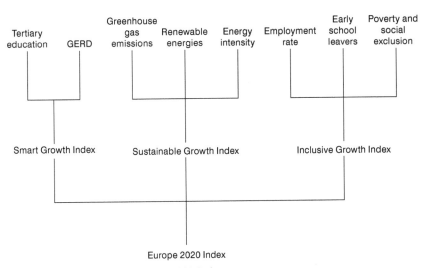

Figure 5.1 Structure of the Europe 2020 Index

$$X_{ic} = \frac{x_{ic} - \min_k \{x_{ik}\}}{\max_k \{x_{ik}\} - \min_k \{x_{ik}\}} \tag{5.1}$$

where i is the indicator (TEDU, GERD, RNEW, or EMPL), c the country, and $\max_k$ and $\min_k$ are the maximum and minimum value of that indicator across the whole period available. For "negative" indicators, those for which a higher value represents worse performance, like GGE, EINT, SCHO, and POV, I apply:

$$X_{ic} = \frac{\max_k \{x_{ik}\} - x_{ic}}{\max_k \{x_{ik}\} - \min_k \{x_{ik}\}} \tag{5.2}$$

where i is the indicator (GGE, EINT, SCHO, or POV), c the country, and $\max_k$ and $\min_k$ are the maximum and minimum value of that indicator across the whole available time series.

The normalized indicators can now be aggregated in order to build the three indices. These, in turn, can be further aggregated to produce the synthetic Index. In the aggregation, I use equal weights, giving the same relevance to all the components of the index. The three sub-indices represent three major pillars of the Europe 2020 Strategy, and they have been conceived as equally important. The indicators that compose each sub-index are also equally weighted, in order not to give any priority to one or another. I use a geometric aggregation method, instead of the linear one: the main difference is that by aggregating indicators through a geometric mean, high differences between the values of the components are taken into account and "penalized," with respect to a series with more homogeneous values for its components. The geometric mean accounts for the deviation from the average and satisfies the property of interval-scale unit comparability, while the arithmetic one does not (Ebert and Welsch 2004).[3]

In other words, for our purposes of cross-country comparison, choosing the geometric method means rewarding those countries presenting more equilibrated values of the three main components of the Index, i.e. including a mechanism

Table 5.1 Descriptive statistics of the normalized indicators

Indicator	Max.	Min.	Average	Median	Standard deviation
GERD	0.951	0.008	0.327	0.275	0.237
TEDU	1.000	0.034	0.547	0.550	0.244
GGE	0.985	0.001	0.570	0.565	0.238
RNEW	0.786	0.002	0.206	0.147	0.169
EINT	1.000	0.001	0.808	0.892	0.184
EMPL	0.853	0.266	0.591	0.599	0.132
SCHO	0.992	0.089	0.803	0.835	0.153
POV	0.962	0.130	0.775	0.809	0.161

to reward more balanced profiles of development. Therefore the formula[4] to be applied is:

$$I_g = \left(\prod_{i=1}^{n} X_i \right)^{\frac{1}{n}}$$ (5.3)

The first aggregation generates the three sub-indices, corresponding to the three main pillars of the strategy (smart, sustainable, and inclusive). Figure 5.2 shows the Europe 2020 profiles for the six biggest countries, in terms of population, of the EU. France and Germany have similar values in all the three dimensions, similar to the UK, which differs from the other two only for the "sustainability" dimension, where it performs lower than the other countries. Spain and Italy show similar profiles, with Italy slightly exceeding Spain in the "sustainable" and "inclusive growth" dimensions, but Spain performs much better in the "smart growth" dimension. Poland has a profile that is close to the Italian one, performing a bit better in the INGI and SMGI, and a bit worse in the SUGI.

The second aggregation generates the overall Europe 2020 Index. This instrument allows a yearly monitoring of the progress made by each country. With the last data available[5] the three sub-indices and the index can be built for ten consecutive years from 2003 to 2012.

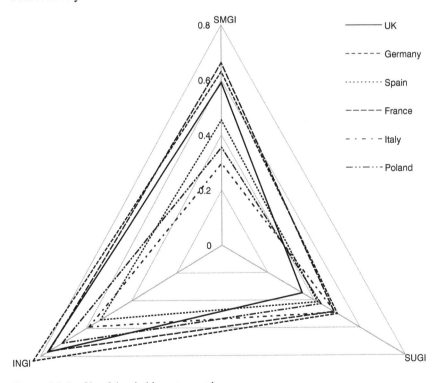

Figure 5.2 Profile of the six biggest countries

Table 5.2 Europe 2020 Index overall score (2003–2012)

	2003	2004	2005	2006	2007	2008	2009	2010	2011	2012
Belgium	0.445	0.445	0.456	0.476	0.490	0.503	0.530	0.540	0.547	0.571
Bulgaria	0.133	0.231	0.236	0.254	0.273	0.324	0.349	0.355	0.339	0.359
Czech Rep	0.355	0.356	0.366	0.378	0.396	0.417	0.444	0.468	0.504	0.540
Denmark	0.643	0.655	0.671	0.664	0.661	0.688	0.714	0.712	0.725	0.744
Germany	0.513	0.523	0.530	0.540	0.560	0.572	0.601	0.606	0.624	0.640
Estonia	0.453	0.462	0.491	0.530	0.527	0.557	0.572	0.588	0.651	0.647
Ireland	0.391	0.414	0.424	0.437	0.454	0.476	0.510	0.509	0.521	0.532
Greece	0.327	0.331	0.342	0.349	0.354	0.354	0.364	0.378	0.386	0.390
Spain	0.390	0.377	0.382	0.405	0.407	0.442	0.466	0.479	0.474	0.466
France	0.558	0.557	0.563	0.571	0.581	0.593	0.613	0.612	0.609	0.626
Italy	0.336	0.338	0.350	0.365	0.377	0.392	0.409	0.417	0.426	0.441
Cyprus	0.261	0.264	0.272	0.278	0.261	0.192	0.300	0.325	0.335	0.351
Latvia	0.341	0.360	0.393	0.432	0.458	0.467	0.428	0.458	0.497	0.510
Lithuania	0.412	0.451	0.476	0.498	0.504	0.519	0.519	0.514	0.546	0.563
Luxembourg	0.343	0.382	0.418	0.423	0.457	0.474	0.508	0.491	0.492	0.502
Hungary	0.341	0.343	0.346	0.365	0.379	0.397	0.425	0.435	0.452	0.472
Malta	0.085	0.151	0.159	0.186	0.179	0.183	0.187	0.197	0.229	0.252
Netherlands	0.469	0.454	0.471	0.486	0.498	0.516	0.533	0.524	0.549	0.564
Austria	0.538	0.542	0.553	0.567	0.580	0.597	0.626	0.624	0.629	0.654
Poland	0.279	0.302	0.320	0.335	0.357	0.385	0.417	0.430	0.445	0.476
Portugal	0.318	0.322	0.329	0.367	0.401	0.442	0.465	0.485	0.505	0.507
Romania	0.213	0.240	0.261	0.281	0.309	0.345	0.336	0.342	0.359	0.368
Slovenia	0.481	0.504	0.503	0.527	0.535	0.540	0.580	0.602	0.626	0.651
Slovakia	0.268	0.270	0.285	0.294	0.309	0.322	0.344	0.388	0.409	0.433
Finland	0.693	0.707	0.734	0.727	0.737	0.762	0.772	0.754	0.769	0.777
Sweden	0.734	0.744	0.771	0.792	0.802	0.822	0.834	0.819	0.836	0.849
UK	0.442	0.423	0.437	0.453	0.462	0.482	0.509	0.514	0.534	0.540

Countries are listed alphabetically in their original languages, as the official EU alphabetical ranking prescribes.

All the countries have improved their scores in the reference period, for which all the data are available. There is, however, some change in these trends, for instance Latvia in 2009 suffered an abrupt worsening of the overall index, mainly driven by the "inclusive growth sub-index," due to the critical deterioration of its employment rate, as a consequence of the crisis. The same happened to Cyprus in 2008, when the "sustainable growth sub-index" registered an abrupt fall, driven by the peak in greenhouse gas emissions the country had in that year. Since then the situation has constantly improving.

Table 5.3 Europe 2020 Index overall ranking (2003–2012)

	2003	2004	2005	2006	2007	2008	2009	2010	2011	2012
Belgium	10	11	11	11	11	11	10	9	10	9
Bulgaria	26	26	26	26	25	24	23	24	25	25
Czech Rep	15	17	17	17	18	18	17	17	15	13
Denmark	3	3	3	3	3	3	3	3	3	3
Germany	6	6	6	6	6	6	6	6	7	7
Estonia	9	8	8	7	8	7	8	8	4	6
Ireland	13	13	13	13	15	13	12	13	13	14
Greece	20	20	20	21	22	22	22	23	23	23
Spain	14	15	16	16	16	16	15	16	18	20
France	4	4	4	4	4	5	5	5	8	8
Italy	19	19	18	20	20	20	21	21	21	21
Cyprus	24	24	24	25	26	26	26	26	26	26
Latvia	18	16	15	14	13	15	18	18	16	15
Lithuania	12	10	9	9	9	9	11	11	11	11
Luxembourg	16	14	14	15	14	14	14	14	17	17
Hungary	17	18	19	19	19	19	19	19	19	19
Malta	27	27	27	27	27	27	27	27	27	27
Netherlands	8	9	10	10	10	10	9	10	9	10
Austria	5	5	5	5	5	4	4	4	5	4
Poland	22	22	22	22	21	21	20	20	20	18
Portugal	21	21	21	18	17	17	16	15	14	16
Romania	25	25	25	24	23	23	25	25	24	24
Slovenia	7	7	7	8	7	8	7	7	6	5
Slovakia	23	23	23	23	24	25	24	22	22	22
Finland	2	2	2	2	2	2	2	2	2	2
Sweden	1	1	1	1	1	1	1	1	1	1
UK	11	12	12	12	12	12	13	12	12	12

Countries are listed alphabetically in their original languages, as the official EU alphabetical ranking prescribes.

At the same time we observe some outstanding relative performances throughout the period, like Bulgaria, Poland, and to a certain extent also Malta, who are clearly catching up, though starting from lower levels. We also significantly see Estonia in the last few years for which data are available. In 2011 the Baltic country managed to considerably increase its relative performance and jumped four places up in the ranking, to number four. In the last two years, we observe a significant decrease in the score of Spain, mainly driven by the "inclusive growth sub-index," due to the dramatic fall in employment levels.

In Table 5.3 we can actually observe how relative positions have changed throughout the period considered. Some countries have lost ground; notably Spain lost six positions and France four, followed by Greece, which lost three. Others, instead, have remarkably improved their position, in particular Estonia, Latvia, Poland, and Portugal, which are clearly catching up throughout the period. The Estonian exploit in the index is mainly due to the "smart growth sub-index," driven by an important increase (+46 per cent) of the gross domestic expenditure on R&D in 2011. The constant improvement of Poland in the index throughout the period was initially driven by a particularly strong improvement of the "inclusive growth" pillar until 2008, and by the "smart growth" one, since then. Portugal's positive performance has been driven by a steady increase in the tertiary education attainment and a considerable reduction in early school leaving. Falling employment rates, however, have slowed down its performance in the last years. The Latvian performance is positively influenced by a particularly high score in the "environmental sustainability" dimension, mainly due to the share of renewable energy in gross final energy consumption, where it is already well above the EU target for 2020.

Table 5.4 presents the values of the three sub-indices composing the Europe 2020 Index for the most recent year for which data are available. Sweden stands out as the first in all rankings, but most of the other Member States show more heterogeneous profiles, performing quite differently in the three dimensions of the strategy. We can observe great variation in the performances among countries and across time.

Policy context

The descriptive analysis based on the Europe 2020 Index allows a proper monitoring of the achievements of the Member States in the strategy. However it does not allow us to understand which factors determine these results, what helps improving performances and what causes divergences over time and between countries. The analysis will try to understand which factors are more likely to be associated with positive performances of the countries in the Europe 2020 Strategy.

The years since the Europe 2020 Strategy was launched have been intensely characterized by deep changes in the governance of the EU. The focus has been put on a new macroeconomic governance, for the Eurozone in particular, but not exclusively. A wide set of legislative acts has been agreed upon to reform the Stability and Growth Pact (Regulation (EU) 1175/2011 and 1177/2011), to prevent and correct macroeconomic imbalances (Regulation 1176/2011), to enforce measures that correct excessive macroeconomic imbalances in the euro area (Regulation 1174/2011), and to guarantee the effective budgetary surveillance in the euro area (Regulation 1173/2011, and to set the requirements of the budgetary framework for the Member States (Directive 2011/85EU).

The so-called "six-pack," the "two-pack," and the Treaty on Stability, Co-ordination and Governance in the Economic and Monetary Union (the "fiscal

Table 5.4 "Smart growth," "sustainable growth," and "inclusive growth" sub-indices (values and ranking, 2012)

SMGI (2012)			SUGI (2012)			INGI (2012)		
Sweden	0.870	1	Sweden	0.787	1	Sweden	0.895	1
Finland	0.865	2	Latvia	0.724	2	Netherlands	0.871	2
Denmark	0.758	3	Finland	0.653	3	Austria	0.846	3
Slovenia	0.693	4	Denmark	0.653	4	Czech Rep	0.835	4
France	0.662	5	Lithuania	0.621	5	Denmark	0.833	5
Belgium	0.657	6	Austria	0.614	6	Germany	0.832	6
Germany	0.630	7	Romania	0.597	7	Finland	0.831	7
Netherlands	0.629	8	Estonia	0.582	8	Luxembourg	0.805	8
Ireland	0.619	9	Portugal	0.522	9	Slovenia	0.787	9
Estonia	0.603	10	Slovenia	0.506	10	Estonia	0.773	10
UK	0.590	11	Germany	0.501	11	UK	0.768	11
Luxembourg	0.553	12	Italy	0.492	12	France	0.761	12
Austria	0.538	13	France	0.486	13	Slovakia	0.743	13
Spain	0.455	14	Slovakia	0.456	14	Cyprus	0.730	14
Czech Rep	0.420	15	Hungary	0.451	15	Belgium	0.725	15
Lithuania	0.405	16	Greece	0.450	16	Lithuania	0.709	16
Portugal	0.385	17	Czech Rep	0.448	17	Poland	0.705	17
Hungary	0.377	18	Poland	0.429	18	Latvia	0.663	18
Poland	0.355	19	Spain	0.415	19	Ireland	0.658	19
Italy	0.296	20	Bulgaria	0.408	20	Portugal	0.647	20
Latvia	0.277	21	Belgium	0.392	21	Hungary	0.619	21
Greece	0.254	22	Ireland	0.370	22	Malta	0.611	22
Cyprus	0.244	23	UK	0.348	23	Italy	0.587	23
Slovakia	0.239	24	Netherlands	0.328	24	Romania	0.555	24
Malta	0.233	25	Luxembourg	0.284	25	Spain	0.537	25
Bulgaria	0.219	26	Cyprus	0.242	26	Greece	0.520	26
Romania	0.151	27	Malta	0.113	27	Bulgaria	0.519	27

compact") have focused the EU policy-making on the main macroeconomic indicators, while at the same time the Europe 2020 Strategy remained the overarching strategy, setting the long-term objectives for the EU.

The importance of the economic growth and of the sustainability of public finance is central in the new macroeconomic architecture of the EU. The aim of this work is to understand how relevant they are in ensuring the success and sustainability of the Europe 2020 Strategy, and to disentangle their specific impact on countries' performances. In the analysis of the potential determinants of performances in the strategy, we take account of these factors, together with another set of indicators aiming at considering the role of institutions.

The level of general government gross debt and the general government deficit (or surplus) are key fiscal parameters, introduced already by the Maastricht Treaty. They were introduced as building criteria for the Economic and Monetary Union (EMU), and were considered necessary for its sustainability. For a review of the process conducting to the establishment of these parameters and for their macroeconomic significance, see Buiter et al. (1993), Dornbusch (1996, 1997) and Delors (2013). We test them in order to assess their importance in the strategy.

While none of the indicators of the Europe 2020 Strategy is based on the GDP, a good overall economic performance of the country could also determine good performance in the strategy. For this reason a measure of the GDP growth is introduced in the model to understand to what extent it influences the results.

We also observe from the data that many of the top performing countries according to the index, happen to be relatively wealthier than the average. Richer countries might be better equipped to progress in the different dimensions of the strategy. In order to disentangle this possible effect, I introduce the measure of the GDP per capita, in purchasing power standards, into the model.

Another possible line of thought, instead, emphasises the role of institutions in promoting processes of development. The question of how institutions influence progress has long been central in the study of economic development (Veblen 1898; Commons 1931; Williamson 1975; Coase 1984; North 1991; Rodrik 2008; Dixit 2009). I include this perspective in the analysis, applied to the study of the Europe 2020 Strategy.

Institutions

The so-called "institutionalism" has become increasingly central in the economic literature (Coase 1998; Hodgson 1998; Williamson 2000; Parada 2001). It attempts to incorporate a theory of institutions into economics (North 1993).

Ronald Coase (1937) first introduced explicitly the notion of transaction costs into economic analysis. Oliver Williamson (1975) and Douglas North (1991) used the concept of reduction of transaction costs to explain why a more efficient institutional system promotes development by "creating order and reducing uncertainty." Since these seminal works, the role of institutions has been studied and recognized as central in the process of economic development.

North (1991: 97) defined institutions as "the rules of the game." They are "humanly devised constraints that structure political, economic and social interaction," and "they consist of both informal constraints, and formal rules" (North 1991: 97). Dixit (2009) highlighted "the structure and functioning of the legal and social institutions that support economic activity and economic transactions by protecting property rights, enforcing contracts, and taking collective action to provide physical and organizational infrastructure" (North 1991, 5).

Many authors have studied the relationship between institutions and economic performances (Olson 1982; Knack and Keefer 1997; Hall and Jones 1999; Rodrik

2008; Acemoglu and Robinson 2010; Chang 2011). All of these studies focus on the effect of institutions on economic growth, on the level of investment, or on development.

Acemoglu and Robinson (2010) argued that institutions are the main determinants of differences in prosperity across countries; and in particular Acemoglu et al. (2003) suggested the existence of a "robust and strong effect of institutions on the volatility of economic activity," which in turn has strong implications for economic development.

Dollar and Kraay (2003) studied the relations between institutions and trade, finding that the good quality of the institutions was related to higher levels of trade and that both were particularly important in determining the growth prospects of countries. Rodrik et al. (2004) estimated the contribution of institutions, geography, and trade in determining income levels around the world, finding that the quality of institutions outranks by far all other factors.

Some authors (Chang 2011), on the other side, have criticized the dominant view of institutions as determinants of economic development, and have argued that an improvement in the quality of institutions might be the consequence of the process of economic development, mainly driven by a better human capital (Glaeser et al. 2004).

In order to study if and how formal and informal institutions can be associated with success or failure in the Europe 2020 Strategy, the distinction between formal and informal institutions must be introduced.

Formal institutions

Formal institutions are laws, rules, and mechanisms that define the system in which economic agents can operate. They include the constitutional rules of the political game, the legislature that makes specific regulations within this context, the courts, the police, as well as licensing and regulatory agencies, which interpret and enforce these rules.

Knack and Keefer (1997) suggest using property rights enforcements as main indicators of institutions; others look at measures of corruption (Mauro 1995), or at the levels of entry barriers (Djankov et al. 2002), as good proxies. Formal institutions are linked, in literature, to the concept of good governance.

The World Bank developed a set of indicators aimed at measuring all different aspects of good governance: the Worldwide Governance Indicators[6] (WGI) (Kaufmann et al. 2010). Their use in the economic literature is growing exponentially, in parallel with the greater focus on institutional factors as explanatory variables for the process of economic development.

These indicators are widely used, but they are also subject to some criticism, because they may suffer from perceptual biases, adverse selection in sampling, and conceptual conflation with economic policy choices (Kurtz and Schrank 2007), or because their construction is based on untested hypotheses (Glaeser et al. 2004). However, the need to operationalize the concept of institutional quality and to develop robust models to assess their relevance implies that these indicators currently are the best source of data to perform an institutional analysis of the process of economic development.

The analysis of institutions as a key element of good governance moved from the field of development economics, and was initially applied to the study of developing countries. Subsequently, however, it has been found relevant for developed countries as well, and this is of particular relevance for this work.

Sachs and Warner (1997) studied the relation between trade openness and institutional quality and found that such factors are particularly relevant to explain economic development in all countries, not just in developing ones. The role of good institutions is key in explaining the integration in international trade, in particular why rich countries trade with each other, but developing countries less so (Anderson and Marcouiller 2002). The idea that institutional differences are an important determinant of trade flows is confirmed by Levchenko (2004), who shows how countries with better institutions capture larger import shares in industries that are more "institutionally complex."

Institutional quality, moreover, is considered to be the prime determinant of capital flows and investment across countries (Lambsdorff 2003; Alfaro et al. 2005), it explains most variations in per capita incomes across countries (Acemoglu et al. 2001), and seems to be associated with higher investments in R&D (Clarke 2001) and lower volatility of macroeconomic policies (Acemoglu et al. 2003), which in turn leads to higher growth.

The concept of government effectiveness is the one on which we focus our attention. Among the governance indicators produced by the World Bank, government effectiveness tries to measure the general quality of public administration in one country, based on perceptions of the quality of public services, the quality of the civil service and the degree of its independence from political pressures, the quality of policy formulation and implementation, and the credibility of the government's commitment to such policies. We consider it as the most appropriate indicator to test the relevance of formal institutions in determining good performance in a wide, governmental, development agenda like the Europe 2020 Strategy.

Government effectiveness is found to be strictly associated with the existence of transparent budget rules (Blume and Voigt 2013), with higher levels of fiscal decentralization (Kyriacou and Roca-Sagalés 2011), and with better credit rating rates of sovereign debts (Afonso et al. 2007).[7] It leads to better social outcomes, like lower rates in some crime categories (Azfar and Gurgur 2005), and is the strongest macro-level predictor of support for democracy (Magalhães 2014).

According to Lee and Whitford (2009), much of the variation in the levels of government effectiveness is explained by national income, with wealthier countries experiencing greater perceptions of effectiveness. But in a more recent analysis Adams-Kane and Lim (2014) reverse the causality link, arguing that it is government effectiveness affecting per capita income, and they identify human capital formation as the key channel. The quality of institutions, as measured by government effectiveness, is central to learning and education, and human capital is found to have a significant and positive effect on per capita income levels.

The literature on government effectiveness emphasizes the importance of having all the leverages of policymaking work in an institutional environment with a high quality of governance. This is why I use this indicator as a potential explanatory variable in the model.

Informal institutions

A fundamental question of political economy has been the impact that informal institutions shaping the organization of a society may have on the economic performance of countries (Cole et al. 1992: 1095; Sabatini 2008). "Features of social organization, such as trust, norms, and networks that can improve the efficiency of society by facilitating coordinated actions" (Putnam 1993: 167) are what is commonly referred to as "social capital."

The concept of social capital has often been prone to multiple interpretations, having multiple dimensions and possible effects (Serageldin and Grootaert 2000). Its definition has several variations across the social sciences (Bourdieu 1986; Coleman 1988; Putnam 1993; Fukuyama 1995; Woolcock 1998; Ostrom 1999; OECD 2001). In sociology and political science, the concept is often used as a property of organizations or countries, while in economics it is linked to the characteristics of individuals (Pugno and Verme 2012).

Economists have often used it to explain the role social interaction plays in promoting better functioning markets (Greif 1993). The literature on game theory, and in particular on repeated games, has highlighted at the microeconomic level how cooperation can be enhanced thanks to social capital (Kreps et al. 1982; Abreu 1988). Social connections can even sometimes substitute legal structures and produce the same effect of reducing transaction costs, as we have seen for formal institutions (Arrow 1972; Glaeser et al. 2002).

Informal institutions, synthesized by the concepts of social capital and trust, are extremely relevant even in the most advanced market economies (Dixit 2009), since "reputation and the trust it fosters are the core attributes of market capitalism" (Greenspan 2007: 256). As Arrow (1972: 357) pointed out: "Virtually every commercial transaction has within itself an element of trust, certainly any transaction conducted over a period of time. It can be plausibly argued that much of the economic backwardness in the world can be explained by the lack of mutual confidence."

The dimension of "trust" is considered to be the most important in explaining the economic function of social capital (Coleman 1988; Fukuyama 1995; Knack and Keefer 1997; Ostrom 1999; Zak and Knack 2001; Sabatini 2008), as an engine for enhanced efficiency and economic growth (Pugno and Verme 2012), and as a key to overcoming market failures linked to the difficulty in enforcing or observing contracts (Karlan 2005). Most of the economic analyses of social capital use a generalized measure of interpersonal trust, as provided by the World Values Survey[8] (WVS) (Inglehart 1999; Sabatini 2009; Toya and Skidmore 2012).

The positive effect of social capital on growth and productivity has been highlighted by a very large body of literature (Fukuyama 1995; Knack and Keefer

1997; La Porta et al. 1997; Sobel 2002; Glaeser et al. 2002). Among these studies, it is worth highlighting the macro-econometric analysis by Knack and Keefer (1997), who found that an increase in the WVS measure of trust in one country increases economic growth too.

The same results, but on a wider sample, were found by Zak and Knack (2001), who argued that "growth rises by nearly 1 percentage point on average for each 15 percentage point increase in trust (a one standard deviation increase)" (Zak and Knack 2001: 307–309). They also argued that formal institutions may affect growth through their impact on trust: a better institutional setting is likely to enhance trust, thus reducing transaction costs and overcoming potential market failures, leading to higher growth. Beugelsdijk et al. (2004) tested the robustness of these results, finding that if the first analysis (Knack and Keefer 1997) could be considered as "limitedly robust," the Zak and Knack (2001) results, instead, are highly robust both in terms of the statistical significance of the estimated coefficients and in terms of the estimated effect sizes.

The literature on the effects of social capital, as measured by trust, suggests a series of positive effects: on trade (Greif 1993; Woolcock 1998), health (Putnam 2000; Rose 2000), school performance (Coleman 1988), entrepreneurship and innovation (Brüderl and Preisendörfer 1998; Dakhli and De Clercq 2003), the well-functioning of formal institutions (Williamson 2000), in terms of judicial efficiency, control of corruption and civic involvement (La Porta et al. 1997), crime prevention (Wilson 1987), and democratic stability (Inglehart 1999; Uslaner 2003). Social capital is also associated with higher reported levels of happiness (Uslaner 2003; Bjørnskov 2003), and life satisfaction (Helliwell et al. 2009; Pugno and Verme 2012).

Social capital, as measured by trust, seems to be the best variable to include the role of informal institutions into the model, and to test whether or not it is a key factor in determining the performances of EU countries.

Econometric analysis

The key question is how and to what extent the Europe 2020 Index is influenced by other measures and, if so, which are the most significant factors. The main hypothesis is that institutional factors might be the key explanatory variables, even more than the indicators of economic growth and public finances. For this reason we perform a set of multiple linear regression analyses.

The empirical strategy is to compose a large panel of 270 observations, covering 27 countries for ten years, from 2003 to 2012, which are those for which the Europe 2020 Index can be calculated. The model has the Europe 2020 Index as the dependent variable (E2I).

Formal institutions are included in the model through the concept of good governance. The indicator of Government Effectiveness, from the World Governance Indicators,[9] is used as a measure of good governance. Informal institutions are included through the concept of social capital. I use the generalized measure of trust (Trust), from the World Values Survey,[10] as a proxy for social capital.

The indicators of sustainability of public finances considered in the model are the general government gross debt (Debt), and the general government deficit or surplus (Deficit), both calculated in percentage of the GDP and provided by the AMECO database. Finally we test two additional independent variables: the GDP growth (Growth) and the GDP per capita in purchasing power standards (GGDPpps), as provided by Eurostat.

The model tests the role of the six explanatory variables in influencing the Europe 2020 Index:

We first test the two institutional variables alone, and find a coefficient of determination of 56 per cent, which means the two variables explain more than half of total variation in the index. Both institutional variables, moreover, are strongly significant ($p = 0.000$) and have positive coefficients.

We gradually include the other variables, in order to understand whether they add explanatory power to the model, and find that debt and deficit do not add much, and that they moreover are not significant and have coefficients close to zero. The level of GDP per capita in purchasing power standards has the same null effect on the dependent variable. GDP growth is the only one that shows certain

Table 5.5 Europe 2020 Index and institutional and economic factors

Explanatory variables	Dependent variable: Europe 2020 Index					
	(1)	*(2)*	*(3)*	*(4)*	*(5)*	*(6)*
GovEffectiveness	.074***	.077***	.071***	.078***	.073***	.079***
	(0.013)	(0.013)	(0.013)	(0.016)	(0.012)	(0.015)
Trust	.566***	.573***	.562***	.564***	.552***	.548***
	(0.060)	(0.061)	(0.059)	(0.060)	(0.060)	(0.060)
Debt		.000			−.001*	−.001*
		(0.000)			(0.000)	(0.000)
Deficit		−.002			.002	.000
		(0.002)			(0.002)	(0.002)
Growth				−.004*	−.005**	−.005**
				(0.002)	(0.002)	(0.002)
GPDpps				.000		.000
				(0.000)		(0.000)
Constant	.208***	.215***	.220***	.212***	.250***	.257***
	(0.015)	(0.019)	(0.016)	(0.018)	(0.022)	(0.024)
Observations	270	270	270	270	270	270
R^2	0.560	0.565	0.571	0.561	0.580	0.581
No. countries	27	27	27	27	27	27

Robust *t*-statistics in brackets. *** $p < 0.001$; ** $p < 0.01$; * $p < 0.05$. Test (F): Prob $> F = 0.0000$. The main assumptions are verified: linearity of the relationship; independence of the observations; normality of the residuals; homoscedasticity.

significance, but it is associated with extremely low coefficient, close to zero. It might be considered significant in the regression, but it does not influence the variation of the Europe 2020 Index.

Government effectiveness and trust, on the contrary, maintain their strong significance in all specifications of the model and the estimated effects are quite relevant. An increment of one unit of the government effectiveness indicator, holding constant all the other variables, leads to an increase in the Europe 2020 Index by 0.079 units, while the same increment in the generalized measure of trust leads to an increase in the index by 0.548 units. None of the other variables has a coefficient considerably different from zero in any of the specifications of the model.

Discussion

The attempt to disentangle the main factors affecting the performance of EU Member States in pursuing the goals of the Europe 2020 Strategy points to the importance of institutions. Formal and informal institutions seem to play a decisive role in explaining the different performances of European countries in the Europe 2020 Strategy, more than the other economic variables, based on GDP, which have been tested through the model. Both formal and informal institutions play a prominent role in such a complex development strategy, with social capital being the first and most relevant factor.

These results confirm the "institutional" view, suggesting that the effectiveness of policy making strongly depends on context factors, and that the institutional environment in which it takes place may actually determine a great deal of its chances to succeed.

The results of the analysis give robust support to the hypothesis that good governance is particularly important in such a strategy. As we saw before, many of the policy fields on which the Europe 2020 Strategy focuses fall out of the direct competences of the EU, and this implies that national policy making plays a decisive role in determining the effectiveness of the strategy and the overall European capacity to achieve its goals. This analysis has proved the intuitive idea that much of the variation in performances across countries depends on the quality of governance at the national level.

The role of social capital, then, appears as particularly strong. More cohesive societies are also those that are better equipped to pursue a broad development strategy. A strategy based on several pillars, whose scope goes well beyond the strict concept of the GDP growth, seems to require a high level of social capital, measured by its component of interpersonal trust.

These results also find support in previous analyses (Easterly 2002; Rodrik 2003; Dixit 2009), which suggested that the quality of institutions becomes more decisive for higher levels of development, which is a particularly interesting suggestion for our case of a developing strategy for a group of developed economies, like the MS of the EU.

The finding that both social capital and good governance are the main determinant factors of success in the Europe 2020 Strategy also confirms the suggestion by some authors (Grootaert and Van Bastelaer 2002: 5) that an "encompassing view of social capital includes the social and political macro environment that shapes social structure and enables norms to develop ... this view also includes the macro-level formal institutional relationships and structures."

Others, like Gros and Roth (2012), specifically mentioned the relevance of institutional factors for the Europe 2020 Strategy. They argued that it can be best achieved with appropriate and sufficient investment in human and social capital and with efficient government institutions. They claim that the quality of the institutions is more important than other factors, and that "a sufficient level of government effectiveness throughout the EU-27 is a critical condition for making the EU as a whole more competitive," even arguing that that "a clear implication would be that the structural funds should be used to build social capital and effective institutions rather than airports and highways" (Gros and Roth 2012: 85).

Conclusions

The inherent complexity of the Europe 2020 Strategy, focused on areas where the European Commission does not have full jurisdictional competence, increases the relevance of a timely and precise monitoring system and of an effective and efficient institutional setting. A supranational strategy so dependent on initiatives and actions by national governments requires a strong monitoring mechanism and a high degree of accountability for the Member States. In order to achieve the best possible results, it is important to understand which are the key factors determining countries' performances. This paper makes contributions in both directions.

The Europe 2020 Index represents a powerful tool to monitor the performances of the EU countries towards the achievements of the strategy goals, as defined by the eight official headline indicators. The index allows a yearly monitoring and can already be built for ten consecutive years, since 2003. It can play an important role in enhancing the transparency and accountability of policies implemented at the EU and national level in the current context.

We observe certain differences in performances, both between countries and across time. The need for a better understanding of the determinants of those differences inspired an analysis of potential success factors, such as level of wealth, growth, sustainability of public finances, and institutions.

The analysis looks at the institutional economics literature in search of explanation. The underlying idea is that such a wide, supranational, complex strategy characterized by multilevel governance, by a need for continuous political commitment, and by policy areas falling beyond the strict competences of the European Commission may require something more than the coordination of economic policies. I conjectured that institutions, in the sense of North (1991), could be the key explanatory variable, and decided to test both measures of formal and informal institutions against the economic criteria based on the GDP.

The econometric analysis performed in this paper confirmed the key importance of formal and informal institutions, both in absolute and in relative terms, compared with the other factors considered. Institutional variables are the most significant ones and have the strongest estimated effects. The results do not imply that economic growth, levels of the GDP per capita, and fiscal sustainability are not important objectives *per se*. The main policy implication of this analysis would be that in order for the goals of the Europe 2020 Strategy to be achieved, policy making should adopt a broader focus that includes the role of institutions.

Notes

1 The opinions expressed in this chapter are the author's alone and do not reflect those of the European Commission.
2 The EU had 27 Member States until 1 July 2013, when Croatia joined, becoming the 28th.
3 When we use the geometric aggregation method, the marginal utility of an increase in the score is much higher for low absolute values of the score; consequently, a country has a greater incentive, compared to the linear method, to address those areas where it performs badly, as this would give it better chances to improve its position in the ranking (OECD 2008).
4 In some cases, where the value of the indicator for one country equals the lower bound in the normalization formula, the value would become zero, and the geometric aggregation method would imply a value of zero for the overall index. This problem has been solved by assigning, in those three cases, the lowest possible score different from zero to the value of the normalized indicator (i.e. 0.001).
5 Accessed 10 July 2014.
6 The Worldwide Governance Indicators report aggregate and individual governance indicators for 215 economies over the period 1996–2012, for six dimensions of governance: (1) voice and accountability; (2) political stability and absence of violence; (3) government effectiveness; (4) regulatory quality; (5) rule of law; (6) control of corruption.
7 Interestingly, the study by Alfonso et al. was performed before the start of the financial crisis and of the consequent sovereign debt problems in the Eurozone.
8 The WVS measures generalized trust through the question developed by Rosenberg (1956): "Generally speaking, would you say that most people can be trusted or that you can be too careful in dealing with people?"
9 Available at info.worldbank.org/governance/wgi.
10 Available at www.worldvaluessurvey.org.

References

Abreu, D. 1988. "On the Theory of Infinitely Repeated Games with Discounting." *Econometrica* 56(2): 383–396.
Acemoglu, D. and J. Robinson. 2010. "The Role of Institutions in Growth and Development." *Review of Economics and Institutions* 1(2) (Fall): 133–164.
Acemoglu D., S. Johnson and J. Robinson. 2001. "The Colonial Origins of Comparative Development: An Empirical Investigation." *American Economic Review* 91(5): 1369–1401.
Acemoglu, D., S. Johnson, J. Robinson and Y. Thaicharoen. 2003. "Institutional Causes, Macroeconomic Symptoms: Volatility, Crises and Growth." *Journal of Monetary Economics* 50(1): 49–123.

Adams-Kane, J. and Lim. 2014. *Institutional Quality Mediates the Effect of Human Capital on Economic Performance*. Policy research working paper 6792. Washington, DC: World Bank.

Afonso, A., P. Gomes and P. Rother. 2007. *What "Hides" Behind Sovereign Debt Ratings?* Working paper no. 711. Frankfurt: ECB.

Alfaro, L., S. Kalemli-Ozcan and V. Volosovych. 2005. *Why Doesn't Capital Flow from Rich to Poor Countries? An Empirical Investigation*. Working paper w11901. Cambridge, MA: National Bureau of Economic Research.

Anderson, J. E. and D. Marcouiller. 2002. "Insecurity and the Pattern of Trade: An Empirical Investigation." *Review of Economics and Statistics* 84: 342–352.

Arrow, K. 1972. "Gifts and Exchanges." *Philosophy and Public Affairs*,(1): 343–362.

Azfar, O. and T. Gurgur. 2005. "Government Effectiveness, Crime Rates and Crime Reporting." *Crime Rates and Crime Reporting* (May): 2–42.

Beugelsdijk, S., H. L. De Groot and A. B. Van Schaik. 2004. "Trust and Economic Growth: A Robustness Analysis." *Oxford Economic Papers* 56(1): 118–134.

Bjørnskov, C. 2003. "The Happy Few: Cross-country Evidence on Social Capital and Life Satisfaction." *Kyklos* 56(1): 3–16.

Blume, L., and S. Voigt. 2013. "The Economic Effects of Constitutional Budget Institutions." *European Journal of Political Economy* 29(C): 236–251.

Bourdieu, P. 1986. "Forms of Capital." In *Handbook of Theory and Research for the Sociology of Education*, edited by John G. Richardson, pp. 241–260. Westport, CT: Greenwood Press.

Brüderl, J. and P. Preisendörfer. 1998. "Network Support and the Success of Newly Founded Businesses." *Small Business Economics* 10: 213–225.

Buiter, W. H., G. Corsetti and N. Roubini. 1993. "Excessive Deficits: Sense and Nonsense in the Treaty of Maastricht." *Economic Policy* 1: 57–100.

Chang, H. J. 2011. "Institutions and Economic Development: Theory, Policy and History." *Journal of Institutional Economics* 7(4): 473.

Clarke, G. R. 2001. "How Institutional Quality and Economic Factors Impact Technological Deepening in Developing Countries." *Journal of International Development* 13(8): 1097–1118.

Coase, R. H. 1937. "The Nature of the Firm." *Economica* 4(16): 386–405.

Coase, R. H. 1984. "The New Institutional Economics." *Journal of Institutional and Theoretical Economics* 140(1): 229–231.

Coase, R. H. 1998. "The New Institutional Economics." *The American Economic Review* 88(2): 72–74.

Cole, H. L., G. J. Mailath and A. Postlewaite. 1992. "Social Norms, Savings Behavior, and Growth." *Journal of Political Economy* 100(6): 1092–1125.

Coleman, J. S. 1988. "Social Capital in the Creation of Human Capital." *American Journal of Sociology* (94): S95–S120.

Commons, J. R. 1931. "Institutional Economics." *American Economic Review* 21: 648–657.

Dakhli, M. and D. de Clercq. 2004. "Human Capital, Social Capital, and Innovation: A Multi-Country Study." *Entrepreneurship and Regional Development* 16: 107–128.

Delors, J. 2013. "Economic Governance in the European Union: Past, Present and Future." *Journal of Common Market Studies* 51(2): 169–178.

DGINS ESSC. 2010. "Sofia Memorandum: Measuring Progress, Well-being and Sustainable Development." Available at www.dgins-sofia2010.eu.

Dixit, A. 2009. "Governance, Institutions and Economic Activity." *American Economic Review* 99(1): 3–24.

Djankov, S., R. LaPorta, F. Lopez-de-Silanes and A. Shleifer. 2002. "The Regulation of Entry." *Quarterly Journal of Economics* 117(1): 1–37.

Dollar, D. and A. Kraay. 2003. "Institutions, Trade and Growth." *Journal of Monetary Economics* 50(1): 133–162.

Dornbusch, R. 1996. *Debt and Monetary Policy: The Policy Issues.* Working paper w5573. Cambridge, MA: National Bureau of Economic Research.

Dornbusch, R. 1997. "Fiscal Aspects of Monetary Integration." *American Economic Review* 87(2): 221–223.

Easterly, W. 2002. "The Elusive Quest for Growth: Economists' Adventures and Misadventures in the Tropics." *Journal of Macromarketing* 22(1): 136–144.

Ebert, U. and H. Welsch. 2004. "Meaningful Environmental Indices: A Social Choice Approach." *Journal of Environmental Economics and Management* 47: 270–283.

Erixon, F. 2010. "The Europe 2020 Strategy: Time for Europe to Think Again." *European View* 9(1): 29–37.

European Commission. 2010. "EUROPE 2020: A Strategy for Smart, Sustainable and Inclusive Growth." *COM* (March): 1–35.

Fukuyama, F. 1995. *Trust: The Social Virtues and the Creation of Prosperity.* New York: Free Press.

Glaeser, E. L., D. Laibson and B. Sacerdote. 2002. "An Economic Approach to Social Capital." *The Economic Journal* 112(483): F437–F458.

Glaeser, E. L., R. La Porta, F. Lopez-de-Silanes and A. Shleifer. 2004. "Do Institutions Cause Growth?" *Journal of Economic Growth* 9(3): 271–303.

Greenspan, A. 2007. *The Age of Turbulence.* New York: Penguin Books.

Greif, A. 1993. "Contract Enforceability and Economic Institutions in Early Trade: The Maghribi Traders' Coalition." *American Economic Review* 83(3): 525–548.

Grootaert, C. and T. Van Bastelaer. 2002. *Understanding Social Capital.* Washington DC: The World Bank.

Gros, D. and F. Roth. 2012. *The Europe 2020 Strategy: Can it Maintain the EU's Competitiveness in the World?* No. 7260. Brussels: Centre for European Policy Studies.

Hall, R. E. and C. I. Jones. 1999. "Why do Some Countries Produce So Much More Output Per Worker than Others?" *The Quarterly Journal of Economics* 114(1):83–116.

Helliwell, J. F., C. P. Barrington-Leigh, A. Harris and H. Huang. 2009. *International Evidence on the Social Context of Well-Being.* Working paper w14720. Cambridge, MA: National Bureau of Economic Research.

Hodgson, G. M. 1998. "The Approach of Institutional Economics." *Journal of Economic Literature* 36(1): 166–192.

Hooghe, L. and G. Marks. 2010. "Types of Multi-Level Governance." *Handbook on Multi-Level Governance.* pp. 17–31.

Inglehart, R. 1999. "Trust, Well-Being and Democracy." In *Democracy and Trust*, edited by M. Warren, pp. 88–120. Cambridge: Cambridge University Press.

Jachtenfuchs, M. 2010. "The Institutional Framework of the European Union." *Handbook on Multi-Level Governance.* pp. 203–223.

Karlan, D. S. 2005. "Using Experimental Economics to Measure Social Capital and Predict Financial Decisions." *American Economic Review* 95(5): 1688–1699.

Kaufmann, D., A. Kraay and M. Mastruzzi. 2010. *The Worldwide Governance Indicators: Methodology and Analytical Issues.* Policy research working paper no. 5430. Washington, DC: World Bank.

Knack, S. and P. Keefer. 1997. "Does Social Capital have an Economic Payoff? A Cross-Country Investigation." *The Quarterly Journal of Economics* 112(4):1251–1288.

Kreps, D. M., J. Roberts and R. Wilson. 1982. "Rational Cooperation in the Finitely Repeated Prisoner's Dilemma." *Journal of Economic Theory* 27: 245–52.

Kurtz, M. J. and A. Schrank. 2007. "Growth and Governance: Models, Measures, and Mechanisms." *Journal of Politics* 69: 538–554.

Kyriacou, A. P. and O. Roca-Sagalés. 2011. "Fiscal Decentralization and Government Quality in the OECD." *Economics Letters* 111(3): 191–193.

Lambsdorff, J. G. 2003. "How Corruption Affects Persistent Capital Flows." *Economics of Governance* 4(3): 229–243.

La Porta, R., F. Lopez-de-Silane, A. Shleifer and R. W. Vishny. 1997. "Legal Determinants of External Finance." *Journal of Finance* 52(3): 1131–1150.

Lee, S. Y. and A. B. Whitford. 2009. "Government Effectiveness in Comparative Perspective." *Journal of Comparative Policy Analysis* 11(2): 249–281.

Levchenko, A. A. 2004. *Institutional Quality and International Trade*. Washington, DC: IMF.

Magalhães, P. C. 2014. "Government Effectiveness and Support for Democracy. *European Journal of Political Research* 53(1): 77–97.

Martens, W. 2010. "Europe 2020 and Beyond." *European View* 9(1): 29–37.

Mauro, P. 1995. "Corruption and Growth." *Quarterly Journal of Economics* 110(3): 681–712.

North, D. C. 1991. "Institutions." *Journal of Economic Perspectives* 5(1): 97–112.

North, D. C. 1993. *The New Institutional Economics and Development*. EconWPA Economic History (9309002). Available at www2.econ.iastate.edu/tesfatsi/NewInstE. North.pdf.

OECD. 2001. *The Well-Being of Nations: The Role of Human and Social Capital*. Paris: OECD Publishing.

OECD. 2008. *Handbook on Constructing Composite Indicators: Methodology and User Guide*. Paris: OECD Publishing.

Olson, M. 1982. *The Rise and Decline of Nations*. New Haven, CT: Yale University Press.

Ostrom, E. 1999. "Social Capital: A Fad or a Fundamental Concept?" In *Social Capital: A Multifaceted Perspective*, edited by P. Dasgupta and I. Serageldin. Washington, DC: The World Bank, pp. 195–198.

Papadopoulos, Y. 2010. "Accountability and Multi-Level Governance: More Accountability, Less Democracy?" *West European Politics* 33(5): 1030–1049.

Parada, J. J. 2001. "Original Institutional Economics: A Theory for the 21st Century?" *Oeconomicus* 5 (Fall): 46–60.

Pasimeni, P. 2011. "The Europe 2020 Index." *Social Indicators Research* 110(2): 613–635.

Pasimeni, P. 2012. "Measuring Europe 2020: A New Tool to Assess the Strategy." *International Journal of Innovation and Regional Development* 4(5): 365–385.

Pugno, M. and P. Verme. 2012. *Life Satisfaction, Social Capital and the Bonding-Bridging Nexus*. Working paper 5945. Washington, DC: World Bank.

Putnam, R. D. 1993. *Making Democracy Work: Civic Traditions in Modern Italy*. Princeton, NJ: Princeton University Press.

Putnam, R. D. 2000. *Bowling Alone: The Collapse and Revival of American Community*. New York: Simon & Schuster.

Rodrik, D. (ed.). 2003. *In Search of Prosperity: Analytic Narratives on Economic Growth*. Princeton, NJ: Princeton University Press.

Rodrik, D. 2008. *One Economics, Many Recipes: Globalization, Institutions, and Economic Growth*. Princeton, NJ: Princeton University Press.

Rodrik, D., A. Subramanian and F. Trebbi. 2004. "Institutions Rule: The Primacy of Institutions Over Geography and Integration in Economic Development." *Journal of Economic Growth* 9(2): 131–165.

Rose, R. 2000. "How Much Does Social Capital Add to Individual Health? A Survey Study of Russians." *Social Science and Medicine* 51: 1421–1435.

Rosenberg, M. 1956. "Misanthropy and Political Ideology." *American Sociological Review* 21(6): 690–695.

Sabatini, F. 2008. "Social Capital and the Quality of Economic Development." *Kyklos* 61(3): 466-499.

Sabatini, F. 2009. "Social Capital as Social Networks: A New Framework for Measurement and an Empirical Analysis of its Determinants and Consequences." *The Journal of Socio-Economics* 38(3): 429–442.

Sachs, J. D. and A. M. Warner. 1997. "Fundamental Sources of Long-Run Growth." *American Economic Review* 87(2): 184–188.

Sarcinelli, M. 2010. "'Europa 2020', Nuovo Governo Economico e Ri-Regolamentazione Finanziaria: Incentivi o Vincoli Alla Crescita?" *Moneta e Credito* 63(252): 285–319.

Serageldin, I. and C. Grootaert. 2000. "Defining Social Capital: An Integrated View." In *Social Capital: A Multifaceted Perspective*, edited by P. Dasgupta and I. Serageldin, pp. 40–58. Washington, DC: World Bank.

Sobel, J. 2002. "Can We Trust Social Capital?" *Journal of Economic Literature* 40: 139–154.

Toya, H. and M. Skidmore. 2012. *Do Natural Disasters Enhance Societal Trust?* Working paper no. 3905. Munich: CESifo.

Uslaner, E. M. 2003. "Trust, Democracy and Governance: Can Government Policies Influence Generalized Trust?" In *Generating Social Capital: Civil Society and Institutions in Comparative Perspective*, edited by M. Hooghe and D. Stolle, pp. 171–190. New York: Palgrave Macmillan:.

Veblen, T. 1898. "Why is Economics Not an Evolutionary Science?" *The Quarterly Journal of Economics* 12(4): 373–397.

Williamson, O. E. 1975. *Markets and Hierarchies*. New York: Macmillan.

Williamson, O. E. 2000. "The New Institutional Economics: Taking Stock, Looking Ahead." *Journal of Economic Literature* 38(3): 595–613.

Wilson, W. J. 1987. *The Truly Disadvantaged*. Chicago, IL: University of Chicago Press.

Woolcock, M. 1998. "Social Capital and Economic Development: Toward a Theoretical Synthesis and Policy Framework." *Theory and Society* 27(2): 151–208.

Zak, P. and S. Knack. 2001. "Trust and Growth." *Economic Journal* 111: 295–331.

Annex 1: Indicators used in the Europe 2020 Index

Tertiary education attainment (TEDU)

The share of the population aged 30–34 years who have successfully completed university or university-like (tertiary-level) education with an education level ISCED 1997 (International Standard Classification of Education) of 5–6. This indicator measures the Europe 2020 strategy's headline target to increase the share of the 30–34-year-olds having completed tertiary or equivalent education to at least 40 per cent in 2020. Data source: Eurostat.

Gross domestic expenditure on R&D (GERD)

The indicator provided is GERD (gross domestic expenditure on R&D) as a percentage of GDP. "Research and experimental development (R&D) comprise creative work undertaken on a systematic basis in order to increase the stock of knowledge, including knowledge of man, culture and society and the use of this stock of knowledge to devise new applications" (Frascati Manual, 2002 edition, §63). R&D is an activity where there are significant transfers of resources between units, organizations and sectors and it is important to trace the flow of R&D funds Data source: Eurostat.

Greenhouse gas emissions (GGE)

This indicator shows trends in total man-made emissions of the "Kyoto basket" of greenhouse gases presenting annual total emissions in relation to 1990 emissions. The "Kyoto basket" of greenhouse gases includes carbon dioxide (CO_2), methane (CH_4), nitrous oxide (N_2O), and the so-called F-gases (hydrofluorocarbons, perfluorocarbons and sulphur hexafluoride, SF_6). These gases are aggregated into a single unit using gas-specific global warming potential (GWP) factors. The aggregated greenhouse gas emissions are expressed in units of CO_2 equivalents. The indicator does not include emissions and removals related to land use, land-use change and forestry (LULUCF); nor does it include emissions from international aviation and international maritime transport. CO_2 emissions from biomass with energy recovery are reported as a Memorandum item according to UNFCCC Guidelines and not included in national greenhouse gas totals. The EU as a whole is committed to achieving at least a 20 per cent reduction of its greenhouse gas emissions by 2020 compared with 1990. This objective implies: a 21 per cent reduction in emissions from sectors covered by the EU ETS (emission trading scheme) compared to 2005 by 2020; a reduction of 10 per cent in emissions for sectors outside the EU ETS. To achieve this 10 per cent overall target each Member State has agreed to country-specific limits for 2020 compared to 2005 (Council Decision 2009/406/EC). Data Source: European Environment Agency.

Share of renewable energy in gross final energy consumption (RNEW)

This indicator is calculated on the basis of energy statistics covered by the Energy Statistics Regulation. It may be considered an estimate of the indicator described in Directive 2009/28/EC, as the statistical system for some renewable energy technologies is not yet fully developed to meet the requirements of this Directive. However, the contribution of these technologies is rather marginal for the time being. More information about the renewable energy shares calculation methodology and Eurostat's annual energy statistics can be found in the Renewable Energy Directive 2009/28/EC, the Energy Statistics Regulation

1099/2008, and in the transparency platform of the Directorate General for Energy (http://ec.europa.eu/energy/renewables/index_en.htm). Data source: Eurostat.

Energy intensity of the economy (EINT)

This indicator is the ratio between the gross inland consumption of energy and the gross domestic product (GDP) for a given calendar year. It measures the energy consumption of an economy and its overall energy efficiency. The gross inland consumption of energy is calculated as the sum of the gross inland consumption of five energy types: coal, electricity, oil, natural gas, and renewable energy sources. The GDP figures are taken at chain-linked volumes with reference year 2000. The energy intensity ratio is determined by dividing the gross inland consumption by the GDP. Since gross inland consumption is measured in kgoe (kilogram of oil equivalent) and GDP in thousands of euros, this ratio is measured in kgoe per thousand euros. Data source: Eurostat.

Employment rate of the population aged 20–64 (EMPL)

The employment rate is calculated by dividing the number of persons aged 20–64 in employment by the total population of the same age group. The indicator is based on the EU Labour Force Survey. The survey covers the entire population living in private households and excludes those in collective households such as boarding houses, halls of residence and hospitals. Employed population consists of those persons who, during the reference week, did any work for pay or profit for at least one hour, or were not working but had jobs from which they were temporarily absent. Data source: Eurostat.

Early leavers from education (SCHO)

Percentage of the population aged 18–24 with at most lower-secondary education and not in further education or training. From 20 November 2009, this indicator is based on annual averages of quarterly data instead of one unique reference quarter in spring. "Early leavers from education and training" refers to persons aged 18–24 who fulfil the following two conditions: first, the highest level of education or training attained is ISCED 0, 1, 2 or 3c short; second, respondents declared not having received any education or training in the four weeks preceding the survey (numerator). The denominator consists of the total population of the same age group, excluding no answers to the questions "highest level of education or training attained" and "participation to education and training." Data source: both the numerators and the denominators come from the EU Labour Force Survey.

Population at-risk-of-poverty or exclusion (POV)

The Europe 2020 strategy promotes social inclusion, in particular through the reduction of poverty, by aiming to lift at least 20 million people out of the risk of poverty and exclusion. This indicator summarizes the number of people who are either at risk-of-poverty and/or materially deprived and/or living in households with very low work intensity. Interactions between the indicators are excluded. At risk-of-poverty are persons with an equivalized disposable income below the risk-of-poverty threshold, which is set at 60 per cent of the national median equivalized disposable income (after social transfers). The collection "material deprivation" covers indicators relating to economic strain, durables, housing, and environment of the dwelling. Severely materially deprived persons have living conditions severely constrained by a lack of resources and have experienced at least four out of the nine following deprivations items: cannot afford (i) to pay rent or utility bills, (ii) keep home adequately warm, (iii) face unexpected expenses, (iv) eat meat, fish, or a protein equivalent every second day, (v) a week holiday away from home, (vi) a car, (vii) a washing machine, (viii) a colour TV, or (ix) a telephone. People living in households with very low work intensity are people aged 0–59 living in households where the adults worked less than 20 per cent of their total work potential during the past year. Data source: Eurostat.

6 Reinforcing Europe's failed fiscal regulatory state

Scott Greer and Holly Jarman

Introduction

Europe's monetary policymakers have saved the Euro. They protected the European monetary system. They prevented obvious defaults on government debt and ended speculative attacks on individual countries. They defended a currency union that has all the deflationary properties of the gold standard, which is a notable achievement in democratic states, and fought off the first real challenge to their decisions from a democratically-elected member state government. They have done all this while advancing a certain kind of European integration, giving the EU a range of powers and responsibilities to oversee essentially the fiscal and public policies of its member states. They have, in other words, built a much more complex, legally entrenched, and powerful fiscal regulatory state for the EU.

The EU has long been a nearly ideal case of a "regulatory state", capable of regulating but not redistributing or even paying the costs associated with implementing its rules (Majone 1994; Schelkle 2009). This is because its core tool for public policy, whether labour law, environmental law, or competition law, is law. EU policy is mostly about the development, deployment, and centralized or decentralized enforcement[1] of regulations on markets and on member states. Unlike most other governments, it has few of its own resources. The Commission is a small and policy-focused organization, and its budget is a derisory one per cent of the EU GDP, most of which goes to structural funds projects or agricultural policy and does not meaningfully compensate for the effects of the internal market or EU law (Pasimeni 2014). The costs of regulations are borne by the regulated, after all.

This European regulatory state has long had a fiscal side, with the EU deploying regulations to constrain member state fiscal policy, but it was weak – persistently violated, and rewritten in 2005 to suit Germany and France when they were in violation. The EU's response to its various debt crises has been to substantially expand the breadth, automaticity, and punitiveness of this regulation over member state finances, rather than add other policy tools, such as redistribution, that would stabilize its union. The ambition and integrative drive of the reforms is striking and underappreciated. The breadth and intimacy of fiscal surveillance and the mechanisms for punishing transgressions of the Stability and Growth Pac is a dramatic increase in the formal powers of the EU. It is intended to have significant, constraining effects on domestic democratic politics.[2] The EU now has a competency over the detailed shape of every aspect of the welfare state, with member states' health, education, pension, and other policies subject to EU review and censure in the name of fiscal stringency.

It is a big step for EU integration, but a step in the same direction as before; towards reinforcing its fiscal regulatory state. The next two sections discuss the content of their choice in more detail. European integration did not have to be a product of the crisis, and neither did a redoubled commitment to a fiscal regulatory approach that puts all the burden of adjustment to the Euro on domestic budgets and workers. Europe's political leaders have opted for neither a breakup of its unstable currency zone nor the kind of redistribution that would take the burden of adjustment off of their populations. As of late summer 2015, the Greek government, despite strong support for its challenge to the Eurozone, caved in and accepted an agreement that keeps it in the Euro at a very high price. Even the left-wing government of Alex Tsipras, with a platform opposed to austerity, popular support ratifying its position, and an invitation from the German finance minister to a (wholly illegal) five-year holiday from the currency (Taylor 2015), would not take the step to leave the Euro that is so strongly associated with austerity and economic crisis. Breakup was averted. Meanwhile, traditional side-payments in the EU budget such as structural funds, or even the newer investment schemes, are clearly inadequate to cope with the disparities in the EU, while the substantial sums of money spent on rescuing government debt of the countries in receivership constitutes a transfer of public money from creditor states to the bondholders more than the citizens and is not supposed to continue. Instead, the new EU fiscal governance regime that they have designed extends and strengthens the EU's regulatory policies over fiscal policy while effectively requiring that signatories of its Fiscal Compact treaty constitutionalize restrictive EU budget rules.

We conclude that the success of this arrangement is unclear and frankly unlikely – as we would expect from the difficulties that the Eurozone fiscal regulatory state experienced before 2010. It is unlikely that the putatively credibility-enhancing powers of the fiscal governance system saved the Euro. As we argue below, there is a strong case that the European Central Bank, rather than a convincing preventative regime with credible commitments to austerity, has been maintaining the European monetary system. Nor is it clear that it will work on its own terms. Reformed EU fiscal governance builds in multiple, redundant, and much tougher mechanisms for monitoring and punishing member state decisions, reinforced by a treaty; incorporates an ambitious new European Semester in order to "reform" areas such as health and education long thought beyond the EU's competencies; and extends its decentralized enforcement provisions with domestic constitutional amendments. Nonetheless, the problems governments face, the effects of economic cycles, party politics, and domestic politics could still create a coalition that could blunt its implementation, notably in the Council.[3] Nor is it clear that it will produce broader benefits that justify such major changes. There is essentially no evidence that austerity on its own produces economic growth, and without economic growth it is very difficult to satisfy the expectations of bond markets or voters.

In short, we argue that the Eurozone fiscal governance system is a major increase in EU power, but one that perpetuates a regulatory approach to fiscal policy that has historically failed to address the problems of the Euro, and that while fiscal governance can constrain member states it is unlikely to be a credible constraint on overall fiscal policy. We make the argument in the following sections. First we discuss the crisis measures taken by the "troika" in peripheral Eurozone member states, where the EU became involved in extremely intimate domestic policymaking in areas such as healthcare and labour law. The subsequent section discusses the EU's formal, institutional response, which was a block of legislation, an intergovernmental treaty (with constitutional effects in its signatories), and a large new apparatus dedicated to making EU fiscal rules more effective by broadening them into more policy areas and increasing the force and automaticity of their punishments. This structure has significant effects on politics, with limited participation by member state legislatures, the European Parliament, or interests (civil society) relative to older EU politics – and use of the data from often-derided soft law mechanisms to formulate arguments and targets.

There are a variety of political reasons why the EU might have preferred an expanded fiscal regulatory state over more obvious options such as breaking up the currency union or creating redistributive mechanisms to cushion the effects of speculation and economic change. It is clear, however, that fiscal governance did not stop the bond market crisis. As the fourth section explains, the ECB did that, while also taking on a set of unorthodox roles that neither treaties nor economic theory suggest it should. The EU's mostly right-wing governments are not alone worldwide in opting for austere fiscal policy for themselves and others but accepting more exotic monetary policy interventions by central banks to avoid deflation, albeit with disturbing distributional effects.

Our conclusion is that the Eurozone fiscal regulatory state will continue to malfunction. There is no clear reason to expect that it will succeed on its own terms (constraining member state fiscal and public policy), or produce growth or equity. The European Union faces a dangerous situation. It is equipped with big new claims of authority over member states and their policies, but is at risk of those claims being rejected by states and their voters.

Eurozone crisis measures: conditional lending for structural adjustment

Economic Adjustment Programmes, aka Memoranda of Understanding, are the conditions on the loans that the Troika of IMF, ECB and Commission (on behalf of the European Financial Stability Fund and the European Financial Stabilization Mechanism and, as of September 2012, the European Financial Stability Mechanism) oversee.[4] They emerged as the ad hoc responses to real or expected crises in the debt markets of peripheral states but, as subsequent sections below explain, have now been formalized (in the two-pack, below) as a response and deterrent to future crisis. The basic structure of conditional lending is simple: lenders set a number of requirements for policy change and fiscal targets, and "tranches" of the loan are contingent on fulfilling the policy requirements. EAP conditionality is tough, but it is worth noting that it comes with support far beyond what indebted countries in the rest of the world could receive: the two Greek bailouts so far total about €190 billion, for a country with a GDP of just under €300 billion per year.

The EAPs are intended to change the trajectories of countries in deep trouble, some of which had clear structural problems even before the boom that busted in 2008, and deter countries from behaviour that might lead them to similar crises. They assume that moral hazard and bad public policy caused the crises of the Eurozone, and can be addressed with painful reforms (pain, to address the moral hazard; reforms, to address the lack of competitiveness; and painful reforms, to overcome domestic interests that otherwise would block change). Moral hazard, meanwhile, has apparently been redefined from its original meaning into something that applies to debtors rather than lenders. Deterring borrowing, rather than rash lending, is the new meaning of moral hazard and is the purpose of the policy.

This is not good economic history. Specific stories varied in both the causes of the crises and the specific origins of the EAPs. Ireland and Cyprus did not request their EAPs but were forced into them by other member states worried about financial contagion. Spain received a bailout but escaped an EAP in name and conditionality, probably because the Spanish government knew that a formal bailout for Spain would be too expensive and risky. Likewise, the underlying problems and proximate causes of their debt problems were also different. Only in Greece and possibly Cyprus was there a strong argument that distinctively bad government, rather than speculative private financial activities, was the main problem. Ireland and Spain had been compliant with Eurozone fiscal targets and enjoyed fiscally stronger positions than Germany in 2008. Their problem was that the good times were financed by speculative capital inflows, and that the chosen solution was the nationalization of bad banking debts rather than sharing losses with speculative investors. It is not at all clear why structural adjustment lending was the solution for them.

The operation and effects of structural adjustment conditional lending have been much discussed in a large international literature reviewed by Greer (2014a) and summarized in the rest of this section (also Rodrik 2006). The form is of a conditional loan, and the content is "structural adjustment", which means liberalization (e.g. deregulation of markets, including labour protection), privatization (of state-owned enterprises), reduction in state expenditure (e.g. through reduced pay and conditions for civil servants) and, in the EU cases, some increased taxes and improved tax collection.

The form of conditional lending turns out to be a disppointing vehicle for reform.[5] Compliance tends to be poor. In general, compliance with ultimata without a sense of ownership tends to be poor. Structural adjustment lending is just that – an ultimatum. Proliferating complex demands for policy change, meanwhile, creates more opportunities for noncompliance. It is often hoped that structural adjustment will displace corrupt elites and practices, but they frequently manage to pass on the cost of the cuts to more vulnerable populations. It is not hard to see how budget cuts in health or education might lead to reduced access rather than reduced corruption. These problems produce a running debate: do structural adjustment policies produce undesired outcomes, or does poor compliance with the good ideas explain the repeated failures of states to escape poverty through accepting conditional structural adjustment loans (Vreeland 2007)?

The content of structural adjustment reforms is focused on budgetary constraint, labour market liberalization, privatization, and deregulation. In the EAPs, it means policies including liberalization of markets in areas such as energy, transportation, and services; reductions in salaries and benefits for public employees; privatization of some state owned firms; changes in labour law to make hiring and firing easier; and a few targeted investments such as health IT. In content, the record is also bad. This package, found in the EAPs as well as most other structural adjustment programmes, has mostly negative effects on society and social investment that are not reliably balanced by economic improvements (Huber and Stephens 2012). It does not produce economic growth on average (Easterly 2005), and the dispersion in economic growth among countries exiting structural adjustment is large (so if we remove successful outliers like developmental South Korea, whose success is hardly due to obeying the IMF, its record becomes worse). Nor does it produce social gains, and it costs those who cannot delay activities such as ill health, intrauterine development, labour market entry, or primary education until better economic times (Peabody 1996). It usually seems to increase income inequality. It also produces complex unexpected outcomes when structural adjustment plans are put into practice, as a vast literature cataloguing policy failures attests.[6]

The record of the EAPs in Europe is, as the structural adjustment literature would predict, poor. Compliance with specific policies must be inferred from the periodic EAP reports; what it suggests is that Greece was strikingly noncompliant and Ireland especially compliant. As of mid-2015 Ireland and Portugal have exited their full-scale EAPs, as has Spain its partial EAP. As of the end of 2014, according to Eurostat, the debt-to-GDP ratio of the four Eurozone countries was between 177.1 per cent in Greece, and 107.5 per cent in Ireland. For comparison, the equivalent numbers are 74.7 per cent for Germany, 95 per cent for France, 91.9 per cent for the Eurozone overall, and a low of 10.6 per cent for Estonia. The ex-Troika countries are all still vulnerable to speculative attack, and are, like most of the EU, nowhere near the shared target of a 60 per cent debt-to-GDP ratio. Most economic indicators remain worrisome, notably unemployment. In December 2014, Eurostat's reported unemployment rates were: Greece, 25.8 per cent, Cyprus, 16.4 per cent, Portugal 13.4 per cent and Ireland 10.5 per cent, which is concentrated among the youth. Such unemployment is by this point probably structural and difficult or impossible to reverse without rapid economic growth and effective, expensive, active labour market policies.

The EAPs were chronologically the first major part of post-2008 Eurozone fiscal governance, and have been entrenched in subsequent law as the EU's emergency response to future sovereign debt crises. They were an intrusive and expensive policy intervention better known in developing countries than in Europe, but their policy prescriptions have been quite conventional for decades, and it is unsurprising that they have faced serious implementation problems and have been unable to create growth or resolve the debt problems of the peripheral countries in EAPs. Their structure, however, reaffirmed the regulatory approach, assuming that crisis was down to bad behaviour by their governments, that pain was a solution to an assumed moral hazard problem cantered in public sector borrowers, and that reforms to produce growth would create a sustainable future fiscal profile.

When the newly elected Syriza-led government of Alex Tsipras challenged the Troika in 2015, it failed. Despite a referendum specifically rejecting the terms set by the Eurogroup of Eurozone finance ministers, negotiating on behalf of the Troika, the government caved and accepted a new and longer list of conditions for structural adjustment as the price of receiving ongoing ECB support and starting negotiations on a new EAP. The pain in Greece might demonstrate to voters in other creditor states that challenging the Eurozone power structure is futile. It also showed how some of the provisionality of the Troika is becoming entrenched. For example, the Eurogroup, despite being the key body negotiating on behalf of the ECB, Commission, and member states, was an informal group that refused to meet with the Greek Finance minister. Such informal groups are quite conventional in European governance, but it is something of a novelty for one to assume such power with so little formalization. Likewise, the ECB's restrictions on support for the Greek banking sector forced the economic crisis which caused sryiza to back down, another remarkable action for a central bank with no such remit.

The permanent reforms

The Troika was a crisis measure with no clear basis in the treaties and a highly unorthodox relation to the legal and theoretical role of the Commission and ECB. Since 1992, Eurozone policymakers, unwilling to break up the monetary union or make sufficient internal transfers to cushion against economic shocks and imbalances, have instead focused on trying to make sure that states run tight enough budgets to withstand shocks. In practice, that has meant a long series of efforts to incorporate a bias towards tight fiscal policies and internal devaluation into fiscal policies across the EU.

There were a variety of theoretical ways to save the currency union, involving redistribution between people and governments, but the only ones adopted are the ones that advance the European fiscal regulatory state (Hodson 2013). European elites, especially those of Northern European creditor countries, seem more willing to share rules than money (which makes sense if we assume that their voters do not trust the voters of other countries – if I do not trust you, regulating your behaviour is more sensible than giving you money). Given that France had both Northern (large private bank exposure to peripheral government debt) and Southern (criticized for an overgrown state) characteristics, its position was ambiguous, which cemented Germany's position as the key actor.

The origins of the plan seem to lie with German Chancellor Angela Merkel's office, which wanted to support massive intervention to preserve the Eurozone but needed to promise German voters and possibly the German Constitutional Court that debtor countries were getting no free lunch and that no such interventions would happen in the future (e.g. Bastasin 2012; Hewitt 2013). There was little question that Germany would act to preserve the Euro. The Eurozone is a major market for German exports, and German banks were heavily exposed to European sovereign debt markets.

Stated theoretically, the idea is to harden the ineffective budget constraint on profligate nations. Lenders acted like the weaker Eurozone economies were ultimately guaranteed by the stronger Eurozone economies, creating what might be seen as a soft budget constraint (though as with much in this episode, the stated rationale is weak: it is not clear whether peripheral governments did ever assume they would be bailed out; the assumption that they thought they faced a soft budget constraint might be just empirically wrong). If there is a soft budget constraint, runs the argument, it will be exceeded, and lead to either bailouts with attendant moral hazard problems or crises (Rodden 2005 presents the argument well).

If repeated violations of the Stability and Growth Pact (SGP) meant a soft budget constraint then the EU certainly had one. The SGP was violated by every Eurozone state but Finland at some point after 2000 and was rewritten when enforcement proceedings threatened France and Germany. The accompanying Broad Economic Policy Guidelines (BEPG) were ignored the one time they actually led to a sanction on a member state (Ireland) (Hodson and Maher 2001; Hodson 2011). It is not hard to see why the old rules were not credible even before the EU commenced a series of enormous bailouts.

Member states would continue to have many reasons to violate the SGP, including principled disagreement with its theories or limitations on sovereignty, or desires to spend in order to maintain their own careers in government, or even the action of automatic stabilizers in bad economic times. What might look from one angle like credible commitment to responsibility by otherwise short-termist politicians could look from other angles like an effort to entrench certain right-wing approaches into law, or a manifesto for electoral ruin. As a result, runs the logic, a reformed SGP would have to be automatic and tough in order to effectively constrain the future policy decisions of democratic governments. The reformed EU fiscal regulatory architecture is an effort to make it automatic and tough enough to overcome all the reasons one might expect democratic politicians to break its rules.

The "six-pack"

The 2011 reform of the SGP was known as the "six-pack", consisting of four regulations and two directives. These six pieces of law were designed to formalize and strengthen the EU's fiscal surveillance regime – the regime that had failed to prevent the Eurozone countries from heading into a deep recession that threatened monetary union itself. Thanks to the crisis, member states that had failed to discipline themselves in previous years were now more willing (or more easily pushed) to bind themselves to a formal fiscal disciplinary regime.

The SGP has two arms: a preventative arm (Art. 121 TFEU), which focuses on monitoring member states' economies and economic policies, and a corrective arm (Art. 126 TFEU), which comes into play when states are non-compliant. Regulation 1175/2011 reformed the SGP's preventative arm, establishing an annual cycle of economic monitoring called the European Semester (elaborated below). It empowers the Commission and Council to formulate guidelines for economic and employment policy, monitor their implementation, and conduct surveillance to prevent and correct broadly defined "macroeconomic imbalances"

Council Regulation 1177/2011 reformed the SGP's corrective arm, which consists largely of the Excessive Deficit Procedure (EDP). It expands the EDP to focus not only on the Maastricht criterion for an excessive deficit, but also that for an excessive debt. The Commission decides if a member state has broken or is at risk of breaking either or both rules, with the Council deciding if an excessive deficit or debt then exists. Together, they make recommendations to the member state, which come with the risk of penalties – including changes in European Investment Bank lending policy, non-interest bearing deposits, and fines.

Regulation 1173/2011 enforces both arms of the SGP, specifying lodgements and fines for non-compliance with both the corrective and the preventative arms and penalties for falsifying statistics. The application of these penalties is made more automatic through the use of Reverse Qualified Majority Voting (RQMV), where recommendations are adopted unless a qualified majority vote passes the Council within 10 days. The regulation also formalizes methods of working introduced in a more ad hoc way to combat the crisis by allowing the Commission to establish "permanent dialogue" with states under the EDP.

Regulation 1176/2011 and Regulation 1174/2011 define the preventative and corrective arms of a new Macroeconomic Imbalance Procedure (MIP), a similar but parallel mechanism to the EDP that allows the Commission and Council to conduct much broader fiscal surveillance that is not just limited to the Maastricht criteria. Imbalances are defined as "any trend giving rise to macroeconomic developments which are adversely affecting, or have the potential to adversely affect, the proper functioning of the economy of a Member State or of the economic and monetary union, or of the Union as a whole" (Regulation 1176/2011, Art. 2(1)). Like the SGP, the Commission monitors and formulates recommendations under the preventative arm, creating a "scoreboard" of economic indicators, while penalties for non-compliance are dealt with under the Excessive Imbalance Procedure, a parallel to the EDP that involves interest-bearing deposits, annual fines, and decision-making by RQMV.

Finally, Council Directive 2011/85/EU requires EU member states (except the UK) to adopt national fiscal rules that support compliance with the Maastricht reference values. These national rules must not only specify the target, but also outline the procedure for monitoring compliance and the consequences of failing to comply.

The Treaty on Stability, Coordination and Governance

The Treaty on Stability, Coordination and Governance (TSCG) was an attempt to build the six-pack's new emphasis on fiscal discipline into treaty law and tie it to a formal bailout mechanism – but it is not itself an EU law. Rather, it is a separate international treaty signed in 2012. Currently in force, the TSCG is binding on Eurozone states, while other states can choose to be bound in whole or in part once they adopt the Euro. The United Kingdom and the Czech Republic did not sign the treaty.

Because the TSCG is not an EU law, it runs in parallel with the six-pack, although there are many similarities between the two. The TSCG re-states the SGP's debt rule and definitions of excessive deviation and exceptional circumstances. States are required to move towards the same goals – medium-term objectives – they outline through the SGP.

But the TSCG goes further than the SGP in several key respects. It commits contracting states to a structural deficit no higher than 0.5 per cent of the GDP (or 1 per cent of the GDP for member states with debt below 60 per cent of the GDP). States must convert their commitments into national law of a "binding force and permanent character, preferably constitutional", and create independent bodies to monitor their budgetary discipline. The TSCG, therefore, essentially constitutionalizes budget rules, taking the kind of "debt-brakes" (*schuldenbremsen*) seen in Germany and Switzerland to the EU level and diffusing them in member state constitutions.

Rather than the Council and Commission playing roles in enforcement, the Court of Justice of the European Union (CJEU) can require a state to implement the new rules, and impose fines for non-compliance. That is a far cry from the SGP's dependence on the Council doing the sanctioning, which obviously meant countries with voting power would never be willingly sanctioned. Eurozone members' fines will go to the ESM. Non-Eurozone member states under pressure, determined to stay close to the core of Europe, or with a taste for this kind of fiscal policy, can join the treaty. If they are fined, the funds go to the EU general budget.

The bailout mechanism is the European Financial Stability Mechanism (EFSM), which is a fund to be used to stabilize economies – in most cases, by buying debt. It is a change from the Maastricht framework because it envisions financial support to countries in trouble; the original Maastricht theory had no provision for bailouts as a condition of its passage. Receiving a bailout from the EFSM is conditional on adhering to the TSCG.

The "two-pack"

To consolidate the six-pack reforms, the TSCG, and the ad hoc arrangements created to deal with states facing the worst economic situations, two more regulations were passed in 2013, known as the "two-pack".

Regulation 473/2013 applies to Eurozone states not in distress – those not operating under Economic Adjustment Programmes. It adds a common timeline to the European Semester, strengthening the cycle of monitoring and policy recommendations carried out by the Commission. States must submit their draft budgetary plans to the Commission by October, which must contain "relevant information on the general government expenditure by function, including on education, healthcare and employment, and, where possible, indications on the expected distributional impact of the main expenditure and revenue measures". If a draft plan is non-compliant with the SGP, the Commission can ask the member state to revise it. The Commission assesses each plan and adopts an opinion on each by the end of November, along with a report on the budgetary situation within the Eurozone overall. Plans must be approved by national parliaments by the end of December.

Regulation 472/2013, the other half of the two-pack, applies to Eurozone states in distress – those receiving financial aid. It essentially formalizes and regularizes the Troika procedure for the future (necessary, given the fragile legal bases for the constitution and actions of the Troika in the 2010 and 2011 bailouts). These states can be made subject to "enhanced surveillance that goes beyond that required of other member states. Member states under enhanced surveillance must adopt corrective measures in consultation with the Commission and possibly other bodies including the ECB, ESAs, ESRB, or the IMF. In consulting with member states, the Commission can draw on the body of information it has gathered through the SGP and MIP, as well as information gained from interactions with the state (e.g. through the OMC), and analysis carried out by the ECB, ESAs and ESRB (stress tests, sensitivity analysis).

All of this consultation can be used to move member states in a particular direction. Through QMV, the Council can formally recommend that a state should adopt certain precautionary corrective measures or prepare a draft Economic Adjustment Programme. The Commission proposes the approval of the draft EAP, and the Council votes by QMV. Once approved, the Commission, in liaison with the ECB and IMF where necessary, is responsible for monitoring the EAP's implementation.

The reformed fiscal governance regime can seem like a logical next step in fiscal surveillance, the European integration, and the credible commitment that European policymakers say markets demand of countries with the debt and poor demographic prospects of the EU members. It implements what are called debt-brakes in the original German (balanced budget rules), something a number of countries had been doing anyway, whether out of general worry (Germany) or when under market pressure during the crisis (Spain). As for surveillance, that principle has long been established – since Bretton Woods at least – and the specific power of an EU institution to discipline states for bad budget problems was established in the SGP.

This version, unlike the SGP or recommendations from economists, promises to effectively hold governments to a new rule that is enforced by a mixture of domestic courts, EU agencies, and the CJEU. Budgets now must be constitutionally regulated by third party enforcers – if not the new domestic agencies or member state courts, then the CJEU itself. It might not be a good idea for a democracy to decide to run a structural deficit of more than 0.5 per cent of GDP; in the EU it is illegal. The magnitude of this change is stunning: in 2010, when many countries were dealing with the effects of a revenue collapse and financial crisis, they all ran far higher deficits: the United States (8 per cent), the UK (7.9 per cent), Spain (7.5 per cent), the Netherlands (5.7 per cent), Ireland (8.6 per cent) and Greece (7.4 per cent). Even relatively prosperous Germany (3.1 per cent) and parsimonious Italy (3.6 per cent) were delinquent by this standard (Kumhof and Rancière 2010). In general, we know a great deal about the effects of balanced budget rules from the American state government. They are procyclical, discourage social policy innovation and long-term planning, are generally regressive in effect (social welfare and education get cut) and produce budgetary trickery.

With the Fiscal Compact, a contestable if not falsified economic theory (Blyth 2013) is now constitutional law in Europe. Governments are to be suitably constrained, with negative effects on their citizens' ability to participate in the decisions of a meaningful political power.

The European Semester

The European Semester's name might suggest a one-off academic exercise, but it is a core part of the EU's new fiscal governance regime and arguably an ambitious, coherent, and agenda-driven example of "new governance" that goes beyond older and less effective models such as the BEPG and OMC. It draws on extensive Commission surveillance, as well as member state self-review, and the intent is to go far deeper into member state decisions. In the European Semester, the Commission Directorate-General and Council formation for economic and financial affairs manage a process that debates every country's budget in detail for not just macroeconomic compliance, surveillance compliance, and budgetary compliance, but also for policy content that reinforces the desired outcomes (ensuring that heterodox routes to the orthodox outcomes are not tried). The centrepiece of the European Semester is the Country Specific Recommendations (CSRs), in which the European Union, after receiving data and plans from governments, makes suggestions about what the governments should do.

The Semester has three separate legal bases, and each CSR is clear about which recommendations have which legal bases. One is the SGP, and is punitive. One is the MIP, and is also punitive. The third is Europe 2020, a strategy adopted by the Barroso Commission to replace the Lisbon Agenda as a theme for EU action. It highlighted "differentiated, growth-friendly fiscal consolidation, restoring normal lending to the economy, promoting growth and competitiveness, tackling unemployment and the social consequences of the crisis, and modernising public administration" as the EU's goals (European Commission 2011). Predictably, the new Juncker Commission has no investment in their predecessors' project, but there is no clear sense as of late summer 2015 of what might replace it. The 2015 CSRs still draw on it for a variety of their suggestion. Unlike the MIP and SGP bases, there is no base for coercive action should a member state ignore a CSR based on Europe 2020 or any strategy that replaces it.

Each country submits statistics (newly structured and better collected, if the rest of the six-pack is taken seriously) and its plans to improve its performance in these areas. The "semester" comes about because it runs on an annual cycle, starting in 2012, of two six-months periods during which states must make and report adjustments that will allow them to hit their targets. The Commission is the principal judge of their compliance.

While it remains to be seen if the agenda expands and contracts, in the manner of the Open Method of Coordination (OMC), the initial goals are tightly bound to the founding Regulation and the context of the six-pack. In an echo of the OMC, there is an apparatus for local and regional governments to participate in monitoring the Semester's progress. Civil society is encouraged to participate in the member states' formulation of their national action plans, and is otherwise supposed to be represented by the participation of the Economic and Social Committee in the Semester evaluations. The European Parliament has an opportunity to comment. The situation within the Commission is still evolving, but it seems that through strenuous internal politics DGs other than ECFIN are finding a role in the Semester and CSRs (for example, DG EMPL is invited to develop social and labour policy advice, and it invites health policy ideas from DG SANTE– though EMPL decides what it accepts from SANTE and ECFIN decides what it accepts from EMPL in its recommendations to the ECOFIN council).

This process largely excludes civil society, social policy ministries, and legislative accountability in most countries, but the advisory mechanisms that produce opinions and soft law are open to bureaucratic infiltration. More socially inclined politicians and bureaucrats in Brussels are especially using these fora to argue against reforms they find objectionable and ways to include their priorities in "promoting growth and competitiveness" (through human capital strategies, probably), and "tackling unemployment and the social consequences of the crisis" (Vanhercke 2013). These consultative mechanisms are the main vehicle by which some ideas from the more left-leaning "social" sector of the EU can enter the Commission's thinking in what Jonathan Zeitlin calls the "socialization" of the European Semester (Zeitlin and Vanhercke 2015). This is not the first time, after all, that the EU leaders have agreed on an essentially right-wing competitiveness agenda that slowly incorporated more and more social and environmental policies. That is the experience of the Lisbon agenda, for example. Even if the Lisbon agenda did little to advance social or environmental policy, the incorporation of social and environmental goals diffused its political force.

Three things stand out about the European Semester. One is the breadth and depth of its claims about member state policymaking. Country-Specific Recommendations (CSRs)[7] can be very specific indeed; Austria, for example, is told that its health system requires clearer lines of authority, greater use of primary care and less hospitalization, and a better medium-term financing mechanism (Austria is hardly a country in obvious crisis, but the CSRs did almost perfectly mirror the reform plans of the incumbent Austrian government). In 2015, the French were told, with the SGP as a treaty base, to reform (remove) the *numerus clausus* limiting admission to education for health professions. In theory, at least,

France, which is in an Excessive Deficit Procedure, could be fined for endangering the Eurozone with its rash fiscal policies if it were to ignore the recommendation to review admissions policies of medical schools.

Even if it is unlikely that France will be fined for its approach to medical education, this is a quite astonishing change in the governance of the EU. The EU had previously limited authority to address member state policies, let alone make clear recommendations in areas such as health, where the Lisbon Treaty reaffirmed member state responsibility for the organization and finance of health care services. Now it does, so long as the objective is fiscal rigor. The Semester procedure includes attention to both expensive welfare services such as pensions and health, and calls for reform in areas such as labour market policy – in other words, most of the areas of social policy that member states have been reluctant to turn over to the EU responsibility. It is also a clearly political process, with the Commission making sectoral recommendations based not on its own risk assessment but rather focusing on areas where it judges its impact greatest (Greer, Jarman, and Baeten in press). That includes not making tough recommendations to non-Eurozone or notably Eurosceptic governments; the UK notably escapes CSRs that are otherwise indicated.

The second aspect is the hardening of the soft law. Where do the detailed recommendations in the EAPs or CSRs come from? The answer is the large fund of data and reform proposals assembled by often-derided EU soft law projects such as the OMC, in particular the Economic Policy Committee. Even if the OMC's effects in the expected areas (learning, peer review, etc) were generally limited and contingent on local politics (e.g. De la Porte 2010; Greer 2011), they created a large fund of detailed and superficially consensual policy reform ideas. Member states rarely paid much attention to the processes producing their recommendations and reform plans, but those reform ideas and comparative data sets are now being used by DG ECFIN and the ECOFIN council, as well as the Troika, to propose detailed interventions into member state policies. Soft law paved the way for some very much harder law. How much harder remains to be seen.

The third is the extent to which the Semester process is structurally biased towards austerity – its purpose is to promote fiscal sustainability and "competitiveness" and its ultimate rationale fiscal policy coordination – but it might be losing some of its focus. Within the Commission, for example, it is run by DG ECFIN, and other DGs with more social interests are in an essentially subservient advisory role; in the Council, it is ECOFIN, the finance ministers, who run the process.[8] Since the arrival of the Juncker Commission ("a German commission" as a Commission official told one of us in May 2015), DG ECFIN has lost some of its role because its commissioner is a French Socialist, and the Secretariat General, responsible to Juncker, has taken a more commanding role.

The process systematically excludes legislatures and civil society, empowering the EU vis-à-vis states, and states vis-à-vis social interests. A study of the increasingly numerous health policy CSRs concludes that they "are framed as a means to the objective of ensuring sustainability of public finances and no as part of the pillar on combating poverty and social exclusion" and finds "a shift away from concentrating only on the financing of health systems as a lever for policy reform but also shows how health care organization and delivery is also recently being targeted as an area for policy reform;" it finds an association between public debt and CSRs, "indicating that the performance of the health system is a secondary consideration to the overall country financial situation" (Azzopardi-Muscat et al. 2015: 6), while other studies suggest that the CSRs are indeed changing member state policies in detailed areas (Stamati and Baeten 2015; Greer, Jarman and Baeten in press). The "socialization" of the Semester seems to be proceeding slowly.

The ECB as microeconomic and macroeconomic policymaker

The EU, then, has multiple complex and overlapping mechanisms, not to mention a long history of policy experiments, all intended to enforce the Stability and Growth Pact. Compliance with the SGP is supposed to compensate for the otherwise serious problems of a currency union with serious deflationary tendencies and a constant risk of debt crisis: if every member state pursues the combination of strict fiscal policy and liberalized economics, runs the theory, then the Eurozone will be safe from crisis. On one hand, the argument has little obvious validity. Spain and Ireland were model SGP-compliant states when Germany was breaking the rules (justified by the costs of its own labour market liberalization, Hartz IV) and were undercut by the combination of speculative capital outflows, private banking extravagance, and a rigid currency union. On the other hand, it is not clear that the multiple, and multiplying, SGP enforcement mechanisms developed by the EU since 2010 had any positive effect on the survival of the Eurozone. Rather, the ECB seems to be what saved the Euro by convincing bond traders that they could not win by betting on a Eurozone member state exiting the currency union.

Dyson (2001) realized immediately that the political order of the Eurozone was "ECB-centric", with a largely unaccountable central bank prominent in an institutional landscape otherwise prone to gridlock, but it took a decade to show just how right he was. It is unsurprising that a gridlocked political system such as the EU, in which the only area of intergovernmental agreement is on fiscal constraint, does not produce activist economic policies among governments, and that the unelected central bank is therefore freest to make new policy.

The ECB was designed to be unaffected by democracy, as part of both a recent worldwide move towards anti-inflation independent central banks and a concession to Germany, where the hard-money Bundesbank, *in the context of the German political economy*, contributed greatly to growth and stability (Dyson and Featherstone 1999; Hall 1994; Hall and Franzese 1998). Dyson (2014) notes the remarkable success of the Bundesbank in spreading its eccentric theories about German economic history, economic policy, and German preferences despite the inaccuracies of its ideas. The theory, broadly endorsed by the economics profession, is that the way to make a group of people such as bankers more predictable is to make them less accountable. The micro-foundations of this proposition are unclear (Adolph 2013). This means that while the continent was binding itself to the SGP goals, the ECB was autonomous and able to pursue much more radical and supportive policies (the combination of a fiscally austere political system with an activist central bank was hardly unique to Europe, as the UK and USA both showed).

The European Central Bank might have been set up – in treaty and in culture – to have very limited interventionist powers, but, as many central banks have done, it took dramatic action in a crisis. There are two clear ways it has done so. One is by the classic central banker's actions, supplemented by newer forms of quantitative easing: Mario Draghi famously promised to do "whatever it takes" to preserve the Euro (Carrel et al. 2012), and bond yields in peripheral Europe immediately began to stabilize (Hodson 2013). After he outlined the "Outright Monetary Transactions" (OMT) programme on 6 September 2012, interest rates on government debt from weaker Eurozone economies dropped further and have remained stable or shifted downward since. OMT would involve buying government debt subject to government compliance with conditions set by the rest of the EU. It is also not clear that the OMT would be legal under EU (or German) law. Fortunately, markets were reluctant to bet against a fully engaged central bank, and speculative attacks ceased (allowing the Cypriot operation, involving a Troika intervention and currency controls, to take place without causing another crisis). Second, the Eurozone economy has been stagnant, leading to announcements in September 2014 that the ECB would consider unorthodox quantitative easing, followed by a specific programme announced in January 2015.

The ECB, as a guardian of the Eurozone monetary system and an actor free to intervene, also carved out a surprising role for itself in the Troika, one reinforced by the promise of selectivity in the OMT programme (the condition for participation). The ECB is completely opaque about its operations, including its role in the Troika. There were essentially no public statements by the ECB explaining the conditions under which it would engage in any kind of unusual activity in support of a country, but its new self-appointed role in public administration, labour law reform, land use planning, and other aspects of the EAPs suggested that it would use its monetary tools to treat countries differently based on its perception of their public policies, its help to treasuries and private banks dependent on compliance with EU policy views.

Among other things, this means that the ECB can reasonably be said to have changed at least two Eurozone governments' compositions. First, it seems that the ECB forced out Silvio Berlusconi. A central bank manipulating market expectations to change a Prime Minster is possibly the only thing worse for Italian democracy than Berlusconi himself (Jones 2012; Hopkin 2012).[9] In 2015, then, the ECB chose not to expand support for Greek banks during the bank run caused by failed negotiations between the Greek government, Troika, and Eurogroup. This was the precipitating factor in the Greek government's capitulation and the resignation of its highly visible finance minister. There might be a theory under which this action has democratic legitimacy, but it would be an unusual one.

Conclusion

There are now multiple redundant, overlapping mechanisms for imposing austerity on member states. They include the kind of receivership currently being experienced in the EAP countries as well as a variety of formal structures built into the Fiscal Compact, six-pack and two-pack, and older mechanisms such as the EU strategies and the OMC. Why does the EU need so many Rube Goldberg policy regimes, all aimed at accomplishing the same, conceptually simple goal – low deficits and debts relative to the GDP? These redundant mechanisms only make sense in the context of European policymakers who, correctly, fear that democratically accountable politicians will not abide by those austere and essentially arbitrary goals, that debt markets will be aware of that and that electorates in creditor countries will want a pound of flesh from their debtors. In other words, they are trying to re-create the discipline of the gold standard through a mixture of hard and soft law.

Put together, the result is a big step forward for European integration, but a big step in the same direction it was heading before the crisis: towards a fiscal regulatory state, one built on regulations that are hard to enforce, intrude deeply into domestic public and social policy, and create losses without any compensation. The area of possible compromise between European leaders – on a fiscal regulatory state – did not change with the crisis, even if there was little or no evidence that the resulting policies worked on their own terms or supported broader objectives such as growth or equity. But even if the whole apparatus of fiscal governance and conditional lending was a smokescreen to permit the bailouts and central bank activism that ended the crisis, it remains in place nonetheless. Even if it looks like it was set up to fail, it is entrenched in law, treaties, and member state constitutions, and in theory subjects member states to a broad, deep, and automatic mechanism that shapes their fiscal and therefore public policies.

The long-term fate of the structure remains to be seen. On paper it is a substantial increase in power and responsibility for the EU vis-à-vis member states, and member state governments vis à vis actors such as parliaments and social partners, but there are good reasons to expect that it will fail on its own terms. Right-wing governments that are intellectually sympathetic to the agenda, such as Spain's, have had difficulty hitting their targets and have had to engage in the coalition-building necessary to avoid sanctions. Less right-wing governments, such as that of France, are openly threatening to break the fiscal rules. The responses to their challenges tends to blur the supposedly clear and automatic rules and decisions of the EU institutions; one possible outcome over time is that the whole mechanism remains, invasive and complex, but becomes as toothless as the BEPG or OMC (Greer 2014b).

What would happen if the EU were not dominated by parties of the right? What if policymakers began to conclude, after a long time, that their competitive liberal orientation is unjustified and inflation tolerable (McNamara 1998)? Or what if governments of the right could not hit the SGP targets in a bad economy without destroying automatic stabilizers and creating a social emergency that could have electoral consequences? The best evidence is that fiscal performance in Europe is affected by economic conditions, almost to the exclusion of other factors (LeMay-Boucher and Rommerskirchen 2014). That suggests that even a small downturn in the European economic performance will push member states away from compliance.

And finally, there is not much evidence that the programme, were it to be enforced, would produce growth. An enormous amount of research shows that there is no simple relationship between fiscal rigor and growth, including comparative political economy that points out the ways in which different economies respond to monetary and fiscal policies (the central preoccupation of the study of political economy; for an example applied to the Euro crisis; see Hall 2012). The work of Alesina, Reinhart, and Rogoff on "expansionary austerity" (Alesina 2010; Alesina and Ardagna 2010; Rogoff and Reinhart 2010; Reinhart, Reinhart and Rogoff 2012) that provided the intellectual colouring for many crisis policies has been falsified (Herndon, Ash and Pollin 2013; Guajardo, Leigh, and Pescatori 2011). At most, crisis-hit countries seem to be reverting to the mean, with some positive but minimal growth. European politicians frequently seem to talk as if growth is a binary variable, with growth present or absent. In reality, it is possible to have very low growth, and that is the situation of much of the Eurozone. If the ECB were not defending the Eurozone, and the Eurozone states it deems worthy, it is hard to say that they would be escaping debt or economic crisis.

In short, Europe's fiscal regulatory state has a very poor record on any terms but European leaders have increased their bets on it. Without any distributive or redistributive policies, the fiscal crisis response mechanisms of the EU and its member states are very weak. That means that avoiding crisis by avoiding fiscal problems is the only clear EU strategy, and that means betting heavily on a mechanism whose deficiencies are clear, whether we regard their weaknesses in terms of the difficulty of fiscal self-binding by short-termist politicians, or the highly political, distributive nature of the decisions it is taking, or the weakness of the economic theory underlying the policies. The most successful part of the system – as in, the part with any apparent success on its own terms as a discipline on member states – is probably the Semester, where it can empower governments who wish to pursue liberalizing policies against domestic opposition.

As Karl Polanyi (1944) explained in the context of the gold standard, a rigid monetary policy that pushes all the burden of adjustment onto society, without countervailing regulation and welfare states, will be unstable and deflationary at best, and create far greater crisis at worst. Europe's regulatory fiscal state has all the drawbacks of the gold standard but without its simplicity and brutal enforcement mechanisms. Policy since the crisis has been an effort to create that simplicity and power through surveillance and punishment, but for all its redundancy and intrusiveness it probably still falls short. Europe's fiscal regulatory state can do much to constrain public policy and advance a certain kind of European integration, but it is still unlikely that it will be able to force on democratic member states the degree of suffering the Euro seemingly requires. That might be a blessing.

The effort to recreate the economics of the gold standard through regulation sets up a potentially dangerous situation for the EU. The EU has taken a big step forward with the expansion of its fiscal regulatory state and it is already influencing policy. But its success on its own terms as a disciplinary mechanism or in light of broader objectives remains doubtful. The consequences are easy to view in the combination of unpalatable dilemmas that face voters and governments in Eurozone states, in the inevitable fudging of supposedly clear rules, and in the policies enacted in a continent where, as ECB President Draghi says, the "European social model is already gone" (WSJ 2012).[10] Whether such a structure can persist remains to be seen.

Acknowledgements

We would like to thank Robert Fannion, Kate McNamara and participants in the Chapel Hill conference in September 2014 for their excellent comments. This paper draws heavily on Greer et al. (2014).

Notes

1 For which, see Kelemen (2011).
2 A number of authors have argued that this crisis response is not a step forward for the EU; unlike previous crises, it produced not enough or the wrong kind of integration (Boyer 2013; Lefkofridi and Schmitter 2014). It seems to us that a significant increase in EU power vis-à-vis member states, even if ill-advised or supported by governments, fits most definitions of European integration.
3 The most extensive experiment with austerity rules, the United States, does not seem to support the idea that the rules enforce budgetary stability. Bond markets appear to do the enforcing by charging higher interest rates to what buyers see as weaker governments (Kelemen and Teo 2012).
4 For the EAPs see the "Occasional papers" site of DG ECFIN http://ec.europa.eu/economy_finance/publications/occasional_paper/index_en.htm or the country pages on the IMF website.
5 See Greer (2014a) for the literature review underpinning this and the next paragraph.
6 Perhaps the most obviously catastrophic of them all was the introduction of user fees for AIDS testing in some African structural adjustment programmes (Stein 2008).
7 For which, see http://ec.europa.eu/europe2020/making-it-happen/country-specific-recommendations/index_en.htm.
8 Council formations cannot directly comment on each other's work, so when the health ministers' Council wanted to register concerns about the austerity focus of the Semester's health policies, it had to do it through an extended commentary on a working group's report. See Council of the European Union (2013).
9 See also Donadio (2011).
10 Draghi was arguing that high youth unemployment shows that the social model in question is gone.

References

Adolph, C. 2013. *Bankers, Bureaucrats, and Central Bank Politics: The Myth of Neutrality*. Cambridge: Cambridge University Press.

Alesina, A. 2010. "Fiscal Adjustments: Lessons From Recent History." Presentation to ECOFIN Meeting, Madrid, April 15.

Alesina, A. and S. Ardagna. 2010. "Large Changes in Fiscal Policy: Taxes Versus Spending." In *Tax Policy and the Economy 24*, edited by D. Brown, pp. 35–68. Chicago, IL: University of Chicago Press.

Azzopardi-Muscat, N., T. Clemens, D. Stoner, and H. Brand. 2015. "EU Country Specific Recommendations for Health Systems in the European Semester Process: Trends, Discourse and Predictors." *Health Policy* 119(3): 375–383.

Bastasin, C. 2012. *Saving Europe: How National Politics Nearly Destroyed the Euro.* Washington, DC: Brookings Institution Press.

Blyth, M. 2013. *Austerity: the History of a Dangerous Idea.* Oxford: Oxford University Press.

Boyer, R. 2013. "Origins and Ways Out of the Euro Crisis: Supranational Institution Building in the Era of Global Finance." *Contributions to Political Economy* 32: 97–126.

Carrel, P., N. Barkin and A. Breidthardt. 2012. "Special Report: Inside Mario Draghi's Euro Rescue Plan." Reuters (25 September). Available at www.reuters.com/article/2012/09/25/us-ecb-draghi-plan-idUSBRE88O09A20120925.

Council of the European Union. 2013. *Council Conclusions on the Reflection Process on Modern, Responsive and Sustainable Health Systems.* 10 December. Brussels: Council of the European Union. Available at www.consilium.europa.eu/uedocs/cms_data/docs/pressdata/en/lsa/140004.pdf.

De la Porte, C. 2010. "State of the Art. Overview of Concepts, Indicators and Methodologies Used for Analyzing the Social OMC." Working Papers on the Reconciliation of Work and Welfare in Europe: Edinburgh: RECWOWE Publication, Dissemination and Dialogue Centre. Available at www.era.lib.ed.ac.uk/handle/1842/4775.

Donadio, R. 2011. "From Ceremonial Figure to Italy's Quiet Power Broker." *New York Times* (2 December). Available at www.nytimes.com/2011/12/03/world/europe/president-giorgio-napolitano-italys-quiet-power-broker.html?pagewanted=all&_r=0.

Dyson, K. 2001. *The Politics of the Euro-Zone: Stability or Breakdown?* Oxford: Oxford University Press.

Dyson, K. 2014. *States, Debt, and Power: 'Saints' and 'Sinners' in European History and Integration.* Oxford: Oxford University Press.

Dyson, K., and K. Featherstone. 1999. *The Road to Maastricht: Negotiating Economic and Monetary Union.* Oxford: Oxford University Press.

Easterly, W. 2005. "What Did Structural Adjustment Adjust?: The Association of Policies and Growth with Repeated IMF and World Bank Adjustment Loans." *Journal of Development Economics* 76: 1–22.

Greer, S. L. 2011. "The Weakness of Strong Policies and the Strength of Weak Policies: Law, Experimentalist Governance, and Supporting Coalitions in European Union Health Care Policy." *Regulation and Governance* 5: 187–203.

Greer, S. L. 2014a. "Structural Adjustment Comes to Europe: Lessons for the Eurozone From the Conditionality Debates." *Global Social Policy* 14(1): 51–71.

Greer, S. L. 2014b. "The Three Faces of European Union Health Policy: Policy, Markets and Austerity." *Policy and Society* 33(1): 13–24.

Greer, S. L., N. Fahy, H. Elliott, M. Wismar, H. Jarman and W. Palm. 2014. *Everything you Always Wanted to Know About European Union Health Policy but Were Afraid to Ask.* Brussels: European Observatory on Health Systems and Policies.

Greer, S. L., H. Jarman and R. Baeten. (in press) "The New Political Economy of Health in the European Union. *International Journal of Health Services.*

Guajardo, J., D. Leigh and A. Pescatori. 2011. *Expansionary Austerity: New International Evidence*. Washington, DC: International Monetary Fund.

Hall, P. A. 1994. "Central Bank Independence and Coordinated Wage Bargaining: Their Interaction in Germany and Europe." *German Politics and Society* 31(1): 1–23.

Hall, P. A. 2012. "The Economics and Politics of the Euro Crisis." *German Politics* 21: 355–371.

Hall, P. A. and Franzese, R. J. 1998. "Mixed Signals: Central Bank Independence, Coordinated Wage Bargaining, and European Monetary Union." *International Organization* 52(3): 505–535.

Herndon, T., M. Ash and R. Pollin. 2013. *Does High Public Debt Consistently Stifle Economic Growth? A Critique of Reinhart and Rogoff*. Amherst, MA: Political Economy Research Institute, University of Massachusetts Amherst. Available at www. peri.umass.edu/236/hash/31e2ff374b6377b2ddec04deaa6388b1/publication/566/.

Hewitt, G. 2013. *The Lost Continent: Europe's Darkest Hour Since World War Two*. London: Hodder & Stoughton.

Hodson, D 2011. *Governing the Euro Area in Good Times and Bad*. Oxford: Oxford University Press.

Hodson, D. 2013. "The Eurozone in 2012: 'Whatever It Takes to Preserve the Euro'?" *JCMS* 51: 183–200.

Hodson, D. and I. Maher. 2001. "The Open Method As a New Mode of Governance: The Case of Soft Economic Policy Co-ordination." *JCMS* 39: 719–746.

Hopkin, J. 2012. "A Slow Fuse: Italy and the EU Debt Crisis." *The International Spectator* 47: 35–48.

Huber, E. and Stephens. 2012. *Democracy and the Left: Social Policy and Inequality in Latin America*. Chicago, IL: University of Chicago Press.

Jones, E. 2012. "Italy's Sovereign Debt Crisis." *Survival* 54: 83–110.

Kelemen, R. 2011. *Eurolegalism: The Transformation of Law and Regulation in the European Union*. Cambridge, MA: Harvard University Press.

Kelemen, R. and T. Teo. 2012. "Law and the Eurozone Crisis." APSA 2012 Annual Meeting Paper. Available at http://papers.ssrn.com/sol3/papers.cfm?abstract_id=2107426#. UcaqZjN7sZQ.twitter.

Kumhof, M. and R. Rancière. 2010. *Inequality, Leverage and Crises*. Working paper 1-37. Washington, DC: International Monetary Fund.

Lefkofridi, Z. and P. C. Schmitter. 2014. "Transcending or Descending? European Integration in Times of Crisis." *European Political Science Review* 7(1): 3–22.

LeMay-Boucher, P. and C. Rommerskirchen. 2014. "An Empirical Investigation Into the Europeanization of Fiscal Policy." *Comparative European Politics* 13: 450–470.

Majone, G. 1994. "The Rise of the Regulatory State in Europe." *West European Politics* 17: 77–102.

McNamara, K. R. 1998. *The Currency of Ideas: Monetary Politics in the European Union*. Ithaca, NY: Cornell University Press.

Pasimeni, P. 2014. "An Optimum Currency Crisis." *European Journal of Comparative Economics* 11(2): 173–204.

Peabody, J. W. 1996. "Economic Reform and Health Sector Policy: Lessons From Structural Adjustment Programmes." *Social Science and Medicine* 43: 823–835.

Polanyi, K. 1944. *The Great Transformation: The Political and Economic Origins of our Time*. Boston, MA: Beacon.

Reinhart, C. M., V. R. Reinhart and K. S. Rogoff. 2012. "Public Debt Overhangs: Advanced-economy Episodes Since 1800." *The Journal of Economic Perspectives* 26: 69–86.

Rodden, J. A. 2005. *Hamilton's Paradox: The Promise and Peril of Fiscal Federalism.* Cambridge: Cambridge University Press.

Rodrik, D. 2006. "Goodbye Washington Consensus, Hello Washington Confusion? A Review of the World Bank's Economic Growth in the 1990s: Learning From a Decade of Reform." *Journal of Economic Literature* 44: 973–987.

Rogoff, K. and C. Reinhart. 2010. "Growth in a Time of Debt." *American Economic Review* 100: 573–578.

Schelkle, W. 2009. "The Contentious Creation of the Regulatory State in Fiscal Surveillance." *West European Politics* 32: 829–846.

Stamati, F. and R. Baeten. 2014. *Healthcare Reforms and the Crisis.* Brussels: ETUI/OSE.

Stein, H. 2008. *Beyond the World Bank Agenda: An Institutional Approach to Development.* Chicago, IL: University of Chicago Press.

Taylor, P. 2015. "Analysis: IMF Threat to Pull out of Greek Bailout Challenges Germany." Reuters (15 July). Available at www.reuters.com/article/2015/07/15/us-eurozone-greece-imf-threat-analysis-idUSKCN0PP1IS20150715.

Vanhercke, B. 2013. "Under the Radar? EU Social Policy in Times of Austerity." In *Social Developments in the European Union 2012*, edited by B. Vanhercke and D. Natali, pp. 91–120. Brussels: ETUI/ OSE.

Vreeland, J. R. 2007. *The International Monetary Fund: Politics of Conditional Lending.* Abingdon: Routledge.

WSJ. 2012. "Q&A: ECB President Mario Draghi." *The Wall Street Journal* (23 February). Available at http://blogs.wsj.com/eurocrisis/2012/02/23/qa-ecb-president-mario-draghi/.

Zeitlin, J. and B. Vanhercke. 2015. *Socializing the European Semester? Economic Governance and Social Policy Coordination in Europe 2020.* Report prepared for the Swedish Institute of European Studies. Brussels: European Social Observatory (OSE).

7 The monetary union and migration

Bruno Dallago

Introduction

After nearly eight years in the crisis, the overall situation is so different from what appeared as natural in the 1980s and the first half of the past decade, that various analysts and observers formulate the hypothesis of a new secular stagnation in the world economy.[1] The first revival of the hypothesis dates back to a speech by the former US Secretary of the Treasury Lawrence Summers (2014) in 2013.[2] In Summers' view, the main problems are the long-run effects of short-run developments when monetary policy is ineffective because of the extremely low level of interest rates.

This hypothesis found wide appeal when the IMF devoted particular attention to its discussion in the October 2014 World Economic Outlook (IMF 2014) and in its following session (IMF 2015). In the former Outlook, the IMF maintains that "[s]ecular stagnation and low potential growth in advanced economies remain important medium-term risks, given the modest and uneven growth in those economies despite very low interest rates and the easing of other brakes to the recovery" (IMF 2014: XVI). To these, the effect of protracted supply-side constraints on growth in some major emerging market economies should also be added. This risk is particularly great for the euro area and Japan, countries that "could face an extended period of low growth reflecting persistently weak private demand that could turn into stagnation" (IMF 2014: 17).

In the 2015 Outlook, the IMF observes that the decline of potential output growth in advanced market economies started already in the early 2000s and worsened with the global financial crisis. Conversely, the decline in emerging market economies began only after the crisis. Secular stagnation will likely remain as long as demand is weak, inflation is expected to stay below target for an extended period, and monetary policy is constrained at the zero lower bound. The deep reasons of long-term stagnation, according to the IMF, are aging populations in both advanced and emerging market economies. In the former, stagnation is also the outcome of the gradual increase in capital growth that the recovery from the crisis is expected to bring from current rates. In emerging market economies, additional factors of stagnation are the further decline of the potential output growth, due to aging populations, weaker investment, and lower total factor productivity growth coming from their successful technological catching-up.

It is in this context that the European crisis should be placed: as one of the victims of such stagnation and also as one of the causes. There are two components that are worth stressing. Over the years preceding the crisis, there was a significant build-up of debt and asset bubbles also in the European Union. This left a legacy of high levels of debt, which in the European Union were in large part converted into sovereign debts. This created in some countries a dramatic spiral of high financing needs for keeping the debt under control, which fuel further debt accumulation over GDP when growth rates are lower than real interest rates. A debt-deflation spiral could be the consequence.

While macroeconomic imbalances can be fixed through policies even in the EU if a common understanding is found, there is a long-run structural factor that is bound to remain. This is the demographic factor, that is generally negative all over the European Union and particularly so in some countries, such as Portugal, Italy, Greece, Germany – all countries with crude birth rates below 0.9 per cent. In various other countries the rate is between 0.9 per cent and 1.0 per cent, including Spain, Romania, Croatia, Hungary, Bulgaria, Austria, Malta, and Poland. The European Union is barely above 1 per cent on average and the Eurozone is at 0.7 per cent. According to the Economist, the EU is set to have a decline of 96 million workers over the next 40 years (Buttonwood 2014). Considering that various EU countries have problems with productivity growth (Dallago 2016), losing such an impressive number of workers clearly threatens deal a major blow to the future of European economies. Here is where the fundamental role of immigration comes in (according to *The Economist*, the demographic deficit could decrease to 40 million workers over the next 40 years as a result of immigration; Buttonwood 2014).

Monetary unification and labour

The theory of the optimum currency area (OCA) offers a technical explanation of the fact that a monetary union works well only if certain conditions are given and suggests what could compensate for their absence (Baldwin and Wyplosz 2012).[3] An optimum currency area is usually defined as a group of countries or regions with such economic and institutional features that make the use of a common currency economically efficient compared to having two or more currencies.

The classical analysis of the OCA (Mundell 1961; Kenen 1969; McKinnon 1963) stresses that member economies must be open, their production profiles wide, their production diversified, and their resources and labour in particular mobile, and prices and wages flexible. Under those conditions the common currency assures its benefits without major costs or threats. Yet a common currency is after all a political undertaking and countries may decide to proceed with a currency union for the sake of its political benefits even if the above named criteria are not fully respected (Dallago 2015). In these conditions, the currency union has additional instruments to be sustainable.

The working of the labour markets is particularly important for the monetary union approaching an OCA. Price and wage rigidity makes adjustment processes difficult, lengthy and costly. It is the institutional features of labour markets, often related to undeveloped welfare systems, that establish the degree of rigidity of wages. It is the nature of enterprises and their interaction, and particularly their control over markets and their ability to establish monopoly prices, that define price rigidity.

Eurozone countries have different labour markets and other types of institutions. The type of trade unions existing in a country and the degree of centralization of wage bargaining are particularly important features. Another important difference lies in the legal systems. Different legal systems lead to different transmissions of symmetric shocks, since they define the constraints to economic activity and the incentives for economic actors (Acemoglu and Robinson 2012; North 1990).

The OCA theory highlights that a monetary union needs flexible wages and prices or, alternatively, labour mobility to adjust the effects of asymmetric shocks. Under those conditions labour would flow where it is more needed and better remunerated and capital would flow where labour is more abundant and cheaper. This would help re-balance the economy and avoid massive involuntary unemployment, thus easing financial and political tensions within the union.

Unfortunately, labour mobility in the Eurozone is low and wage and price flexibility are also low compared to the United States benchmark. Thus, the adjustment that could not go through prices and wages goes primarily through quantities in the form of unemployment, falling production, and decreasing market shares in the international market. Internal devaluation policies that put labour under great economic and political pressure gave some results – in Ireland, Greece, Portugal, Spain, and Italy (Dallago 2016; O'Rourke et al. 2013) – to the disadvantage of overall economic performance and social and political stability. With time, wages were reduced, but this did not increase employment, which instead declined. Public finances suffered as a consequence, and public debts increased.

Given the difficulties of re-establishing a viable economic situation through internal devaluation policies, are there better ways to reach the desired outcome in the labour market? In particular, would a better management of immigration offer any opportunity to increase labour mobility? Migration is a synonym for an open and integrated world. This primarily concerns migration for economic reasons, but may also explain (at least partly) migration for other reasons (to avoid wars, persecution, discrimination or authoritarian regimes).[4] One problem with migration is that it flows in two directions: to the individual country and out of it; although one flow typically prevails. The "normal" flow is from poorer, less democratic or politically unstable countries to richer, more democratic and politically stable countries. Wage and labour conditions differentials as well as job opportunities play important roles in determining the labour flows between countries. The interesting question here is to consider whether the inflow of migrants, particularly skilled ones, can guarantee to the Eurozone vulnerable countries a labour market effect that is similar to that of an internal devaluation without having the negative economic and social consequences typical of the latter.

On migration

Migration increased at an accelerated rate since the mid-1980s in coincidence with globalization. Other components of globalization, such as world trade, increased at a similar pace while others, such as foreign direct investments and financial flows, grew at a definitely higher pace than migration since the 1990s. When measured over the period since 1960, migration expanded at approximately the rate of the world population. It should also be noted that the growth of migration since the 1990s is overestimated by political events, because it includes the dislocation of people following the disruption of the former Soviet Union and Yugoslavia as well as the separation of the former Czechoslovakia. These observations would lead to the conclusion that migration plays a secondary role in globalization, whose main aspects are finance and trade.

The situation in the South-North flows of migration shows a different picture, which should lead to the conclusion that migration is a major component of globalization and a strategically important one (Docquier and Rapoport 2012). Two aspects are worth stressing. First, the share of immigrants (foreign-born people) tripled since 1960 and doubled since 1985 as a share of the population of high-income countries (OECD area) and grew in line with international trade. Second, immigrants to the high-income countries are increasingly skilled and educated (brain drain).

High-skill migration to the OECD countries accounted for a rapidly increasing share of the total migration. While the number of low-skill immigrants living in the OECD countries increased by 30 per cent during the 1990s, the number of high-skill immigrants increased by 70 per cent.[5] A part of high-skill migrants came from other developed countries. However, the number of those who came from developing countries doubled in the decade. About half of total world migration and 85 per cent of high-skill migration is directed towards the OECD countries. In 2000, the total number of high-skill immigrants recorded in the OECD was 20.5 million. Most of them were recorded in six countries: the United States, Canada, Australia, Germany, the United Kingdom and France. It should be noted that some OECD member countries, such as Mexico, Poland, and Turkey, are countries of out-migration. Considering that approximately 15 per cent of the high-skill migrants go to non-OECD countries, the overall estimate of brain drain is approximately 24 million (Docquier and Rapoport 2012).

The findings of a recent OECD study covering the first decade of the new century (2000/01 to 2010/11) reach similar results (Arslan et al. 2014). In this period, the number of migrants aged 15 and older in OECD countries increased by 38 per cent and reached the overall number of 106 million. The education level of migrants increased even more: one third of overall migrants, or about 35 million in 2010/11, had tertiary education, an increase of 70 per cent over the previous decade.[6] A third of the migrants with tertiary education came from Asia. The economic crisis interrupted the successful assimilation of immigrants in the labour market of OECD countries. Due to the deterioration of the economic situation in destination countries, unemployment rates of emigrants increased between 2005/06 and 2010/11, particularly among Latin American and African migrants.

Brain drain is one of the major problems related to migration. It is at the same time a potential loss for the sending country and a potential gain for the recipient country. In recent decades, the number of high-skill migrants has increased dramatically. In relative terms the situation is variegated. The highest emigration rates are from middle-income countries. This observation apparently supports the interpretation that migrating is a rational decision for which incentives are needed, but also that the means to migrate are necessary. This pattern is particularly evident in high-skill emigrants: incentives to look for a higher remuneration for one's human capital and better jobs are high. Potential emigrants also have the means to afford emigration, and their human capital is of a higher value and more transferable. The Caribbean, the Pacific, Sub-Saharan Africa, and Central America are the regions with the highest brain drain rates (Docquier and Rapoport 2012). It is also interesting to note that emigrating as a student appears to be a particularly profitable strategy: getting a degree in the immigration country guarantees on average higher wages and employment rates compared to those of emigrants who received their degrees in their countries of origin (Coulombe and Tremblay 2009).

Immigration in general, and high-skill immigration in particular, appear critically important for the development of rich countries. Employment of high-skill immigrants is an increasingly important feature of US firms, and the role of firms in immigration is bound to become more important in order to match the increasing heterogeneity of production. In the United States, substantial parts of the immigration framework were designed to allow firms to choose the immigrants that they want to hire. Kerr et al. (2013) studied the impact of skilled immigrants on the employment structures of the US firms and found both local and immigrant skilled workers. There is consistent evidence linking the hiring of young skilled immigrants to greater employment of skilled workers by the firm; a greater share of the firm's workforce being skilled; a higher share of skilled workers being immigrants; and a lower share of skilled workers being over 40 years of age. In 2008, immigrants represented 16 per cent of the US workforce with a bachelor's degree, and they accounted for 29 per cent of the growth in this workforce during the 1995–2008 period. In occupations closely linked to innovation and technology commercialization, the share of immigrants was almost 24 per cent.

The United States is the country that perhaps relied most on immigrants and whose economic development was the most dependent upon high-skill immigrants. Their experience is therefore an important benchmark for other countries. The processes of workforce aging and fertility slow-down are significant also in the United States and consequently the importance of skilled immigration has the potential to increase significantly. These conclusions offer important hints for the role that immigration could have in helping developed countries exit the crisis and start to grow again.

There are also cases that demonstrate the waste of the high-skill immigrants' potential – waste brain, as defined by Reyneri (2007) – where high-skill immigrants are offered under-qualified jobs and low opportunities for their professional mobility. Although Italy fares fairly well in international comparison on the conduct of immigration (Huddleston et al. 2011), there are numerous cases of over-qualified immigrants compared to the jobs available to them, particularly among women (Fullin and Reyneri 2011; Pintaldi and Pontecorvo 2013). Based on the Italian Labour Force Survey, Fullin and Reyneri (2011) found that a great majority of immigrants to Italy do not run a higher risk of unemployment than Italians do. However, immigrants are highly disfavoured in the socio-professional status of their jobs. Their disadvantage increases at higher levels of educational attainment.

In 2012, 962,000 highly educated immigrants, or 41.2 per cent of employed immigrants, had an excess of education compared to what was requested for their job, a share that was more than twice the comparable share for Italians (Pintaldi and Pontecorvo 2013). The share was particularly high in services to families. Over-qualification of foreigners tends to last for years. High-skill immigrants, and women in particular, suffer from further disadvantages that are evident from both the number of hours worked (9.5 per cent of degree-holder immigrants are under-employed, compared to 3.0 per cent of Italians) and their wages. The net wage received by immigrants is nearly 26 per cent lower than that received by Italians with comparable jobs and education. Wage differentials have been growing since 2008 and they tend to increase with the level of education and age. In 2012, wage differentials on average amounted to nearly 30 per cent for degree holders and to 16.7 per cent for immigrants with a general school certificate.

In spite of negative developments, high-skill immigration is undergoing important transformations. According to the findings of the workshop on skilled labour, held at Macquarie University in Australia, the surge in international migrants and students from rapidly developing countries contributed to new forms of international migration, such as brain circulation and international students' flows (Guo et al. 2014).[7] These forms of migration opened up the way for the migration policies of traditionally host countries to affect the economy and skill base of the sending countries as never before. Migration policy is and remains a domestic tool for managing population flows. It is becoming evident, however, that it is also evolving into a tool that can be used to foster economic development and international relations.

Migration to the European Union and migration within the European Union

Migration to the European Union shares many of the features of migration to developed rich countries. Immigration within a monetary union is a politically sensitive issue, perhaps more than in a sovereign country.[8] Billiet et al. (2014) used the fifth round of the European Social Survey data for 23 countries to estimate the perceived threat from immigrants. They found the perceived threat to be higher in countries with a lower GDP growth, particularly when coupled with unemployment.

A further problem is that the member states of the European Union do not have a united approach to migration (Cardwell et al. 2013). The EU strives to achieve coherence in its policies regarding immigration, particularly with its most advanced attempt to integrate the non-member states' interests into its policy agenda. However, in the EU policy the security measures, such as border control and readmission, dominate over "migration and development" and labour migration measures (Wunderlich 2013). This is certainly a politically easy, yet economically ineffective approach.

Two aspects of immigration stand out: first, the features of the employment of immigrants and their remuneration compared to local employees, and second, irregular immigration and employment. Venturini and Villosio (2008) use a matched employer-employee panel dataset with data for the years 1990–2003 to study the labour market assimilation of foreign workers in Italy. They found that foreigners receiving higher wages are the least likely to stay. When entering into employment in the private sector, foreigners earn the same wages as natives. However, wages diverge with on-the-job experience. Moreover, foreigners are disadvantaged in job opportunities even upon entrance and the disadvantage increases over time. Differences vary across sectors (wage and employment differentials are the largest in the construction sector) and provenience of immigrants (Africans have the worst career prospects while Eastern Europeans and Asians have the best prospects among immigrants). Venturini and Villosio (2008) have also found that the general pattern for foreign workers appears to be a fragmented career, either being confined to seasonal or temporary jobs or alternating between regular and irregular employment.

Irregular employment is traditionally spread throughout various countries and so is irregular employment among immigrants. Irregular employment of immigrants is spread in unskilled jobs, while it is definitely contained in high-skill jobs. Venturini (1999) used official statistics to examine how immigrants working in the irregular economy affected employment in the regular economy in Italy between 1980 and 1995. She found that an increase in irregular units of labour produced a reduction in the use of regular labour, but the effect was very limited. Moreover, there was a relevant variance among sectors: the effect was the strongest in agriculture, while the two types of labour in non-tradable services were complementary (see also Zanfrini 2013).

Immigrants, especially from outside the European Union, are particularly successful as entrepreneurs, which may result from necessity entrepreneurship following the discrimination of immigrants in the labour market and on the job (OECD 2013). According to the Register of enterprises at the Italian chamber of commerce (Unioncamere 2014), the share of enterprises owned by foreigners reached 8.20 per cent of all registered enterprises in 2013 and their growth rate was well above the average for all enterprises. Particularly dynamic were enterprises owned by non-EU immigrants, which accounted for 77 per cent of foreign-owned firms and 6.3 per cent of all enterprises. Foreign-owned enterprises were primarily in trade and constructions. These findings for Italy are roughly in line with those of other developed countries.

The OECD (2011) analysed the features of migrant entrepreneurs and their contribution to employment creation in OECD countries in the years 1998–2008. Although there were significant variations between countries and over time, on average the percentage of migrant entrepreneurs was almost the same as that of natives: 12.6 per cent versus 12.0 per cent were self-employed persons as a share of all employed persons in non-agricultural activities in 2007–2008. However, this near parity is the outcome of a higher propensity to establish a business among immigrants in most OECD countries and a lower survival rate of those businesses. Overall, immigrant entrepreneurs had also been successful in increasing employment during the examined period, although the average number of employees at immigrant entrepreneurs was slightly lower than in the case of native entrepreneurs.

According to an OECD study presenting the updated results of the Database on Immigrants in OECD Countries for the years 2005/06 (Widmaier and Dumont 2011), there were considerable regional and national differences concerning labour market outcomes of immigrants within a significant general improvement since 2000. In many OECD countries, highly educated migrants had lower employment rates and higher unemployment rates than their native-born counterparts. At the same time, immigrants with less education fared better than their native-born counterparts. The problem of over-qualification was widespread and the study found that, on average in the OECD, 30 per cent of immigrants holding a university degree work in middle- or low-skilled jobs. This is an important aspect of recent immigration, since in 2005/06 the number of highly educated immigrants holding a tertiary diploma accounted for a third of the total number of recent immigrants. Indeed, on average the immigrants to OECD countries are better educated than natives. The presence of highly educated immigrants is particularly high and growing in the United Kingdom, Ireland, and Germany, while in Italy it is less than half the OECD average and stagnating as a share of the entire immigrant population.

According to Eurostat (2011), the activity rate of foreign-born persons was 5 per cent lower in 2008 than that of native-born persons aged 25–54 years in the EU-27. This difference was due to the significantly lower activity rate of foreign-born women – which was 9 per cent lower than for native-born women – and particularly to a much lower activity rate of women who migrated from the non-EU countries. Activity rates of male immigrants aged 25–54 years were similar to those of native-born men. In the same period, the employment rate of immigrants aged 25–54 years was nearly 10 per cent lower than that of native-born persons: of this employment rate, the difference for non-EU immigrants was 13 per cent and only 2 per cent for EU-27 immigrants. This difference was due mainly to a lower rate of migrant women and greater labour market integration difficulties faced by non-EU migrants.

According to the findings of Docquier and Rapoport (2012), high-skill migration is becoming a dominant component of international migration and is also a fundamental feature of globalization. High-skill migration is the source of brain drain, a phenomenon that is often considered to negatively affect the sending countries. However, there is evidence in the recent empirical literature that high-skill emigration does not necessarily deplete a country's human capital stock. Indeed, brain drain can generate positive network externalities to the advantage of sending countries, including the positive effects created by remittances and learning effects. According to Docquier and Rapoport, remittances "may help overcome liquidity constraints, stimulate education investments, and reduce poverty at origin. The size of the effect depends on the amounts transferred and on their distributional impact" (2012: 704). Moreover:

> Temporary high-skill emigration is beneficial to the source country if enough additional skills are accumulated abroad, if returnees contribute directly or indirectly to the diffusion of new technologies, and/or if the perspective of temporary migration stimulates education investments ex ante. A net positive effect is likely to be obtained if the fraction of time spent abroad is not too large and if the productivity differentials with destination countries are neither too large nor too small.
>
> (Docquier and Rapoport 2012: 706)

Finally, "[b]y reducing international transaction costs and facilitating the diffusion of knowledge and ideas, highly skilled diasporas settled in the developed countries encourage technology diffusion, stimulate trade and FDI, and contribute to improving domestic institutions" (Docquier and Rapoport 2012: 709).

As mentioned earlier in this section, a problem with high-skill immigrants is their over-qualification (i.e. the situation where a person has a level of skills or education higher than required for the job). Eurostat (2011) defines the over-qualification rate as the proportion of the population having completed tertiary education and having low- or medium-skilled jobs among employed persons having attained a high educational level. In 2008 in the EU-27 the over-qualification rate of immigrants – particularly significant for recent immigrants – was 34 per cent and 36 per cent in the case of non-EU immigrants. This share was much higher than the one for native-born persons (19 per cent). Although the phenomenon exists in all EU-27 countries, it was particularly marked in Greece, Italy, Spain, Cyprus, and Estonia, where the gaps were over 25 per cent. With the exception of Estonia, these are all vulnerable Eurozone countries.

Inequalities in the labour market are reflected in incomes: the median annual equivalized[9] disposable income for immigrants in 2008 was considerably lower than that for natives in almost all member countries (Eurostat 2011). As one would expect, considering the average per capita income of individual member countries, the lowest annual income of immigrants was observed in Hungary, Slovakia, Estonia, Lithuania, Latvia, Greece, and the Czech Republic, while the highest was in Luxembourg, United Kingdom, Ireland, and the Netherlands. However, relative differences in median incomes between migrants and natives were the highest in Belgium, Greece, and Austria.

In spite of a certain waste of the immigrants' potential due to their over-qualification and unemployment, the effect of immigration is positive for immigration countries. Huber and Tondl (2012) studied the impact of migration on the EU27's NUTS2 regions in the period 2000–2007 by means of an econometric analysis. According to their findings, migration has no significant impact on regional unemployment and does not support convergence among European regions. In fact, immigration has positive consequences for both GDP per capita and productivity. This is true immediately after the employment of immigrants and the effect increases substantially in the long term: the effect of 1 per cent increase in immigration on GDP per capita is respectively 0.02 per cent in the short term and 0.44 per cent in the long term; the effect on productivity is respectively 0.03 per cent and 0.20 per cent. The effect is similar, but reversed in its sign, for emigration regions. Since these regions are generally poorer and the immigration regions richer, migration does not seem to promote convergence.

An important component of migration is migration within the EU. In the recent years, and particularly after the accession of new member countries from Eastern Europe in 2004, 2007 and 2013,[10] the dominant flow of migrants within the EU was from new member countries to old member countries in the Western and Southern Europe (EU15). Unfortunately, the statistics on these flows is not particularly reliable, but the main migration trends are nevertheless clear.

Considering migration from EU8, Fihel et al. (2006) found that the most distinct characteristic was its temporariness. This pattern is in sharp contrast with pre-1989 migration, when individuals and entire families were migrating permanently. Indeed, most migration is now linked to seasonal work in agriculture and, to a lesser extent, to construction or tourist industry particularly in Germany, Spain, France, Austria, Greece, Norway, and the United Kingdom. Another important form of temporary migration, which often takes the form of false tourism and where Italy is a major recipient, is linked to work in the household sector, including care for children and the elderly, as well as housekeeping. Ethnic networks appear to have played a rather important role in many cases in fostering and addressing migration flows whereby older migrants from the same country or ethnic group attracted new migrants.

These features of migration internal to the EU show that the dominant pattern of migration from new to old member countries was of a complementary nature rather than a substitutive one. Although migrants often had a high-skill level, they usually took jobs that did not require high qualifications and were avoided by the natives. However, one should also notice that unconditional opening of labour markets also in the Northern European countries (notably the United Kingdom Ireland, and Sweden) on 1 May 2004 brought about not only an intensification of labour mobility from EU8, but also favoured the regularization of the employment status of many migrants who had arrived prior to the accession date and who had an irregular status. The social and economic impact of the post-2004 wave of migration from the East is overwhelmingly positive in both host countries and sending countries. Fihel et al. (2006) found that the effects for labour market imbalances were likely to be rather moderate. As for the sending countries migration was paired with a high inflow of remittances, while fears of brain drain was not substantiated.

The effects of migration in a monetary union

Understanding the impact of immigration on the host economy is important for assessing the consequences of migration for the sustainability of the common currency. Kahanec and Zimmermann (2014) studied theoretically and empirically the effect of migration in the OECD countries. They considered that flows of labour and human capital through migration contributed to a more efficient allocation of resources. This explanation is based on the standard economic law of diminishing marginal product of production factors. According to this, as the share of skilled workers in the economy increases, its value decreases and thus also the wage differential between high and low-skilled labour decreases. Thus, if immigrant workers have an average skill level that exceeds that of the workers of the receiving country, by changing relative wages the skilled migration alters the distribution of skills and promotes economic equality in advanced economies. The empirical results showed that the share of immigrants in the labour force and the quality of their human capital as measured by the educational attainment show throughout a strong and positive association, which strongly supports the conclusion that immigration is negatively associated with inequality. The opposite holds for low-skilled immigration.

The role of high-skill immigrants is thus important for the host country's domestic situation and for the viability of the common currency. In a detailed study of the EU experience of the mobility of skilled labour migrants, Kahanec (2012) considered the intra-EU migration after the 2004 and 2007 EU enlargements and the migration to the European Union from the European Neighbourhood Policy (ENP) countries.[11] In general, free labour mobility among countries provides for the increased allocative efficiency of human capital and labour in the labour market of immigration countries and is an important aspect of an optimum currency area. However, in spite of significant EU progress in harmonizing legislation in order to facilitate internal mobility, there still remain significant barriers to labour mobility, including barriers of an administrative and technical nature. Migration increased following the 2004 enlargement; however, this increase was only temporary since it was followed by a slowdown in the late 2000s and early 2010s.

In line with other sources, Kahanec (2012) found that immigrants had an educational level comparable to that of EU citizens, although there was significant variation across countries and immigrant groups. In spite of this, and with the exception of EU15 and EFTA immigrants, the occupational status of immigrants from the new member countries and from outside the EU was generally lower than that of natives and was characterized by over-qualification (or down-skilling, according to Kahanec). There was no sign of negative wage or employment effects of migration in receiving countries. In spite of the positive effects of immigration, after the mild liberalization of immigration in the early 2000s, the EU reversed many of these efforts during the late 2000s and early 2010s. Here lies a serious problem for the EU: restrictive immigration policy measures tend to discourage precisely high-skill immigrants, who are the most needed and easy to integrate, but also the most sensitive to such negative attitudes and policies, also because they have alternative destinations. The effect is that the EU falls victim to a negative selection that results in attracting fewer high-skill immigrants than the United States and more low-skill immigrants.

Labour mobility and flexible wages are important components of an optimum currency area and are important prerequisites of a viable monetary union that has many internal differences and disparities and lacks institutional completeness. When the monetary union is under the effect of asymmetric shocks, the labour market flexibility supports the adaptation of the economy to the new situation by moving labour to where jobs are and by the flexibility of wages. In this way and by increasing high-skill labour supply, migrants contribute to decrease labour costs and prices in the immigration countries and regions of the monetary union. At the same time, they contribute to support incomes and prices in the vulnerable emigration countries through remittances. High-skill migrants thus contribute to the restoration of the conditions for the competitiveness of both strong and vulnerable countries in a monetary union. This is all the more important in the Eurozone where most countries have unfavourable demographic situations.

An increase in labour mobility and flexibility and a decrease in wages are part of a mainstream response to the crisis and are important components of internal devaluation policies. These policies have important negative consequences for the economy through their contribution to a decrease in demand in the domestic market and an increase in social conflicts. Immigration, particularly that of high-skill people, offers a better alternative.

Jauer et al. (2014) compare pre- and post-crisis migration at the regional level in Europe and the United States in order to assess the migration response to asymmetric labour market conditions. The authors' finding that prior to the crisis the migration response to the labour market shocks was stronger in the United States confirms the results of other studies. However, during the crisis migration reacted to changes in labour market conditions more intensely in Europe than in the United States, also because the internal mobility in the United States seems to have declined during the crisis. Thus, the enlargement strengthened the adjustment capacity of the European labour markets to asymmetric shocks.

The importance of this finding for the European Union is reduced by two considerations. First, labour migration to the Eurozone came mostly from two sources: the new member countries (many of them outside the Eurozone, particularly the largest ones) and countries outside the European Union. Indeed, the increase in labour mobility within Europe was mostly caused by the EU enlargements of 2004 and 2007. This effect may be due to threshold effects in Europe, namely the fact that the membership of countries with much lower wages and worse labour market conditions pushed East-West intra-European mobility vigorously upward. In the EU this effect was more than twice as large as in the United States. However, a significant part of the labour market effect of immigration from the named two sources seems to have stemmed from the regularization of previous illegal immigrants.

Second, intra-Eurozone migration contributed much less to the adjustment processes within the Eurozone. Jauer et al. (2014) estimated that migration would absorb nearly a quarter of the asymmetric labour market shock within a year if all measured population changes in Europe were due to migration for employment purposes – which is certainly an overestimation. However, most migrants within the Eurozone came from non-Eurozone countries, and even in the case of intra-Eurozone migration a significant part of mobility originated from third-country immigrants who obtained the nationality of their Eurozone host countries. Although migration from outside the Eurozone had important benefits in terms of additional labour supply and skills, it is the intra-Eurozone labour mobility that would contribute in the most effective and direct way to alleviate the effects of asymmetric shocks in the common currency area in terms of reducing the labour market disparities and increasing price flexibility. Indeed, the effect of a prevailing high-skill immigration from outside the Eurozone into the economically strongest Eurozone countries would improve the latter countries' situation while leaving vulnerable countries in even greater difficulties.

While recognizing that migration – being an equilibrating force in the labour market – is an important criterion for an optimal currency area, two caveats have to be stressed. First, labour mobility requires institutions and structures. According to Kahanec (2012), the EU is recognizing some of the challenges and is taking appropriate, though partial, measures in order to better manage immigration and the adaptation of immigrant workers to the labour market (the European Blue Card, for instance), enabling the entry of skilled third-country nationals on relatively favourable terms. However, it is undoubtedly the provision of labour market institutions covering the whole single market that can contribute most to solving the problem. Also, the hosting country facilities, including housing at affordable prices, are important, particularly in countries with tight housing market.

Second, inter-Eurozone labour mobility from vulnerable to strong countries may also have negative effects in terms of economic development, specialization, and innovation. While emigration of high-skill citizens of vulnerable countries eases unemployment in those countries, it also has negative effects. While emigration contributes to keeping the remuneration of high-skill workers in vulnerable countries higher – thus keeping them at home and supporting incentives for investment in human capital – the level of remuneration and job opportunities are hardly the same as in strong countries. This probably induces the best qualified and most entrepreneurial among the high-skill people to migrate, thus impoverishing the quality of the high-skill labour force in vulnerable countries. This contributes to weakened international specialization and innovation in vulnerable countries. If this effect dominates, high-skill migration makes human capital more abundant where it is already abundant and, conversely, scarcer in those countries and regions where it is already scarce. In this way the high-skill migration contributes to an increase in long-term inequalities across regions and countries. Within the Eurozone this effect would weaken the chances for emigration countries to develop and in the end would lessen the sustainability of the incomplete monetary union..

Empirical analyses of the determinants of high-skill emigration show that poor economic performance and correlated factors – including poverty, weak institutions, inequality, discrimination, and political repression – are important determinants of emigration, particularly of high-skill emigration. However, recent literature also shows that high-skill migration has more complex and less deterministic effects, including relative wages, the availability of jobs, living conditions, and the existence of more attractive working conditions in destination countries relative to emigration countries (Boeri et al. 2012; Driouchi et al. 2009; Peri 2009). In particular – and depending on such features as governance, technological distance, population size of the sending country, and the public policies adopted in the receiving and sending countries – high-skill migration can generate positive network externalities which counteract the drain of the sending country's human capital stock (Docquier and Rapoport 2012).

It generally appears that the bidirectional link between high-skill emigration and economic development can generate both vicious and virtuous circles. An adverse economic shock can endogenously determine the emigration of high-skill workers, and this emigration can in turn have negative effects on the economy, thus propagating shocks across regions. Alternatively, the network effects activated by such emigration can ultimately have positive effects for the sending economy.

In a dynamic perspective, the third aspect is important, too. As already noted, the immigrants – though being a source of entrepreneurship – are discriminated against. Since entrepreneurship is an important source of wellbeing and development, it makes sense to identify institutional and technical ways of supporting immigrant entrepreneurship. According to the OECD (2011), several OECD member countries have implemented specific migration policies. These are of two types: targeted measures to support migrant entrepreneurs already established in the host country, and specific immigration policies that regulate the entry and stay of foreign entrepreneurs and investors. The former type is more important as it is aimed at overcoming the relative disadvantages faced by immigrant would-be entrepreneurs (compared to the native ones), with particular reference to equal access to finance. The latter type – of minor importance, since most would-be migrant entrepreneurs enter the country through other channels – are designed to identify and support the would-be entrepreneurs whose features and projects are likely to be successful and meet the country's economic needs.[12]

Conclusion

The effects of high-skill migration in a monetary union are more complex than in sovereign countries. A member country of a monetary union does not have sovereignty over its monetary policy and is deprived of an exchange rate policy, while its fiscal policy is severely restricted. Under these conditions, vulnerable countries cannot use depreciation to restore the competitiveness of their economy when this decreases, nor can they use expansionary monetary policies, while they are also constrained over the use of expansionary fiscal policies.

Since high-skill immigrants are attracted to a country of destination by job opportunities and employment and life conditions better than the other countries, chances are that a vulnerable country is unable to attract high-skill immigrants from third countries and from within the Eurozone and is losing its own high-skill citizens to the advantage of stronger Eurozone countries. There is a vicious circle here. High-skill immigration could offer a smooth way to internal devaluation. The ability by a vulnerable country to attract high-skill immigrants at wages lower than the prevailing ones would improve the supply of high-skill labour, contribute to a soft decrease in wages and a higher labour flexibility and mobility. However, the economic and financial conditions in a vulnerable country that goes through devaluation policies are not such that it attracts high-skill immigrants, while at the same time it loses its own high-skill citizens.

Yet vulnerability is not due to emigration, which is rather a consequence. The outflow of high-skill workers in vulnerable countries is due to both an income effect (the domestic decrease of wages and worsening work conditions and welfare) and a structural effect (decreasing jobs and specialization in weaker economies characterized by lower technical progress – at least relative to the number of high-skill citizens). Thus, and although high-skill immigration could contribute to solve the problems of vulnerable countries in a monetary union, the general conditions of their economy and society do not attract high-skill immigrants and represent a push factor to emigration of their high-skill citizens.

If vulnerability is due, among other things, to the dismal state of the vulnerable countries' labour markets and related institutions, the effect of their loss of high-skill immigrants and citizens could be doubly negative, since it could even diminish the pressure to reform the labour market. It appears that the first step in solving the issue of vulnerability is a political determination to reform the labour market, thereby creating better conditions for high-skill workers. Reforms may consist of a greater flexibility of the labour market, but also – and in vulnerable countries perhaps primarily – of improvements in the labour market efficiency by means of, among other things, lower transaction costs for the management of employment and technical progress applied to the search of jobs. Yet these reforms are costly and may even jeopardize for some time the smooth progress of production. Chances of success can improve considerably if the European Union would provide common support to the vulnerable countries that start undertaking credible reforms and structural change.

Acknowledgements

I thank Serena Piovesan of Cinformi for the support with regard to data and information gathering, and Gert Guri, University of Trento, for comments on a previous version of this paper. Special thanks goes to professor Nada Stropnik (Institute for Economic Research, Ljubljana) for helpful comments and suggestions on an earlier version of this paper and for the careful revision of the manuscript. The ideas and statements presented here reflect solely the author's views. Parts of this paper were prepared in the framework of SEEMIG (Managing Migration and its Effects in SEE), a strategic project funded by the European Union's South-East Europe Program.

Notes

1 The original formulation of the "secular stagnation" hypothesis and the introduction of the term "secular stagnation" date back to the 1938 American Economic Association presidential address by Alvin Hansen (1939). Hansen ascribed secular stagnation to slowdowns in population growth and the pace of technological advance, which decrease consumption and investment spending. These prevent the attainment of full employment.

2 For a broader range of opinions and positions, see Teulings and Baldwin (2014). Although positions differ in this book, a fairly strong consensus emerges on the facts that negative real interest rates are needed to equate saving and investment with full employment and that secular stagnation increases the difficulty of achieving full employment with low inflation and a zero lower bound on policy interest rates. For a criticism of the hypothesis in the present situation, see Hamilton et al. (2015), according to whom the disappointing post-2008 recovery is better explained by contingent factors: protracted but ultimately temporary headwinds from the housing supply overhang, household and bank deleveraging, and fiscal retrenchment.

3 For a Keynesian criticism to the OCA theory see Goodhart (1998). For an Austrian criticism see Glăvan (2004) and Hayek (1990).

4 On migration, its explanations and historical and spatial aspects, see Fassmann et al. (2014).

5 High-skill immigrants are defined as foreign-born individuals aged 25 or more and holding an academic or professional degree beyond high school (i.e. a "college graduate") at the census or survey date.

6 Migrant women with tertiary education increased by 79 per cent over the period, much more than migrant men. Also higher than the average was the emigration of persons with tertiary education from low-income and lower-middle income brackets.

7 Zanfrini (2013) uses official sources to show that from 1999/2000 to 2011/2012 the number of foreign students in Italy increased 6.3 times, from 1.4 per cent of the total student population to 8.4 per cent.

8 See the recent European Agenda on Migration (EC 2015) and the political bargaining around its formulation and implementation.

9 Eurostat defines equivalized income attributed to each household member as the household's total income divided by its 'equivalent size' in order to take account of the size and composition of the household (see http://epp.eurostat.ec.europa.eu/statistics_explained/index.php/Glossary:Equivalised_disposable_income). Household equivalent size is calculated using the so-called modified OECD equivalence scale (this scale gives a weight of 1.0 to the first adult, 0.5 to any other household member aged 14 and over and 0.3 to each child under 14 years).

10 These were respectively EU8 in 2004 (eight new member countries), EU2 in 2007 (two new member countries) and one new member country in 2013.

11 These countries are divided into two groups: the ENP-East countries (Armenia, Azerbaijan, Belarus, Georgia, Moldova, and Ukraine) and the ENP-South countries (Algeria, Egypt, Israel, Jordan, Lebanon, Libya, Morocco, the occupied Palestinian territory, Syria, and Tunisia).

12 Mahuteau et al. (2014) assessed the impact of a change in the immigration policy on migrants' probability of becoming entrepreneurs in Australia. The new policy was introduced in the mid-1990s and consisted of stricter entry requirements and restrictions to welfare entitlements. According to the author's findings, immigrants who entered under more stringent conditions had a higher probability of becoming self-employed, an effect that time spent in Australia positively affected.

References

Acemoglu, D. and J. A. Robinson. 2012. *Why Nations Fail. The Origins of Power, Prosperity and Poverty.* London: Profile Books.

Arslan, C., J.-C. Dumont, Z. Kone, Y. Moullan, C. Ozden, C. Parsons, T. Xenogiani. 2014. *A New Profile of Migrants in the Aftermath of the Recent Economic Crisis.* OECD Social, Employment and Migration Working Paper no. 160. Paris: OECD.

Baldwin, R. and C. Wyplosz. 2012. *The Economics of European Integration,* 4th edn. New York: McGraw-Hill.

Billiet, J., B. Meuleman and H. D. Witte. 2014. "The Relationship between Ethnic Threat and Economic Insecurity in Times of Economic Crisis: Analysis of European Social Survey Data." *Migration Studies* (March): 1–27.

Boeri. T., H. F. D Brücker, .and H. Rapoport, eds. 2012. *Brain Drain and Brain Gain: The Global Competition to Attract High-skill Migrants.* Oxford: Oxford University Press.

Buttonwood. 2014. "Secular Stagnation: The Long View." *The Economist* (November). Available at www.economist.com/blogs/buttonwood/2014/11/secular-stagnation.

Cardwell, P. J., C. Kaunert and S. Léonard. 2013. "Introduction." In *International Migration* 5(6): 24–25 (special issue on Migration in the European Union's Area of Freedom, Security and Justice after the Treaty of Lisbon and the Stockholm Programme, edited by P. J. Cardwell, C. Kaunert and S. Léonard).

Coulombe, S. and J.-F. Tremblay. 2009. "Migration and Skills Disparities across the Canadian Provinces." *Regional Studies* 4(1): 5–18.

Dallago, B. 2016. *One Currency, Two Europes.* Singapore: World Scientific.

Docquier, F. and H. Rapoport. 2012. "Globalization, Brain Drain, and Development." *Journal of Economic Literature* 50(3): 681–730.

Driouchi, A., C. Boboc and N. Zouag. 2009. "Emigration of Highly Skilled Labour: Determinants & Impacts." MPRA Paper no. 21567. Available at http://mpra.ub.uni-muenchen.de/21567/.

EC. 2015. *A European Agenda on Migration: Communication from the Commission to the European Parliament, the Council, the European Economic and Social Committee and the Committee of the Regions.* 13.5.2015 COM(2015) 240 final. Brussels: European Commission.

Eurostat. 2011. *Migrants in Europe, 2011 Edition: A Statistical Portrait of the First and Second Generation.* Luxembourg: Publications Office of the European Union.

Fassmann, H., E. Musil and Kathrin Gruber. 2014. *Dynamic Historical Analysis of Longer Term Migratory, Labour Market and Human Capital Processes in the SEEMIG Region.* Working paper (3) (August). SEEMIG. Available at www.seemig.eu/downloads/outputs/SEEMIGWorkingPapers3.pdf.

Fihel, A., P. Kaczmarczyk and M. Okólski. 2006. *Labour Mobility in the Enlarged European Union: International Migration from the EU8 Countries.* Working paper 14/72 (December). Warsaw: Centre of Migration Research.

Fullin, G. and E. Reyneri. 2011. "Low Unemployment and Bad Jobs for New Immigrants in Italy." *International Migration* 49(1): 119–147.

Glăvan, B. 2004. "The Failure of OCA Analysis." *Austrian Economics* 7(2) (Summer): 29–46.

Goodhart, C. 1998. "The Two Concepts of Money: Implications for the Analysis of Optimal Currency Areas." *European Journal of Political Economy* 14(3): 407–432.

Guo, F., G. Hugo and M. Tani. 2014. "Introduction." *International Migration* 52(2): 1–2 (special issue on The Globally Mobile Skilled Labour Force: Policy Challenges and Economic Opportunities, edited by F. Guo, G. Hugo and M. Tani).

Hamilton, J. D., E. S. Harris, J. Hatzius and K. D. West. 2015. *The Equilibrium Real Funds Rate: Past, Present and Future.* March. San Diego, CA: University of California at San Diego. Available at http://econweb.ucsd.edu/~jhamilto/USMPF_2015.pdf.

Hansen, A. H. 1939. "Economic Progress and Declining Population Growth." *The American Economic Review* 2(1): 1–15.

Hayek, F. A. 1990. *Denationalisation of Money: The Argument Refined. An Analysis of the Theory and Practice of Concurrent Currencies*, 3rd edn. London: The Institute of Economic Affairs.

Huber, P. and G. Tondl. 2012. "Migration and Regional Convergence in the European Union." *Empirica* 39: 439–460.

Huddleston, T. and J. Niessen in cooperation with E. Ni Chaoimh and E. White. 2011. *Migrant Integration Policy, Index III, Italia.* Brussels: British Council and Migration Policy Group.

IMF. 2014. *World Economic Outlook: Legacies, Clouds, Uncertainties.* October. Washington, DC: International Monetary Fund.

IMF. 2015. *World Economic Outlook: Uneven Growth – Short- and Long-Term Factors.* April. Washington, DC: International Monetary Fund.

Jauer, J., T. Liebig, J. P. Martin and P. Puhani. 2014. *Migration as an Adjustment Mechanism in the Crisis? A Comparison of Europe and the United States.* Social, Employment and Migration Working Paper 155 (January). Paris OECD. Available at www.oecd.org/els/workingpapers.

Kahanec, M. 2012. "Skilled Labour Flows: Lessons from the European Union." *IZA Research Report* 49. (December).

Kahanec, M. and K. F. Zimmermann. 2014. "How Skilled Immigration may Improve Economic Equality." *IZA Journal of Migration* 3(2). Available at www.izajom.com/content/3/1/2.

Kenen, P. 1969. "The Theory of Optimum Currency Areas: An Eclectic View." In *Monetary Problems in the International Economy*, edited by R. Mundell and A. K. Swoboda. Chicago, IL: University of Chicago Press, pp. 41–60.

Kerr, S. P., W. R. Kerr and W. F. Lincoln. 2013. Skilled Immigration and the Employment Structures of US Firms. Working paper 14-040 (November). Cambridge, MA: Harvard Business School.

Mahuteau, S., M. Piracha, M. Tani and M. V. Lucero. 2014. "Immigration Policy and Entrepreneurship." *International Migration* 5(2): 53–65.

McKinnon, R. 1963. "Optimum Currency Areas." *American Economic Review* 53 (September): 717–724.

Mundell, R. 1961. "A Theory of Optimum Currency Areas." *American Economic Review* 51(4): 657–665.

North, D. C. 1990. *Institutions, Institutional Change and Economic Performance.* Cambridge: Cambridge University Press.

OECD. 2011. *International Migration Outlook, Part II: Migrant Entrepreneurship in OECD Countries.* Paris: OECD. Available at www.oecd.org/migration/imo.

OECD. 2013. *International Migration Outlook.* Paris: OECD. Available atwww.oecd.org/migration/imo/2013.htm.

O'Rourke, K. H. and A. M. Taylor. 2013. "Cross of Euros." *Journal of Economic Perspectives* 27(3): 167–192.

Peri, G. 2009. *The Determinants and Effects of Highly-Skilled Labour Movements: Evidence from OECD Countries 1980–2005.* London: CEPR.

Pintaldi and Pontecorvo. 2013. *Dossier Statistico Immigrazione 2013*. Rome: Centro Studi e Ricerche IDOS.

Reyneri, E. 2007. *Immigration in Italy: Trends and Perspectives*. Rome: Consiglio Nazionale dell'Economia e del Lavoro. Available at www.portalecnel.it/portale/ indlavdocumenti.nsf/0/466486C57FF3FF42C125737F0050A9EC/$FILE/ Reyneri-%20Immigration%20in%20Italy.pdf.

Summers, L. H. 2014. "US Economic Prospects: Secular Stagnation, Hysteresis, and the Zero Lower Bound." *Business Economics* 49(2): 65–73.

Teulings, C. and R. Baldwin, eds. 2014. *Secular Stagnation: Facts, Causes, and Cures*. London: CEPR Press.

Unioncamere. 2014. *Unioncamere: nel 2013 le imprese straniere sfiorano quota 500mila*. Rome: Unioncamere. Available at www.unioncamere.gov.it/P42A2224C160S123/Nel-2013-le-imprese-straniere-sfiorano-quota-500mila--Napoli--Roma--Monza-e-Milano-le-province-che-corrono-di-piu.htm.

Venturini, A. 1999. "Do Immigrants Working Illegally Reduce the Natives' Legal Employment? Evidence from Italy." *Journal of Population Economics* 1: 135–154.

Venturini, A. and C. Villosio. 2008. "Labour Market Assimilation of Foreign Workers in Italy." *Oxford Review of Economic Policy* 24(3): 517–541. Available at http://dev3.cepr.org/meets/wkcn/2/2395/papers/VillosioFinal.pdf.

Widmaier, S. and J.-C. Dumont. 2011. *Are Recent Immigrants Different? A New Profile of Immigrants in the OECD based on DIOC 2005/06*. OECD Social, Employment and Migration Working Papers 126. Directorate for Employment, Labour and Social Affairs, Paris: OECD Publishing. Available at http://dx.doi.org/10.1787/5kg3ml17nps4-en.

Wunderlich, D.. 2013. "Towards Coherence of EU External Migration Policy? Implementing a Complex Policy." *International Migration* 51(6): 26–40.

Zanfrini, L. 2013. *Immigration in Italy*. Berlin: Netzwerk Migration in Europa. Available at http://migrationeducation.de/fileadmin/uploads/CountryprofileItaly_aggiornamento.pdf.

8 The future of the German model after the labour market reforms

Joachim Möller

Introduction

Max Weber, Werner Sombart and others have already used the notion of the "German" or "Rhine" model of capitalism to describe some specific characteristics of the German economy in the early twentieth century. Several decades later, in the mid-1970s, the social-democratic chancellor Helmut Schmidt started his election campaign using the motto "*Modell Deutschland*" as a specific response to the structural challenges experienced after the deep supply shocks of the oil-price crisis that took place at that time. Today the *German model* plays a central role in the debate on the *varieties of capitalism* (Esping-Andersen 1990; Albert 1993; Streeck 1992, 1997; Hall and Soskice 2001a). The basic claim in the debate is that "capitalism" or market societies may be organized in rather different forms. These differences include wage bargaining and other labour market institutions, the stance towards active labour market policy, the organization and generosity of the social security system, forms of cooperation between social partners or interest groups, educational systems, and forms of economic specialization, among others. The German model has been characterized along these dimensions in the literature.

Since the early 1990s there has been growing scepticism about the chances that the specific "German" variety of capitalism would survive in the face of financial strain and "globalization" (i.e. under conditions of growing integration into the world economy, offshoring and high capital mobility; Streeck 1997). This scepticism culminated after the burst of the new economy bubble at the beginning of the millennium. The worries about the future of the model led to Chancellor Gerhard Schröder's "Agenda 2010" and the deep labour market reforms of 2003–2005. These reforms strengthened the German economy in general and the labour market in particular. However, the German model was transformed along several dimensions. Some of the core elements of the system were weakened and others were strengthened. Overall, the German variety of capitalism is still intact, although an increasing dualism might threaten the concept of a solidaristic society. Hence, this raises the question of how these tendencies can be counteracted without jeopardizing the indisputable economic successes and marked favourable labour market development of the country.

he salient features of the German model

efinitions of the German model

here are varying definitions of the German model in the literature. They differ
ith respect to their emphasis on different features and structural elements of
ie system. Wolfgang Streek defines the German model as "(an) institutionalized
igh wage economy combining high competitiveness in world markets with
rong social cohesion and, in particular, low levels of inequality along a variety
f dimensions" (Streeck 1995: 2), whereas Albert (1993) emphasizes the highly
pecific industrial relations in combination with a productive model based on
iversified quality production. Ten years later, Hall and Soskice (2001a) described
ie German type of market economy as "an emblematic example of a coordinated
apitalism, which should be juxtaposed to the liberal market capitalism typical
f the American configuration" (Boyer 2006: 135). Similarly, Freeman (2000)
haracterizes what he calls the "Rhineland Model".

Streeck describes the German productive model as a "'diversified quality
roduction': a unique multiple palette of demanding and qualitatively outstanding
roducts being designed for world market niches that could justify the high
nd low differentiated wages of their producers through the realization of high
rices in international competition (Streeck 2005: 9, translation by the author).
treeck argues that the described productive model has especially favoured strong
iedium-size manufacturing firms, which are often denoted as hidden champions
.e. world-market leaders in their specific field of specialization).

The fuzziness of these definitions from the perspectives of different
isciplines is not surprising. In a recent article, Kathleen Thelen criticizes the
ne-dimensional classification of socio-economic systems along a continuum,
egardless of whether it is called "corporatism" or "coordination". The varieties
f capitalism can be described along several political, institutional, historical,
tructural, and behavioural dimensions. Thelen stresses the coalitional
oundations on which political-economic institutions rest: "A coalitional
pproach reveals that institutions that in the past supported the more egalitarian
arieties of capitalism survive best not when they stably reproduce the politics
nd patterns of the Golden Era but rather when they are reconfigured – in both
orm and function – on the basis of significantly new political support coalitions"
Thelen 2012: 3).

There are various salient features of the German model. The central pillars of
ie system are effectively corporatist structures and a strong social partnership,
relatively generous social security system that is at the core of Bismarck-type
ocial security (status-oriented and mainly financed by social contributions). The
conomy is geared toward export-oriented manufacturing, benefiting from a well-
eveloped system of dual vocational training and a well-educated workforce.
luctuations are relatively minor. Wage bargaining takes place at the intermediate
sectoral, regional) level; however, through wage-leadership (*Lohnführerschaft*),
he outcomes at the aggregate level are rather similar. Although union coverage
akes place only at the intermediate level, the strong role of unions in the bargaining

process leads to a solidaristic wage policy (low wage dispersion). Federal institutions are engaged in active labour market policy and the buffering of labour market shocks through short-term working allowances and other instruments. The financing of companies depends on a house-bank system. Finally, the German system relies on a solid infrastructure, especially with respect to transport and logistics but also in relation to the legal system.

It is important to regard these various dimensions not as isolated, but rather as strongly interrelated. Hall and Soskice (2001b: 17) coined the notion of institutional complementarities (i.e. the presence of one institution increases the efficiency of another). To illustrate these interrelationships, consider the following example.

Robert Boyer emphasizes the "strong complementarity between product strategy and human resource management" (Boyer 2006: 137). An important characteristic of labour relations in the German model is the priority of within-firm flexibility relative to external flexibility.[1] The preference for retaining a qualified workforce even during severe recessions stems from the high importance of firm-specific capital, which originates from the needs of export-oriented diversified quality production. This product strategy requires the flexible use of equipment by highly skilled workers that is crucial for specialized firms facing highly volatile product demand in the world market. Labour hoarding during periods of slack demand is a suitable measure, especially if this behaviour is publically supported through generous short-term working allowances. However, labour hoarding in combination with massive reductions in working hours and temporary earnings moderation requires mechanisms of social partnership and trust. Work councils serve as intermediaries to arbitrate between the conflicting interests of management and workers. Hence, this institution plays a key role in organizing within-firm flexibility through various measures to stabilize employment. Moreover, a social partnership is also required in regard to fostering training measures and high workplace security standards. Traditionally, the system of well-functioning labour relations in Germany is especially developed in the manufacturing sector, where there are high levels of unionization and collective bargaining coverage.

The dual vocational training system fits well with diversified quality production. The dual system combines the acquisition of both theoretical and practical knowledge. An important aspect of this system is that it offers corresponding training resources such as the working time of experienced workers who are able to transfer firm-specific and general skills to their apprentices. Because the curricula within professions are codified, a worker who completed an apprenticeship in a specific field can be expected to possess the standard skills that are typical of related professions. Hence, a corresponding certificate in a certain profession serves as a signifier of a bundle of skills and competences.

The German model as an in-between case

In a variety of respects the German model appears as an intermediate case between the Anglo-Saxon-type market economies on the one hand (deregulated, in egalitarian, neo-liberal) and Scandinavian-type societies on the other (coordinated at the national level, egalitarian, highly unionized). First, there is a grouping of types of welfare states corresponding to this classification. In the cluster of Anglo-Saxon "liberal" states, one finds strict entitlement rules, means-tested assistance, meagre universal transfers and social insurance plans. Germany belongs to a second cluster of corporativist welfare states, where "the granting of social rights was hardly ever seriously contested. What was predominant was the preservation of status differentials" (Esping-Andersen 1990: 111). The third cluster described by Esping-Andersen is the Scandinavian "social democratic regime", where social rights were extended to the new middle classes.

Second, Germany is an in-between case also with respect to corporatism. This became obvious in the Calmfors/Driffill debate and has also been examined by economists dating back to the late 1980s by stressing the relationship between the degree of centralization of wage bargaining and macroeconomic performance. It is argued that the best economic results are derived from either a completely decentralized system, like in the Anglo-Saxon countries, or a system allowing for wage bargaining at the aggregate level. As the authors put it, "extremes work best" (Calmfors and Driffill 1988: 13). Germany, among others, is seen as being "between these polar cases, with wage setting mainly at the industry level" (Calmfors 1993: 161).

Third, the German model is an in-between case also with respect to Egalitarianism. The slogan of Ludwig Erhard, minster of economic affairs and chancellor during the period of the German *Wirtschaftswunder* in the 1950s and 1960s, was "Prosperity for All". For almost five decades after World War II, the rising economic tide was lifting all boats, both large and small. Supported by high unionization and a solidaristic wage policy, the system was accompanied by relatively strong wage compression. According to indicators of earnings inequality, Germany was traditionally closer to the Scandinavian than Anglo-Saxon countries until the mid-1990s.

The crisis of the German model

Globalization and the fall of the iron curtain

In the mid-1990s, Wolfgang Streeck (Streeck 1997) and others expressed scepticism over whether the German model, as a relatively egalitarian high-wage economy, could survive in the face of "globalization" (i.e. under conditions of growing integration into the world economy, offshoring and high capital mobility). This is akin to what Thelen and van Wijnbergen call the neoliberal offensive position, meaning the thesis that "globalization pushes all countries toward neoliberalism and deregulation, encouraging firms to lower labour cost and increase labour market flexibility while undermining the power of unions to prevent these" (Thelen and van Wijnbergen 2003: 859).

It should be stressed that in the tradition of Bismarck, the financing of the social security net is strongly tied to the wage bill. There is therefore a broad consensus that the traditional German model presupposes a sufficiently high share of active workers paying social contributions. Consequently, elevated unemployment puts the system under pressure. According to Streeck (2005: 9), the organized solidarity within the system underwent a tensile test in the late 1990s, when an additional surge in internationalization generated competitive pressure on German enterprises. This started to increasingly affect, as well, the formerly very successful niche producers. With steadily increasing systemic unemployment since the mid-1970s, the foundations of the model were undermined.

Most authors agree that perhaps these problems were not caused but rather aggravated by the dramatic economic consequences of the German re-unification. West Germany absorbed a nation with a non-competitive industrial base and a desolate public infrastructure. From the early 1990s onwards, the high financial burden of German re-unification became an additional challenge for public and private budgets. As a result, the German economy was plagued by low growth and job creation rates.

In the late 1990s, the German economy additionally felt some additional negative effects immediately after the introduction of the Euro. Capital flows were re-directed to formerly high-interest countries within the Eurozone, which was detrimental to home investment. After profiting in the first years subsequently to the opening of the borders to the East, the West German industry ran into problems. Germany appeared to be increasingly sclerotic, unable to cope with the challenges of the structural changes demanded by the new period of globalization. As a consequence, the German economy entered into a critical phase. In 1999, *The Economist* mocked Germany as the "sick man of Europe" (Economist 1999). It was doubtful whether the system was sustainable. According to some authors, the erosion of the "German model" already started (Driffill 2006: 746). In particular, at least two manifestations of greater flexibility have to be mentioned: (i) the emergence of company-level alliances between employers and employees to secure employment and competitiveness and (ii) the spread of contingent pay arrangements.

Structural problems

According to some observers, the structure of the economy was at the heart of the poor employment record. Rather evidently, Germany did not manage to boost new job creation in some labour-intensive branches of the service sector, especially eating and drinking, care facilities, and retail trade. In a comparison between Germany and the U.S., Richard Freeman and Ronald Schettkat show that a large proportion of the marked differences in employment rates stems from differences in these low-wage services (Freeman and Schettkat 2001). "Mediocre employment growth in these three service sectors is thus key to understanding Germany's employment woes" (Kenworthy 2006: 42). Burda, Sachs find that wage rigidity in services – due to unionization, minimum wage provisions or overly generous unemployment benefits – has obstructed rapid labour-intensive growth in service activities (Burda and Sachs 1988: 560). This conclusion is somewhat at odds with a later analysis, according to which wage levels were not the primary cause of the discrepancies between Germany and the US (see Glyn et al. 2007).

Before the Great Recession, the relative strength of the manufacturing sector as a constituting element of the German model was seen as a disadvantage rather than an advantage. Barry Eichengreen reflects on Hans-Werner Sinn's argument that Germany is becoming a bazaar economy. He argues that the country "is losing its manufacturing prowess" and that "expensive German labour cannot compete with equally skilled but immensely less expensive workers in the east" (Eichengreen 2007: 1).

In the aftermath of the financial crisis in the US and the Great Recession, the view on the adequate size of the manufacturing sector has changed once again. Today, it is widely accepted that the German economy did rather well in recent years and was even seen as a growth engine within Europe, not *despite* but *because* of its "hypertrophic" manufacturing sector. A debate on re-industrialization recently started taking place even in the US (e.g. Sperling 2013; see Möller 2014 for more details).

The labour market reforms

Rationale behind the reforms

In retrospect, the foundations of the traditional German model of the *Wirtschaftswunder* have been eroding since the mid-seventies. More and more, mass unemployment became a menacing phenomenon. The striking ratchet effect in the unemployment figures that first appeared after the first oil price crisis led to a steady increase in systemic unemployment. This can be described as a result of significant hysteresis effects due to, for instance, the depreciation of human capital through periods of long-term unemployment. Fatally, these mechanisms were reinforced by the relatively generous unemployment insurance system. Hence, the favourable elements of the traditional system that served as a buffer against demand shocks now achieved the opposite of the intended effect.

Furthermore, the structure of labour demand underwent a deep structural transformation. In the 1980s, the nature of technical progress and work place organization began to change. Low-skilled workers in particular were hurt by skill-biased technical progress resulting from computerization and other developments. Unions tried to fight against these fundamental forces by bargaining for a fixed component in wage increases (*Sockelbeträge*) in order to allow the lowest income groups to profit more than proportionally from the economic development. However, growing unemployment among low-skilled workers, which became a severe problem starting in the late 1980s, increasingly undermined this strategy.

In the first years of the new century, the situation that developed called for drastic reforms to secure basic social attainments. The result was a courageous political program (Agenda 2010), which Michael Burda called the "teutonic turnaround". In his programmatic speech in March 2003, Chancellor Schröder argued: "If Germany refrains from modernizing its labour market institutions, then it will be modernized by the brute forces of the global markets, leaving barely enough room for a social protection net" (Deutscher Bundestag 2003: 2481, translation by the author). This can be seen as the expression of a widely shared sentiment that far-reaching reforms were necessary to keep the basic functioning of social security institutions alive. It might be argued, however, that the deep structural changes that came along with the reforms sacrificed basic elements of the German model. Hence, the controversial question is whether the reforms have thrown the baby out with the bathwater.

The reform agenda

The key elements of Agenda 2010 aimed at reforming the labour market institutions. The so-called Hartz reforms, which represented the core of the Agenda, were implemented in different steps between 2003 and 2005. In addition to improving the effectiveness and efficiency of the Federal Employment Services, the fundamental concept to improve the functioning of the labour market and reduce unemployment can be characterized as "supporting and demanding". In other words, the reforms adopted a "carrot and stick" approach. On the "carrot" side, several instruments aimed to facilitate the integration of the unemployed, such as support for training measures, wage subsidies and improved conditions to place workers in new jobs. Concrete elements on the "stick" side include the – albeit moderate – weakening of job protection standards, the reduction of the maximum entitlement period for unemployment insurance benefits, the tightening of job acceptance regulations for the unemployed as well as the de-regulation of temporary work agencies. Perhaps the most substantial change, however, was the merger between unemployment assistance and welfare (Hartz IV). The implication of this change is that, after receiving unemployment insurance for 12 months, workers typically fall back into the basic welfare system. The former unemployment assistance system (*Arbeitslosenhilfe*) was related to previous earnings. Basic welfare, however, provides lump-sum, means-tested benefits only. Compared to the pre-reform situation, this meant a substantial deterioration in the positions of workers. Three important aspects have to be mentioned in this context. First, the social security system was traditionally status-oriented. The new institutional system, however, implies the possibility of a deep fall in social status after only one year of unemployment. This represented a credible threat. Second, compared to the pre-reform situation, the position of long-term unemployment recipients was significantly weaker. Third, the criteria under which workers could reject a job offer became stricter.

Taken together, these three elements of the reform placed strong pressure on the unemployed to find a new job quickly. Not surprisingly, this pressure led to changes in behaviour. In particular, effects on the reservation wage of the unemployed, job search intensity, and willingness of job seekers to make concessions could be expected. Moreover, the bargaining power of workers was also generally affected by these profound changes in the institutional environment.

Reform effects

The German labour market reforms of 2003 to 2005 were a drastic and painful but ultimately effective cure. Although not all parts of the reforms were well designed, strong positive labour market effects were rapidly visible. Supported by a favourable external economic environment, the German economy experienced an extraordinary boom period in the three years following the reform. Between 2004 Q4 and 2008 Q2, real production growth was 9.4 per cent in the aggregate economy and 18.8 per cent in manufacturing. From 2005 until the eve of the Great Recession at the end of 2008, unemployment fell from its peak level of more than 5 million to less than 3 million. Furthermore, the disastrous trend in systemic unemployment was reversed: For the first time since the 1960s, the unemployment rate at the beginning of the economic downturn (2008 Q3) was lower than at the beginning of the previous recession. Moreover, as shown by Fahr and Sunde (2009), Möller (2010), Klinger and Rothe (2012), or, more recently, Stops (2015), a marked increase of the efficiency parameter in the matching function (or an inward-shift of the Beveridge curve) indicated the improved functioning of the labour market due to behavioural and institutional effects as well as better performance of labour services.

The turnaround of systemic unemployment is documented in Figure 8.1. The figure shows the evolution of unemployment in West Germany since the 1950s. The arrows connect the troughs of the unemployment series. As seen, the

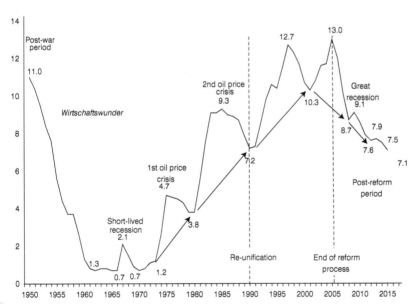

Figure 8.1 Long-run development of the German unemployment rate (as a percentage of the civil labor force, 1950 to 2014)

Source: German Federal Employment Agency; Arbeitsmarktberichterstattung

recession in the sixties did not lead to an increase in the systemic unemployment (i.e. the troughs before and after the recession were at about the same levels). With the OPEC I crisis of the mid-1970s, the situation changed markedly. In the post-reform period after 2005, the upward trend dating back to the early seventies was reversed. Simultaneously, long-term unemployment decreased markedly.

The response of the labour market to the Great Recession can be seen as a first litmus test of whether the resilience mechanisms of the German model would survive the reforms. The degree of cushioning of employment in face of the extraordinarily sharp decline in external demand has been described as a miracle (for an explanation, see Möller 2010 or Burda and Hunt 2011). As an export-oriented economy, the country was hit harder than other advanced countries by the collapse of orders for exports. Relative to trend growth, German GDP decreased by approximately 6.5 per cent. Despite this huge shock, the unemployment rate remained relatively stable. An unprecedented level of within-firm flexibility was the main explanation for this.

The behaviour during the Great Recession shows that the basic mechanisms of the German model evidently remained quite intact. The crisis was a confirmation of a healthy social partnership. Within-firm flexibility proved to be extremely effective in absorbing the enormous shock to GDP. The support of the Federal Labour Services' labour market policy helped confine the financial consequences of labour hoarding. Moreover, the strategy of retaining their qualified workforces paid off for firms. When the recovery gained momentum, firms were ready to respond very quickly to expanding production.

After 2005, the strategy of diversified quality production turned out to be very successful. German firms could expand their market shares not only vis-à-vis their traditional trading partners but also in emerging markets. This can partly be explained by their provision of right mix of products that have been in high demand in recent years (machine tools, automobiles, chemical products). Hence, the traditional strength of the German economy in core manufacturing industries was very favourable.

Long-run trends and Hartz reforms

In this context, perhaps the most important long-run trends in the labour market are (i) wage moderation, (ii) increasing wage dispersion and segmentation and (iii) declining union coverage. All these trends started long before the Hartz process was initiated. Rather than being caused by Agenda 2010, they are related to factors such as technical progress, the re-organization of industrial production in an increasingly integrated world economy, and, finally, to the fall of the iron curtain. There is no doubt that these factors caused deep structural changes in the German economy. With respect to the fall of the iron curtain, at least three channels must be mentioned. First, the opening to the East meant the emergence of low-wage countries like Hungary, Poland or the Czech Republic as direct neighbours of the German economy. The threat of the re-location of production sites weakened substantially the bargaining positions of workers and their unions

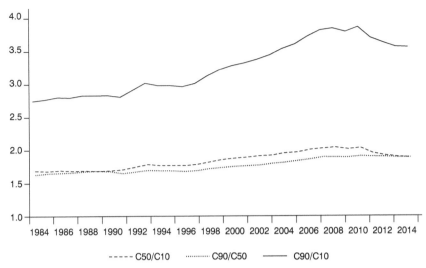

----- C50/C10   ·········· C90/C50   ——— C90/C10

Figure 8.2 Indicators of wage inequality among full-time workers aged 25 to 55 in West Germany, 1984–2014 centile ratios

Source: own calculation with IAB-IEB data

Second, the market potential of the German economy increased considerably. Third, the re-structuring process after re-unification – especially the collapse of manufacturing industries in East Germany – weakened the overall union coverage in Germany.

Several authors have addressed the fact that wage inequality has risen substantially in Germany over the last two or three decades (see, for instance, Dustmann et al. 2009 and Card et al. 2013). Figure 8.2 shows indicators of wage inequality for prime-age full-time workers in West Germany in the period from 1984 to 2014. Until the mid-1990s, the 90/10-percentile ratio remained more or less constant. This was true also for the equivalent measures of wage inequality in the lower and upper tails of the distribution (i.e. the 50/20 and 90/50 percentile ratios, respectively). Since then, wage inequality has followed a markedly upward trend. In the mid-1980s, the earnings of workers in the ninth decile were approximately 2.5 times greater than the earnings of workers in the first decile. At the end of the observation period, the corresponding value was 3.5.

A further important aspect concerns the wage structure related to skill differentials. Figure 8.3 depicts the development of an index of real earnings for full-time male workers aged 40 in West Germany according to three skill levels (low-skilled, workers with vocational training, and university graduates). It turns out that until the re-unification (1991), real wages were increasing among all skilled groups. In the first half of the nineties, real wages were stagnating among all groups. Since the mid-nineties however, the development of real earnings among the skilled groups has clearly diverged. Whereas workers with a university degree experienced sharp increases in their real earnings, the earnings of low-skilled workers declined. This is especially true after 2005. For one and a half

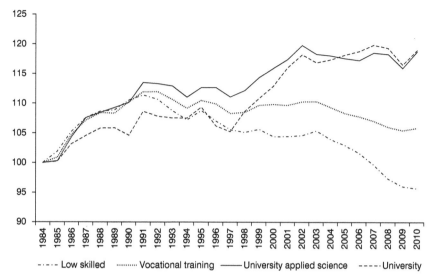

- - - - Low skilled   ·········· Vocational training   ——— University applied science   - - - - University

Figure 8.3 Real wage index by qualification type for full-time male workers in West Germany, 1984–2010

Source: own calculation with SIAB data

decades after 1990, the real earnings of the intermediate skilled group more or less stagnated, but then decreased as well. Hence, sizeable groups of workers suffered losses in real earnings, especially in the years after the labour market reforms. With stagnating or even declining real earnings among the majority of workers, unit labour costs have fallen considerably.

At the same time, the share of low-wage earners increased markedly. This is true for total employment as well as for subsamples divided by region (east/ west) or gender. The trend towards a higher share of low-pay employment has accelerated only to a certain extent since 2005.

To sum up, it seems that the German economy has become much less egalitarian than it has been traditionally. The low-pay sector has risen dramatically, as noted by Rhein (2013). Almost a quarter of all employees received less than the low pay threshold of €9.54 per hour in 2010. According to Rhein (2013), Germany has moved from being a country with intermediate earnings inequality to belonging to the group with the greatest levels of inequality in Europe. If all employees are considered, the size of the low-pay sector even exceeds that of the United Kingdom.

A further change in the structure of the German labour market is related to the rising share of non-standard employment. Non-standard employment comprises part-time and minor employment as well as employment with all types of fixed-term contracts. It should be emphasized that not all forms of non-standard employment imply low-quality jobs. For example, part-time work might be voluntarily chosen for family reasons. The same applies to some fixed-term contracts when they correspond to the preferences of workers. In general, however, non-standard employment is more likely to be associated with low job quality.

Table 8.1   Share of standard employment contracts in total employment by age and skill
groups (percentage)

	1991	2000	2013	2000/1991	2013/2000
Age					
15–24	56.0	35.8	30.5	–36.1	–14.8
25–49	71.1	65.3	59.0	–8.2	–9.6
50–64	67.6	61.2	57.5	–9.5	–6.0
Skill level					
Low	53.2	44.0	30.6	–17.3	–30.5
Intermediate	73.0	66.0	59.5	–9.6	–9.8
High	68.5	62.5	58.2	–8.8	–6.9

Share of employees with permanent contracts and working hours > 31 h/per week.
Source: Destatis (Mikrozensus).

Table 8.1 shows that standard employment follows a declining trend in the long run. For the youngest age group, the share of standard employment contracts is almost halved from the beginning of the 1990s to the latest period. Looking at sub-periods reveals that the lion's share of the decline occurred in the 1990s. For prime-age employees (age 25–49), the shrinking share of standard employment accelerated slightly in the 2000s, whereas this is not the case for older workers. Looking at the skill level, there is a clear indication that the increase in non-standard employment is highly concentrated among low-skilled workers. This might also be due to the de-regulation over the course of the labour market reforms.

Overall, one can conclude that the creeping process of erosion in standard employment was not initiated by the Agenda policy during the period from 2003 to 2005. However, some of the elements of the reform have favoured this development.

The future of the German model

Assessing labour market performance in general, it is fair to recognize the sizeable merits of the reform efforts. Although the labour market reforms came at some significant costs for large groups of workers, it seems that some basic ingredients of Agenda 2010 have not destroyed but have rather strengthened the German variety of capitalism. They clearly helped overcome the most dangerous threats to the foundations of the German model (i.e. the increase in systemic unemployment and the loss of competitiveness in export markets). The "teutonic turnaround" has substantially contributed to the employment records and reductions in short- and long-term unemployment in the last ten years. Moreover, the reform agenda was also relevant for the German "labour market miracle" during the Great Recession of 2008/2009. These statements are partly at odds with the conclusion of a widely recognized recent study:

The scale of the reforms is modest enough that they seem unlikely to have triggered the dramatic increase in competitiveness or the enormous drop in German unemployment or to have led Germany's labour market through the deep recession in 2008–2009.

(Dustmann et al. 2014: 184)

As I argued above, it is true that wage restraint and the increase in wage dispersion started well before the labour market reforms, approximately in 1995. It is also true that the substantial improvement in competitiveness of the German exporters is closely linked to the relative decrease of Germany's unit labour costs vis-à-vis its trading partners, which was mainly due to this wage moderation. However, it is a severe misunderstanding to assess the scale of the reforms as "modest". The Hartz reforms, especially the merger between unemployment assistance and welfare, deeply changed the fundamental labour market institutions. What Dustmann et al. (2014) fail to explain is the precise temporal coincidence of the reform process and the obvious break in the unemployment trend, the change in the parameters of the matching function, and the indicators of the behaviour of workers and the unemployed. The change in competitiveness has been occurring gradually since the mid-1990s, but for 10 years or so, no successes were apparent in the labour market. Only after the end of the reform process in 2005 did the unemployment figures decrease by approximately 40 per cent in three years. Although an empirical macroeconomic analysis of the situation does not allow for a causal inference to be made in the strict sense, it is very likely and highly plausible that the drastic reforms implemented under chancellor Schröder had first- rather than second-order effects on labour market performance. Yet it should be emphasized that the timing of the German labour market reforms was well chosen because they occurred during a period of an expansionary world market. My reading of the facts is that the combination of the structural reforms with the external boom helped to overcome the most dangerous threat to the foundations of the German model (i.e. the increase in systemic unemployment). Although not all parts of the reform process were well designed, the Agenda policy sharpened awareness that the acceptance of various forms of flexibility for firms to cushion against external economic shocks is mutually advantageous to employers and employees. This relates to working time and working-time accounts as well as remuneration schemes. Especially in the export-oriented manufacturing sector, these new forms of flexibility improved responsiveness to market signals and reinforced the effects of the long period of wage moderation on international competitiveness. Hence, one salient feature of the German model – its export-orientation based on a strong manufacturing sector – was even strengthened by the effects of the reform. Other features – like the dual training system, long-tenures of prime-age skilled workers or well-functioning social partnerships – were not negatively affected by the reforms. In particular, the system of labour relations is still rather distinct from that of the Anglo-Saxon approach.

In the light of the presented evidence, Hartz reforms did not destroy the German model. However, it has undergone transformations in order to adapt to new conditions of the functioning of the economy and there are aspects of these transformations, which could be seen as representing the creeping erosion of some of its cornerstones. It would therefore be wrong to sweep the challenges to the German model under the rug. These challenges relate to the decline in the importance of collective bargaining agreements, growing labour market segmentation and an increase in wage inequality. It should again be emphasized that all these phenomena – although often attributed to the reforms – were not caused by the Agenda policy implemented under chancellor Schröder from 2003 to 2005. They are due to long-run trends that had already started in the 1990s or even before. At most, the labour market reforms have led to a certain acceleration of these erosion processes, such as the increase in atypical employment among certain groups.

The reform process might be blamed, however, for ignoring and not counteracting the erosion of some of the fundamentals of the German model. This raises the question of whether there is some scope for the reform process to be rectified. In other words, we can ask whether the trends in segmentation and inequality can be reversed without jeopardizing the obvious employment-related successes of the reforms.

Traditionally, the German economy ran successfully with a rather low level of earnings inequality. At the same time, at least the important group of trained workers enjoyed a comfortable social security network. Today, workers are in much greater danger of losing their social status within a quite short period of time. Given the regulatory framework in place after the reforms, they are much more pressed to accept unfavourable working conditions and low-paid jobs. Wage inequality has risen sharply. Furthermore, social permeability has decreased over the years. Among recent criticisms of the German system, the education inheritance (*Bildungsvererbung*) is of major concern. The job and income risks borne by specific groups, namely the young and the low skilled, also seem to be increasing.

In light of this discussion, is seems that what is necessary is not a reversal of the reform process but a further, prudent and gradual development of reforms. The segmentation and inequality issues have to be addressed without throwing the baby out with the bathwater (i.e. without jeopardizing the employment-related successes). Adequate measures should include all efforts to enhance qualification among the disadvantaged and the labour market integration of the long-term unemployed. The introduction of a statutory minimum wage on 1 January 2015 was helpful in mitigating the inequality trend, but possible dis-employment effects should be monitored carefully.

To summarize, the German labour market reforms were a necessary painful cure to stop the harmful trend of increasing systemic unemployment. However, their negative side effects should not to be overlooked. Mitigating the damage that increasing segmentation has inflicted on the German model will pose an important challenge in the future.

Acknowledgement

The article is a shortened and modified version of J. Möller, "Did the German Model Survive the Labour Market Reforms?", forthcoming in *Journal for Labour Market Research*.

Note

1 This point has already been stressed by the profound analysis of the differences between the German and US systems by Abraham and Houseman (1995).

References

Abraham, C. G. and S. N. Houseman. 1995. "Labour Adjustment under Different Institutional Structures: A Case Study of Germany and the United States." In *Institutional Frameworks and Labour Market Performance: Comparative Views on the US and German Economies*, edited by F. Buttler, W. Franz, R. Schettkat and D. Soskice, pp. 285–315. Abingdon: Routledge.

Albert, M. 1993. *Capitalism vs. Capitalism: How America's Obsession with Individual Achievement and Short-term Profit Has Led It to the Brink of Collapse*. New York: Four Walls Eight Windows.

Boyer, R. 2006. "What Is the Future for Codetermination and Corporate Governance in Germany?" In *Transformationen des Kapitalismus: Festschrift für Wolfgang Streeck zum sechzigsten Geburtstag*, edited by J. Beckert, B. Ebbinghaus, A. Hassel and M. Philip, with assistance of W. Streeck, pp. 135–157. Schriften aus dem Max-Planck-Institut für Gesellschaftsforschung vol. 57. Frankfurt: Campus Verl.

Burda, M. C. and J. Hunt. 2011. "What Explains the German Labour Market Miracle in the Great Recession?" *Brookings Papers on Economic Activity* 42(1): 273–335. Available at http://ideas.repec.org/a/bin/bpeajo/v42y2011i2011-01p273-335.html.

Burda, M. C. and J. D. Sachs. 1987. *Institutional Aspects of High Unemployment in the Federal Republic of Germany*. NBER working paper 2241. Cambridge, MA: National Bureau of Economic Research.

Burda, M. C. and J. D. Sachs. 1988. "Assessing High Unemployment in West Germany." *World Economy* 11(4): 543–563.

Calmfors, L. 1993. "Centralisation of Wage Bargaining and Macroeconomic Performance: A Survey." *OECD Economic Studies* 21 (Winter): 161–191.

Calmfors, L. and J. Driffill. 1988. "Bargaining Structure, Corporatism and Macroeconomic Performance." *Economic Policy* 3(1): 13–61.

Card, D., J. Heining and P. Kline. 2013. "Workplace Heterogeneity and the Rise of West German Wage Inequality." *The Quarterly Journal of Economics* 128(3): 967–1015.

Deutscher Bundestag. 2003. *Stenographischer Bericht*. Berlin: Plenarprotokoll.

Driffill, John. 2006. "The Centralization of Wage Bargaining Revisited: What Have we Learnt?" *JCMS: Journal of Common Market Studies* 44(4): 731–756.

Dustmann, C., J. Ludsteck and U. Schönberg. 2009. "Revisiting the German Wage Structure." *Quarterly Journal of Economics* 124(2): 843–881.

Dustmann, C., B. Fitzenberger, U. Schönberg and A. Spitz-Oener. 2014. "From Sick Man of Europe to Economic Superstar: Germany's Resurgent Economy." *Journal of Economic Perspectives* 28(1): 167–188.

Economist. 1999. "The Sick Man of the Euro." *The Economist* (3 June). Available at www. economist.com/node/209559.

Eichengreen, B. 2007. "The German Economy: Be Careful What You Ask For." Available at www.eurointelligence.com/news-details/article/the-german-economy-be-careful-what-you-ask-for.html?cHash=050f9ab081c28f7499b4f565d2b00754 (accessed 5 January 2014).

Esping-Andersen, G. 1990. *The Three Worlds of Welfare Capitalism*. Princeton, NJ: Princeton University Press.

Fahr, R. and U. Sunde. 2009. "Did the Hartz Reforms Speed-Up the Matching Process? A Macro-Evaluation Using Empirical Matching Functions." *German Economic Review* 10(3): 284–316.

Freeman, R. 2000. *Single-Peaked Versus Diversified Capitalism: The Relation Between Economic Institutions and Outcomes*. NBER working paper 7556. Cambridge, MA: National Bureau of Economic Research. Available at www.nber.org/papers/w7556.

Freeman, R. B. and R. Schettkat. 2001. "Marketization of Production and the US-Europe Employment Gap." *Oxford Bulletin of Economics and Statistics* 63(0): 647–670.

Glyn, A., J. Möller, W. Salverda, J. Schmitt and M. Sollogoub. 2007. "Employment Differences in Distribution: Wages, Productivity and Demand." In *Services and Employment. Explaining the U.S.-European Gap*, edited by M. Gregory, W. Salverda and R. Schettkat, pp. 141–175. Princeton, NJ: Princeton University Press.

Hall, P. A. and D. W. Soskice (eds). 2001a. *Varieties of Capitalism: The Institutional Foundations of Comparative Advantage*. Oxford: Oxford University Press.

Hall, P. A. and D. W. Soskice. 2001b. "An Introduction to Varieties of Capitalism." In *Varieties of Capitalism: The Institutional Foundations of Comparative Advantage Vol. 1*, edited by P. Hall and D. W. Soskice, pp. 1–68. Oxford: Oxford University Press.

Kenworthy, L. 2006. "Germany's Employment Problem in Comparative Perspective." In *Transformationen des Kapitalismus: Festschrift für Wolfgang Streeck zum sechzigsten Geburtstag*, edited by J. Beckert, B. Ebbinghaus, A. Hassel and M. Philip, with assistance of W. Streeck, pp. 37–59. Schriften aus dem Max-Planck-Institut für Gesellschaftsforschung vol. 57. Frankfurt: Campus Verl.

Klinger, S. and T. Rothe. 2012. "The Impact of Labour Market Reforms and Economic Performance on the Matching of the Short-term and the Long-term Unemployed." *Scottish Journal of Political Economy* 59(1): 90–114.

Möller, J. 2010. "The German Labour Market Response in the World Recession – Demystifying a Miracle." *Journal for Labour Market Research*, 42(4): 325–336.

Möller, J. 2014. "Prosperity, Sustainable Employment and Social Justice: Challenges for the German Labour Market in the Twenty-first Century." *International Journal for Educational and Vocational Guidance* 14(1): 1–12.

Rhein, T. 2013. "Erwerbseinkommen: Deutsche Geringverdiener im europäischen Vergleich." *IAB-Kurzbericht Nürnberg* 15: 1–8. Available at doku.iab.de/kurzber/2013/kb1513.pdf.

Sperling, G. 2013. *The Case for a Manufacturing Renaissance: Prepared Remarks by Gene Sperling*. Washington, DC: The Brookings Institution. Available at www.brookings.edu/~/media/events/2013/7/25-manufacturing/the-case-for-a-manufacturing-renaissancegenesperling7252013finalp.pdf.

Stops, M. 2015. *Revisiting German Labour Market Reform Effects: A Panel Data Analysis for Occupational Labour Markets*. IAB Discussion Paper 2. Nürnberg: Institut für Arbeitsmarkt- und Berufsforschung.

Streeck, W. 1992. *Social Institutions and Economic Performance. Studies of Industrial Relations in Advanced Industrialized Countries*. London: Sage.

Streeck, W. 1995. *German Capitalism: Does it Exist? Can it Survive?* Cologne: Max-Planck-Institut für Gesellschaftsforschung.

Streeck, W. 1997. "German Capitalism: Does it Exist? Can it Survive?" *New Political Economy* 2(2): 237–256.

Streeck, W. 2005. *Nach dem Korporatismus: Neue Eliten, neue Konflikte.* MPIfG working paper 05/4. Cologne: Max-Planck-Institut für Gesellschaftsforschung. Available at http://hdl.handle.net/10419/44269, checked on 2/24/2014.

Thelen, K. A. 2012. "Varieties of Capitalism: Trajectories of Liberalization and the New Politics of Social Solidarity." *Annual Review of Political Science* 15: 137–159.

Thelen, K. A. and C. van Wijnbergen. 2003. "The Paradox of Globalization: Labour Relations in Germany and Beyond." *Comparative Political Studies* 36(8): 859–880.

Part II
The external context and the European Union

Between threats and opportunities

John McGowan

Ever since the post-World War II economic recovery really took hold in the early 1950s, Europe has been an oasis of peace, prosperity, and stability in a troubled world. The events of the past ten years have revealed how completely interdependent these three goods – peace, prosperity, and stability – are. A threat to one quickly undermines the ability to sustain the others.

It was natural to ascribe much of Europe's success to two supranational organizations created in the 1950s: the Common Market, which evolved into the European Union (EU) and NATO (North Atlantic Treaty Organization). Of course, prior to 1990, that success was confined to western Europe. But the collapse of the Soviet Union saw western Europe reach out toward its Eastern European cousins. Surely it made sense to want more of a good thing. The European Union and NATO would be expanded to include the newly liberated nations of the east. Europe on a grand scale would accomplish what German reunification achieved at the national level.

The effects of this European overreach, occurring in the 1990s, did not become apparent immediately. The prosperity of the 1990s covered a multitude of sins. But the economic weakness afflicting both Europe and the rest of the globe after 2008 revealed the troubles lurking just beneath the surface of Europe's actions. For this reason, the ongoing Ukraine crisis should be seen as a symptom of a wider set of problems, not just as an isolated crisis.

In particular, the EU (perhaps over-influenced by an America that seemed incapable of revising Cold War attitudes) squandered the opportunity to open the door to economic and diplomatic cooperation with the Russia that emerged from the ashes of the Soviet Union. How could this new Russia not feel threatened when NATO now extended to its very borders, and when the EU worked to develop economic ties to all of the former Soviet satellites? Russia, as Eric Brunat shows in Chapter 12, became a natural resource dependent economy in the period from 1995 to the present, thus standing in the same relation to the Western democracies as states such as Nigeria or Saudi Arabia. In hindsight, we have to at least wonder if that fate could have been averted if Europe had engaged Russia instead of isolating it.

The Ukraine crisis also highlights what has remained the biggest obstacle to its success since the EU's inception: nationalism. It would be the height of naiveté and wishful thinking to believe that the national states joined in the EU project were willing to sacrifice national sovereignty and national self-interest to the European parliament or the European bureaucrats. As has often been noted, it was precisely the EU's inability to forge a truly supranational political structure that led to the decision to create a common currency. The hope, quite clearly, was that closer economic union would lead to the kind of political union for which, quite obviously, adequate support still did not exist to institute. And, of course, several EU states declined to join the common currency.

But I think it fair to say that the EU had crafted a reasonably workable compromise between national sovereignty and supranational institutions prior to 1990. At least, nationalism at that juncture did not seem a threat to the whole enterprise. The collapse of Yugoslavia in the 1990s was the beginning of the change. Two consequences of the Yugoslavian crisis stand out today. First, it began the movement of various ethnic groups to demand their own nation-state (a reprise, if you will, of the self-determination doctrine of Woodrow Wilson in 1915). In other words, against the move toward a more unified Europe, there was now a strong counter-movement toward the proliferation of smaller, discrete political units. By the time the smoke had cleared, where Yugoslavia and Czechoslovakia once stood, there were now eight new states.

Second, the Yugoslavian troubles marked the first time that NATO was out into action. Not only did the military aggression against Serbia alienate the Russians, but it also broke the long-standing European abstention, in practice if not in theory, from the adventurism that characterized (and characterizes) American foreign policy since World War II. From the Balkans followed European involvement in the Middle East following 9/11. With the end of peace also came the end of stability. Not only was the political map of Eastern Europe redrawn, but the whole Middle East descended into chaos.

In this context, the Ukraine crisis looks like more of the same. Ukraine as a state appears unworkable in the context of reawakened ethnic loyalties, while Russia feels compelled to resist US and European incursions into areas it considers within its sphere of influence. And, as Jake Kipp notes in Chapter 13, Russia is also pushed to devise an Asian strategy to counter-balance what it can only perceive as the European threat.

Three further points about nationalism are worth making here. First, passions that might have seemed only Eastern European are now evident in the West. The futures of Spain, the United Kingdom, and Belgium as the unified nations we now know are uncertain. Paradoxically, this break-up into smaller units is enabled by the existence of the EU. An independent Scotland is more thinkable precisely because it would be able to piggy-back on the larger institutional framework provided by the EU. Of course, it is possible that if the EU welcomed a newly independent Scotland (or Catalonia) into its ranks, the nation from which that new entity was formed might quit the EU in protest. An even larger paradox, to which I will return, is this movement toward smaller and smaller political entities even as globalization leads to larger and larger economic enterprises. It is hard to see how these smaller political units can hold their own against accumulations of economic power.

Second, Herman Schwartz (Chapter 11) notes that Germany's economy constitutes 28 per cent of the entire GDP of the EU. If other nations split into smaller units, the relative power of Germany in the EU can only increase. After witnessing what happened to Greece in the spring and summer of 2015, it is (to say the least) unclear why any smaller nation would want to trust its fate to the EU. As Paul Marer shows in Chapter 9, these kinds of calculations are already at play in the countries that are scheduled to join the euro. But I think we should expect such calculations about the very feasibility of EU membership going forward. The pending UK referendum on EU membership will be a crucial moment in this process of re-examination.

Third, the awakening of nationalistic passions undermines European peace and stability – and that rise is augmented by the declining prosperity after 2008. The emergence and growing popularity of the nationalist parties, with their hostility to the EU, is an understandable response to a European project that was pursued in the face of popular scepticism and was never truly endorsed by a fully democratic process. Certainly, the majority were willing to go along so long as there was prosperity. And even since 2008 there has been impressive willingness among Europeans to face economic pain in order to keep the euro and the European project more generally alive. But the chasm between the elites in Brussels and the populace back in the member states, which was always there, has certainly intensified as prosperity wanes. Now that nationalism has found a convenient target in the flood of refugees coming into Europe as a result of the destabilization of the Middle East and Northern Africa post 9/11. The nationalistic violence first experienced in Yugoslavia in the 1990s and currently afflicting the Ukraine has become increasingly possible in Western Europe.

Turning now to economic concerns, the hostility to the migrants is as misguided as it is tragic. As Bruno Dallago explains in Chapter 7, migration into Europe is an economic plus, not an economic drain. The larger issue here is Europe's economic standing in the world – or the issue of secular stagnation (discussed in Chapter 11 by Herman Mark Schwartz). Everyone agrees that Europe's demographics, primarily its aging population and low birth rates, means that the growth rate of its various economies (or its economy measured as one whole) will lag behind the US and various "emerging" economies around the world. The disagreements come with how to respond to this situation. Importing a younger population in the form of immigrants is one remedy, although hardly a cure-all. The more traditional approach has been to turn one's economy in the direction of exports. In the current globalized economy, such a strategy requires reductions in wages in order to make the economy's products competitive on the world market - and Germany (as Joachim Möller, in Chapter 8, and Herman Mark Schwartz describe) has aggressively pursued that policy. Of course, the same effect can also be achieved by devaluation of a currency, but that option is off the table for Eurozone members. The larger issue is that not every country in the world can be

Table II.1 Annual GDP growth for France, Germany and the US

Country	2010	2011	2012	2013	2014
France	2.0	2.1	0.2	0.7	0.2
Germany	4.1	3.6	0.4	0.1	1.6
United States	2.5	1.6	2.3	2.2	2.4

Source: http://data.worldbank.org/indicator/NY.GDP.MKTP.KD.ZG

a net exporter – and it is really not sustainable over the long run to keep expecting the United States to be the consumer nation for the rest of the world. There are also ecological issues to consider. What would be the environmental costs if the Chinese, for example, were to begin consuming at even a fraction of the rate of America's consumption of goods like oil, water, and beef?

Economists are fond of pointing to the inefficiencies in European economies, contrasting France (usually the whipping boy in such accounts) unfavourably to the more open and more dynamic business environment in the United States.[1] But once we discount the impact of demographics on economic growth, it is not obvious that France lags so far behind the US – and the French do reap a variety of benefits from structuring their economy the way they do (longer vacations, better health care, more job security). A comparison of French, German, and US growth rates (Table II.1), for example, does not provide an obvious case that France is an outlier. Both France and Germany reveal Europe's weak recovery as compared to a stronger US recovery, and while France's 2014 results are disappointing, in 2013 France had a higher growth rate than Germany. While France did not achieve the robust growth rates of Germany in 2010 and 2011, neither did the United States, and there are various reasons, including the demographic ones, to believe that 4 per cent growth in any of the mature economies will be extremely difficult to achieve in the short to medium-range future.

Pessimists keep insisting that Europe cannot afford, in the long run, its generous social safety net. Or, in other words, that the long run of European prosperity is bound to end – and sometime fairly soon, unless some drastic changes are made. But the changes suggested are so unpalatable, and exact such costs on large segments of the population, that it is not obvious that such changes would be, in that same long run, beneficial. What would it benefit a nation to reform its economy at the cost of impoverishing its people? The larger issue here is what prosperity is for. Yes, France has higher unemployment rates than Germany and the US: 10.3 per cent in France as compared to 5 per cent in Germany and 6.2 per cent in the United States according to the most recent OECD figures. But those same data sets place France's poverty rate at 8.1 per cent while Germany's sits at 8.4 per cent with the US's at 17.9 per cent. This apparent anomaly in the employment and poverty figures reflects not only France's robust safety net, but the fact that extremely low wages means you can have a job in the US but still have an income under the poverty line (OECD 2015). So it is certainly arguable that a larger percentage of citizens in France enjoy the fruits of prosperity than in the United States, even if France's aggregate economic performance is not quite as robust as that of the US. And despite claims that France's model is unsustainable, it has managed to keep its head above water to date. It is worth reminding the economic fundamentalists that household debt in France is 104.2 per cent of disposable income and government debt is 110.2 per cent of GDP; the comparable figures for the US are 114.1 per cent for household debt and 122.6 per cent for government debt (OECD 2015a). So, which country is on an unsustainable path?

My larger point is that "weakness" can mean a variety of things. France, and other European states, have been relatively strong in relation to economic forces that would push for lower wages and increasing inequality, while in the United States the state's power vis à vis such forces has waned. Weaker economic results may very well be an acceptable price to pay for more control over the distribution of economic benefits, especially when the gap between the weaker results and those in the US are not huge. Western Europe has consistently, over the past fifty years, had the best record in the world of distributing the benefits of prosperity. The GINI coefficient, which measures inequality, with 0 representing perfect equality and 1 representing perfect inequality, stands at 0.29 in Germany and 0.31 in France as contrasted to 0.40 for the United States (all figures for 2013). Of the 31 OECD countries, only Turkey, Mexico, and Chile are more unequal than the US (OECD 2015b).

Of course, these comments are predicated on the belief that France (and Europe more generally) can return to something close to 2 per cent growth per annum. If the results of the past three years are a long-term trend, and not just the fruits of Europe's slow recovery, then all bets are off. This is another way of saying that if secular stagnation is Europe's future, then the ability of Europe to both enjoy prosperity and to distribute that prosperity generally among its citizens may be lost forever. The consequences of such a collapse of European prosperity and of the European model for sharing its fruits would almost certainly be increased instability and social unrest. I agree with Thomas Piketty that rolling back prosperity in the direction of the inequities prevalent in the Gilded Age prior to World War I would generate the kinds of conflict also characteristic of that period.[2]

In order to avoid such an impoverished future, Europe needs to position itself within the world economy even as it comes to term with the rising economic inequality that the globalized economy has produced over the past forty years. John Pickles (Chapter 10) points to one way of viewing changes that are already underway. We may, in fact, be misrepresenting national GDPs since we ascribe all the revenue to the US (for example) when a car is produced in Tennessee, even though various parts of that car are produced in Mexico, Peru and Japan.[3] The movement of goods in Global Value Chains (GVCs) offers an opportunity for nations around the world to participate in productive processes, with different nations finding suitable niches. Pickles is even cautiously optimistic that the existence of such chains can underwrite global trade agreements that establish wage levels along with safety and environmental regulations that are not simply a race to the bottom. European economies, in this scenario, must find what they are good at doing, while the EU as a whole must work toward establishing the trade relations and regulatory frameworks that enable GVCs even while protecting workers and the environment. It is here that the EU has a significant function as a political entity large enough to counterbalance globalized capital.

I share Pickles' cautious optimism. I don't think the EU's woes are primarily economic. I think they are political. Of course, the European economy took a severe hit in the recession, as did the US economy. And, of course, in some ideal universe, European economies could be more efficient. But to think that somehow differences in efficiency or regulation between the US and the EU amount to huge differences in economic outcomes is, I think, delusional – and ultimately not borne out by the numbers. All economies are less than ideally efficient, and all modern economies are highly regulated. (Surely the financial crisis of 2008 should make it clear that regulation, despite its real costs, is on the whole a better thing than non-regulation). The very real strengths of Europe – not the least of which has been its peace and stability, not to mention its high levels of education – counter-balance its institutional and/or structural weaknesses. If the past eight years have taught us anything, they have shown that plenty of capital prefers stability and safety (even with significantly lesser returns) to volatility and risk. In an ever-dangerous world, European stability will generate prosperity even if growth rates are not robust. It would be a shame if growth rates lower than those characteristic of the boom years of 1950 to 1980 were to serve as an excuse for rising poverty rates and a weaker safety net.

What the economic crisis of the past eight years has revealed are significant political weaknesses. The European project has been caught mid-stream. It is obvious now that a common currency is dysfunctional absent true political unity. And yet Europe – both its elites and its ambivalent peoples – can't seem to decide to go one way or the other: whether to dissolve the common currency or build the supranational political institutions that the euro requires to work. The response to Greece in 2015 tells us that the dissolution of the euro is off the table for the most powerful players in Europe; but those same players apparently lack the will to create the institutional and legal framework needed to make the euro viable. The timid response to the crisis, and the adherence (for the most part) to austerity measures, has turned a serious downturn into a severe and prolonged one. The fact that Europe followed America's lead in the response to the Ukraine crisis is just another indication of the political weakness that has produced such a feeble response to the economic crisis. Europe's interests in relation to Russian oil are not the same as America's (as Eric Brunat points out). But Europe lacks the ability to conduct a foreign policy of its own, and so is left to go along (albeit reluctantly) with what America initiates. The chaos attending the refugee crisis is still another example of political weakness.

The inability to make a decision one way or the other can be attributed, finally, to the democratic deficit. The European elites do not dare to put the European project to a vote because they think they would lose. But in the absence of a vote their hands are tied. They have very little mandate to do anything, so what we get are continual half-measures and kicking of the can down the road as well as a tendency to follow the lead of the Americans. And their dithering has only inflamed popular hostility to the European project and the recourse to nationalism that is the default position for those who wish to spurn the EU. After the overreach of the 1990s, we have now the overly cautious approach that has characterized EU policy since 2008. The result is an endless economic crisis, simmering along with low growth and high unemployment, just as the Ukraine crisis also simmers along with low-level violence and no resolution in sight. Politically enfeebled, the EU cannot find the means to bring either crisis to an end, even if we can give it credit for managing, time and again, to avert total disaster. To date, Europe has avoided truly extreme economic depredation, political instability, or civil unrest, but it is not doing well on any of these fronts even if it is muddling along. A severe disruption of any one of these three pillars of European success – and it is not hard to imagine such disruptions – would place the other two pillars in jeopardy. Certainly, the current course of teetering on the edge of disaster seems unwise as well as unsustainable.

Notes

1 See Economist (2012) for a typical claim that France's economy is headed toward disaster. In his blog (Krugman.blogs.nytimes.com), Paul Krugman's entries for 9 November 2013, 16 January 2014 and 27 August 2014 offers a vigorous counter-argument to those bullish about France.
2 Thomas Piketty (2014) makes the case that income and, especially, wealth inequality is returning to pre-World War I levels, while also suggesting that such inequalities must, eventually, disrupt the stability of democratic societies.
3 See Ash (2015) for an excellent explanation of how accounting for Global Value Chains would alter statistical measurements of GDP.

References

Ash, K. 2015. "The Emergence of Global Value Chains: Implications for Trade Policy and Trade Agreements." In *Crises in Europe: Transatlantic Perspectives*, edited by B. Dallago and J. McGowan, pp. 21–34. Abingdon: Routledge.
Economist. 2012."The Time-Bomb of Europe." *The Economist* (17 November). Available at www.economist.com/news/leaders/21566640-why-france-could-become-biggest-danger-europes-single-currency-time-bomb-heart.
OECD. 2015a. "OECD Factbook (Edition 2014)." OECD Factbook Statistics (database). Available at www.oecd-ilibrary.org/economics/data/oecd-factbook-statistics/oecd-factbook-edition-2014_g2g5582b-en.
OECD. 2015b. "OECD Income Distribution Database (IDD): Gini, Poverty, Income, Methods and Concepts." Available at www.oecd.org/social/income-distribution-database.htm.
Piketty, T. 2014. *Capital in the Twenty-First Century*. Cambridge, MA: Harvard University Press.

9 The euro and eastern Europe

Six insiders, six outsiders – why so?

Paul Marer

Introduction

For a plausible understanding of why a particular EE country had taken or is taking its own approach regarding the euro, a discussion of several background issues will be helpful.

The first is the legal–political–economic requirements for an EE country to adopt the euro. As latecomers to the European Union (EU) as well as to the EMU, the EE countries were not given the same options that the earlier candidates had. Specifically, all the newer members of the EU have a treaty obligation to eventually adopt the euro, although without a specific timetable on when to do so. By contrast, when the EMU had been agreed upon in Maastricht in 1992, all EU members at the time could decide whether or not to adopt the euro.

The second issue is a benefit-cost analysis of the EMU membership. There are unconditional as well as conditional advantages and costs of adopting the euro. The *conditional* benefits and costs depend on a country's historical, political, ideological, economic, social, cultural, and legal situation, which of course may change over time. Understanding the conditional benefits and costs is essential for interpreting the actions of each of the EE countries at the time when it made the decision to adopt (or to link its currency) to the euro, as well as to assess the likelihood that today's euro outsiders will join the EZ in the foreseeable future.

The third issue concerns the complex design of the EMU, including the institutions and the policies that are supposed to make the arrangement work smoothly. While there was much controversy all through the 1980s and early 1990s when the EMU was still on a drawing board, during the EMU's first decade (1999–2008), it became the conventional wisdom that the original architects, who prevailed at Maastricht, were clearly right, and that everything was turning out as well, if not better, than EMU's advocates had expected. This favourable perception was clearly a factor in Slovenia's and Slovakia's decisions to jump on the EZ bandwagon at the time when they did (2007 and 2009, respectively). In 2009 came the Great Recession. The hitherto hidden or forgotten design problems of the EMU had suddenly appeared. It has also become evident that the hope and the expectations of the EZ's architects – that if and when the time came to fix the Euro's design shortcomings, the political will to do so would be found – have remained unrealized. Therefore, perceptions about the EMU became strongly negative, with a growing realization that Europe's common currency had several major design faults. This new conventional wisdom certainly has dampened the interests of the EE's euro outsiders in becoming euro insiders today, or any time soon. And the perception in the EE that in the EZ's smouldering sovereign debt crisis, the North had treated the heavily indebted Southern members of the EMU rather harshly has been reinforcing the euro outsiders' caution about adopting the euro.

This chapter underscores the fact that monetary integration in Europe is not only, or even mainly, a financial or an economic issue; it is also a political one. In certain situations, politics dominates all the others, in some cases for the better (at least that is how it may appear at first); in others, for the worst, standing as an obstacle to the resolution of various crises. The EMU itself, and the relationship between it and the EE countries, also involves historical, ideological, social, cultural, and legal aspects. One intended contribution of this chapter is a multidisciplinary perspective on the issues.

EE is defined here as the 11 countries in the region that were members of the EU at the beginning of 2015, Serbia – a candidate country for EU membership. In January 2014, the first intergovernmental conference took place between Serbia and the EU, signalling the formal start of Serbia's accession negotiations. Although it may take years before Serbia is admitted as a full member, the country appears to be the next in line to join the EU, assuming of course that enlargement will continue. A further reason for including Serbia is that the country is adjacent to one of the region's euro insiders, Slovenia, as well as the country's extremely high level of (informal) Euroization.

Legal aspects of Eurozone membership

The Maastricht Treaty of 1992 had established the EMU; the common currency was introduced in 1999. Along with subsequent amendments, the Treaty specified that while the then members of the EU had a choice on whether or not to join the EMU, countries that would be admitted to the EU later, as full members, would have the legal obligation to eventually adopt the euro, thus joining the Eurozone (EZ).[1] When the government of a new EU member thinks that the country is ready to adopt the euro, it must formally apply. At that point, the country must be found to have fulfilled all the Maastricht criteria (listed below), and that EMU's current members and the European Central Bank (ECB) would have to agree that the country was ready to adopt the euro.

Provisions of the Maastricht Treaty

Below is the list of the Maastricht "convergence" criteria that an EZ candidate country must comply with before it can be permitted to adopt the euro.

1   The government's annual budget deficit cannot exceed 3 per cent of GDP.
2   Its stock of public debt cannot exceed 60 per cent of GDP.

3 The inflation rate must be within 1.5 percentage points of the average of those three members with the lowest-inflation figures.

4 Long-term interest rates must be within 2 percentage points of the average of the three best anti-inflationary performers.

5 A candidate country must spend a minimum of two years in ERM II, during which fluctuations of its exchange rate vis-à-vis the euro must remain within +/–15 per cent of the central rate.[2]

6 Full domestic political independence of the central bank.

The logic of these requirements is indicated by their "convergence criteria" label. By fulfilling criteria 1–5 before adopting the euro, candidate countries were supposed to have converged, in terms of key macroeconomic performance indicators, toward the "core" countries of Germany, France, and the Benelux nations. The assumption was that the more economically alike the members of the EMU were, the easier it would be for the ECB to decide and implement common monetary policies appropriate for the entire group and for each of its members.

The logic of criterion 6 is to make sure that each EZ member's national central bank would be able to carry out, without fail, the monetary policy instructions of the ECB, whose local subsidiary they would, in effect, become.

EMU's designers were aware that for the EZ to function well, it would be insufficient just to fulfil the Maastricht criteria prior to entry. It is also important that those key economic decisions such as fiscal policy, which will remain in the hands of the member governments, should continue to be aligned among the members. It is with this objective in mind that prior to the birth of the euro, the so-called Stability and Growth Pact (SGP) had been agreed upon, namely, that Maastricht criteria 1 and 2 would continue to be permanently observed by EZ members.[3]

Adopting the euro: benefits and costs

To better understand the motives of those EE countries, which have become euro insiders, as well as the attitudes of those that have remained euro outsiders (and their euro adoption prospects), let's enumerate the benefits as well as the costs of the euro adoption.

Certain benefits are unconditional; that is, they are (or would be) benefiting any country adopting the euro, irrespective of the country's economic circumstances, while the existence and extent of certain other benefits depend upon the specific circumstances of the country at the time. The costs of membership are also partly unconditional and partly conditional, depending upon a country's circumstances.

Unconditional benefits

1 The EZ members save transactions costs when doing business with other EZ members. The more "open" an economy and the larger the share of its external economic transactions with other EZ members, the greater the savings. This

means that the smaller an EZ member economy, the more open it is likely to be, and thus the larger will be this benefit of the EMU membership relative to its GDP.

2 Competition is enhanced, due to an increase in cross-border transactions as well as the ease with which prices and costs can be compared across countries, since they are now stated in a common currency. This improves economic efficiency.

3 The irrevocable fixing of the exchange rate insulates the economy from currency speculation and from economic fluctuations caused by such speculation. This benefit will disappear for the country, which is expected to leave the EZ, whether voluntarily or being forced to do so. (An example is Greece today: euro bank deposits and other euro assets in Greece, except cash, face a "redenomination" risk).

4 A combination of the above three benefits is likely to improve economic efficiency and thus macroeconomic performance, especially in terms of GDP growth rates.

5 Having formally adopted the euro, a new member country participates in designing the ECB's institutions and policies, including those of the EZ's special funds, such as the European Stability Mechanism (ESM), which was established to assist the EZ members.

Conditional benefits

1 A country with a history of high inflation, which is usually accompanied by economic, social, and political upheavals, benefits from credibly and permanently transferring monetary policy decisions to a strong, prestigious, and independent central bank, such as the ECB. Such a transfer can be made directly, by joining the EZ; or indirectly, by credibly pegging the domestic currency to that of the euro. In either case, becoming a euro insider also means a firm commitment to responsible fiscal policies.

2 An EZ member running large, sustained current-account deficits can be assured of the financing of those deficits via a combination of (a) private (voluntary) capital inflows and (b) the automatic granting of Target2 credits by the European System of Central Banks.[4] Target2 credits automatically make up the difference between a country's current-account deficit and that portion of the deficit not covered by the private capital inflows.

3 Being a euro insider can also be a financial "shelter" in case of global economic turbulences, such as the financial meltdown and the last Great Recession. *Ceteris paribus*, a euro insider is likely to obtain financial assistance more promptly and more adequately from the EU, thanks to certain EZ facilities (such as the ESM), from the partner EU governments, and perhaps also from the IMF, than those which are euro outsiders.

4 Becoming a euro insider is also a strong political declaration that the country places a high value on joining "Western" economic and monetary arrangements. Such a benefit can be very important to certain successor states

of the Soviet Union, such as the Baltic nations, as a way of further distancing themselves from Russia's orbit.

Similarly to benefits, some costs are certain; others depend on a country's circumstances.

Unconditional costs

1   The *financial costs* of membership includes subscriptions to the ECB's capital and to various EZ "rescue funds," such as the ESM. Although each member country's contribution is based on its economic size, such costs are relatively more burdensome for the poorer members. For example, the requirement that Slovakia contribute to the EZ's bailout fund for Greece had caused a political crisis in Slovakia, on the grounds that it is unjust to require a poorer country's taxpayers to subsidize their counterparts in a richer country.

Conditional costs

1   Joining the EZ means *giving up key aspects of national sovereignty* to unelected EU officials in Brussels and to their counterparts at the ECB in Frankfurt. Therefore, there were/are monetary economists as well as politicians who view the EMU itself as a highly undesirable and unwelcome undertaking, whether from the point of view of political philosophy, economic efficiency, or both.[5]
2   Giving up two key instruments of the monetary policy – the exchange and interest rate – can be costly if the business cycles of a new member are not synchronized with those of the other members and if the new member's domestic *adjustment capabilities are constrained.* Adjustment capabilities are limited if a country has large public and/or external debts relative to the GDP; high and inflexible budget expenditures, such as welfare-type payments; inflexible wage-setting practices, such as indexing wages to inflation; and low labour mobility.
3   If a prospective EZ member is at a much lower level of development than are the current members, then becoming a euro insider is likely to cause inflation in the new member state to be permanently higher than the EZ average *and* to trigger a credit boom. The above-mentioned are likely to happen for several interdependent reasons. First, the poorer EU countries – eager to converge toward the more developed ones in terms of per capita GDP levels – are more likely to experience above-average inflation to begin with. Furthermore, upon joining the EZ, the poorer new member is likely to experience fast productivity growth in its tradable sectors (typically helped by large capital inflows), leading to wage rises both in the tradable and non-tradable sectors, causing total-economy unit labour costs to rise.[6] This was certainly the case during the EMU's "sunshine decade" (1999–2008).[7] Since both short-term and long-term interest rates had converged quickly to the EZ, different national inflation rates resulted in substantial differences in *real* interest rates, becoming much

lower (in some cases even negative) in the lower-income new members than in the higher-income older members.[8] Low nominal and especially low real interest rates in countries whose businesses and households were used to high nominal rates inevitably trigger a credit boom (especially in the construction, real estate, and service sectors), contributing to cost-push as well as to demand-pull inflation. And the longer and stronger is a credit boom, the more likely that it will cause severe economic problems when the credit bubble bursts.

4   Just as the assurance of a more or less automatic financing of current-account deficits within the EZ is a membership benefit by the countries running sustained, large balance-of-payment deficits, countries running sizable payment surpluses within the EZ, such as Germany, may view them as costs, especially if they perceive a risk that the surpluses might not ever be fully settled.[9]

5   All euro outsiders have been frightened by the EZ's multiple crises that began in 2009 and have been continuing with greater or lesser intensity ever since. These include the crisis of sovereign debt service, the extreme weakness of many systemically important banks and other financial institutions, severe problems of intra-EZ competitiveness, as well as deep recessions and disappointing growth throughout the EZ. Influential voices have argued that some of the crises were triggered or exacerbated by the fundamental design faults of monetary integration among a large group of diverse countries.[10] Concerned about the very future of the EZ, and also about being "infected" if they join the group, most euro outsider countries have been assuming a "let's wait and see" attitude about becoming euro insiders.

Economic and Monetary Union design debates and design faults

The likelihood of the euro outsiders joining the EMU has diminished in recent years with a better understanding *today* of the EMU's fundamental design faults than when the Maastricht Treaty was signed, and later, during the EZ's "sunshine era," which preceding the Great Recession.

Although there were debates during the 1980s and early 1990s on whether establishing a common currency at that time might be premature, the leading expert on what constitutes an "optimum currency area" (OCA), 1999 Nobel Laureate in economics Robert Mundell endorsed the speedy establishment of the EMU. In fact, the Nobel Committee cited Mundell for his contribution in laying the foundations of the EMU, with the year of his Nobel award coinciding with the introduction of the euro.[11]

Mundell and other "monetarists" believed that the fixing of exchange rates and the adoption of a common currency would ensure sufficient convergence of the economies *after* the introduction of the euro so as to make the monetary union work. The EMU was also seen as stimulating structural reforms, especially in the Mediterranean countries, where labour market rigidities, non-competitive business sectors, excessive state regulation, and corruption were seen as incompatible with the EMU membership (Csaba 2014: 23). However, in those countries, complacency about fixing those problems became the rule, not the exception. Furthermore, Mundell also supported the EMU on the grounds that the euro would help counterbalance the USD as the world's pre-eminent reserve and vehicle currency, even if the USD would remain the globe's dominant currency.

Opposed to Mundell and other monetarists were the "economists" who believed that the introduction of a single currency should be the crowning of a lengthy process of convergence of the economies seeking to adopt the euro. German economists were the most vocal representatives of this group and were thus always the strongest advocates of the most rigorous conditions possible for establishing the EMU and for countries to join it (Swoboda 1999).

As we can clearly see now, by hindsight, the sceptics were proven right. They correctly identified the most basic design flaw of the EMU (number 1 below), to which several other design problems must be added:

1   The most fundamental design fault with the EMU was the establishment of a monetary union *prior to fiscal and political union*. Such a never-before sequencing in economic history can be likened to putting horses before an imaginary cart, hoping that the cart (fiscal and political union) will materialize when needed. Of course, this problem is much easier to pinpoint with hindsight. Many also thought that to link countries monetarily but not politically would be a good idea.[12] Be that as it may, one should note that the *dominant political objective* of the EMU was *not* the establishment of a truly well-functioning monetary arrangement among a group of countries, but to "control" the prospective economic and therefore political might of Germany following reunification.[13]

2   A design fault related to the above was proceeding with the EMU *without a banking union*. During a financial crisis, like the Great Recession, banking problems (due in no small measure to lax banking supervision by *national* banking supervisors) spilled over into fiscal difficulties as the states had to intervene to stabilize financial institutions in trouble. The effective transmission mechanism of a single monetary policy requires a healthy financial system in the member countries to create near-uniform monetary conditions in every part of the EMU. This requires a banking union as a complement to monetary union, with a centralized banking supervision, a common bank resolution mechanism, and a unified deposit insurance system.[14] If a banking union would have been in place, it is doubtful that the excessive indebtedness of corporate and household sectors in several countries, which eventually caused such havoc in those countries' public finances, would have been allowed.

3   Another basic design fault of the EMU was its *exclusive focus on the convergence of a few key macroeconomic indicators*, neglecting large differences among prospective members in their formal and informal institutional arrangements (such as the role of the state in the economy and wage-determination practices) as well as in culture (the mindset, such as the scale of, and the attitude toward, corruption). Differences in those areas were especially large between the

EZ's "Northern" members (Germany, Belgium, Austria, The Netherlands and Finland) and its "Southern" members (Italy, Greece, Spain and Portugal).[15] As it is easy to see in retrospective, huge divergences in the latter areas have caused, cumulatively, basic incompatibilities between the two groups of countries. The design problem was to assume that the EZ would operate like the US, where lasting economic-level differences between, for instance, California and Mississippi, have not been causing irreparable harm to the United States to remain united. One important reason for the difference between the US and the EMU is the fundamentally weaker solidarity among the nations of Europe historically, politically, and culturally as compared with the "melting pot" tradition and institutional features of the US.

4   Another design fault was the *absence of effective sanctions enforcing* the Maastricht criteria as well as the provisions of the SGP.[16]

5   Still another design fault was the non-recognition that the very creation of a monetary union without fiscal and political union might give rise to *sovereign debt problems* for which effective solutions were not designed. Specifically, sovereign debt problems are much more likely to arise in the most heavily indebted members of the EMU where all public debt is, in effect, in a "foreign" currency (that is, mostly in Euro) whose issue member governments do not control. Hence, member countries facing debt-servicing problems are not in charge of their money supply and consequently don't have the option of reducing debt-to-GDP ratios via inflation, which would be an option if a significant part of the public debt would be in the debtor country's domestic currency.

6   Serious *competitiveness problems* are also more likely to arise in an EMU because the EZ membership means that national governments give up the two main tools for improving intra-EZ competitiveness, exchange rate devaluation, and interest rate adjustments. Competitiveness problems are not design faults *per se,* only the assumption that such problems will not arise – or if they do, what agreed procedures will be used to fix them – can be considered as design faults.[17]

Euro insiders and euro outsiders in eastern Europe

Having traced the historical, theoretical, and factual backgrounds of the EMU, we are now ready to present and interpret the relationship between the dozen countries of the EE and the euro (Table 9.1). The first six countries listed are euro insiders: the first five had already adopted the euro during 2007-2014; the last having had its currencies pegged firmly to the euro since 1997.[18]

If a similar tabulation had been compiled in 2008, on the eve of the financial meltdown and the Great Recession, the ratios would have been reversed: only two EE countries had adopted the Euro; the currencies of the four others were pegged to the euro. The other six EE countries have remained euro outsiders. Strong circumstantial evidence suggests that none of them have a near-term or medium-term interest in adopting the euro.

Table 9.1 East European countries and the Euro

Country	EU Member	ERM II start date	Euro adopt date	Euro peg date	ER regime today or prior to the euro or peg
Slovenia	2004	6/2004	2007		Managed floating
Slovakia	2004	11/2005	2009		Managed floating (1998–2005)
Estonia	2004	6/2004	2011	2002	Pegged to DM (1992–2002)
Latvia	2004	5/2005	2014	2005	SDR peg (1993–2005)
Lithuania	2004	6/2004[1]	2015[2]	2002	USD peg (1994–002)
Bulgaria	2007	not member	no plan	1997[3]	Hyperinflation/depreciation Euro outsiders
Czech Republic	2004	not member	no plan	none	Basket peg (1993–95);[4] Managed floating (since 1997)
Hungary	2004	not member	no plan	none	Adjustable peg (1990–94); crawling band (1995–2001); Euro target zone (2001–08);[5] Managed floating (since 2008)
Poland	2004	not member	no plan	none	Peg/crawling (1990–2000); Managed floating since 2000
Romania	2007	not member	no plan	none	Managed floating[6]
Croatia	2013	not member	no plan	none	Managed floating
Serbia[7]	–	not member	–	–	Peg/crawling peg 2000–06; Managed floating since 2006

Notes

1 In 2006, the EU found that while Lithuania met 4 of the 5 Maastricht criteria, its average annual inflation in 2005 was 2.7 percent vs the limit of 2.6 percent.

2 In June 2014, the EU Commission and the ECB found that Lithuania has met the Maastricht criteria so it can be expected to introduce the Euro on January 1, 2015, for which legislation has also been cleared in Lithuania.

3 Pegged at the time to the DM.

4 Between Feb 1996 and May 1997, had an ER regime with +/− 7 percent fluctuations allowed. Speculative attacks on the koruna during the 1997 Asia crisis led to the switch to managed floating.

5 This was strikingly similar to ERM II: permitting +/−15 percent fluctuations against the euro. For a brief explanation of the reasons for changing the exchange rate regime multiple times, see Marius A Zoican, "The Quest for Monetary Integration: The Hungarian Experience. (Munich: MPRA, April 5, 2009), available in full: http://mpra.ub.uni-muenchen.de/17286/

6 Details about the early 1990s: M. Birsan and M. Plesca, "Exchange Rate Policy during Transition: Romania" in Z. Sevic and G. Wright (eds.), Transition in Central and Eastern Europe (Belgrade: 2007), pp. 399–407.

7 Serbia's system transformation had begun in 2000. For details, see Radovan Jelasic, "Serbia: On the De-Euroization Road to the Euro" in E. Nowotny, P. Mooslechner and D. Ritzberger-Grünwald, The Euro and Economic Stability (Cheltenham: Edward Elgar), pp. 23–33.

Hypotheses to explain country choices

In a section above I listed a combined *nine* unconditional and conditional *benefits* of being or becoming a euro insider and *six* combined certain and conditional *costs* of being tied to the euro. Instead of attempting to prepare country-specific balance sheets of benefits and costs, perhaps also giving weights to each factor's presumed importance for a country – an exercise that would likely yield an unsatisfactory "on the one hand and on the other hand" type of outcome – the following plausible hypotheses are offered:

- Hypothesis 1: Every euro insider country in the EE has had one overriding and important political or economic motive (in some cases a combination of such motives) to adopt the euro or to tie its currency to the euro.
- Hypothesis 2: For the EU member EE countries that have remained euro outsiders, the expected political and economic benefits of joining the EMU have not been demonstrably greater than the costs; their euro policies can be simply labelled as "drifting". (Note that not qualifying for euro adoption on the basis of unfulfilled Maastricht criteria is not included as a reason because if the country had an overriding political or economic reason to adopt the euro, it would have found a way to qualify).

It will be easier to marshal arguments and examples consistent with hypothesis 1 than to do the same, convincingly, for hypothesis 2. For one, it is more plausible to give reasons why an action was taken rather than the opposite. Also, there are significant differences among the euro outsiders on why and how each country has been "drifting," as discussed in the following sections.

Nevertheless, giving to all outsiders uniformly the "drifting" label does have a rationale: no country could officially state that it would never adopt the euro since each has a treaty obligation to do so. Therefore, whether a government is really against euro adoption "forever" or whether it is taking a genuine "wait and see" attitude on the issue, each must address the question in more or less the same way, whether it really means what it says or just prevaricates.

Country choice rationales

Next follows a brief country-by-country discussion of key facts and my interpretation of the main reason(s) that brought a country into the EZ or kept it out of the EMU.

Focusing on the euro insiders first, the three Baltic States – Estonia, Latvia, and Lithuania – offer the most clear-cut cases: each has had overwhelmingly important political as well as significant economic reasons for adopting the euro. The political reason: they place a high value on joining this "Western" economic and monetary arrangement, too, as an additional way of distancing themselves as far as possible from Russia's orbit (benefit 9). All three are tiny economies, so that the benefits of having a *de facto* fixed exchange rate vis-à-vis their major economic partners are much greater than those benefits would be for larger countries (benefit 1). All three had entered ERM-II almost immediately after the EU accessions (Table 9.1), and in all three there was (and remains) broad-based political and social support for the EZ membership.[19] Until each country finally qualified to join the EZ, they took the closest available substitute by pegging their currencies to the euro.

Slovenia's circumstances were/are quite similar to those of the Baltic States. It left Yugoslavia as soon as possible, establishing itself as an independent state in 1991. It, too, joined ERM II immediately after becoming an EU member in 2004 and was the first EE country to adopt the euro in 2007.[20] The step had strong domestic political and public support. And, as a tiny country with exports representing 50 per cent or more of the GDP – by joining the fellow EZ countries – it has been benefiting from a fixed exchange rate vis-à-vis its main economic partners. However, following the global financial crisis and the Great Recession, Slovenia experienced one of the steepest GDP declines in Europe. Its loss of competitiveness vis-à-vis neighbouring non-EZ countries whose exchange rate had declined was certainly a factor. However, by far more important in Slovenia's poor performance are the following factors: (1) a large part of its economy has been sheltered from competition; (2) extreme structural rigidities; (3) lagging privatization of large enterprises; and (4) high corruption. These had all contributed to its severe banking crisis (2012–2014), with many predicting at the time that Slovenia would also have to be bailed out by its EZ partners (a fate it had escaped, barely). It is important to note that Slovenia has been the only EE member of the EU that kept foreign banks largely out of the country. Slovenia preserved some of the most dysfunctional features of its pre-transformation economic system: banks continuing to have much too cosy relationships with enterprises, many still state owned. For all these reasons, I would *not* conclude that Slovenia had made a mistake in adopting the euro.

Slovakia's is the most interesting case. During its first eight transformation years (1990–1998) it was considered to be an unusually corrupt country, greatly lagging in political and economic reforms behind the rest of the Visegrad Four (the Czech Republic, Hungary and Poland). In September 1998, the opposition that won the election and formed a new government engineered the region's quickest and most dramatic changes in politics, economic system reforms, and economic policy. Simultaneously with the EU accession negotiations (beginning in 2000), its new government also decided on a strategy of introducing the euro as quickly as possible. The reasons for this dramatic about-face were the economic philosophy and unusual political and economic expertise of key persons in the new government, a determined wish to irrevocably break with the recent past policies, and the fervent desire to catch up to and perhaps leapfrog the Czech Republic – a rival against which it has long been considered a junior and lagging partner. Ever since it had joined the EU (in 2004), entering the ERM II (in 2005), and adopting the euro (in 2009), Slovakia's relative economic performance, as well as its reputation, has improved considerably, evidence of which is the rapidly growing size of foreign investment inflows. Slovakia did well to adopt the euro as an integral part of a comprehensive economic reform package.

Bulgaria had no strong political but an overwhelming economic reason to tie its currency to the euro. After a terribly difficult early post-communist period, during 1996–1997 Bulgaria experienced twin banking and currency crises, including hyperinflation, bringing the country to the verge of collapse. A radical new approach was needed and it was found by the newly elected government. This approach pegged the currency to the DM (preparation and implementation during 1997–1999), with the peg automatically switched to the euro in 2001.[21] Pegging a currency has meant that the monetary authorities gave up control over the money supply as well as the interest rates and the exchange rate, just as if the country had adopted the euro. That Bulgaria has been able to maintain its currency's peg, at the same fixed rate, for nearly two decades is a credit to its authorities' determination and to its public's support. While Bulgaria has periodically been toying with the idea of moving toward the full EMU membership, that step is not a plausible option for it as long as its economy and politics continue to suffer from many serious ills.

Turning to the six euro outsiders, those four that had joined the EU during the decade of the 2000s – the Czech Republic, Poland, and Hungary (in 2004) and Romania (in 2007) – had been toying, off and on, with the idea of moving toward adopting the euro. "Off and on" is an apt phrase. Each has published, and frequently revised, timetables of planned milestones to reach on the road to the EZ membership. Depending on such factors as the preferences of the government in power, the experiences of the EZ members from the EE and the Mediterranean area, and the prevailing global mood about the strengths and weaknesses of the EZ (that has fluctuated between lauding its benefits during 1999–2008 and damning its shortcomings since about 2010), the authorities in those four countries have vacillated between making a seemingly strong commitment to implementing their own timetable to introduce the euro, to repeatedly revising the timetable, or simply stopping any concrete discussion of euro adoption.

Given the legal obligation of each EU member country to eventually adopt the euro, none has made an official statement that it would never do so. Today, the evasive statements we hear most often can be paraphrased as "we'll wait and see about developments in the EZ and will only join if and when it is the right time for us to do so." For most of them, the evasiveness of such declarations reflects not the hiding of policies on euro adoption, but the fact the policymakers in those countries really do not know if and when their country will be ready to join the EZ.

Apart from the aforementioned commonalities, there are also important differences within the four countries. Most interesting is the stand of the Czech Republic. Already noted was the strong and principled opposition of one of the country's most influential politicians and statesmen, Václav Klaus, to the entire EMU concept. Since he has supporters, the political-social consensus essential for a smooth euro accession has not been materializing. Most informative also is the domestic debate on whether the Czech Republic would really gain economic benefits by adopting the euro. The country's consistently prudent fiscal and monetary policies have allowed it to control inflation and maintain price rises and interest rates at levels similar to those achieved by the EZ's northern group.

Thus, the Czech Republic does not need "imported credibility." Based on this considerable achievement, its experts conclude that the Czech Republic doesn't need the membership in the EZ to bring down inflation and the real interest rates. Therefore, the debate about euro adoption boils down to an exchange rate regime choice: would it be better to have a fixed exchange rate vis-à-vis the euro by joining the EZ or would it be preferable to continue to maintain flexible exchange rates vis-à-vis the euro as well? The reasoning then goes: the EZ membership would prevent potentially large exchange rate shocks, which, *ceteris paribus*, *reduces macroeconomic volatility*. However, at the same time, giving up exchange rate flexibility would also remove a channel of stabilization in case the economy suffers asymmetric shocks as compared with those experienced by the EZ's larger economies. That, in turn, would *increase macroeconomic volatility*. Economic models of the Czech Republic do not suggest that potential gains of improved macroeconomic stability arising from EZ membership would be greater than the prospective losses of the same attributable to EZ membership (Hurnik et al. 2010).

Among the Visegrad countries, key aspects of Hungary's economic performance has been the opposite from those of the Czech Republic: irresponsible fiscal policies for a sustained period (2001–2007), resulting in the entire EU's largest cumulative budget deficits for that period and by far the highest public debt to GDP ratio among the EE members of the EU. The global financial crisis of 2008 pushed Hungary to the precipice of a sovereign debt default, which would have occurred if it were not for a quick bailout loan of $25 billion arranged jointly by the EU and the IMF. Hungary did not – and still has not – met most of the Maastricht criteria.[22] For the past decade, no serious government program has given priority to pursuing economic policies that would qualify the country for the EZ membership. And with the increasingly open antagonism of Viktor Orban's FIDESZ government toward the EU, who argues that Hungary must remain independent, there is little chance that more than lip-service will be given at any time soon to eventually adopting the euro. And, regrettably, public opinion has been so poisoned by the two successive FIDESZ governments' (2008–2012 and 2012–2016) relentless anti-EU rhetoric that it is doubtful whether political and public opinion could easily be switched to support EZ membership. An influential official of the ruling Party stated in January 2015 that (1) Hungary would be worse off if it abandoned the forint; (2) EE countries that have adopted the euro have obviously not benefited from it, by for example, stating: "Slovenia's economy is in serious trouble, and in Slovakia prices went up when it adopted the Euro"; and (3) adoption of the euro would require an amendment to the Basic Law (the constitution) since it specifies that the legal tender of Hungary is the forint.[23] A year earlier, the Governor of the Hungarian National Bank said that the Great Recession "crisis has shed light on the detrimental consequences of the premature adoption of the single currency. Hungary wishes to and will introduce the euro, but unless it is strong enough to do so, its best interest is to stay out of the euro area" (Matolcsy 2014: 8).

Poland is different from both the Czech Republic and Hungary. Its policymakers and experts have been debating for years the pros and cons of the *timing of euro adoption.* Generally speaking, there appears to be more fundamental support f the euro, as well as for the EU than in the Czech Republic and in Hungary. T main reason seems to be Poland's pursuit of increased political and econom influence within the EU. One reason that Poland has a friendlier attitude towa the EMU is its interest in helping to shape the future of the EZ, as also that of t EU. What influential Polish supporters of the EZ membership stress, based on t lessons learned from the experiences of the Southern members of the EZ, is t importance of the country being well prepared prior to adopting the euro. Th will require implementing a further range of fiscal and labour market refor necessary for the economy to become sufficiently flexible to be able to absorb a external economic shock that it might be experiencing. At the same time, being relatively large economy, Poland likes, *ceteris paribus*, the flexibility that com from retaining independent monetary and exchange rate policies.

Romania has also been "on and off" with respect to the EZ membershi However, in contrast to Hungary, its repeated postponements of the date wh it expects to join have had more to do with making insufficient progress towa qualification than any kind of a serious political or economic doubt wheth adopting the euro would be a positive step. When Romania submitted i Convergence Program to the European Commission in 2013, Prime Minist Victor Ponta stated that "Eurozone entry remains a fundamental objective f Romania but we can't enter poorly prepared." He then added that 2020 was more realistic target than the earlier dates that have been targeted and repeated postponed. Romania's central bank has recently prepared amendments to t Constitution to make it legally possible to transfer its tasks to the ECB and introduce the euro as the legal tender.

Croatia has become a full EU member only in 2013. In contrast to Slovenia ar Slovakia, it has not pushed, simultaneously with the EU accession, negotiatior toward joining the EZ. One likely reason is that while attitudes toward the EM had been glowingly positive during the mid-2000s when Slovenia and Slovak became EU members, attitudes today range from critical, to sceptical, to uncertai And since Croatia has much less political imperative to adopt the euro than t Baltic States and Slovenia did a decade ago (nor is Croatia's economy quite s small as those just mentioned), its "let's wait and see" attitude is prudent.

For Serbia, not being an EU member – and with many years to go before would qualify for EU accession – it is premature even to speculate about t pros and cons and the likelihood of the euro adoption. In fact, one of Serbia most pressing economic problems – wrote the then Governor of the Nation Bank of Serbia in 2010 – is how to "de-Euroize" its monetary system. Owin to the population's still fresh memory of hyperinflation and repeated dramat depreciation of the domestic currency, businesses and households are relucta to hold the *dinar*. Even in the face of interest rate incentives by Serbia's centr bank to hold the dinar, there has remained strong preference for the euro and oth foreign currencies. Serbia's heavily Euroized economy limits the effectivenes of domestic monetary policy and makes the country vulnerable to speculatior driven depreciation of the local currency.[24]

Five years after Governor Jelasic's 2010 statement, I contacted the former Governor and asked him whether Serbia would not have done better by pegging its currency to the euro, as Bulgaria did in 1997 (to the DM at that time, switching the peg later to Euro). He replied affirmatively:

> I was fully convinced ten years ago that it does make sense to carry out an independent monetary policy even in the case of a small open economy. I would do it differently today. The cost of trying to convince people to trust the unpegged local currency simply does not work. Look at Croatia, where even today the majority of the deposits are in Euros! If I had it in my power, I would peg the dinar to the euro tomorrow.[25]

Summary and conclusions

Let the statements in italics below serve as the contribution's summary and conclusions, while the in-between text (not in italics) focuses on explanations and examples.

> *Every euro insider country in the EE has had one overridingly important political or economic motive (in some cases a combination of such motives) to adopt the euro or to peg its currency to it.*

In the case of the three Baltic States of Estonia, Latvia and Lithuania, the principal motive was political: to distance themselves from Russia's orbit by joining a Western monetary arrangement. This motive was reinforced by all three being small, open economies, with the other EZ members as their main commercial partners. Having the same currency as their partners reduces substantially the transaction costs; the smaller and more open an economy, the greater are the savings so generated. Before and after their severe economic downturns during the Great Recession (due in large part to allowing similar credit bubbles to arise as those experienced by the Mediterranean countries, Ireland, and several other countries in the EE), these Baltic Tigers have been performing well. First pegging to and then adopting the euro were not the only reason for their economic success. But those steps certainly did not hurt and almost certainly helped them to maintain sound economic policies and to correct earlier policy mistakes by "internal devaluation."

Slovenia shared with the Baltic States the same economic and similar political motives: being a small, open economy and distancing and distinguishing itself from the economically and politically more troubled other ex-Yugoslav countries.

Slovakia was the most unexpected, relatively early euro adopter (in 2009). The trigger was domestic politics manifested by the government's strong belief, which came to power in 1998, that it must break with the economically dysfunctional past. Aiming to adopt the euro as quickly as possible provided the blueprint. The new government's market-oriented ideology and its implementation expertise gave the country a political window to take such a daring step, and made good use of the opportunity. The country's fervent desire to catch up to and perhaps leapfrog the Czech Republic reinforced the decision, as did being a small, open economy. There is domestic as well as international consensus that, on a net basis, Slovakia gained substantial, long-term benefits by adopting the euro.

Other than being a small, open economy, Bulgaria had a fundamentally different reason for pegging its currency to Euro: following a major economic crisis, including runaway inflation, it wished to import economic credibility and stability from the EZ. For such a step to be successful, the importer must subsequently follow prudent economic policies. In this respect, Bulgaria can be said to have been partly successful (for example, in terms of fiscal issues, especially public debt and performance) and partly unsuccessful (weak structural reforms and continued high levels of corruption).

> *The five EU member EE countries that have remained euro outsiders typically did so because the expected political and economic benefits of joining the EMU have not been demonstrably greater than its costs. In brief, it was convenient for them simply to "drift."*

Beyond this broad generalization, there are significant differences among the five. The Czech Republic has long been pursuing relatively prudent economic policies so that it had no need to try to import stability from the EZ. Opposition to adopting the euro has also been vocal and influential on the economic philosophy as well as on the political ideology grounds. In the view of the EZ's opponents (such as Václav Klaus), EMU requires an excessive and unwelcome degree of economic centralization and the granting of too much political power to unelected officials. Poland by and large shares the Czech Republic's prudent economic policy. And by being a relatively large economy, it prefers exchange rate flexibility to a loss of independent monetary policy. Romania has had too many economic and political problems, so it has not been ready to apply to, nor be received by, the EZ. Hungary has been the *enfant terrible* of the EE outsider group; because it had been in the breach with most Maastricht convergence criteria before the Great Recession; since 2008 because the FIDESZ governments in power since then have been conjuring up enemies and are preaching maximum economic, financial, political, and legal independence, an attitude that would not be compatible with EZ membership. Croatia, which joined the EU only recently, does not as yet qualify for euro adoption.

Serbia, the sixth euro outsider in EE, is the most interesting case. Since its EU membership is far from imminent, it cannot as yet contemplate the euro adoption. However, influential voices today think that Serbia would benefit from becoming a euro insider by tying its currency irrevocably to the euro, as Bulgaria did almost two decades ago.

> *Perceptions of economists, politicians, and the general public about the benefits and costs of having an EMU and of being a member of it have changed dramatically from 1999-2008 and since 2009. The initial euphoria,*

engendering great expectations about the EZ's bright economic future, has crumbled during and since the Great Recession. Negative perceptions about the EZ and its many "design faults" are reducing consistently the likelihood that the EE's euro outsiders will be interested in adopting the euro.

This statement can be applied with confidence to the region's current euro outsiders. This is so in spite of the three Baltic States appearing to be counter examples because all three adopted the euro on or after January 2009.

Two reasons can explain the apparent paradox. First, each Baltic country valued highly the political benefit of additional distance from Russia. No euro outsider in the region has a similar, strongly held political agenda. Second, their decisions to adopt the euro were made from euro insider positions already. Therefore, a decision to break their peg to the euro by substantially devaluing their currencies – strongly advocated at the height of the economic crises by many famous economists (including Nobel Laureate Paul Krugman) – would have had devastating domestic economic impacts, triggering massive bankruptcies of their heavily Euro-indebted businesses and households.

Even a minimum understanding of why and how the EMU was designed, how it is functioning, what are its prospects, and the evolving relationship between the euro and the EE countries requires a multidisciplinary approach. History, domestic and international politics, political philosophy, economics, economic ideology, finance, culture, and the law are all relevant.

Examples of the relevance of each area can be found even in this contribution. For example:

* *History* is relevant because France's historical-memory-induced fear of Germany was the ultimate reason for the signing of the Maastricht Treaty, just after German reunification.
* *Domestic politics* was crucial in Slovakia's unexpected leapfrogging of the other Visegrad countries in introducing the euro. Domestic politics in Germany and in Greece are the main obstacles why an EMU-saving compromise on Greece's monumental sovereign debt has been so incredibly difficult to find.
* *International politics* had been a factor in the UK's decision to opt out of the EMU.
* *Political philosophy* and *economic ideology* were the twin reasons for Václav Klaus's vociferous and effective opposition to the EMU.
* Most of the benefits and costs of the EMU membership are *economic*.
* Central to the operation and continued survival of the EMU are the *financial* decisions of the ECB as well as by actors on the financial markets.
* *Culture* is a fundamental determinant in how seemingly identical institutions function differently in the various countries; it also helps to shape the long-term economic competitiveness of countries.

- The *law* is always central; for example, most countries wanting to adopt the euro must first modify their constitutions to make this adoption legally possible.

Acknowledgements

I would like to thank my colleagues at Central European University, Laszlo Csaba, Mel Horwitch, Julius Horvath, and Laszlo Urban, as well as my other colleagues, Gabor Oblath and Imre Tarafas, for valuable comments and suggestion on an earlier version of this essay. Any remaining errors of fact or interpretation are the authors.

Notes

1   EZ is a term used here interchangeably with the EMU. The UK and Denmark had formally opted out while Sweden decided not to enter ERM II (see next note) in order not to meet the exchange rate criterion because Sweden's EZ membership was rejected by its voters in a referendum.
2   ERM stands for the exchange rate mechanism. ERM I was a system introduced by the European Economic Community in 1979 as part of the European Monetary System (EMS), which was designed to reduce exchange rate variability among EMS currencies.
3   The provisions of the SGP were tightened by the so-called fiscal compact of 2012 (subsequently ratified by all EZ and several non-EZ countries of the EU). Some of the SGP's new rules aim to prevent fiscal policies from heading in potentially problematic directions, while others are supposed to correct excessive budget deficits or excessive public debt burdens.
4   For details, see Whelan (2014). "Target" is an abbreviation of "Trans-European Automated Real-time Gross Settlement System," which has been operating in some form in the EU for decades. In November 2007 the system was transformed to meet the requirements of a settlement system within the EZ, and was renamed Target2.
5   One of the most influential political figures holding this view is the Czech Republic's former Minister of Finance and former President of the Republic, Václav Klaus. In 2010, when still President, he wrote this in *The Wall Street Journal*: "Many of us [are] in favor of a looser form of European integration [but] against the so-called deepening of the EU and against the creation of a political union in Europe. People like me understood very early that the idea of a European single currency is a dangerous project which will either bring big problems or lead to the undemocratic centralization of Europe."
6   This is the famous Balassa-Samuelson effect, amply documented in the literature.
7   The EZ's "sunshine decade" is the author's term for that initial period when the establishment of the common currency was generally viewed as being an unmitigated success, based largely on the more rapid rate of "catching up" the growth of the EZ's poorer members (Portugal, Italy, Greece, and Spain).
8   On the convergence of EZ interest rates, see Agnes Bénassy-Quéré et. al. (2010: 136).
9   One of Germany's most influential economists and policy advisers, Hans-Werner Sinn, wrote in 2012: " if the Euro breaks up and if the TARGET claims are not honored as legally valid titles, or the TARGET debtors are unable to repay while the TARGET-neutral countries object to share in the losses…the TARGET surplus countries would lose their TARGET claims."
10 See Soros (2013).
11 For a comprehensive review of the OCA literature, see Horvath (2003).

12 One of the EE's leading economists, Leszek Balczerowitz, former Minister of Finance and former Governor of the Central Bank of Poland, still believed, as of 2010, such a purely monetary linking to be a good idea. Balczerowitz attributed the EMU's current crises to the dysfunctional fiscal policies of several EMU members and to their lagging structural reforms (Balczerowitz 2010: 26–27). Balczerowitz argues that the EMU could work even without a political union and without a common treasury if the fiscal incentives and safeguarding mechanisms would have been properly designed and implemented.
13 For a discussion of the political background of the EMU, see Marer (2014).
14 See Noyer (2014).
15 France and Ireland sort of "straddle" between the two groups, in certain areas and at certain times exhibiting features characteristic of the Northern group; in other areas and at other times showing "Southern" characteristics.
16 Italy and Belgium were accepted as EMU founding members even though both exceeded, by very large margins, Maastricht criterion 2. Greece was admitted even though it was common knowledge that it "complied" with the fiscal criteria only on paper, falsifying its economic statistics. And even Germany, as most other EMU members, has breached the provisions of the SGP numerous times. Altogether, there were more than 100 breaches of the SGP during the EMU's first decade.
17 For a comprehensive account of the history of the Euro and the many ups and down of EZ policy debates and outcomes, see Dallago (forthcoming).
18 In 1997, Bulgaria tied its currency to the DM, switching automatically to the euro once the new currency was introduced in 1999.
19 See, for example, Banerjee et al. (2011: 134).
20 How Slovenia prepared for Euro adoption and how its membership in the EMU constrained its government's ability to mitigate the impact of the Great Recession is told in Bole and MacKellar (2010).
21 For more info on Bulgaria's economic problems and its decision to peg, see Atanasov and Valchanov (2011).
22 The most comprehensive scientific assessment of what Hungary will need to do to successfully adopt the Euro is a major essay by Judit Nemenyi and Gabor Oblath (2012). The main conclusion of the essay is that irrespective of the timing of Euro adoption, it would be in Hungary's interest to meet as quickly as possible the EMU's Maastricht conditions because that would enhance international confidence in Hungary's economic policies and would improve prospects for Hungary's economic performance and convergence.
23 Antal Rogan, FIDESZ majority leader in Parliament, as reported in *Origo News*, 19 January 2015.
24 For details, see essay by the former Governor of the National Bank of Serbia, Radovan Jelasic (2010: 23–33).
25 Mr. Jelasic is quoted with his permission.

References

Atanasov, Y. and D. Valchanov. 2011. "Currency Board as An Exchange Rate Arrangement: The Bulgarian Experience." MS in Finance Thesis, Aarhus School of Business, Aarhus University, Denmark.
Balczerowitz, L. 2010. "A More Perfect Monetary Union." *Finance: The Magazine for Emerging Europe* (Summer): 21–39.
Banerjee, B. et al. 2011. "The Road to Euro Adoption: A Comparison of Slovakia and Slovenia." In M. Beblavy et al. (eds), *The Euro Area and the Financial Crisis*. Cambridge: Cambridge University Press, pp. 131–150.

Bénassy-Quéré, A. et al. 2010. "Economic Divergence within the Euro Area: Lessons for EMU Enlargement." In *The Euro and Economic Stability: Focus on Central, Eastern and South-eastern Europe*, edited by E. Nowotny et al., pp. 131–143. Cheltenham: Edward Elgar.

Bole, V. and L. MacKellar (eds). 2010. *From Tolar to Euro*. Ljubljana: Center of Excellence in Finance.

Csaba, L. 2014. "Developmental Perspectives on Europe." *Society and Economy* 36(1): 21–36.

Dallago, B. Forthcoming. *One Currency, Two Europes*. Singapore: World Scientific.

Horvath, J. 2003. *Optimum Currency Area Theory: A Selective Review*. Bank of Finland Discussion Paper 15. Oslo: Institute of Economies in Transition. Available at www.suomenpankki.fi/pdf/110655.pdf.

Hurnik, J., et al. 2010. "The Czech Republic on Its Way to the Euro: A Stabilization Role of Monetary Policy Revisited." In *The Euro and Economic Stability: Focus on Central, Eastern and South-eastern Europe*, edited by E. Nowotny, et al., pp. 48–68. Cheltenham: Edward Elgar.

Jelasic, R. 2010. "Serbia: On the De-Euroization Road to the Euro." In *The Euro and Economic Stability*, edited by E. Nowotny, P. Mooslechner and D. Ritzberger-Grünwald, pp. 23–33. Cheltenham: Edward Elgar.

Klaus, V. 2010. "The Euro Zone Has Failed." *WSJ* (June 1): http://www.wsj.com/articles/SB10001424052748704875604575280452365548866.

Marer, P. 2014. "The Eurozone Crises and Central and Eastern Europe." In *Free Market in Its Twenties: Modern Business Decision Making in Central and eastern Europe*, edited by M. Kisilowski. Budapest: CEU Press, pp. 111–120.

Matolcsy, G. 2014. "Hungary on Uncharted Waters." In *The Euro Dilemma: Inside or Outside*. Lamfalussy Lectures Conference series. Budapest: Hungarian National Bank pp. 71–90.

Nemenyi, J. and G. Oblath. 2012. "Rethinking Adopting the Euro." *Kozgazdasagi Szemle* 59 (June): 569–684.

Noyer, C. 2014. "Why the EMU Needs a Banking Union." In *The Euro Dilemma: Inside or Outside*. Lamfalussy Lectures Conference series. Budapest: Hungarian National Bank pp. 41–59.

Sinn, H.-W. 2012. "Target Losses in Case of a Euro Breakup," Available at www.voxeu.org/article/target-losses-case-Euro-breakup.

Soros, G. 2013. "A European Solution to the Eurozone's Problem." Available at www.project-syndicate.org/blog/a-european-solution-to-the-eurozone-s-problem.

Swoboda, A. 1999. "Robert Mundell and the Theoretical Foundation for the European Monetary Union." Available at www.imf.org/external/np/vc/1999/121399.htm.

Whelan, K. 2014. "Target2 and Central Bank Balance Sheets." *Economic Policy* 29(77): 79–137.

10 Global value chains, changing divisions of labour, and the regulation of work in EU28 and Euro-Med

John Pickles

Introduction

In 2013 the OECD argued that transnational enterprise-coordinated value chains now account for 80 percent of global trade. This trade is "increasingly dominated by the complex and circuitous routes followed by goods and services as they are upgraded into finished products" with "ever more complex webs of investment and trade", allowing more countries to participate in the process (OECD 2013). Global value chains (GVCs) are complex supplier networks coordinated by lead-firms in which design, contracting for production, as well as wholesale and retail are all controlled by the lead firm, while the processes of design, production, and retailing are disaggregated and manufacture is increasingly outsourced and off-shored to first, second and even third-tier suppliers in lower-cost locations.

The increasing importance of such coordinated intra-firm trade is rapidly altering the dynamics of global sourcing and the governance structure of industrial production. It has particular consequences for Europe and Euro-Med.[1] Amador et al. (2015) have made this point clearly, showing how the regional integration of production among Euro area economies has deepened, with particularly important effects on emerging economic geographies of eastern and southern countries in the wider Europe. Most active, but not alone, in this process of integration have been the German and to a lesser extent the Austrian economies. In their analysis of global value chains and macroeconomic imbalances in Europe, Ederer and Reschenhofer (2014: 1–2) have also pointed to the differential export/domestic demand profiles of northern and southern European countries in an attempt to assess "whether surpluses in the North correspond with deficits in the South" (ibid.: 23). In one reading of these differentials, "the surplus countries in the 'North' benefitted from booming demand in the 'South'" and, "as a consequence they should now strengthen their demand expenditures to boost demand and exports in the South" (ibid.: 24). By contrast, others have suggested that the rapid expansion of Chinese and other emerging market economy exports mean that expanded domestic demand would have little effect on the export performance of southern Europe.[2] Whichever reading of these issues ends up being validated, the crucial point remains that the contemporary economy is now organized through large intra-firm value chains dominated largely by northern lead-firms, which are highly inter-woven networks, and they have become important determinants of the structures of economic governance in northern, eastern and southern European economies. Somewhat ironically, under the banner of economic and trade liberalization, European capital, labour, and state institutions have worked assiduously – at least since the 1970s – to create non-market intra-firm arrangements to manage this process of differential insertion into the global economy (Pickles and Smith 2016). The resulting new regional divisions of business and employment are not just the outcome of these transformations, but they also act to re-form the economic life of European regions themselves.

This chapter focuses on three such emerging dynamics and their consequences with particular focus on the effects of the transformations in southern and southeastern Europe following the revolutions of 1989 and economic accession in 2004 and 2007, as well as the 2007/8 financial crisis and subsequent austerity politics across the regions.

- The expansion and deepening of global value chains have contributed to a significant re-configuration of the regional and international divisions of labour in Europe and Euro-Med, with important consequences for the changing character of industrial structure and geographies.
- As the integration of global trade through GVCs increases the coordination costs of global sourcing it also stimulates new initiatives to benchmark economic performance and standardize sourcing practices and standards across a lead-firms' global supplier network. These benchmarking and coordination efforts have positive potentials for generalizing minimum labour standards, but uncertain consequences for national and regional efforts (especially EU efforts) to raise the floor on wages and workplace standards and compliance.
- The expansion of global value chains is now seen to have been an important contributory factor in amplifying the speed of transmission of the 2007/8 financial crisis regionally and internationally. For many, "the global financial and economic crisis that started in 2007 strongly impacted not only on international trade and GVCs but also on the overall macroeconomic situation of countries running larger foreign imbalances, notably within the Euro area" (Amador et al. 2013: 2). It was the interdependence of the global economy that quickly spread the effects of the financial crisis with devastating consequences for debt and decline in Eurozone countries. In this sense, economic integration created heightened systemic risk, while also allowing for differential rebound.

At the core of each issue is a deeper concern about the ways in which we interpret the 2007/8 crisis and how we see post-crisis restructuring. In particular, I would like to ask whether it helps to see the post-crisis situation as a short-lived rupture that – like other recessions – will return to a normal situation that is familiar. Or are we experiencing something much more profound – a structural transformation whose social and political consequences are only now becoming manifest?

The European Union was not slow to begin its own scenario-planning in the face of these challenges. In its report *Global Europe 2050* (European Commission 2012) three scenarios are outlined:

* *Scenario 1: If Nobody Cares.* In this scenario Europe muddles along with no clear vision or direction. Economic growth will remain lower than in the US and China global competitiveness will decline.
* *Scenario 2: Protectionism.* This scenario paints a bleak picture of global economic decline followed by the rise of protectionism. The result (according to the European Commission report) would be that share of the world GDP would fall by almost a half by 2050.
* *Scenario 3: European Renaissance.* In this scenario the EU continues to enlarge and become stronger. It consolidates its political, fiscal and military integration. Innovation systems become more efficient with an increased role given to users. Investment in technological and services innovations will have a direct impact on economic and social development. Member States will work together to make the European Research Area fully functional with research agendas being decided in common across Europe. The EU GDP will be almost doubled by 2050.

These scenarios are developed to address the need to plan with crises in mind. But the fact that the report outlines Scenario 3 as the only real option, characterizing the other two variously as muddled or reactionary, suggests that this notion of crisis is about finding the correct technical fix. By contrast, the now nearly 50-year decline in the adjusted share of the GDP going to labour across all OECD countries suggests that the globalization of manufacturing and services has a much deeper systemic role than such policies of economic upgrading and innovation-led renaissance can address. Indeed, the Report provides no explicit discussion on how to actually address in its proposals the repeated experience of crisis that typifies the European and US experience. Moreover, without more serious efforts to understand how the emerging structures of global value chains are deepening financial risk, public policy will continue to reflect an overly Pollyanna outlook, while workers in both the core and semi-peripheral economies of Europe will feel the consequences of crisis and austerity politics on a regular basis.

Personally, I am not pessimistic about the ability of the EU to sustain its structures and perhaps even to extend them further, particularly through limited eastern and Euro-Med partnerships. Indeed, I think there are strong reasons that favour continued EU expansionary institutions and norms, although these may not – and probably will not – take the form of expanded accession agreements. Nonetheless, it does seem that the conditions of the contemporary world of Europe have changed fundamentally from those that guided the formation of the Union and the creation of a common currency. In this sense, the EU is going through – not temporary crises of indebtedness and unemployment – but deep structural crises of classic combined and uneven development. The attempt to forge a regional economy of stable relations predicated on full employment, demand-led growth, and social welfare provision has itself been made more unstable by the geographical extension of production networks and the deepening of their inter-dependencies. What has changed? And what are the possibilities for economic regeneration in conditions of tightly integrated networks and chains of economic interdependence?

Two related issues are important aspects of this restructuring. First, and the focus of this chapter, the rapid emergence of global value chains with deep regional effects has altered the ways in which markets operate and crises are transmitted through the economy. Second, global value chains are driven to expand, interiorize operations, and push to innovate production, logistics, and retail systems by the declining production of value and the ever-deepening crisis of the need to generate profits through rents (Reyes, Havice and Pickles 2016). I focus on one of the most ubiquitous forms of manufacturing industry, one of the largest employers in both advanced, transitional, and emerging economies, and the industry that has most typified the emergence of intra-firm managed networks: the clothing industry.

The structural re-organization of manufacturing and work in EU and Euro-Med global value chains

Since the 1970s, older Fordist and Stalinist organizational forms of the economy were predicated in large part on the development of and support for large-scale, fully integrated manufacturing industries driven by national energy and resource sectors, locally concentrated firms, industrial clusters, and a wide variety of state supports and parastatal industries. Since the 1980s, this organizational form of the economy has given way to disaggregated production systems organized around ever more globally distributed supply chains.

The delocalization of western European manufacturing industries and the offshoring and near-shoring of assembly production to east central Europe (ECE) began as early as the 1970s, led by textile and clothing manufacturers and buyers (Fröbel et al. 1980; Gereffi 2006: 1). It intensified with trade liberalization – particularly the end to quota-constrained trade in textiles and clothing under the World Trade Organization's Agreement on Textiles and Clothing (ATC) – and has continued with the integration of the new Member States of the EU into the European Single Market in 2004 and 2007. In this new liberalized trade regime, European manufacturers and buyers were free to source product in any amount from any country and suppliers could compete for contracts without quota restraint, subject only to a system of national and regional trade agreement tariffs, non-tariff barriers, and WTO-sanctioned safeguards.

The model of global economic organization that emerged was essentially an input-output chain disaggregated and distributed across an ever broader Euro-Med region, coordinated by a lead-firm sourcing from a distributed and complex system of input suppliers and manufacturers. Such GVCs represent a distinct organizational form for managing specialization across space, in which managerial

ntrol and high value-added activities are centralized organizationally and
:ographically in the headquarters of large multinational corporations (MNEs),
hile the value chain is fragmented into specialized geographically-distributed
:tivities. This specialized and fragmented structure of production requires the
ireful coordination of diverse actors in which traded goods and services are
rgely internal to the chain and its network of input and intermediary suppliers.
he lead-firm drivers of the chain capture the vast bulk of the value-added in the
·ocess, mobilizing their dominant position in the chain to capture rents through
e careful control, coordination, and normalization of participants across the
iain.

Initially, as Gereffi (1994) has shown, GVCs were manufacturer-driven, but
·anded and retailed companies creating buyer-driven chains quickly superseded
ese. Both manufacturer-driven and buyer-driven global value chains were
.storically controlled and coordinated by northern lead-firms, a structure of
overnance that largely remains the case today, although in recent years trading
)mpanies such as the Hong Kong based Li and Fung have also emerged as
gnificant chain coordinators. Supplier firms were generally dependent on these
U15-based lead-firms for their orders, intermediate inputs, and know-how, but
ie asymmetries of this relationship severely limited their ability to be more than
<port processors disconnected from other regional exporters. Cost pressures
uickly resulted in chain adaptation as orders for weaker suppliers were reduced
r re-assigned and production was relocated to other cheaper locations, while a
iore limited number of suppliers were able to mobilize longstanding outward
rocessing arrangements into strategic partnerships, upgrading, and higher value
roduction.

The incorporation of proximate assembly producers in low-wage countries
n the margins of the European Union was part of a broader EU strategy of
ibour market reform orchestrated under pressure from large industry and retailer
ssociations. As these fractions of north European capital sought to extend the
·ontiers of accumulation opportunities by establishing supplier networks in
astern Europe, north Africa, and – most recently – the Middle East, national and
U policies created ever more conducive policy frameworks for them. This so-
alled "Golden Bands" approach was a driving motif for both enlargement and
·ade integration in and beyond Europe.[3] The principal instrument of this strategy
·as the OPT customs arrangement.

This emerging regional structure of production was driven by a conjoined
ffort by European firms to increase their regional footprint, access cheaper labour
iarkets, and enhance their business efficiency, and by state policies favouring
:gional trading systems focused on the outsourcing and offshoring of low-value
ianufacturing activities. The result was expanded opportunities for eastern and
outhern firms to enter into the value chains of northern European economies,
xpanded job opportunities in low-wage sectors, and highly constrained forms of
)cal and regional development.

Post-socialist enterprises and their workers offered to western European
ianufacturers and retailers an opportunity to recapture some competitive

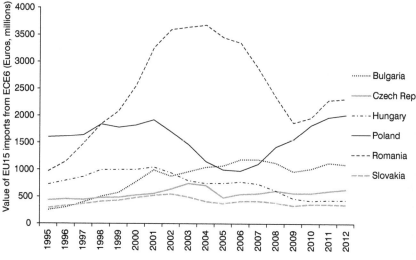

Figure 10.1 Apparel exports to selected ECE suppliers EU15 markets, 1995–2012

Source: elaborated from Comext database

advantage by extending their production systems into low wage labour markets (Fröbel et al. 1980; Graziani 1998; Coe et al. 2004; Smith, Buček, Pickles and Begg 2003). At the cost of relatively small (and rapidly diminishing) increases in logistical and transaction costs, regionally extended supply chains were able to tap into large, low-cost yet skilled labour pools in settings in which industrial infrastructures, laws, and norms were well established. These were settings in which existing product capabilities – high quality men's and women's suits for example – fed into niche markets in EU countries requiring regionalized production, stock replenishment, and tighter control over logistics and quality control (Abernathy et al. 2006; Pickles 2006; Pickles et al. 2006; Smith et al 2008).

The expansion and deepening of global value chains have re-configured regional and international divisions of labour in Europe and Euro-Med with important consequences for the changing character of industrial structure and geographies. In similar research on the European auto industry, Pavlínek (2012) has referred to these outsourced production facilities as export processing islands in the desert with few if any local forward and backward linkages. Kia/Hyundai in Slovakia is one of the extreme cases, importing all inputs (including workers' uniforms) from Asian suppliers. In his research on Slovak service centre providers, Chovanec and Rehák (2012) have described how even high tech computer and financial services have emerged in Bratislava as basic service work centres without any noticeable forms of integration with the local economy. But, apparel is perhaps the archetype for these kinds of regional economic integration models, driven by trade policies, preferences, and rules that constrain opportunities for economic upgrading through rules of origin and transformation rules aimed at protecting northern textile manufacturers. This creates instead weak clusters of independent supplier firms dependent on contracts from northern buyers and lacking any real backward and forward linkages in the regional economy (Pickles and Smith 2016). The EU clothing value chain produced what EU policymakers themselves refer to as the "three golden bands" of apparel production and export. These bands were central to the accumulation strategies of western European industrial and retail capital in the clothing sector: core EU/European, central Europe and north Africa, as well as wider eastern European locations. Beyond these three golden bands, and in the context of the significant trade liberalization that the end of quota constrained trade in 2004 and 2008 represented, the rise of certain Asian production sites was profound. Chinese and Bangladeshi exports to the EU15 grew significantly over this period. In the face of this dramatic relative increase of certain Asian producers, exports from ECE to EU15 markets continued to constitute between 0.5 and 4 percent of EU15 apparel imports. While many ECE countries saw a relative reduction in their exports to the EU over this period, many continued to operate in those markets and some even saw absolute growth of apparel exports.

These macro-regional systems of golden bands production are part of wider geo-political and geo-economic integration projects between the EU and its neighbouring states. Partly concerned with restricting migrant labour flows, partly connected to the consolidation of dictatorial governments controlling the rise of radical Islam in north Africa, and partly connected with the geographical expansion of the economic interests of the EU capital to enable EU-based firms to access cheaper labour reserves in neighbouring states, these frameworks underpinned in important ways a much larger system of macro-regional integration (see, for example, Smith 2013).

This process was heavily managed by EU trade and customs policies, and was particularly sharply figured in the pan-European policy agenda to cope with these changes set out in the 2003 European Communication Report on "The Future of the Textiles and Clothing Sector in the Enlarged European Union" (European Commission 2003a). The Communication Report stressed several important policy commitments that have shaped the deepening regional economic integration processes more generally. First, EU policy initiatives for EU15 were to concentrate on high value-added processes of innovation, research, and design, underpinned by the use of new technologies, enabling the creation of sustainable and "positive industrial relations" (European Commission 2003a: 15). The process was dependent on encouraging the networking of small and medium enterprises (SMEs) and the creation of regional clusters of firms. Such expanded production networks were dependent on improved market access to the main markets of the EU15 and the development of preferential access arrangements for accession and partner states in the face of expected Chinese and other Asian imports to the EU. The Communication Report thus figured at its very heart the need to create and enhance a pan-European and Mediterranean zone of production in order to "allow the ... sector to maintain the whole chain of production close to the European market, combining the advantages of reasonable costs, quality and proximity" (European Commission 2003a: 24).

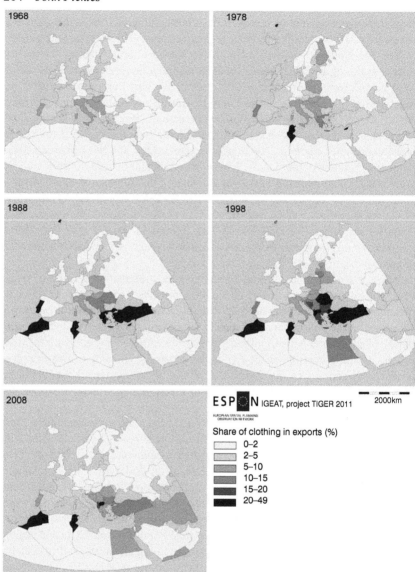

Figure 10.2 Specialization in clothing industry in the Euro-Mediterranean area, 1968–2008
Source: Roukova (n.d.: 19)

   In practice, participation in GVCs has had highly differentiated consequences for firms. Lead-firms in northern Europe have prospered by managing costs, off-setting risk, and gaining access to labour markets and technical know-how for which they bear little responsibility and towards which they have exhibited highly uneven forms of loyalty. Supplier firms and workforces in eastern Europe and Euro-Med have also benefitted from the surge in foreign direct investment, contracting for product, and nter-firm credit and know-how. But many such suppliers and workforces have been ntegrated into European value chains largely for the labour cost advantages they offer and the precarious at-a-distance relationship to the core business of the lead-irm. Supply chains have, in this sense, operated like a concertina, expanding and contracting as domestic demand in major EU markets expands and contracts.

Such risk-prone value chains operate within the constraints of trade and customs rules.[5] Glasmeier et al. (1993), Pickles (2012) and Pickles et al. (2015) describe the role of trade rules in the creation of conditions for "constrained upgrading" in which rules of origin, accumulation and transformation differentially restrict the range of operations that lead-firms are willing or able to devolve to their supplier networks. Initially, these were largely stitch-up functions with some value-added activities such as labelling, packaging, and perhaps some minor in-house design functions. Driven by the interests of EU textile manufacturers, few GVC supply firms in eastern Europe or Euro-Med were able to integrate their own domestic fabrics and yarns into exported product, and few have been able to source such fabrics and yarns themselves. In those cases where this has emerged, the supplier firm has nearly always benefitted from a triaging of the supply chain in favour of strategic partners where delivery time, flexibility, and quality have emerged as countervailing demands to narrower cost management strategies.

In sum, European GVCs emerged in Europe and Euro-Med as geographical responses to cost containment. They created webs of supplier networks under highly restrictive trade and customs arrangements that advantages northern manufacturers and buyers at the expense of constrained opportunities for eastern and southern suppliers. These were managed for maximum flexibility, including the uneven and precarious placing of orders, intense competition in contracting for cost reduction, and an almost complete disregard for the sustainability of regional industrial districts and labour pools.

The consequences for labour are by now well known; the internationalizing of post-socialist European, Indian, and Chinese labour markets in the same decade effectively doubled the global labour force and intensified downward pressure on contract prices and wages while simultaneously allowing buyers to leverage tighter delivery schedules, increased flexibility, and higher penalties for non-compliance (see Oxfam 2004; Hale and Wills 2005; Freeman 2007). In some cases, these adjustments led to rapid increases in imports from more "cost-effective" locations (especially from China, India and Bangladesh; see Gereffi 2003).

As the networks of value chains were extended across eastern Europe and Euro-Med they became the dominant structures of production, increasingly dependent on the fortunes of northern domestic markets and lead-firm sourcing strategies. It was this structural condition that became the vehicle for the geographical amplification of crisis after 2007.

Trade liberalization was, in this sense, both a managed process for the political protection of northern textile manufacturers and the emerging interests of European retailers, as well as a tool for economic integration and security considerations among emerging markets and newly democratizing states. Importantly, given the events of recent years, this policy agenda and extension of European production networks into eastern European and Euro-Med countries was also predicated on what the above-mentioned report called "sustainable development issues – improved core labour standards, enhanced environmental standards, for example – to create market niches for ethically produced" products. Enhanced regional clusters and the dissemination of information and communication technologies were to create a regionally integrated, economically efficient, industrial system of benefit to all actors.

But, as we now know, the "paths" that emerged out of the ruptures of the 1980s and early 1990s have been more diverse and difficult, the challenges have been highly contested, and the outcomes have been uneven and – in many regions – are still uncertain. Even for new EU member states, the clear if delayed general economic and social benefits of the initial years of harmonization have today turned into serious economic recessionary trends; real wages, the adjusted wage share, real hourly minimum wages, and real GDP growth have all been declining and unemployment has been increasing (Bourgeot 2013).

Global value chains and the amplification of crises

Even in the face of such evidence that economic integration was producing exploitative working conditions and sharp divisions between regional growth and decline, regional economic change has generally (and perhaps increasingly) been understood in terms of narratives of integration, harmonization, stabilization, growth, upgrading, core labour standards, and national development. Indeed, despite their many engagements with the consequences of structural change, regional transformation, uneven development, and spatial and social inequality, regional economists and policy makers working on the region have adopted a generally and overly positive outlook on the nature of change.

There are long traditions of this EU-positivity, both in the original vision for the united Europe and in the accession programs that brought post-socialist countries into the EU. For example, in the 1990s, the word "transition" carried this positive valence, generally being understood as referring to a shift in the organization of administration, economy, and society from one known, stable form to another differently known, stable form. For the World Bank this was the very clear "from plan to market" (World Bank 1996) and the path between the two was largely to be managed technically and politically. In recent years, such ruptural events have increasingly been seen as stimuli to innovation, reform, and regional resurgence; the collapse of the command economy enabled the flourishing of liberal market economies, EU accession normalized and regularized national policies, infrastructures, and even currencies, regional innovation systems, inter-firm networks, and growth centres emerged as key elements of the main narrative of development. In this view, the task of governance and economic management has been to ensure that change is controlled and negative and indirect consequences are minimized.

GVC-led trade has had several important implications for the structure of regional and global economic development. GVC outsourcing and their new dustrial production geographies have created real development benefits. For ample, UNCTAD (2013: x) has estimated that:

> GVCs lead to a significant amount of double counting in trade – about 28 per cent or $5 trillion of the $19 trillion in global gross exports in 2010 – because intermediates are counted several times in world exports, but should be counted only once as "value added in trade".
>
> (UNCTAD 2013: x)

The EU, World Bank/IFC, UNCTAD, and WTO are now involved in ordinated efforts to develop new measures of traded value, measures that could ve significant impacts on how regional benefits of export-oriented development e assessed.

The expansion of integrated intra- and inter-firm networks of specialized oduction and intermediate goods and services trade have also increased oduction efficiencies, reduced costs, and created new much needed low-wage bs in the global South and high-value service jobs in the global North. As di auro et al. have shown:

> along with the increase in GVC participation, the importance of services – both directly and as "embodied" in final manufacturing – has grown in terms of value added and job creation. For instance, from the mid-90s, job creation in service activities in Germany and Spain has more than compensated job losses in declining traditional manufacturing activities.
>
> (Di Mauro et al. 2013: 6)

And, as the integration of global trade through GVCs increased the coordination osts of global sourcing, it also stimulated new initiatives to standardize and armonize sourcing practices and standards across supplier networks. These oordination efforts have particularly positive effects on European value chains for eneralizing minimum labour standards, but uncertain consequences for national d regional efforts to raise the floor on wages and workplace standards and ompliance in what amount to highly dependent (even captured) and precarious iyer-supplier networks.

The expansion and deepening of intra-firm networks and trade through GVCs is another important effect. The expansion of global value chains has been i important contributory factor in amplifying the speed of transmission of the)07/8 financial crisis regionally and internationally. It was the interdependence the global economy that quickly spread the effects of the financial crisis in the S to the rest of the world. In 2009 alone, world trade declined by a massive 13 ercent, with even deeper consequences for the EU than for the US.

The fragmentation of production, the geographical specialization of economic actices coordinated by lead-firms in global value chains, meant that declines in nal demand for commodities was immediately transmitted throughout the value iain, with particularly serious consequences for upstream suppliers and their sub-contractors (Cattaneo, Gereffi and Staritz 2010: xv). In this sense, economic integration heightened systemic risk, but it also enabled faster recovery among the most networked value chains. As Altomonte et al. (2012) have shown in their assessment of the role of global value chains in France during the trade collapse and the "bullwhip effect", intra-group trade originating in hierarchies of firms (GVCs) experienced the negative demand shock following 2007/8 faster and deeper than arm's-length traders, but recovered faster than firms in the same sector operating through arm's-length trade arrangements. That is, global value chains amplified the demand shock faster than arm's-length trade because of the inter-connectedness of firm networks in GVCs. But, the corollary was that GVC embedded firms recovered faster because they were better prepared through their supplier networks to react to demand and manage inventory replenishment.

It is crucial to any interpretation of these amplification effects that they can be linked to three dynamics of the contemporary structure of European capitalisms. First, some EU economies are much more integrated into GVCs than others, and each has its own regional structure. Germany has emerged as the most networked economy, particularly into eastern Europe. Spain and Portugal expanded their GVC networks much later, at a time when Euro-Med and southeast Europe offered the only remaining suppliers with whom to work. Greece barely created European value chains, remaining largely a sub-contracting destination with the exception of small under-resourced and often non-compliant value chains extending into low-cost labour markets in Bulgaria.

Second, strong intra-firm networks exhibit two related dynamics. Their lead-firms are strong vis-à-vis their supplier networks, while their suppliers are generally weak and in an interdependent relation to them. Since northern value chain networks are highly concentrated geographically because of their histories of emergence, domestic demand declines or financial crises have much more significant effects in their supply chain regions as contracting is withdrawn, product mixes change, and/or contract prices are driven down.

Third, GVCs have different relationships to capital markets and financial demands than vertically integrated or arm's length buyers. Suppliers in value chains are much more dependent – in some cases fully dependent – on buyer-provided short-term loans, letters of credit, and equipment. In regions where suppliers are dependent on their embeddedness in the value chains of northern lead-firms, local inter-firm cooperation and learning is often non-existent, with suppliers – whether in automobiles or clothing – operating as stand-alone factories. Regional infrastructures, banking, and other technical and labour market supports that typify northern lead-firm regions are simply absent. Spillovers and inter-firm learning are limited. And state supports have been stripped away by the very politics of liberalization that EU-12 countries enforced on the accession and partnership countries in the east and Euro-Med. Broader macro-economic changes have also left these states with extremely high debt burdens and ever increasing pressures to enact austerity measures that, in the case of Greece, even the IMF has argued cannot lead to any development or growth (Nardelli 2015).

The overall consequence of such combined and uneven development dynamics has been the rapid integration of eastern and southern European economies and societies into the EU and Euro-zone but in ways that remain hierarchical, based on asymmetries of both power and access to capital and know-how, dynamics that remain precarious and continue to re-inscribe north–south divisions in Europe, reflected in unemployment, incomes, health, and other social indicators. The past forty years have certainly been characterized by decades of prosperity and growth on the path to a high-value European economic growth model, but any geographical analysis must take into account the ways in which economic integration created intense networks of uneven inter-dependencies and fragile chains and asymmetries. These value chain networks are the new structure of the European economy and, in times of economic downturn, they are marked by ever-deeper structural and employment crises.

Conclusion: Toto, we're not in Kansas anymore

In his *Afterthoughts on Material Civilization and Capitalism* (1977), the French historian Fernand Braudel suggested the need to understand markets in terms of complex hierarchies of exchange relations.[6] In particular, he argued that markets can function in ways that are far from open and free. He referred to these private markets as "countermarkets":[7]

> English historians have shown that as of the fifteenth century the traditional public market was accompanied by what they have called the private market (I would prefer to stress differences and call it the countermarket) ... Itinerant dealers who collected and assembled merchandise went to the homes of the producers. From the peasant they bought wool, hemp, livestock, hides, barley or wheat, and poultry. Or they might even buy these items in advance, as unshorn wool and uncut wheat. A simple note signed at the village inn or at the farm itself sealed the bargain. Then they shipped their purchases by cart, pack horse, or boat to the major cities or coastal ports ...
>
> (Braudel 1977: 52)

> This type of exchange replaced the normal collective market and substituted for it individual transactions based on arbitrary financial arrangements that varied according to the respective situation of the individuals involved ... It is obvious here that we are dealing with unequal exchanges in which competition – the basic law of the so-called market economy – had little place and in which the dealer had two trump cards; he had broken off relations between the producer and the person who eventually received the merchandise (only the dealer knew the market conditions at both ends of the chain and hence the profit to be expected); and he had ready cash, which served as his chief ally. Thus, long chains of merchants took position between production and consumption, and it is surely their effectiveness that

caused them to win acceptance, especially in supplying large cities, and that prompted the authorities to close their eyes or at least to relax controls.

(Braudel 1977: 52–53)

Who could doubt that these capitalists had monopolies at their disposal or that they simply had the power needed to eliminate competition nine times out of ten? ... Finally, the sheer size of their capital enabled capitalists to preserve their privileged position and to reserve for themselves the big international transactions of the day.

(Braudel 1977: 57–58)

The EU outward processing trade and the "normal" trade that has replaced it have many characteristics in common with the countermarkets of which Braudel wrote. From the 1970s on, eastern European and more recently Euro-Med producers and workers were entrained into well-established outsourcing commercial networks that locked them into assembly production for European buyers. For many such producers contracting became the sole source of work for the factory and managers had little opportunity to either build new markets or experiment with new products or production processes. Capital was scarce and contracts required on-time production of increasing quality. Many producers were simply "locked in" to existing chains of contracting and supply, with little opportunity or hope of "branching out" or understanding alternative market conditions. These were classical private markets, segmented and monopolized by buyers to discipline producers, minimize costs, and increase flexibility (especially during periods when consumption patterns were changing quickly). But they were also the conduits for the rapid transmission of demand shifts in northern markets and financial crises and credit freezes among lead-firms.

EU28 and Euro-Med are built in large part on these extended regional production networks of uneven exchange relations, inter-firm networks that lock-in asymmetries of power, channel value in ways that benefit core firms and regions, and maintain private markets whose sustainability is ever more challenged by the tendency of these commercial relations to amplify risk and uncertainty. A new integrated European economy has certainly been produced, but it is not the stable, high-value, and harmonized one, which Eurocrats envisioned at the start of the process.

Acknowledgements

This chapter has benefitted from discussions with the participants at the University of North Carolina, Chapel Hill 2014 conference on Crisis in the EU, particularly with Grigor Gradev, General Secretary of the International Trade Union Congress. The chapter draws on parallel work with four other groups. First, my longstanding collaboration with Adrian Smith, Robert Begg, Poli Roukova, Milan Bucek and Rudolf Pastor on eastern European economic geographies, particularly our recent book (Pickles and Smith 2016). Second, my collaborators in the University of Manchester UK DFID Capturing the Gains Research Network (PIs Stephanie

Barrientos and Gary Gereffi). Third, with the authors and editors of the special issue of the *Cambridge Journal of Regions, Economy, and Society* on Trade Policies and Global Value Chains (Pickles, Plank, Staritz, and Glasmeier 2015). And fourth, with my UNC value group colleagues Elizabeth Havice and Alvaro Reyes. All interpretations and errors are my responsibility.

Notes

1 Euro-Med has come to refer to the countries of the Euro-Mediterranean Partnership or the Barcelona Process. It currently comprises 39 states; 27 from the EU, 3 Candidate states (Croatia, Macedonia and Turkey), and 9 Mediterranean Partners (Algeria, Egypt, Israel, Jordan, Lebanon, Morocco, the Palestinian Authority, Syria and Tunisia). Libya has had observer status.
2 Ederer and Reschenhofer (2014) do not take into account eastern European countries, but instead focus on a series of countries as proxies for the "north", "west" and "south" of Europe in order to assess bilateral trade balances and to decompose the effects of changes in global demand patterns from structural changes in the geographies of global production.
3 Interview with Director of Economic Affairs, EURATEX, Brussels, 2003.
4 This is currently being further extended by the Deep and Comprehensive Agreements being developed with north African, Middle Eastern and Eurasian states (Badre 2014).
5 For a more detailed analysis of the role of trade policies, preferential access agreements, and rules of origin in shaping these geographies of production and employment see Pickles, Plank, Staritz and Glasmeier (2015).
6 This section draws on Smith et al. (2005).
7 We used Braudel's argument in our 2005 response to the 2003 EU Commission Communication (see Smith et al. 2005).

References

Abernathy, F., A. Volpe and D. Weil. 2006. "The Future of the Apparel and Textile Industries: Prospects and Choices for Public and Private Actors." *Environment and Planning A* 38(12): 2207–2232.
Altomonte, C., F. di Mauro, G. Ottaviano, A. Rungi and V. Vicard. 2012. *Global Value Chains During the Great Trade Collapse: A Bullwhip Effect?* Frankfurt: European Central Bank.
Amador, J., R. Capparielloy and R. Stehrerz. 2015. *Global Value Chains: A View from the Euro Area.* Working paper no. 1761 (March). Frankfurt: European Central Bank.
Badre, A. 2014. *International Negotiations for Economic Diplomacy: EU-Morocco's DCFTA.* July. Berlin: Institute for Cultural Diplomacy
Begg, R., J. Pickles and A. Smith. 2003. "Cutting It: European Integration, Trade Regimes and the Reconfiguration of East-Central European Apparel Production." *Environment and Planning A* 35: 2191–2207.
Bourgeot, R. 2013. "Labour Costs and Crisis Management in the Euro Zone: A Reinterpretation of Divergences in Competitiveness." Robert Schuman Foundation European 289 (23 September). Available at www.robert-schuman.eu/en/european-issues/0289-labour-costs-and-crisis-management-in-the-euro-zone-a-reinterpretation-of-divergences-in.
Braudel, F. 1977. *Afterthoughts on Material Civilization and Capitalism.* Baltimore, MD: Johns Hopkins University Press.

222   *John Pickles*

Cattaneo, O., G. Gereffi and C. Startiz (eds). 2010. *Global Value Chains in a Postcrisis World: A Development Perspective.* Washington, DC: World Bank.

Chovanec, M. and Š. Rehák. 2012. "Exploring Spatial Patterns of Creative Industries with Firm Level Micro Geographic Data." *Regions Direct* 2: 10–35.

Coe, N., M. Hess, H. Yeung, P. Dicken and J. Henderson. 2004. "Globalising Regional Development: A Global Production Networks Perspective." *Transactions of the Institute of British Geographers* 29(4): 468–484.

Di Mauro, F., H. Plamper and R. Stehrer. 2013. *Global Value Chains: A Case for Europe to Cheer Up.* Compnet Policy Brief 03/2013 (August). Frankfurt: European Central Bank.

European Commission. 2003a. "Communication from the Commission to the Council, the European Parliament, the European Economic and Social Committee and the Committee of the Regions on The Future of the Textiles and Clothing Sector in the Enlarged European Union." COM(2003) 649 final. Available at http://europa.eu.int/comm/enterprise/textile/com2003.htm.

European Commission. 2003b. *Commission Staff Working Paper: Evolution of Trade in Textile and Clothing Worldwide – Trade Figures and Structural Data.* SEC(2003) 1348. Brussels: European Commission. Available at http://europa.eu.int/comm/enterprise/textile/documents/sec2003_1348en.pdf.

European Commission. 2004. "Textiles and Clothing: Statistics." Available at http://europa.eu.int/comm/enterprise/textile/statistics.htm.

European Commission. 2012. *Global Europe 2050.* Brussels: European Commission Directorate of Research and Innovation.

Ederer, S. and P. Reschenhofer. 2014. *A Global Value Chain Analysis of Macroeconomic Imbalances in Europe.* Working paper no. 67 (September). Vienna: WWW for Europe.

Freeman, R. B. 2007. "The Challenge of the Growing Globalization of Labour Markets to Economic and Social Policy." In *Global Capitalism Unbound: Winners and Losers from Offshore Outsourcing,* edited by E. Paus, pp. 23–40. New York: Palgrave Macmillan.

Fröbel, F., J. Heinrichs and O. Kreye. 1980. *The New International Division of Labour.* Cambridge: Cambridge University Press.

Gereffi, G. 1994. "The Organization of Buyer-Driven Global Commodity Chains: How US Retailers Shape Overseas Production Networks." In *Commodity Chains and Global Capitalism,* edited by G. Gereffi and M. Korzeniewicz. Westport, CT: Greenwood Press, pp. 95–123.

Gereffi, G. 2003. "The International Competitiveness of Asian Economies in the Global Apparel Commodity Chain." *International Journal of Business and Society* 4(2): 71–110.

Gereffi, G. 2006. *The New Offshoring of Jobs and Global Development.* ILO Social Policy Lectures, Jamaica (December). Geneva: International Labour Organization.

Glasmeier, A., J. W. Thompson and A. J. Kays. 1993. "The Geography of Trade Policy: Trade Regimes and Location Decisions in the Textile and Apparel Complex." *Transactions of the Institute of British Geographers* 18(1) 19–35.

Graziani, G. 1998. "Globalization of Production in the Textile and Clothing Industries: The Case of Italian Foreign Direct Investment and Outward Processing in Eastern Europe." BRIE Working Paper 128 (May). Berkeley: University of California. Available at http://brie.berkeley.edu/_briewww/pubs/pubs/wp/wp128.htm.

Hale, A. and J. Wills (eds). 2008. *Threads of Labour: Garment Industry Supply Chains from the Workers' Perspective.* Oxford: Blackwell.

Nardelli, A. 2015. "IMF: Austerity Measures Would Still Leave Greece with Unsustainable Debt." *The Guardian* (30 June). Available at www.theguardian.com/business/2015/jun/30/greek-debt-troika-analysis-says-significant-concessions-still-needed.

ECD. 2013. *Implications of Global Value Chains for Trade, Investment, Development and Jobs.* A report prepared for the G-20 Leaders Summit, Saint Petersburg. (September). Paris: OECD.

xfam. 2004. *Trading Away Our Rights: Women Working in Global Supply Chains.* Oxford: Oxfam International.

vlínek, P. 2012. The Impact of the 2008–2009 Economic Crisis on the Automotive Industry: Global Trends and Firm Level Effects in Central Europe. *European Urban and Regional Studies* 22(1): 20–40

ckles, J. 2006. "Trade Liberalization, Upgrading and Regionalization in the Global Apparel Industry." *Environment and Planning A* 38(12): 2201–2006.

ckles, J. 2012. *Capturing the Gains.* Working Papers 13. Available at http://www.capturingthegains.org/pdf/ctg-wp-2012-13.pdf

ckles, J. and A. Smith. 2016. *Articulations of Capital: Global Production Networks and Regional Transformations.* Institute of British Geographers Book Series. Chichester: John Wiley.

ckles, J., A. Smith, M. Buček, P. Roukova and B. Begg. 2006. "Upgrading, Changing Competitive Pressures and Diverse Practices in the East European Apparel Industry." *Environment and Planning A* 38(12): 2305–2324.

ckles, J., L. Plank, C. Staritz and A. Glasmeier. 2015. "Trade Policy and Regionalisms in Global Clothing Production Networks." *Cambridge Journal of Regions, Economy, and Society* 8(3): 381–402.

eyes, A, E. Havice, and J. Pickles 2016. "The Thorny Problem of Value and the Emergence of Global Value Chains as the New Structure of (Post-)Capitalism." Forthcoming.

oukova, P., M. Varbanov, A. Ravnachka, G. van Hamme, and P.M. Lockhart (n.d.). "Global commodity/value chain approach to assess the position of regions in the European and global economy." Working paper 8.1. Available at: http://www.espon.eu/export/sites/default/Documents/Projects/AppliedResearch/TIGER/FR/TIGER_working_paper_8.1_-_global_commodity_value_chain.pdf.

mith, A. 2013. "Europe and an Inter-Dependent World: Uneven Geo-Economic and Geo-Political Developments." *European Urban and Regional Studies* 20(1): 3–13.

mith, A., M. Buček, J. Pickles and B. Begg. 2003. "Global Trade, European Integration and the Restructuring of Slovak Apparel Exports." *Ekonomický časopis* 51: 731–748.

mith, A., J. Pickles, R. Begg, P. Roukova and M. Buček. 2005. "Outward Processing, EU Enlargement and Regional Relocation in the European Textiles and Clothing Industry: Reflections on the European Commission's Communication on 'The Future of the Textiles and Clothing Sector in the Enlarged European Union." *European Urban and Regional Studies* 12(1): 83–91.

mith, A., Pickles J., M. Buček, R. Begg and P. Roukova. 2008. "Reconfiguring 'Post-Socialist' Regions: Trans-Border Networks and Regional Competition in the Slovak and Ukrainian Clothing Industry." *Global Networks* 8(3): 281–307.

NCTAD. 2013. *GVCs and Development: Investment and Value Added Trade in the Global Economy.* Geneva: UNCTAD. Available at http://unctad.org/en/PublicationsLibrary/diae2013d1_en.pdf.

orld Bank. 1996. *World Development Report 1996: From Plan to Market.* Washington, DC: World Bank.

11 The euro as a house of straw

Why Europe's crisis is (still) linked to American housing

Herman Mark Schwartz

The most recent GDP data confirms that the recovery in the Euro area remains uniformly weak, with subdued wage growth even in non-stressed countries suggesting lackluster demand. In these circumstances, it seems likely that uncertainty over the strength of the recovery is weighing on business investment and slowing the rate at which workers are being rehired.

(Mario Draghi, Jackson Hole, WY, 22 August 2014)

Introduction

Most analyses blame the euro crisis on the fact that Europe is far from being an optimum currency area. Metaphorically, the Eurozone was a straw house and when the wolf of the American financial crisis arrived at the Eurozone's door, the Eurozone's profound structural problems caused it to collapse around its inhabitants. And as in the old story, the PIIGS suffered most. This view is largely correct, insofar as it describes the structural causes of the Eurozone crisis in terms of permissive conditions. But it is a bit misleading as to both the deeper and proximate causes for the euro crisis, and thus precisely why the US housing bust was so perilous for Europe. The Eurozone might well have been a rickety structure, vulnerable to the emergence of regional imbalances. But why did those imbalances emerge in the first place? The origins of those imbalances explain why the European "real" economy was caught up in the US housing bubble. Likewise the arrival of the wolf, in the form of the US housing collapse, mattered because the European banks were so caught up in the US housing market, and were thus vulnerable to a collapse of the US housing market.

Put simply, the fact that the Eurozone was not an optimum currency area left it vulnerable to anything that might aggravate its own internal imbalances. At the *macro-economic* level, Europe's core political economies, and especially Germany, rely on external demand for growth, and particularly on US and Chinese growth. Without "Chimerican" growth, Europe faces secular stagnation brought on by the combined effects of aging, dual labour markets, female exclusion, and a deeply conservative central bank. Given that Chinese growth also partly relies on continued US growth, European growth was especially hostage to the US economy. At a *macroeconomic* level, Europe's reliance on external markets for growth should not necessarily have generated a problem. Europe has a relatively balanced external current account, on a net basis. But this net position conceals a reliance on a surplus with North America that helps balance net energy imports and a trade deficit with China. That is, gross flows are relatively unbalanced. Internally, Europe was completely unbalanced, with northern Europe running consistent trade surpluses with southern/peripheral Europe. Peripheral Europe in turn relied on the previously mentioned surpluses with North America to help mitigate its deficits with northern Europe. Consequently, Europe had a double reliance on North America and China. It needed excess US growth to generate growth, and it needed excess US growth to ameliorate its internal imbalances. Yet this need not have caused a euro crisis in the absence of specific institutional characteristics and investment choices that made the euro "straw"-like.

At an *institutional* level, European banks were the conduit channelling northern European surpluses back to the southern deficit countries. But as a matter of investment strategy, those banks also recycled smaller European external surpluses and re-intermediated borrowed money into the US housing market. Northern European banks were the conduit for trade surplus, recycling both internally and externally, and thus were the glue holding the not-quite-optimum currency area together. This dual role was the proximate cause for the euro crisis. As with the US banks in the 1970s, the European banks in surplus countries should have been shielded from a pure foreign debt crisis. But in both cases the structure of intermediation exposed them to an external crash. European banks had created risky currency and maturity mismatches in their lending into the US housing market, and moreover had invested heavily in securities built on subprime mortgages. These mortgages were packaged in ways that concealed considerable credit risk. And while the European banks thought they had avoided exchange rate risk by borrowing in dollars to fund dollar denominated mortgage assets, their ability to raise loans in dollars to offset any dollar-denominated losses would be weaker in any emergency, forcing them to liquidate euro-denominated assets in any crash. Thus, the American housing crash – the realization of credit risk and its transubstantiation into a dollar shortage – was also a European banking crash. European banks' capital disappeared in the losses they sustained in the US housing market. The US housing crash thus created a simultaneous growth and financial crisis in Europe as the main channel for European internal rebalancing broke down. The banks were the straws from which Europe's optimum currency area straw house had been built.

This chapter thus proceeds as follows. First, by focusing on the German political economy I argue that Europe and the Eurozone in particular have a tendency towards secular stagnation. This section is profoundly Keynesian. The second section explains how the North American and Chinese growth mitigates the tendency to secular stagnation in northern Europe. The critical link here is the recycling of (northern) European trade surpluses into the US economy in the 1990s and 2000s, and, more importantly, the re-intermediation of the US credit into the US housing market in the 2000s. The third section briefly describes intra-European imbalances to show why losses by the European banks in the US housing market disrupted the flow of capital from north to south, triggering the European crisis. The fourth section concludes by suggesting that massive changes to political institutions would be needed to decouple Europe from the United States and China.

A European tendency toward secular stagnation?

Both demography and political economy tilt Europe towards secular stagnation, or, more narrowly, towards growth rates below those in North America and developing Asia. EU growth rates roughly parallel those in North America or the United States, particularly on a per capita basis. From 2000 to 2012, real net national income in every major economy in the Eurozone grew more slowly than in the United States.[1] But using the aggregated EU or Eurozone growth rates conceals the fact that growth was largely concentrated in the far northern non-Eurozone economies, and, for a time, in the trade deficit southern countries. Figure 11.1 disaggregates and compares growth rates for select European and other economies against the Eurozone 17 average and the EU 28 average from 1999 to 2015. (Using the Eurozone 17, which grew more slowly than the EU28 area, provides a conservative comparison, and using constant local currency removes exchange rate effects.)

What explains this disparity in growth rates? A full-scale explanation of this contentious issue is impossible here. But demographically, Europe has a significantly lower birth rate than the United States, and lower population growth overall. While there are significant regional differences in fertility, these largely favour the faster growing far north rather than core or southern Europe. Germany, for example, had negative population growth some years in the 2000s, partly as

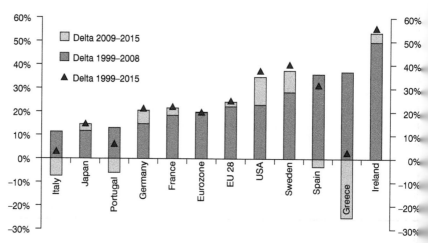

Figure 11.1   Change (delta) in GDP measured in constant local currency, 1999–2008, 2009–2015 and 1999–2015

Source: own calculation from EU AMECO database

a consequence of a total fertility rate averaging 1.33 births per woman over most of the 1990s and 2000s. This is well below the replacement rate of 2.1 and the OECD average of 1.7. The OECD predicts that the Eurozone labour force will grow by only 0.2 per cent annually from 2014 to 2030, versus 0.5 per cent for the United States (OECD 2014a). Lower fertility obviously creates lower absolute growth as the number of consumers and households stagnates. But it also creates lower relative growth as firms shift resources to economies with faster absolute population and thus market growth. Firms in capitalist economies tend to invest where growth is fastest, all other things being equal.

Europe has also historically presented lower female labour force participation on average, though again with big regional differences favouring Northern Europe, and with some rapid catch-up in the 2000s. Figure 11.2 shows the deviation, in percentage points, of select countries' female employment to population ratios from the OECD-22 average. Social support for female labour force participation is low relative to the US or Canada, and in core Europe extremely low relative to the Nordics. But Scandinavia accounts for barely 25 million people versus the 500 million of the EU-28, so this is like noting that Massachusetts had something resembling universal health insurance at a time that the entire United States did not. It does not move the average much. Although female labour force participation has been rising – in some cases sharply – to levels close to or exceeding those in North America, the level of labour intensity remains lower because of the higher prevalence of part time work (Figure 11.3). Thus, while the Netherlands and Germany have rates of female labour force participation

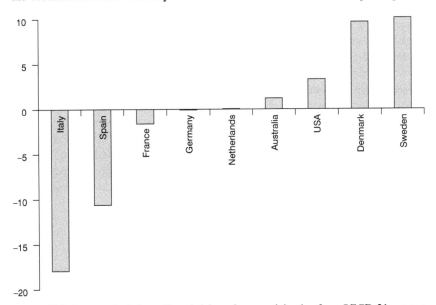

Figure 11.2 Average deviation of female labour force participation from OECD-21 average level of female labour force participation, 1992–2014, percentage points

Source: own calculation from www.OECD-ilibrary.org data

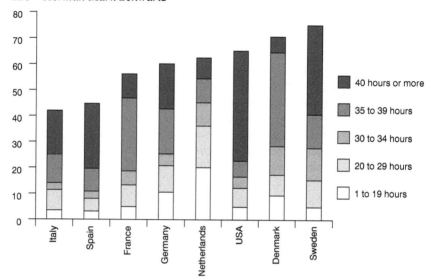

Figure 11.3 Female work intensity: hours worked as a share of employment to population
ratio, average, 1992–2013. Columns do not sum to 100 per cent because of
labour force non-participation (e.g. roughly 60 per cent of Italian women
work zero hours

Source: own calculation from www.OECD-iLibrary.org data

similar to the United States, the bulk of this participation involves many fewer
hours of work on average across the year. In the United States, 75 per cent of
women are working more than 35 hours per week, versus only 23.7 per cent in the
Netherlands and 53.1 per cent in Germany. As with fertility, lower labour force
participation and work intensity translates into lower or slower absolute growth,
which in turn translates into lower relative growth as firms invest in places with
more purchasing power and market expansion.

    Much of this imbalance stems from Germany, whose industrial structure is
oriented towards investment goods, whose political economy is oriented towards
wage restraint, and who in addition has all the problems listed above. Because
Germany accounts for about 21 per cent of EU GDP and about 27 per cent of
Eurozone GDP, it exerts an outsized influence on the European developments. It
is thus the focus of the next section.

The German growth model

The German political economy is characterized by collectively bargained wage
repression and a reliance on capital goods exports to other, more rapidly growing
economies. The latter makes the German economy relatively pro-cyclic and
externally oriented. The former, the deliberate suppression of domestic demand,
reinforces firms' orientation towards the external market. Weak domestic demand
stemming from demography and changes to the welfare state also reduce

consumption, including imports. In the 1990s these forces were relatively weak, and a deliberate policy to incorporate and upgrade the old German Democratic Republic produced mild trade deficits. But in the 2000s, wage restraint became the lodestone of German economic elites at precisely the point in time when changes in pension policy incited extra savings from consumers. These two policy decisions combined with an increasingly elderly population to produce trade surpluses, albeit mostly with the EU countries. German banks then recycled those surpluses to peripheral Europe in order to finance continued German capital goods exports to those deficit economies. Confronted with a stagnant domestic market and EU-mandated reductions in state subsidies, those banks also entered the US housing market in search of increased profits.

Demography is the force least amenable to short-term policy remediation. The share of Germany's population over 65 years of age rose from 15.3 per cent in 1992 to 17.2 per cent in 2000, and then accelerated to 21 per cent in 2012, even though the first post-war cohorts were only just entering retirement.[2] The elderly typically consume fewer imports and more locally provided services as compared to the young. Old people typically have already a well-furnished household and thus decline to purchase cheap imported consumer non-durables on the one hand, and on the other hand typically depreciate their consumer durables less intensively. Old people don't buy much new furniture and they drive less than younger people. By contrast, they consume considerably more health care and other personal services than younger people, particularly as their ability to care for their homes and selves declines. These services are almost by definition usually non-traded. While the old might "import" more in the form of tourism, even there diminished mobility takes its toll. Aging thus reduces Germany's ability to absorb imports in proportion to its ability to generate exports, unless massive numbers of Germans relocate to sunnier parts of Europe. But Germans currently relocate southwards much less than the more adventurous British, and much, much less than Americans.

Short-term policy changes to the welfare state also diminished German consumption overall while shifting consumption away from imports. The most important of these was the 2001 Riester pension reform, which over a three-decade phase in period will raise the retirement age by two years, and decrease the effective replacement rate from 70 per cent to 54 per cent. By way of compensation, the Riester reform permitted (and indeed incentivized via tax concessions and other subsidies) workers to shift 4 per cent of their wage into a private occupational pension (OECD 2014b). Despite the long phase in period for the various Riester changes, workers (over?) reacted much as economists would expect and increased private savings to compensate for their smaller expected public pension pay-out. These extra savings had to find some home. Given that German firms were pursuing wage restraint (see below) and thus domestic real investment was shrinking, and given that increased savings necessarily inhibit domestic consumption growth in the first instance, the excess of savings over local investment necessarily had to be exported to other countries. Individual reactions to Riester thus helped provide part of the financial counterpart to Germany's physical trade surplus.

Table 11.1   Wage levels and rates of change, 2000–2007. Select countries, units as indicated, ranked by last column.

	Average wages in 2011 in current USD	Average wages in 2011 in USD PPPs	Average annual change, 2000–2007
Korea	29,053	35,406	2.5
Sweden	54,459	37,734	1.9
Denmark	73,032	45,560	1.8
UK	50,366	44,743	1.8
Australia	74,512	44,983	1.6
France	47,704	38,128	1.2
United States	54,450	54,450	1.2
Italy	39,112	33,517	0.3
Germany	46,984	40,223	0.2
Spain	37,583	34,387	−0.1
Japan	51,613	35,143	−0.3

Source: OECD Employment Outlook 2012 – Statistical Annex

Finally, and probably most importantly, collectively bargained wage restraint in the export industries dampened Germany's domestic demand. Wage restraint lowers domestic demand and thus wage earner consumption. In turn, this reduces the incentive to hire new workers. Weak hiring leads to higher wage-based taxes to fund social assistance for the unemployed. This in turn makes it harder for employers to hire new workers. Overall, wage restraint reduced the wage share of the German GDP by roughly four percentage points from 1998 to 2007.[3] Though German unions began pressing for higher wages after 2011, this came too late and too little to prevent or ameliorate the euro crisis. Table 11.1 provides comparative data on wage growth in the 2000s; German wage growth lagged considerably behind that in northern Europe, the United States, and Britain. On the other hand wage restraint should – and did – translate into higher profits.

Why didn't these increased profits substitute for the lost purchasing power of the average person? In principle, the bargain behind wage restraint involved increased investment by German firms. German workers accepted wage restraint on the theory that increased investment would secure jobs for the future. And German firms did invest – just not in Germany. The investment share of German GDP fell from its 1992–2000 average level of 22.1 per cent to just 18.1 per cent from 2000 to 2012. In per capita terms, German gross fixed capital formation fell by nearly 10 per cent from 2001 to 2005, and did not re-attain the 2001 level until 2007.[4] Or, to put it more graphically, while German actors had €1,62 billion available to them as savings from 2002 to 2010, they opted to deploy only 34 per cent or €554 billion of that domestically. They instead first voluntarily used €227 billion or 14 per cent of those savings for FDI elsewhere, and they were more or less forced to accommodate the shift of another €308 billion, or

19 per cent of those savings, to the periphery as an accumulation of Target2 claims corresponding to post-2008 capital flight from the periphery (Sinn 2011). Why? Low domestic demand induced firms to export savings into more rapidly growing economies to service demand there. This too became self-sustaining, as the relatively lower level of domestic investment decreased German domestic growth, spurring further export of savings.

German wage restraint in the late 1990s and 2000s kept the growth of German consumption well below that of its European neighbours. Relative to German consumption growth, from 2001 to 2008, Irish consumption grew twice as fast and Spanish, Portuguese, and Greek consumption grew 60 per cent faster, while Italian consumption increased 30 per cent faster. Germany both relied on and funded a faster-growing periphery to help absorb its own excess output. This created imbalances – excess German exports, excess peripheral imports – that gave Germany trade surpluses averaging 4.8 per cent of the GDP in the period 2001 to 2008, versus deficits in Spain, Portugal, and Greece of 6.5 per cent, 9.6 per cent, and 9.3 per cent respectively. Germany's cumulative global trade surplus from 2001 to 2008 of $1,009 billion is almost precisely matched by the GIPS global deficit of $1,007 billion, and is 10 per cent smaller if Italy is added in (International Monetary Fund 2014). Germany's trade surplus accounted for 20 per cent of its GDP growth in the period 1995 to 2009, which is a relatively large share (exceeded among major OECD countries only by Japan's 27 per cent share; Hoshi and Kashyap 2011: 62). Without putting too much weight on it, Germany's goods export surplus with the United States also accounted for 20 per cent of its cumulative goods trade surplus, in the period 1995–2009.

Was this imbalance inherently unsustainable? Clearly, given Europe's deficiencies as an optimum currency area, any shock would be dangerous. The introduction of the euro removed one key mechanism for accommodating regional imbalances, namely currency devaluation. Major economic regions in the United States also lack devaluation as an adjustment tool, and also experience enormous net inflows of capital. But labour flows, fiscal transfers and capital flows in the United States dwarf anything occurring in Europe, and make the United States much closer to being an optimum currency area in terms of its ability to handle inter-regional imbalances. Roughly 2 per cent of the US population moved across a state border in any given year in the 2000s, versus only 0.1 per cent in Europe. (Again, while labour mobility inside Europe is rising, this occurred subsequent and consequent to the crisis.) The EU's budget amounts to only 2 per cent of the European GDP, and half of this is committed to the CAP, which tends not to redistribute much on a net basis to poorer regions. By contrast, the United States federal government runs three major programs with sizeable regionally redistributive aspects: Social Security (the old age pension), Medicare/Medicaid (respectively health insurance for the elderly and poor), and defence. Each of these disburses between two and two and a half times the entire EU budget as a share of the GDP. Finally, the federal tax system also automatically shifts income from high growth to low growth (i.e. high employment, low employment) areas by taxing the former more heavily and the latter more lightly. In effect, the United

States runs a robust transfer union, while the EU is hobbled by its growth and stability pacts.

In the absence of compensatory labour and fiscal flows, only massive financial flows from north to south could accommodate Europe's regional imbalances. Here too the comparison with the United States reveals the EU's relative lack of integration, even though this is the one area where the EU had attained considerable integration. The United States has highly integrated inter-regional capital markets. Money flows seamlessly from one region to another via a variety of instruments, but among the largest are the mortgage finance system and the municipal (i.e. non-central government) bond system. The US federal government incentivizes funding of both markets through tax concessions and, in the case of mortgages, what is now an explicit guarantee of Fannie Mae and Freddie Mac's $1.9 trillion of debt and $5.6 trillion of insured mortgage backed securities (Freddie Mac 2014). By contrast, the entire EU27 mortgage market amounted to roughly €6.7 trillion of outstanding debt in 2012, or less than just the federally guaranteed part of the US mortgage market; the entire US residential mortgage stock amounted to €8.2 trillion (EMF 2013: 85). Outstanding US municipal (i.e. state and local government) bonds currently amount to $3.7 trillion, or about one-third the size of the marketable US federal public debt. The nearest EU equivalent would be bonds related to the as yet unrealized fiscal union.

In the absence of high levels of labour mobility, fiscal transfers, or capital mobility, the only way for the Eurozone to manage regional imbalances emerging from lagging German consumption was the recycling of northern European trade surpluses into peripheral public and private debt. In particular, privately funded construction booms occurred in Spain and Ireland. The Basel 2 accord incentivized this behaviour, because banks did not have to hold equity capital against their holdings of peripheral public debt, while the (apparent) elimination of exchange rate risk in 2001 made lending to private entities more attractive. But this lending created a powerful virtuous cycle that increased both the absolute level of peripheral indebtedness and peripheral reliance on this recycling. Capital inflows stimulated peripheral economic growth. Increasing employment meant more consumption and thus stronger fiscal positions; stronger fiscal positions helped attract more capital at lower interest rates, and lower interest rates incentivized more consumption of housing and consumer durables, closing the loop by increasing employment. Rinse and repeat…until the money stopped flowing. A country running a consistent 6 or 9 per cent current account deficit – as Spain or Greece did in the 2000s – is vulnerable to any sudden stop in foreign lending. The only thing offsetting this increased vulnerability was the ability to run a trade surplus with the non-Eurozone world, which, in the 2000s, mostly meant the United States and other countries making investments to service China's extraordinary demand for raw materials.

As Figure 11.4 shows, the Eurozone net of France and Germany ran modest trade (goods and services) surpluses with the United States as the US housing boom took steam. When that housing bubble collapsed, the peripheral Eurozone states found themselves without trade flows that might compensate for their

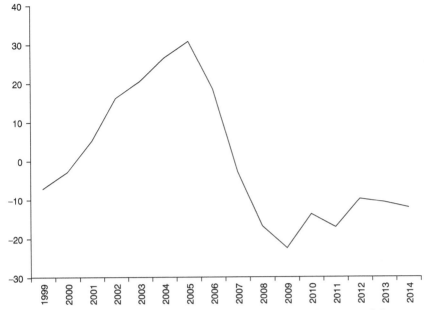

Figure 11.4 Eurozone trade surplus with the United States, net of France and Germany, US$ billions

Source: own calculation from US Bureau of Economic Analysis (www.bea.gov) data

deficit with northern Europe. Even so, had the European banking system not been exposed to the US housing market, northern surpluses might have been available for continued recycling, ameliorating this new, but small macro-economic burden. Unfortunately, northern banks were deeply involved in and thus damaged by the US housing bubble. This damage broke the channel of intermediation between the north and south.

The increased demand for financing for the south occurred at precisely the moment when the German and other northern European banks needed to shore up their own balance sheets in response to the global financial crisis. Part of the problem for northern banks was their losses from speculating in the US mortgage market. But the fear of the Greek default also made southern European public debt look like a problem for bank balance sheets. Banks' individual rationality led them to dump southern debt. Collectively, this produced a sharp spike in interest rates for the south, worsening the fiscal deficits that emerged after the crisis and making it harder to finance those deficits. Far from finding accommodating finance, southern states confronted capital flight. This created a self-fulfilling downward spiral in peripheral economies and the crisis of the euro. Moreover, because the European banks intermediate roughly 80 per cent of the credit in European markets, damage to their balance sheets had immediate and widespread effects (Klein 2014). Why were (northern) European banks so involved in the US housing bubble, and how did they get damaged?

European banks and the US housing bubble

The European banks were damaged by the US housing bubble because they created the same kind of risky maturity mismatch that the US banks created in pursuit of the extraordinary (and ultimately fabricated) profits that they siphoned off as bonuses in the short run. Roughly half of the gross capital inflow into the US economy in 2007 flowed through the European banks. Much of this went into housing-related assets. Notably, the European banks acquired significant volumes of privately originated, subprime (and thus "toxic") backed mortgage securities, unlike the Asian central banks that acquired the much safer Agency MBSs originated by Fannie Mae and Freddie Mac. British banks intermediated half of the European flow, making a precise allocation difficult. Still, the crisis revealed considerable holdings by continental banks, and in any case the euro-area banks directly accounted for a full third (Borio and Disyatat 2011). European banks held roughly $8 trillion in US dollar denominated assets in 2008, and estimates of how much of this involved a maturity mismatch range from a minimum of $1.1 trillion to as much as $6.5 trillion (McGuire and von Peter 2009; Borio and Disyatat 2011).

Indeed, it is somewhat pointless to distinguish the European from US banks in terms of their strategies and the scope of their operations (e.g. see the geographic breakdown of bank assets in McGuire and von Peter 2009: 7). Simplifying a bit, only two meaningful differences emerged as the crisis broke. Both the US and European banks had balance sheets in which long-term, dollar denominated assets (subprime mortgages and mortgage-backed securities) offset short-term, dollar denominated liabilities (asset-backed commercial paper originated by US money market funds, in which the mortgage asset was the collateral or backing for the short-term loan from the money markets to the banks' investment arms). But, while the US banks had dollar denominated capital to offset any losses on those dollar denominated assets, the European banks had euro-denominated capital. Second, the US banks had immediate and unlimited access to funds from the Fed, while European banks had to wait for the Fed and the ECB to work out a swap arrangement to provide the European banks with enough dollars to bail them out of their dollar denominated liabilities. These differences amount to a difference in the timing of the crisis, but not so much to its substance. The European banks, like the US banks, saw their capital, and thus their ability to lend, diminished by their losses on subprime mortgages.

The entire process can be seen in miniature in the balance sheet of Ormand Quay (Table 11.2), which was the off balance sheet structured investment vehicle (SIV) established in Ireland by Sachsen Landesbank so it could speculate in the subprime bubble (Acharya and Schnabl 2010: 7–10; more generally the analysis below draws on Schwartz 2009). Ormand Quay was the ninth largest European conduit engaging in what was effectively a carry trade between the short-term, asset backed commercial paper (ABCP) market and the long-term mortgage market. Its parent bank, Sachsen LB, was one of two canaries in the subprime coalmine, along with IKB Deutsche Industriebank. These banks were the first to suffer losses in their SIVs on a scale that threatened their solvency. IKB was a *ble 11.2* Balance sheet of Ormand Quay structured investment vehicle, as of July 2007

rmand Quay assets (guaranteed by achsen Landesbank)		*Liabilities (all short term debt, i.e. ABCP, with maturity < 1 month)*	
esidential mortgage acked securities RMBS)	$6.3 billion	Asset backed commercial paper	$11.4 billion
ommercial mortgage acked securities CMBS)	$2.7 billion		
onsumer loans	$0.5 billion		
ommercial loans	$0.5 billion		
ther	$1.4 billion		
otal	$11.4 billion	Total	$11.4 billion

urce: Acharya and Schnabl (2010: 51)

pical German bank, specializing in loans to Germany's *mittelstand*, small and edium-sized industrial firms. Yet IKB's Rhineland Funding SIV faced €700 illion in losses on a €17.5 billion offshore investment in derivatives based on S subprime mortgage securities. Fearing panic, the German authorities used the ant state development bank KfW to construct a consortium that provided €3.5 llion in emergency loans and €8 billion in guarantees to IKB, to no avail. IKB ter defaulted on $7 billion of the debt that financed those investments and ended being sold off to a US private equity firm. SachsenLB was the state bank of xony. Its bailout by the federation of savings banks amounted to €17.3 billion imensen and Atkins 2007).

How did the carry trade at the heart of Ormand Quay and similar SIVs work, d why did the German (and Dutch and British) banks engage in this carry trade? erman banks did worse in terms of return to equity than the US or UK banks the early 2000s, reflecting slow growth and increased competition in their mestic market. Moreover, the EU forced a gradual reduction of subsidies to e Landesbanks in the 2000s, putting even more pressure on those institutions well as on similar savings banks in other European countries. This motivated ose banks to search for higher yield. That search took them to Europe's eriphery, where, despite considerable interest rate convergence in the 2000s, iblic debt still yielded a small premium on the public debt of Germany or other orthern European countries. It also took them into the US housing market, where oney could be borrowed on a short-term basis at interest rates annualizing to pproximately 3 or 4 per cent per year (albeit with maturities ranging from 30 to 30 days) and then re-invested into mortgage backed securities (MBS) yielding pproximately 7 per cent per year. By 2008, the European banks were absorbing out 40 per cent of all lending by the American money market funds (Baba, cCauley and Ramaswamy 2009).

Arbitraging between short- and long-term interest rates could be extremely crative, particularly as the typical SIV was using leverage of between 20 and

30 (i.e. for every $1 of its own equity, the typical SIV borrowed between $20 and $30). The risks and rewards here are obvious. In any given year, if everything went well, with leverage of just 20 :1, the 4 percentage point difference between short- and long-term rates would produce a return on equity above 50 per cent. Leverage of 30 :1 would produce a return on equity over 70 per cent. At the same time, the risks were enormous. First, the extreme leverage here made SIVs sensitive to even a small loss. With leverage of 20 :1, a loss of just 5 per cent of an SIV's investments would bankrupt the SIV. At 30 :1, a 3 per cent loss would wipe out its capital.

Second, borrowing short-term money to invest in long-term assets creates a maturity mismatch. The lenders of the short-term money have a legal right to call in their money at the end of term, by refusing to roll over any outstanding loan. As long as those lenders were confident that the underlying collateral for the loan (the assets backing their commercial paper, thus: ABCP), they would probably renew the loan to keep their money working. But if those money market lenders felt that the collateral behind the loan was shaky, the short-term nature of the money they had loaned out meant that they could demand much of it back at once. This created a huge danger for the SIVs. In principle the SIV could liquidate its holdings of MBS and thus have cash on hand to redeem its loans. In practice any panicked selling of MBS by one SIV would cause the price of all MBS to fall, calling into question the security of the collateral behind all SIVs, and thus triggering a wave of loan non-renewal by money market managers.

Or, put in the simplest possible and in many ways most accurate terms, any fear as to the security of the collateral behind the ABCP would start a classic bank panic, with the equivalent of depositors trying to withdraw all their money from banks whose assets were all frozen. (In the movies, this would be Jame Stewart's cue to jump on the table as banker George Bailey and calm everyone down; instead it was Ben Bernanke calming the crowd). To protect their SIV from the risk of forced liquidation, parent banks granted them emergency line of credit. But this exposed the banks themselves to the same risks facing their SIVs, particularly given the large positions these SIVs accumulated. SachsenLB' emergency line of credit to Ormand Quay was more than 10 times its own equity Banks also bought insurance against default – credit default swaps (CDS) · from the likes of AIG. But anything more than a small default could, and die bring everything crashing down. Total European bank liabilities in the US dollar denominated claims amounted to about $2 trillion in mid-2007, of which two fifths came from the money markets, roughly a fifth from other banks, anothe fifth from the central banks, and the last fifth from the euro-denominated deposit converted in the foreign exchange market (McGuire and von Peter 2009: 1! Bernanke et al. 2011). In short, the European banks had a massive exposure t any downturn in the US housing market and, in a crisis, to any upward chang in the US dollar–euro exchange rate. Both occurred from 2007 forward, with rising dollar and falling housing prices forcing the European banks to find eve more dollars to unwind their speculative positions, thus aggravating their losse (Noeth and Sengupta 2012).

The downward spiral of the US housing market in 2007 and the credit crisis subsequent to the Lehman bankruptcy in September 2008 bankrupted the main European banks, and led to the nationalization of Fortis, Dexia, ABN-Amro, Northern Rock, RBS, HBOS, Lloyds TSB, UBS, AIB, and Bankia, among others, as well as government-arranged takeovers or bailouts of a number of other large banks. The US FED and ECB prevented a complete collapse of the European banking system by arranging a currency swap that transferred $600 billion to the ECB, and thus provided the European banks with the dollars they needed to redeem their debts to the panicked US money market funds. This swap prevented an all-out collapse of the European banking system.

Nonetheless, the crisis left the European banks crippled. They were both unable and unwilling to generate credit for the SME sector of the European economy – and SMEs are particularly important in the periphery – or to absorb the huge volumes of new public debt generated for bailing out the banks themselves. Banks reduced their debt levels using the classic tools of deleveraging: strengthening lending standards, calling in or refusing to rollover existing loans, and selling assets.[5] The European banks were thus unable to fulfil their prior role in recycling northern European surpluses to peripheral Europe, at precisely the moment when the peripheral Europe's helpful trade surpluses with the United States disappeared (see Figure 11.4 above), and when oil prices attained an average level three times higher than the pre-crisis level. Instead, the virtuous cycle of capital inflows, higher employment, better fiscal balance, and falling interest rates reversed as northern banks realized that while the euro might remove currency risk, it did not remove credit risk when it came to their holdings of peripheral public debt. With banks unable and unwilling to absorb peripheral public debt, a vicious cycle of the falling GDP, worsening budgets, rising interest rates, and weaker bank assets emerged in the periphery (Lane 2012).

Now what?

The Eurozone crisis is in the most general terms a balance of payments crisis triggered by overinvestment in the non-traded sector. At the same time it is specifically a banking crisis in which the intermediation channels that created and might have ameliorated that imbalance of payments were damaged by the sequelae of the crisis. In many ways it is the twin sister of the US financial crisis. Like peripheral Europe, the United States ran an unsustainable current account deficit, peaking at 6 per cent of the GDP in 2006 (the GIPS deficits amounted to about 7 per cent of their much smaller GDP over the 2000s). As with northern European banks, the American banks compromised their equity by creating SIVs to speculate in MBS built on subprime mortgages. If anything, however, the damage to the US financial system was even greater, as it reached into the money market funds, which supply the commercial credit needed for day-to-day commerce, and into the insurance sector via specialty and general insurers like AIG.

But unlike the United States, peripheral Europe did not have the luxury of simply printing money to rescue its banks, and thus restart the economy. In the

United States, the FED created new money on an enormous scale. The FED of course engaged in emergency lending at the height of the crisis. But over the next five years it also conducted its three Large Scale Asset Purchase programs (colloquially: Quantitative Easing or QE 1, 2, 3), which absorbed roughly $3.5 trillion in US Treasury bonds and Agency (i.e. Fannie Mae, Freddie Mac) mortgage-backed securities (Schwartz 2016). The scale of this intervention can be hard to understand, even though the numbers are large (perhaps precisely because the numbers are so large), and hard to compare to the ECB's more limited interventions. Their scale can be understood in this way: at the height of QE3 in 2012, the FED was buying $45 billion of US Treasuries per month at a time when the federal fiscal deficit amounted to about $90 billion per month. An additional monthly $45 billion absorbed nearly all the MBS thrown off by Fannie Mae and Freddie Mac; so in essence, the FED was funding the bulk of the mortgage market. The ECB has yet to respond with anything approaching this scale of intervention. Moreover, the European political elites largely responded to the crisis with fiscal austerity, rather than the (admittedly underwhelming) stimulus program the US Congress passed at Obama's urging, or the rather larger two year, 2.9 per cent of GDP Chinese stimulus.

Consequently, the ECB, Eurozone, and EU responses have returned Europe both to the structural problems it faced in 2000, and have kept the Eurozone aggregate GDP in 2014 at the same (real) level it attained in 2007. Growth remains hostage to external demand, and the current solutions are deeply deflationary rather than being inflationary or expansionist. Austerity has eliminated peripheral trade deficits by reducing peripheral imports from core. But this makes the core even more reliant on external demand for growth, and in turn implies an accumulation of the USD denominated assets as the United States continues to run modest trade deficits (and thus supplies demand to the world) (Germain and Schwartz 2014). But, sadly, the EU does not have the option of waiting for the rest of the world to grow. First, the EU, at roughly 20 per cent of the global GDP in PPP terms (and roughly 25 per cent in open exchange rate terms), is too big to rely on external growth for salvation. The rest of the world has to grow about 5 percentage points faster than the EU to pull the EU growth rate up by about 1 percentage point, given the EU's current share of global exports. This dimensional issue does not seem to register with export surplus core EU countries, which insist that the troubled periphery emulate their export surpluses. Nor is it clear that a 1 percentage point increase in the growth rate would be enough to save the indebted periphery anyway.

Put aside Greece, which anyway only has an economy a bit smaller than that of Boston metro; Spain, with an economy the size of Texas, has 25 per cent unemployment, has per capita income in constant euro below its 2003 level and aggregate real GDP in 2014 still lower than its 2005 level.[6] When the Texas economy crashed in 1999, the rest of the US economy could pull it out of its slump; likewise Canada (the size of California or Spain plus Denmark) could rely on the US 1990s boom to rescue it from its malaise. But the 1990s saw extremely large falls in nominal interest rates everywhere and a somewhat painless US fiscal consolidation achieved through increased capital gains taxation. Europe is doing exactly the opposite in a more difficult global economic climate. To be sure, many of Europe's structural problems – particularly demography – are not amenable to short-term solutions. Similarly, even if the structural changes in peripheral fiscal practices and labour markets the ECB (and Germany?) desires actually worked, their effects would only manifest themselves in the medium term. But fiscal and monetary policy tools with more immediate effects are right at hand. The ECB rightly fears that these might be inflationary. But creditors are foolish to think that their money is safe in a deflationary scenario. If debtors don't have enough income to service their debts, then creditors' corresponding assets have no value. The only mature choice in rebuilding Europe's house of straw is to suffer a little inflation in the short term rather than deflation in the long term.

Notes

1 Data from the OECD iLibrary (www.OECD-iLibrary.org).
2 Data from the OECD iLibrary (www.OECD-iLibrary.org).
3 Data from EU AMECO database (http://ec.Europa.eu/economy_finance/ameco/user/serie/SelectSerie.cfm).
4 Data from http://ec.Europa.eu/Eurostat
5 The same behaviours occurred in the United States, but (1) US corporations are much less reliant on bank funding than European firms, (2) the US municipal bond market was not connected to the banking system, and (3) the US government ran huge deficits, providing billions of dollars' worth of safe haven assets for banks and investors. In short, while risky securitization helped cause the financial crisis, securitization also helped to limit the fallout from weak bank balance sheets post-crisis.
6 Data from EU AMECO database (http://ec.Europa.eu/economy_finance/ameco/user/serie/SelectSerie.cfm).

References

Acharya, V., and P. Schnabl. 2010. "Do Global Banks Spread Global Imbalances? The Case of Asset-Backed Commercial Paper During the Financial Crisis of 2007–09." *IMF Economic Review* 58(1): 37–73.

Baba, N., R. N. McCauley, and S. Ramaswamy. 2009. *US Dollar Money Market Funds and Non-US Banks*. Basel: Bank for International Settlements. Available at www.bis.org/publ/qtrpdf/r_qt0903g.pdf.

Bernanke, B., C. C. Bertaut, L. DeMarco, and S. B. Kamin. 2011. *International Capital Flows and the Return to Safe Assets in the United States, 2003–2007*. International Finance Discussion Paper 1014. Washington, DC: FRB.

Borio, C., and P. Disyatat. 2011. *Global Imbalances and the Financial Crisis: Link or no Link?* No. 346. Basel: Bank for International Settlements.

Freddie Mac. 2014. *Investor Presentation 2014*. Fairfax County, VA: Freddie Mac. Available at www.freddiemac.com/investors/pdffiles/investor-presentation.pdf.

Germain, R., and H. Schwartz. 2014. "The Political Economy of Failure: The Euro as an International Currency." *Review of International Political Economy* 21(5): 1095–1122.

Hoshi, T., and A. Kashyap. 2011. *Why Did Japan Stop Growing?* NIRA Report. Chicago, IL: University of Chicago.

International Monetary Fund. 2014. "World Economic Outlook Database." Available at www.imf.org/external/pubs/ft/weo/2014/01/weodata/index.aspx.

Klein, M. 2014. "How to Spend it, ECB Bond Buying Edition." *Financial Times* (9 September). Available at http://ftalphaville.ft.com/2014/09/09/1961011/how-to-spend-it-ecb-bond-buying-edition/?.

Lane, P. R. 2012. "The European Sovereign Debt Crisis." *The Journal of Economic Perspectives* 26(3): 49–67.

McGuire, P. and G. von Peter. 2009. *The US Dollar Shortage in Global Banking*. BIS Working PArper 291. Basel: BIS.

Noeth, B., and R. Sengupta. 2012. "Global European Banks and the Financial Crisis." *Federal Reserve Bank of St. Louis Review* 94 (November/December).

OECD. 2014a. *Economic Outlook January 2014*. Paris: OECD.

OECD. 2014b. *Pensions at a Glance 2014*. Paris: OECD.

Schwartz, H. M. 2009. *Subprime Nation: American Power, Global Capital, and the Housing Bubble*. New York: Columbia University Press.

Schwartz, H. M. 2016. "Banking on the FED: QE 1-2-3 and the Rebalancing of the Global Economy." *New Political Economy* 21(1): 26–48.

Simensen, I. and R. Atkins. 2007. "Subprime Hits German State Banks." *Financial Times* (21 August). Available at www.ft.com/intl/cms/s/0/178cbd98-5014-11dc-a6b0-0000779fd2ac.html#axzz3BGMtWr00.

Sinn, H.-W. 2011. "Germany's Capital Exports under the Euro." August. http://www.voxeu.org/article/germany-s-capital-exports-under-Euro.

12 Where goes Russia?

The risks of a continental divide

Eric Brunat

[I]n Russian life, there is a sort of indeterminism which is difficult to understand for rationally-determined Western thought. But this indeterminate character opens wide perspectives. ... One must remember that the Russian is by nature highly polarized; on the one hand, one sees humility and renunciation and on the other, the revolt brought about by pity and the demand for justice. On the one hand, compassion and a warm heart, on the other, cruelty; the love of liberty on one side, and on the other a tendency towards slavery.

(Nicolas Berdiaev 1946)

Introduction

Very sensitive as it is to fluctuations in the international demand for gas, oil, and other fossil resources, in particular to that of European countries, who are themselves in a period of slowed growth during the financial crisis after the year 2000, 2009 was a very difficult year for Russia. Its GDP dropped by 7.8 per cent, which is a more significant drop than in other countries of the BRIC group, the Eurozone, or indeed the Unites States (see Tables 12.1 and 12.2). Russia is thus more than ever dependent on its natural resources, which are sold on international markets, and this ties the country in to fluctuations in demand and is a serious issue revealing structural weakness due to a high degree of specialization. The whole of its macro-economy is dependent on this to a very high degree as "exports of gas and oil represent two thirds of its exports and half of the federal budget, which directly affects internal demand, both public and private" (Brunat and Fontanel 2015).

The economic policy of the first decade of the 21st century

The economic policy of the first decade of the 21st century has repositioned Russia on international markets but the "Ukrainian crisis", in addition to the financial crisis, reveals structural weaknesses

A sharp drop in growth in 2012 and 2013 contrasted to the levels achieved at the beginning of the first decade of this century, and the first two terms of 2014 have not corrected this trend. Despite the growth rates in the years 2010, 2011 and 2012 increased above 3 per cent p.a. but the overall trend is down, to a weak 1.3 per cent in 2013. As we know, it is extremely difficult or indeed impossible for an

Table 12.1 The evolution of GDP: international comparisons (2005–2010)

Region	2005	2006	2007	2008	2009	2010
Russia	6.4	8.2	8.5	5.2	−7.8	4.5
Brazil	3.2	4.0	6.1	5.2	−0.3	7.5
India	9.3	9.3	9.8	3.9	8.5	10.3
China	11.3	12.7	14.2	9.6	9.2	10.4
Euro zone	1.7	3.0	2.8	0.5	−4.1	1.7
EU	2.2	3.5	3.2	0.7	−4.1	1.7
USA	3.3	2.7	1.8	−0.3	−2.8	2.5
World	3.5	4.0	3.9	1.6	−2.0	3.7

Source: IMF World economic outlook, October 2014

emerging or re-emerging country with growth below 3 per cent to finance the costs of economic and social development (institutional change, public infrastructure health, education and social welfare) and in the case of Russia, of economic, social and societal re-emergence (Brunat 2013). However, the "Ukrainian crisis", which occurred as early as the end of 2013, precipitated and deepened these difficulties. It is – after the international financial crisis – a second indicator of the inherent structural problems of the Russian economy, of its institutional and social reality, and of the consequences of the principle options of the economic policy that have been applied over the last 15 years.

The transformation of growth into human development and thus the conditions under which a really dynamic middle class driving growth might appear have been weakened. The Russian economy is running out of steam for fundamental structural reasons. This remark is made outside the context of the mutual sanctions linked to the "Ukrainian crisis" between most of the European countries, the United States and Russia, a highly negative spiral which has undoubtedly considerably impact on the parties concerned; Russia firstly, and to a lesser extent the European macro-economy (even though some sectors of the European agriculture and certain exporters or investors deeply involved in the Russian market have been hard hit by the downturn in trade). The first terms of 2014 have not modified the macro economic trends for growth that appeared in the Russian economy at the end of 2013. Growth stayed very weak in 2014, the IMF (2014) and the World Bank (2014, 2015) forecasted somewhere between +0.2 and +0.4 per cent, which is clearly a poor figure considering that Russia, a nation with a surface area of 17N km², is undergoing social transformation and re-emergence. Accentuated by serious geopolitical tensions, this trend seems unlikely to be inversed before 2020.[1] The growth that is predicted is thus insufficient. It is true that high interest rates do not guarantee an economic policy oriented towards reforms and development as the years before the financial crisis and the "Ukrainian crisis" show, but they are necessary (Voskoboynikov and Solanko 2014).

This situation is largely due to the "political comfort" of an absolute priority given in the early years of this century to a short-term economic policy based on

Table 12.2 Economic indicatiors for Russia (2006–2015)

	2006	2007	2008	2009	2010	2011	2012	2013	2014	2015 as of
GDP (Δ as a %)	8.2	8.5	5.2	–7.8	4.5	4.3	3.4	1.3	0.6	–3.4 Q1–2/15
GDP €bn	789	949	1133	879	1150	1369	1557	1563	1401	233 Q1/15
GDP $bn	991	1300	1658	1223	1525	1904	2001	2077	1850	264 Q1/15
Industrial production (Δ as a %)	6.3	6.8	0.6	–10.7	7.3	5.0	3.4	0.4	1.7	–3.0 –7/15
Investment (Δ as a %)	17.8	23.8	9.5	–13.5	6.3	10.8	6.8	0.8	–2.7	–5.9 –7/15
Exports of goods ($bn)	297.5	346.5	466.3	297.2	392.7	515.4	527.4	523.3	497.8	182.5 1–6/15
Imports of goods ($bn)	163.2	223.1	288.7	183.9	245.7	318.6	335.8	341.3	308.0	92.0 1–6/15
Current balance ($bn)	92.3	72.2	103.9	50.4	67.5	97.3	71.3	34.8	58.4	48.1 Q1–2/15
Unemployment rate. %	6.8	6.0	7.6	8.0	7.0	6.0	5.1	5.6	5.3	5.3 7/15
Population (10⁶) (end of year)	142.8	142.8	142.7	142.8	142.9	143.0	143.3	143.3	143.7	

Source: BOFIT(2014) updated 1 September 2015, BOFIT (2015), Central Bank of Russia, Rosstat, Bank of Poland – BOFIT Russia statistics

production and the export of massive quantities of hydrocarbons and gas sold
high real prices on the world markets. It undoubtedly enabled the country to resto
its financial credibility by radically improving its public accounts after a chaot
decade in the 1990s (strong social differentiation, concentration of private capit
weakness of the country's legal framework, and limited institutional transparency
It enabled the country to refund its federal debts, reinforce its reserves of foreig
currency, and put money into a Reserve fund and a Fund of national well-beir
of significant size (Tables 12.3 and 12.4). The result of all this was of significa
political advantage and was aimed at restoring a certain "Russian greatnes
nationally and internationally while, however, running the risk of slipping into
form of "Dutch disease",[2] a syndrome that distorts economic structures that threate
balanced, diverse, and sustainable economic development. This "profitable" choi
from a political viewpoint, seen initially as positive by the emerging middle class
and also by Russia's Western partners, particularly those in Europe, was mac
to the detriment of institutional reforms on the one hand, which were delayed
left incomplete, and on the other hand, despite their urgency,[3] at the cost of faile
diversification in the priorities of production and of development (educatio
health, justice, public, and private research spending). The development of th
middle classes and the growth of internal demand, a net inflow of foreign currenc
(mainly American dollars and euros) and pressure to increase the monetary ma
(M2), combined with expensive transaction costs particularly because investmel
in infrastructure has remained insufficient compared to the need,[4] have maintaine
a high level of inflation, and have contributed to reinforce the level of the roub
(which is now taking a battering because of the "Ukrainian crisis", resulting in
massive outflow of capital and a serious loss of confidence on the part of nation
and international investors[5]). Over the last 10 years, inflation has never been belo
6 per cent and the latter has begun to rise again in 2013–2014 and again in 2015 (se
Table 12.4; BOFIT 2014).[6] The loss in value of the national currency is hencefort
worrying and requires measures to support it, and a partial but significant use of th
reserves in foreign currency held by the Stabilization Fund (see infra). Exchang
controls are not, for the time being, under consideration (Putin 2014). The preser
situation is, therefore, serious and is made up of:

a low growth rate, inflation on the increase against the backdrop of a wea
Ruble, a drop in exchange reserves and capital flight. However, it must b
underlined that these difficulties occurred in the context of budgetary stabilit
and a positive trade balance. It is true that the active involvement of Russia i
the Ukrainian crisis has increased the specifically Russian risks and has affecte
the macro-economic dynamics of the country, but it would be exaggerated t
explain away the drop in growth, the increase in inflation, the weakness of th
Ruble and the increase in the outflow of capital by purely external factors.

(Gavrilenkov 2014

Table 12.3 Russian federal public finance (2006–2015)

	2006	2007	2008	2009	2010	2011	2012	2013	2014	2015 (as of)
Revenue (% of GDP)	23.3	23.4	22.5	19.5	17.9	20.3	20.7	19.5	20.3	19.2 (7/15)
Expenses (% of GDP)	15.9	18.0	18.4	24.8	21.9	19.8	20.9	20.0	20.8	21.9 (7/15)
National budget surplus (% of GDP)	7.4	5.4	4.1	–5.4	–4.0	0.5	–0.2	–0.5	–0.5	–2.8 (7/15)
Federal public debt (% of GDP)	9.0	7.2	6.5	8.3	9.0	9.5	10.5	11.3	14.4	13.9 (3/15)
Stabilisation fund ($bns)	89.1	156.8	225.1	152.1	113.9	112.0	150.7	176.0	159.1	147.5 (7/15)

Note: In 2008 the Stabilization fund was divided into the Reserve Fund on the one hand, and the National Wellbeing Fund on the other.

Sources: BOFIT (2014 and 2015); Budget: Rosstat 2005 and the Russian Ministry of Finances from 2006; Public federal debt, and Stabilization fund; Russian Ministry of Finances, Bank of Finland – BOFIT Russia Statistics (2014 & 2015)

Table 12.4 Russian monetary indicators (2006–2015)

	2006	2007	2008	2009	2010	2011	2012	2013	2014	2015
12-month inflation (consumption), %	9.0	11.9	13.3	8.8	8.8	6.1	6.6	6.5	11.4	15.6 (7/15)
M2 growth over 12 months, %	48.8	47.5	1.7	16.3	28.5	22.3	11.9	14.6	2.2	7.0 (7/15)
Average salary in € (monthly)	312	388	475	422	520	572	667	704	638	508 (7/15)
Average interest rate for deposits	4.0	5.2	7.0	8.2	4.9	5.7	6.1	5.1	12.3	9.7 (6/15)
Average interest rates for loans	10.5	10.8	15.5	13.7	9.1	9.3	9.4	9.4	18.3	15.5 (6/15)
Exchange reserves in $bns (including gold)	303.0	476.4	427.1	439.0	479.4	498.6	537.6	509.6	385.5	357.6 (7/15)

Sources: BOFIT (2014 & 2015): Russian Central Bank, Rosstat, Bank of Finland – BOFIT Russia Statistics.

The Russian economy seems to be on the point of recession but a proactive budgetary policy is possible and necessary

Structural domestic problems added to the consequences of the present profound geopolitical crisis, harkening back to the "Cold War", and reducing Russia's chances of re-emerging in the medium term as a major power working towards growth and lasting human development. Projections established by international organizations converge on this point.[7] Russia has several structural, institutional, as well as market handicaps (the weight of fossil resources in exports and budget, a legal framework often abstruse, often high transaction costs ...) and they are not compensated by its great assets, which include its human potential, and its skilled workers and engineers in some sectors, a technological savoir-faire inherited from the soviet period (under-estimated but nevertheless and more and more considerably at risk -in quantitative term notably for the sector of machinery for example) and substantial natural resources in all domains. The weight of gas and oil in the major accounts is too heavy, there is a paucity of public and private investment, and the innovation in companies within a flimsy network of small and medium-sized companies (SME/ SMIs) is weak and their life expectancy too short.[8] The foreign debt of companies (debts owed in foreign currency by Russian firms), the extremely worrying level of corruption (see on this subject Transparency International 2013; Stanovaïa 2013[9]), serious regional demographic imbalance, and a drop in the population of almost 6 million since 1992, despite a positive migratory balance,[10] are also part of these structural domestic problems, in addition to intellectual and industrial property law, which are still abstruse and unstable, as well as competition which functions far from the usual rules of a "normal" market economy.

Faced with all this, the government has some tools at its disposal using budgetary leverage and not monetary policy[11] weakened by inflation and the fall in the rouble. The central federal government debt contracted by Russia was hardly over 11 per cent of GDP in 2013 (Table 12.3).[12] This leaves some leeway for the state's economic policies. Furthermore, it must be underlined that the reserves in foreign currency are among the highest in the world relative to the size of the population (Tables 12.2 and 12.4; Brunat and Fontanel 2015) and even if these reserves are being used at the moment to defend the value of the rouble and tend to decline somewhat, their global volume is significant, especially as their decline is compensated partially by new deposits with the Central Bank. Evgeny Gavrilenkov reminds us that:

> the consolidated interventions of the Central Bank (that is to say, the net sales of foreign currency) are significantly higher than the drop in currency reserves. From June 2013 to the end of the first trimester of 2014, these reserves dropped by around $3.2 billion, while the accumulated volume of the Central Bank's interventions in the exchange market was twice as high.

> (Gavrilenkov 2014: 59)

The concerns are related more to the businesses than to the State: their situation radically different. Indeed, with the decline in the rouble, Russian companies, 1ich are heavily indebted, especially in euros, are finding things more and more fficult. The experts estimate that Russian companies have a global debt of $130 llion with large instalments due in the short-term. However, they cannot easily finance in the international financial markets. Help from the state seems inevitable avoid payment default by a number of them (Zlotowski 2014). "An increase in e value of the euro against the rouble thus has a positive impact on the value of its reign currency reserves, of which 40 per cent are in euros. On the other hand, an crease in the value of the euro and the Dollar relative to the rouble is very negative r companies indebted in these currencies, or those which import capital goods eded for industrial modernization" (Brunat and Fontanel 2015). It is thus very obable that without a high price for gas and oil (existing technologies in use for e moment in Siberia being incapable of increasing production[13]), the situation will lly get worse. For the moment, Russia's "country risk" is increasing in the world arket and with it, the interest rates offered by the financial markets.

The Russian economy thus seems close to recession if we consider its insufficient owth, the needs it has to manage structural deterioration, worsened by the present onomic climate, and Western sanctions linked to the events in the Ukraine.[14] eyond this, it has to address challenges such as: how to finance its modernization, e foreign currency debt of its companies, capital flight, insufficient global vestment, the weakening of internal demand, both of consumers and businesses, s dependency on the price of gas (although many contracts have been signed in reign currencies for long periods[15]) and of oil, and a net drop in – or complete ying up of – new flows of direct Western investment.[16] Nevertheless, the country s substantial margins of action and in particular, a margin of financial action, d its macro-economic indicators (other than inflation) are encouraging. President tin (Putin 2014) is wrong to blame the West and its sanctions linked to the Jkrainian crisis" as being the parameters, which have caused Russia's economic fficulties. To assert this, in a purely political stance, hides Russia's fundamental nderlying and long-term economic imbalances. Thus the crisis is a preponderant rt of the structural dimension. He is, on the other hand, right to underline that the untry can resist major short-term macro-economic difficulties. The 2014 budget ows a small deficit of –0.5 per cent of GDP (Table 12.3), and projections are not tastrophic for 2015 varying from around –3 per cent to –3.5 per cent (therefore ose of criteria "such as Maastricht" in an unfavourable global context).

However, these "virtuous" figures inspire the same reserve as that expressed ove concerning the low level of central public debt. There is little transparency day concerning the interweaving of a highly authoritative, not to say autocratic onopolistic State capitalism[17] (Aslund 2013), where private and public interests e mixed in a particularly opaque way (especially in the energy sector, mining, and e defence industries), producing a very conservative form of economic liberalism. he State as owner is a resource allocator. But it does not regulate the economy as rcefully as the state indebtedness of around 10 or 11 per cent of the GDP and a low eficit in the structural budget (apart from 2008 and 2009) and indeed a surplus for

the last 15 years (including no doubt the difficult year of 2014) would have allow
it to happen. To that, one should add central reserves of around $450 billion and t
$170 billion of the Stabilization Fund (which is a reserve fund corresponding to up
10 per cent of the GDP, and the National Well-being Fund supplied by the surplus
the Reserve Fund[18]). Since the end of the 1990s, with the aim of consolidating pov
and restoring the status of the country in the world, many political, geopolitic
economic, and institutional choices have diverted Russia from the road to full a
sustainable development. It has the means to correct these internal problems, but t
attempts to externalize its difficulties can only compromise this hope.

The European Union and Russian neighbourhood policies in the Ukraine: economic impacts of the crisis and consequences of a possible continental divide

After the enlargement of the European Union in 2004 and 2007, the EU proposed tl
Ukraine be part of its "Eastern Partnership" project, including a double agreement
association and free trade. The Association agreement was concluded with Armen
Azerbaijan, Georgia, Moldova, Ukraine, and Belarus, and was officially signed
Prague on 7 May, 2009. This is known as the Prague Declaration, which provic
for the setting up of committees in the framework of thematic platforms to supp
cooperation in specific areas. For the triennium (2014–2017), there are multilate
platforms covering the four main areas of cooperation between countries of t
European Union and their Eastern partners, namely:

- democracy, good governance, and stability;
- economic integration and convergence with the EU policies;
- energy security; and
- facilitated mobility and cultural, political, and economic contacts betwe
  individuals.

Then, the European Union individualizes its relations through bilate
negotiation.

On 21 March 2014, the acting Prime Minister of the Ukraine, Arseniy Yatsenyu
signed, in the framework of the Eastern Partnership, the first part of the Associati
agreement between Ukraine and the European Union.[19] The Association was th
signed with Moldova, the Ukraine, and Georgia, on 27 June. It was the refusal
sign this document by President Viktor Yanukovych in November 2013 in Vilni
that was one of the main reasons put forward by the "Euromaidan" protesters. Th
individualized partnership has been based on several pillars, including:

- respect for international law;
- a commitment to fundamental democratic values, human rights, and the ru
  of law; and
- the establishment of a market economy.

Under this partnership, which is part of the overall "Neighborhood Policy" of the European Union, Ukraine should receive about €400 million in aid per year (which is to be relativized in relation to the amounts received by certain member countries of the Union in the framework of the Common Agricultural and Cohesion Policies – according to the EU budget 2014–2020, Poland for example, receives more than €10 billion annually; Brunat and Fontanel 2014).

Instead, Russia is trying to rebuild a zone of economic and cultural influence and Ukraine was fully included in an ambitious Customs Union. The Customs Union is a Union between Russia, Belarus, and Kazakhstan, which came into force on 1 January 2010. The Union is duty free for goods moving between these three states, allowing free movement in this space. On 29 May 2014 the Eurasian Treaty was signed between Russia, Belarus, and Kazakhstan, and was joined by Armenia on October 9. It came into force on 1 January 2015, and Kyrgyzstan joined the Eurasian Economic Union on 21 May 2015. "The question therefore also relates to the strategy of the Kremlin. Is the creation of the Eurasian Economic Union related, is it a response, a geopolitical calculation that aims to counter the steps towards the East of the European Union?" (Turpin 2015). This is a first step towards creating a Commonwealth of Independent States, an economic alliance similar to the European Union among the States of the former Soviet Union. The Member States have set up a commission to promote closer economic ties, particularly in the functional planning of the Eurasian Union and its possible enlargement in 2015 (Tajikistan has applied; Uzbekistan and Turkmenistan are potential candidates). The Eastern Partnership and the Eurasian Economic Union projects are concomitant and President Viktor Yanukovych has tried to play "in both directions." Moscow has tipped the balance to the Russian side with a double strategy: substantial financial support and preferential prices for gas on the one hand and blockages of Ukrainian exports to Russia on the other.

The end of 2013 marked the end of negotiations with Brussels (the non-signature of the Eastern partnership which was to have taken place in Vilnius, as mentioned above) and irritated the people of Kiev who promptly occupied the Independence Square. In February 2014, Viktor Yanukovych fled. 80 died and hundreds were injured; the Ukrainian crisis deepened and broadened. Part of eastern Ukraine refused to recognize the transitional authorities (especially acting President Oleksandr Turchynov and Prime Minister Arseniy Yatsenyuk). In March 2014, during the Crimea crisis, the Crimean parliament, following a unilateral referendum – and after its refusal to recognize the new interim authorities in Kiev – proclaimed the secession of the Republic of Crimea from Ukraine and its attachment to Russia as a Republic[20] (after 21 February 2014, there was an interruption of constitutional order, when the Constitutional Court was dissolved and the principle of the referendum in the Crimea therefore became neither legal nor illegal; Brunat 2014a). Following Russia's annexation of Crimea, Ukraine officially claimed Crimea as the Autonomous Republic of Crimea, and further asserted control over Sevastopol City, two territorial entities, and parts of continental Ukraine.[21] The risk of a split in the country remains real. Avoiding this risk is certainly one of the main challenges that the new government and President Petro Poroshenko, elected on 7 June 2014, have to face. As a result of serious conflicts in the east of the country that led to the death of thousands of civilians and military, the Kiev authorities signed on 5 September 2014[22] and on 12 February 2015 the cease-fire agreements (known as the Minsk 2 Agreement or Protocol) with the self-proclaimed republics of Donetsk and Lugansk.

The spiral of sanctions seems unstoppable,[23] with damaging consequences for both sides. Russia, on the one hand, is faced with its obvious structural weaknesses, its seriously weakened economic growth, a drop in the value of its national currency, significant capital flight, and the undermining of its middle class's prosperity (see for example Vercueil 2014b). For the European Union on the other hand, the economy is also seriously affected.[24] Escalation of mutual sanctions between Western countries and Russia and the consequent tensions are worsening the situation. In case of a long economic war or an embargo against Russia (which necessarily implies a negative spiral of penalties in both directions), the Europeans would mainly pay the cost. This is especially so with tensions on the price of energy that could ultimately result as well as the measures directly affecting agricultural exports and European agro-food. It is likely that the interests of the United States, rich in oil, natural gas, and shale gas, are not the same as those of Germany, the countries of Central Europe, and the Baltic states, who are particularly dependent in this field.

Through this escalation of sanctions and counter-sanctions, which effect both sides, the central issue is to imagine achieving political goals through economic strategies. For Russia, there is a weakening of its currency and overall trust with the West, a maintenance of inflation at a relatively high level, and a significant drop in the purchasing power of fragile and emerging middle classes, because of the fall of domestic and foreign investment and the generation of massive capital flight. European sanctions that primarily affect certain Russian personalities, its financial capacity on international markets, and access to sensitive and sophisticated Western technologies, were extended in late June 2015 by the Ministers of Foreign Affairs for six months, until early 2016.[25] This dangerous process of outbidding seems inexorable and divides the Europeans themselves: Greece and Italy for example, and other nations, are in favour of a relaxation or even a halt to sanctions; the Baltic States and Poland wish to confirm them and even to deepen them. France and Germany support a more cautious position, trying without much result so far to maintain a dialogue and using the Minsk Agreement 2 as a reference that the two countries have broadly promoted.

We mentioned above how the rent seeking and extroverted Russian economy is dependent on the European markets for the import of goods essential for its industry and for the exportation of its fossil resources. In order to mitigate revenue declines at the national level, Russia is developing a strategy that is much more focused on Asia and especially China for the sale of oil and gas, and for access to emergency liquidities (in addition to the partial mobilization of its own financial reserves), and lastly for the development of prospective, complex, and expensive research of raw materials in the Arctic. Russia, whose counter-sanctions continue to limit agricultural imports from Europe, has started to suffer from the measures that it has taken. This generates higher prices and even some fears (largely artificial) of shortages that have stimulated some local production or new import markets (Belarus, and even Israel for some products),[26] which have so far failed to fully compensate for the shortcoming of agricultural products that until now had come from Europe. Thus, in order to resist in the long-term, Russia will probably have to abandon its model of extroverted and specialized growth. A greater diversification of its economy can therefore partially result from external pressures. This point will probably be positive in the long-term, and as a result of the sanctions, will be an unexpected stimulus. More broadly, it is the Russian model for growth that has to be changed, being now more focused on a strategy of "import substitution." However, the re-conquest of its internal market – some segments of the automobile industry or sensitive goods needed in the extractive industries – requires significant investment (over 90 per cent of industrial machinery is imported) as well as an available skilled workforce in some sectors of production, two essential parameters that are lacking in Russia today (Sapir 2015). Moreover, the risk is significant when the economic vitality and renewed growth is mainly based on domestic capacities and protectionism in the context of a considerable acceleration of innovation and complexification of trade structures internationally. These are to be excluded from the most advanced technologies resulting in a state of poor competitiveness when the situation improves and trade barriers – imposed or chosen – are again eliminated or lowered.

As for the European countries, some recent studies, including those conducted by the Austrian Institute for Economic Research, Wifo[27] (Lena 2015), show that the process of sanctions/counter-sanctions creates negative consequences more serious and complex than initially estimated in 2014 and again in the recent period. Notably, the European Commission seems to have a more optimistic short-term approach, pointing out that only a small number of goods and branches of activities is actually affected by the European export embargo and by the Russian restrictions on imports in response. The Lena study points out that in the context of a very negative scenario of deepening tensions and sanctions with Russia, "more than 2 million jobs and 100 billion euros of wealth produced are under threat … In the first quarter of 2015 only, French exports to Russia fell by 33.6 per cent, year on year" (Lena 2015). In this context, J. Vercueil (2014b) rightly reminds us that European countries are not all affected in the same way and proportionately. The endless case of the sale of two French warships ("Vladivostok", commissioned to be delivered to the Russian Navy in 2014 and "Sevastopol" in 2015) is probably not disconnected to this drastic decline, while French agricultural exports are particularly targeted and affected. But it is Germany, Russia's first European economic partner – especially for the export of individual or heavy vehicles and for the sales of machine tools – that would be the most affected, with a loss of almost 1 per cent of its GDP if the negative trend with Russia continues or worsens (which seems to be the case). Moreover, it is not only the flow of goods that affects each side but also a sudden fall on financial flows of Russian investments and tourists in Europe. The study by Wifo, reported by Lena (2015), points out that the tourism sector is also seriously affected by a sharp decline, observed especially in France.

The official dialogue sounds much like a new "Cold War", although without ideological content as was formerly the case. The latter point is not the least worrying. What is important is that beyond spectacular actions, such as the G7 no longer inviting Russia as its eighth member, or more recently the Russia's establishment of a list of 89 European politicians "banned from entry into Russia", it seems that both sides seek to maintain cultural and human relations as far as possible and seek to strengthen the diplomatic will to keep communications open. Many more discreet companies are maintaining their contacts and positions (some companies – not necessarily from the European Union – are even currently strengthening their position in Russia). The unofficial dialogue seems to be maintained so far. Even some countries (Cyprus, Finland, Hungary, Ireland and others) point out that very few Russian financial assets "have been effectively frozen" so far. If it is positive that the lines of communication of business and – hopefully – reason and common sense have not been stifled, it is very important and urgent to measure correctly the effectiveness and consequences of this spiralling process of economic and human sanctions before it becomes uncontrollable.

Some elements of conclusion

Russia has a need for profound structural reforms in order to set in motion a "normal" market economy, with much more solidarity and less corruption, less concentrated properties in the hands of a few private individuals, and also, individuals within the federal and local State, factors which distort the mechanisms of competition. Secondly, short-term dysfunctions need to be attenuated and regulated by strong public action whose aim should be to support receding internal demand and to, no doubt, recapitalize the banks. With this in mind, the exchange reserves and the Stabilization fund used to defend the rouble at the end of 2014 could, according to the Russian Finance Minister, Anton Siluanov, be made available massively through 2015 and further to finance vast, much more Keynesian reflationary measures.[28]

Beyond the necessary support for the banking system, budgetary policy should indeed finance an industrial policy aimed to protect Russia's inherited know-how; support agricultural production, which is in difficulty (by a policy of revenue support) and no doubt at the cost of a negotiation with the WTO); research in universities (and not only university rectors); the creation and development of SME/SMIs; innovation and industrial property rights. Regional development at the extreme ends of the territory to support the "dissemination of the business culture" (*l'entreprisation des territoires*) (Brunat 2014b) are also essential to facilitate social composition or re-composition. Local government and the advantages of proximity are important to facilitate down-up development (as long as local state institutions are respected and operate in the interest of all and not of an oligarchy and a few potentates). This presupposes strong budgetary decisions and proactive policies in order to support the necessary diversification of the economy with the multiplication of development areas either organized by and from the centre or in facilitating and accompanying the emergence of local initiatives.

This indispensable pragmatism, as it is often the case in political economy, crystallizes under the pressure of circumstances. Russia has always oscillated between "relinquishment and revolt" (Berdiaev 1946); between the justice of men and the justice of the Czar; the reflection of a country, as it sees itself, regaining force since the breaking-up of the Soviet Union. As Andreï Gratchev, Mickhaïl Gorbachev's ex-adviser often reminds us, Russia suffers less from humiliation than from profound frustration. To recover the international status the country merits and has potentials to achieve, Russia must apply a much more interventionist economic policy, with a more determined and peaceful opening towards the world in general, and to Europe in particular (a possible strong drop of oil prices on the world market, beyond the World Bank (2014) low-case scenario, could seriously hamper any improvment or more pro-active policy despite the central financial reserves). The stage would then be set for an improvement in the image of Russia and confidence would return, with – in the place of the old reflexes – the promotion of an attractive "soft power" resolutely turned towards the solid foundations of human development. These could favourably replace force, and postures that are too imperial; postures partly generated by the West itself and indeed by the historical complexity and roots of the Ukrainian case.

The respect of the Minsk 2 peace protocol and the subsequent termination of the process of economic sanctions (poorly efficient and even clumsy) to reach political purposes would certainly revive a desirable and official diplomatic dialogue between the European Union (speaking with a single voice) and Russia. This requires a real political willingness from both parts and probably the fact that Ukraine must be neutral (as Finland, Austria, Sweden, and some others) with the possibility to benefit from the EU eastern partnership, as well as from the deep cultural and economic relations with the Russian Federation.

Acknowledgements

The article is an expanded and modified version of E. Brunat, 'Quelques observations sur la situation économique de la Fédération de Russie', in E. Brunat, G.-H. Soutou and F. Turpin (eds) *Union européenne–Russie : une relation particulière?* (2015, University Savoie Mont Blanc, LLSETI). Special thanks to Frédéric Turpin (USMB) for comments and to James Shepherd (USMB) for editing the English. Any remaining errors of fact or interpretation are the author.

Notes

1 The IMF (2014) suggests the probably forecasts for growth for Russia: 2014 +0.25 per cent; 2015 0.5 per cent; 2016 +1.5 per cent; 2017 +1.8 per cent; 2018 +2.0 per cent; 2019 +2 per cent which will be insufficient to finance the re-emergence of the country. The World Bank has recently revised its growth forecasts for the Russian GDP according to three possible scenarios depending on the possible cost of oil (World Bank 2014).

2 The "Dutch disease" analysis applies to situations in which the mono-exportation of a rent economy, often based on natural resources, engenders disruption in the internal economy, including inflationist pressures and a tendency to de-industrialization.

3 See in particular Vercueil (2014a), Dezhina (2014), Brunat, Lobasenko and Zigone (2015).

4 The percentage, in 2009, of global investment was less than 20 per cent of GDP, and around 20 per cent in 2012 and subsequently. This level is scarcely compatible with a

policy of high-level public and private research and a genuinely proactive modernizat
of the country. The level of global investment, despite the 2010 impetus (+6.3 per ce
that of 2011 (+10.8 per cent) and 2012 (+6.8 per cent) after the severe drop in 2(
(–13.5 per cent), has dropped yet again in 2013 and especially in 2014 and early 2(
(Table 12.2). The global level (as a percentage of the GDP) is still below that of 1!
and is significantly less than that observed in emerging South-East Asian countrie:
the most dynamic of the "transitional" economies (where the levels observed are rar
less than 30 per cent; Brunat 2013).

5   The Russian Central Bank acknowledged on 10 November 2014 that capital outfl
could reach around US$130 billion in 2014 (the lead interest rates were increased to
per cent in mid-December to try to halt the process). At the same time, the rouble 1
lost around 40 per cent of its value relative to the dollar during the second semeste1
2014. At his annual press conference on 18 December 2014 President Vladimir Pt
admitted – while rejecting any idea of exchange controls – that Western sanctions w
the cause of the drop in the value of the rouble to the tune of 25 to 30 per cent agai
the euro and the dollar (Putin 2014).

6   The IMF forecast for consumer prices is a little more optimistic with an expected rat«
2014 of 7.5 per cent and a slide expected in 2015 to 7.3 per cent, 6.0 per cent in 20
and 4.7 per cent in 2018 and 2019 (IMF 2014).

7   See in particular UNCTAD (2014), IMF (2014) and World Bank (2014, 2015).

8   Ex-President Dimitri Medvedev in his speech to the nation (12 November 2009) 1
the accent on the importance of innovation in general, and on the extreme weakness
the contribution companies and especially SME/SMIs make in this field. He underlir
what he saw as still the main cause of their poor development: the weight of an unwie:
bureaucracy, reminding his public that the contribution of Russian SME/SMIs to
national GDP was less than 17 per cent, less than 1 per cent in the knowledge-ba:
economy, and that SME/SMIs were practically non-existent in the field of science ε
information technology. The situation has hardly improved since, despite reforms
universities and the organization of research, and despite the development of so:
scientific parks and special economic zones (Medvedev 2009; Brunat 2012).

9   Tatiana Stanovaïa (2013) writes: "The loyalty of the elite in exchange for the possibil
of appropriating a rent linked to its status has become the key to the "pact" linking
Kremlin and the bureaucracy."

10 The rates of fertility have been among the lowest in Europe over the last few ye
(the rate picks up a bit in 2014 with 1.7 children per woman), and life expectancy
far from those observed in the most advanced countries. Masculine life expectancy
birth dropped sharply, ending up at the end of the 1990s at under 60 years of age (t
complex evolution is linked to the drop in public spending on health subsequent to 1
collapse of the Soviet Union in December 1991–January 1992). The figure has improv
slightly in recent years. A more family-friendly policy (an untaxed "maternity capit.
created in 2007 enables each family to receive around €9000 for a second child, a
subsequent children from 2013, and €9500 in 2014. This capital may not be used,
example, to buy consumer goods and may be used only several months after each bir
seems to have stopped the drop in births (see the work of the demographic specia:
A. Vychnevski 2011). 2013 was the first year in which Russia experienced a positi
natural increase since 1992 (Adomanis 2012) with a birth rate of 13.2 per cent an«
mortality rate of 13.1 per cent (in 2012 the rates are equal at 13.3 per cent and in 20
the improvement seems to have been maintained with a birth rate of 13.3 per cent an«
mortality rate of 13.1 per cent).

11 It is essential to try to stabilize the rouble, to restore as quickly as possible the confider
(and first the domestic confidence) in the national currency (crucial for the investmen1
Thus the monetary policy sounds less obvious than the budgetary policy where roo1
for manoeuvring exist.

12 We can also note that the IMF, which also relies on the figures of the Russian Finance Ministry, publishes statistics on the gross debt of the central government, which lead it to suggest slightly higher figures for the per cent of the GDP: 12.65 per cent in 2012 and 13.91 per cent in 2013. In any case, the levels are low.

13 Difficult new prospection is taking place in Arctic regions with possible help from China (Huotari 2014).

14 These sanctions are aimed at politicians and industrialists, commercial exchanges, mostly of a technological nature, the freezing of certain assets and blocked prospects for refinancing on the financial markets through either explicit means, or indirectly via an increase in interest rates (see in particular for the European sanctions Commission of the European Union 2014). See also the *Official Journal of the European Union*, Council decisions 17 March 2014 (2014/145/CFSP) and 30 July 2014 (2014/508/CFSP).

15 Some contracts are being re-negotiated at the present time or not renewed upon expiration. For example, Lithuania was 100 per cent reliant on imported Russian gas (3.2 billion m^3 imported in 2011; Gazprom 2011; British Petroleum 2011), but in October 2014 it began to import gas from Norway, which can deliver up to 4 billion m^3 per year. The contract with Russia comes to an end in 2015 and Lithuania has already announced that Norwegian gas is a priority.

16 FDIs have been marked by very late growth in Russia in comparison with central and eastern European countries (significantly less than US \$4 billion average yearly flow from 1992 to 1998 and less than US \$1.5 billion from 1992 to 1994) but it strengthened as from 2003 (more than US \$70 billion in 2008 according to UNCTAD 2014). From then on, there is a sharp fall after the financial crisis, then new growth in 2009, followed by the current rapid drop. And yet, these investments are necessary, in particular for cutting-edge technologies.

17 Putin's "vertical power structure" concept, expressed in the first decade of the twentieth century, heavily criticized as a decline of democracy, was no doubt justified in order to reconstruct and to make the State credible and to stop the institutional dislocation which had begun to attack the foundations of the – certainly embryonic – legally founded state from going even further. The risk was that Russian territory might fragment with its Eastern region beyond the Ural Mountains, heavily under-populated but rich in precious raw materials spread over 11 time-zones (after a period during the Medvedev presidency – until 2014 – when there were 9 zones), reaching for independence from the historic Russia whose centre is to the West.

18 It is one of the major sovereign funds in the world sustained by oil revenues and in theory, destined primarily to offset the drop in the value of energy on the one hand and to finance heavy investments on the other hand. The fund can be mobilized as financial leverage in exceptional circumstances for the strategic public and private sectors and as a source of financing for projects which are of interest at the federal level and concern the whole country (see the study of C. Marangé 2015).

19 The Ukrainian parliament – the Verkhovna Rada – ratified this agreement between the Ukraine and the EU on 16 September 2014, which shows how far the Kiev government had moved politically from Russia.

20 On 16 March, the self-determination referendum was held in Crimea; on 19 March the Ukraine left the CIS; on 21 March, Putin "created" two new separate territorial entities: the Republic of Crimea and the city-port of Sevastopol.

21 Almost all countries in the world still consider Crimea as a territory belonging "*de jure*" to Ukraine.

22 On the night of 19–20 September 2014, representatives of the Ukrainian government and the pro-Russian rebels in eastern areas also signed a memorandum for peace that provided a ceasefire, a 15 km withdrawal of heavy artillery from "front lines", creating a 30 km security zone, a no-fly security zone for combat aircraft and drones as well as the departure of foreign mercenaries from both areas.

23 See note 14 above.

24 See the study by the Austrian Institute of Economic Research Wifo, conducted for Lena (2015), the Alliance of seven European newspapers (*Die Welt*, *El Pais*, *La Repubblica*, *Le Soir*, *Tages-Anzeiger*, *La Tribune de Genève* and *Le Figaro*).

25 These sanctions, initiated in early summer 2014, mainly after the annexation of the Crimea, have already been confirmed in March 2015 by the Heads of States and European governments. These will continue until the Minsk 2 peace protocol is fully respected by the belligerents and as long as Russia continues to support separatist actions in east Ukraine.

26 Some new agricultural imports also from Bosnia, Latvia (an EU country), Montenegro, and Uzbekistan are contributing to soften, so far, the real impacts of sanctions and counter-sanctions.

27 Österreichisches Institut für Wirtschaftsforschung (www.wifo.ac.at).

28 This important point is not yet significant in mid-2015, but should be followed very closely by analysts of the Russian economy.

References

Adomanis, M. 2012. "Russia's Population is Growing for the First Time Since The Early 1990's." *Forbes* 29 (November). Available at www.forbes.com/sites/markadomanis/2012/11/29/russias-population-is-growing-for-the-first-time-since-the-early-1990s/.

Aslund, A. 2013. "Putin's Conservative State Capitalism." *Moscow Times*, pp. 22–32.

Berdiaev, N. 1946. *L'idée Russe: Problèmes essentiels de la pensée Russe au XIXe et début du XXe siècle*, translated by H. Arjakovsky. Paris: Editions Mame.

BOFIT. 2014. *Forecast for Russia 2014–2016*. September. Helsinki: BOFIT.

BOFIT. 2015. *Russia Statistics*. September. Helsinki: BOFIT.

British Petroleum. 2011. *Energy Statistical Review*. London: British Petroleum.

Brunat, E. 2012. "The Russian Economy." In *Two Asias: The Emerging Postcrisis Divide*, edited by S. Rosefielde, M. Kuboniwa, and S. Mizobata, pp. 209–248. Singapore: World Scientific Publishing.

Brunat, E. 2013. "Croissance recouvrée et problèmes structurels: les fragilités d'une nouvelle émergence économique et sociale en Russie." In *Basculement économique et géopolitique du Monde, Poids et diversité des pays émergents*, edited by M. Matmati, pp. 99–125 Paris: L'Harmattan.

Brunat, E. 2014a. "Poutine a profité de nos erreurs, Eco des Pays de Savoie." *Journal o, Economic Issues* (11/17 April). No. 15/1291.

Brunat, E. 2014b. "'Entreprisation diffuse' et territoires en Russie: quelques considération théoriques." In L. Bensahel-Perrin, J. Fontanel, B. Pecqueur, A. Silem (eds) *L'économie territoriale en questions: La Librairie des Humanités*, pp. 203–221. Paris: L'Harmattan.

Brunat, E. and J. Fontanel. 2014. "Vingt-cinq ans de transformations économiques." In *L Pologne au cœur de l'Europe*, pp. 74–84. Questions Internationales no. 69. Paris: L Documentation Française.

Brunat, E. and J. Fontanel 2015. "L'économie de la Russie, les grands défis à relever" *Annuaire Français de Relations Internationales*, Vol. XVI. Paris: Université Panthéon Assas, Centre Thucydide, AFRI, DILA, La Documentation Française, pp. 191–204.

Brunat, E., V. Lobasenko and M. Zigone. 2015. "L'Innovation en Russie" in *Unio européenne–Russie: une relation particulière*, edited by E. Brunat, G.H. Soutou and I Turpin, Chambéry: LLSETI, Université Savoie Mont Blanc, pp. 129–155.

Commission of the European Union. 2014. *EU Restrictive Measures in View of the Situatio in Eastern Ukraine and the Illegal Annexation of Crimea*. Press EN, 29 July. Brussel Council of the European Union.

Dezhina, I. 2014. "L'innovation en Russie, entretien au BE Russie." 11 June. Available at www.bulletins-electroniques.com/actualites/76107.htm.

Gavrilenkov, E. 2014. "L'économie russe au premier trimestre 2014." *Bulletin analytique de l'Observatoire franco-russe* 1 (April), pp. 1–19.

Gazprom. 2011. *Annual report*. Moscow: Gazprom.

Huotari, J. 2014. "Arctic Roulette – Will Economic Sanctions Open the Door for Sino-Russian Offshore Operations in the High North." Expert article 1644. *Baltic Rim Economies Review* 5. Available at http://fr.rbth.com/economie/2014/10/10/la_russie_ne_sisole_pas_du_monde_exterieur_31133.html.

IMF. 2014. World Economic Outlook, (October). Available at www.imf.org/external/pubs/ft/weo/2014/02/weodata/weoselgr.aspx

Lena. 2015. "L'impact de la crise russe sur l'économie européenne plus fort qu'attendu, juin." Available at www.msn.com/fr-fr/finance/actualite/limpact-de-la-crise-russe-sur-l%C3%A9conomie-europ%C3%A9enne-plus-fort-quattendu/ar-AAbPmRA?ocid=UP97DHP.

Marangé, C. 2015. "Les sanctions contre la Russie ont-elles un effet dissuasif?" *IRSEM* 37: 44.

Medvedev, D. 2009. "State of Nation Speech." November. Available at http://edition.cnn.com/2009/WORLD/europe/11/12/russia.medvedev.speech/.

Putin, V. 2014. "Annual Press Conference." 18 December, Moscow. Available at http://fr.sputniknews.com/french.ruvr.ru/news/2014_12_18/Grande-conference-de-presse-de-Vladimir-Poutine-le-18-decembre-7483.

Sapir, J. 2015. "Stratégie industrielle russe." RussEurope blog. Available at http://russeurope.hypotheses.org/3879 (accessed 22 June 2015).

Stanovaïa, T. 2013. "Corruption: nouvelle politique, populisme et règlements de comptes, Destins russes." *Revue Internationale Stratégique* 92: 119–127.

Transparency International. 2013. "Corruption Perceptions Index 2013." Available at www.transparency.org/cpi2013/results.

Turpin, F. 2015. Introduction to *Union européenne:–Russie: une relation particulière*, edited by E. Brunat, G.H. Soutou and F. Turpin, Chambéry: LLSETI, Université Savoie Mont Blanc, pp 7–11.

United Nations Conference on Trade and Development (UNCTAD). 2014.World Investment Report 2014, http://unctad.org/en/pages/PublicationWebflyer.aspx?publicationid=937

Vercueil, J. 2014a. "L'économie russe en 2013: les limites du modèle de croissance sont atteintes." In *Russie 2014: regards de l'Observatoire franco-russe*, edited by A. Dubien, pp. 19–30. Paris: Le Cherche Midi.

Vercueil, J. 2014b. "L'économie russe et les sanctions: Une évaluation des conséquences du conflit ukrainien." *Note de l'Observatoire franco-russe* 9 (November), pp. 1–24.

Voskoboynikov, I. and L. Solanko 2014. *When High Growth is Not Enough: Rethinking Russia Pre-Crisis Economic Performance*. Policy brief 6. Helsinki: BOFIT.

Vychnevski, A. 2011. "La Russie pourra-t-elle relever le défi démographique." In *Sous la direction de, La Résurgence de la Russie?*, edited by E. Brunat, pp. 147–156. Société de Stratégie, no. 45. Paris: Agir.

World Bank. 2014. "World Bank Revises Its Growth Projections for Russia for 2015 and 2016." 9 December. Available at www.worldbank.org/en/news/press-release/2014/12/08/world-bank-revises-its-growth-projections-for-russia-for-2015-and-2016.

World Bank. 2015. "Macro-economic Indicators." Available at http://donnees.banquemondiale.org/indicateur/NY.GDP.MKTP.KD.ZG.

Zlotowski, Y. 2014. "Sanctions: la Russie peut tenir … un temps." *AlterEco+* (21 November). Available at www.alterecoplus.fr/sanctions-la-russie-peut-tenir-un-temps.

Annex 1

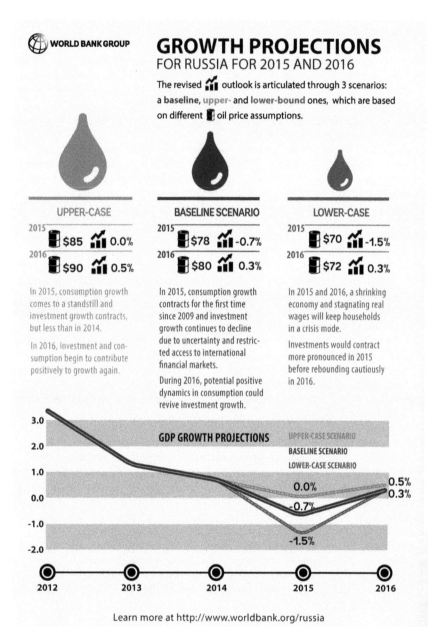

Figure 12A.1 World Bank revises its growth projections for russia for 2015 and 2016 9 December 2014. Available at www.worldbank.org/en/news/press-release. 2014/12/08/world-bank-revises-its-growth-projections-for-russia-for-2015-and-2016.

13 Russia, the European Union, and the Ukrainian Crisis

A European or a Eurasian affair?

Jacob Kipp

Introduction

A decade separated the first Maidan Revolution of 2004 and the Euromaidan Revolution of 2014. At first glance, the crisis that precipitated the Euromaidan Revolution of February 2014 had its roots in the failure of the first Maidan, which promised honest elections, civic reform, an end of corruption, and a check on the power of the oligarchs. Instead, it ended with the election of the very man it was supposed to prevent from becoming president, Victor Yanukovych, in 2010. Rumours of increased corruption, favouritism, the abuse of judicial powers and arbitrary executive actions became increasingly common by 2013.

The immediate crisis, however, had its roots in the negotiations regarding the Association Agreement between the European Union and the Ukraine, exacerbated by American interference in Ukrainian internal politics. The EU had sought a network of relations with non-member, neighbouring states to establish close economic and political cooperation. Putin's Russia, which considered Ukraine part of Russia's "near abroad" and had its own vision of a future Eurasian trading area, saw the Association Agreement between the European Union and Ukraine as adversely affecting vital Russian national interests. The European Union pressed for the signing of the agreement but proved unprepared when this competition became entangled in a smouldering ethnic conflict between eastern and western Ukraine. The EU recognized that within Ukraine there was strong popular support for association with the European Union among the populations of western and central Ukraine. These groups were also more supportive of ending Ukraine's status as neutral and joining NATO. Eastern Ukraine, which included the mining and heavy industry of Ukraine, favoured sustaining close cultural and economic relations with Russia and strongly opposed membership in NATO. That NATO and the EU are not identical organizations only complicated the situation, especially since economic cooperation was the EU priority while defensive cooperation was paramount for the US.

EU pressure on the government of Victor Yanukovych at the time of the Vilnius summit in 2013 did not produce Yanukovych's signature. This fact set off demonstrations in Kyiv and other cities, which became sustained protests known as Euromaidan. In December, demonstrators seized government buildings in Kyiv;

Yanukovych responded with repression at home and negotiated economic aid and assistance from both China and Russia in the hope of sustaining his government without an escalation in violence. After a brief pause in the tensions in Kyiv in conjunction with the Christmas and New Year's holidays, the demonstrations turned into riots and then armed confrontations between special police and radicalized activists. An EU attempt to broker a solution collapsed immediately because political power had shifted from the opposition political parties and to the streets as it does in a revolutionary situation. Yanukovych's flight signalled the triumph of the Euromaidan Revolution but created sufficient chaos for the Russian government to act unilaterally and to covertly occupy Crimea, engineer a plebiscite supporting its annexation to Russia, and then set in motion a popular uprising against Euromaidan in the eastern Ukrainian provinces of Luhansk and Donetsk. Kyiv responded with an Anti-Terrorism Operation to pacify the area. Russia, in its turn, responded by increasing its military assistance to a level where denial of Russian involvement was implausible, even though Moscow officially persisted in denying involvement. The European Union did get its Association Agreement signed by Kyiv's revolutionary government. But its significance was undermined by Moscow's efforts to call into question the *de facto* sovereignty of the government in Kyiv. The European Union and the United States joined in imposing economic sanctions against Russia, but did not provide meaningful military assistance to Kyiv. Germany and France created the Normandy Group (Germany, France, Ukraine and Russia) to negotiate a series of cease-fire agreements, known as Minsk I and Minsk II, reflecting attempts to stabilize the military situation in the east with the assistance of observers from OSCE and to create conditions for a political settlement. So far, what seems to have been achieved is another frozen conflict. Fighting has been reduced. Ukraine exists in limbo between a European Union that fuelled the initial crisis, but failed to aid Ukraine, and a Russia that successfully seized Ukrainian territory, proved willing to support separatists resisting the Euromaidan government, and used diplomacy to dominate the Normandy political process to affirm the existence of another frozen conflict. As a result of the Ukrainian crisis, the post-Cold War order is dead. The European Union has lost credibility as a security player in Europe and the European confrontation is once again between NATO and Russia as the successor to the Soviet Union.

The ongoing Ukraine crisis constitutes a major external threat to the European Union, even as the EU's inability to develop and sustain a consistent response to the crisis exposes the EU's current weakness. Europe's economic woes certainly contribute to its vacillation over how to respond to Russia's annexation of the Crimea and its reluctance to put a strong regime of economic sanction into place. But more significant is NATO's unwillingness to counter Russian military support of the Ukrainian separatists. Most significant, however, is the Eurocentric view that fails to recognize that the Ukrainian crisis should be understood as marking the divergence between a world in which economic and military power is centred in the West and one in which such power resides Eurasia. Russia's goals and its actions are badly misunderstood if its Eurasian ambitions are not taken into account.

The road to the Euromaidan Revolution

Considering the broad challenges Russia faced in the post-Soviet period, especially the relations between Russia and Baltic Republics, Russian–Ukrainian relations, while troubled, were seen by both Kyiv and Moscow as critical bilateral relations. Both capitals were set upon integrating into a dynamic European economy, but both faced daunting challenges involving their domestic, economic, social, and political transformation. Russia looked upon the Commonwealth of Independent States as a vehicle to sustain and gradually reaffirm ties among the successor states to the Soviet Union with Russia assuming the role of dominant power. Bilateral disputes between Russia and Ukraine included the disposition of nuclear weapons deployed within Ukraine, the fate of the Soviet Black Sea Fleet and its infrastructure, and the chronic inability for the new Ukrainian state to pay for Russian natural gas, which was vital to industry, the production of electric power, and domestic heating. The Russian government was also quick to figure out that Russia's integration with Europe's economy would be through the export of natural gas, and recognized that natural gas was also a political lever that could be played as a form of soft power to induce Ukraine and other successor states to adjust their policies in keeping with Russian interests. Ukraine, on the other hand, looked on the Commonwealth as a vehicle by which it could shape its own course and was sceptical about joining any system where Russian hegemony would be the outcome. Ukraine began cultivating ties with the successor states seeking their own connections with the West, especially in the form of energy delivery. Ukraine, Georgia, Azerbaijan, and Moldova in 1997 formed the Organization for Democracy and Economic Development (GUAM) with an expressed interest in creating a Eurasian, Trans-Caucasus transportation corridor, which would bypass Russia.

Ukrainian domestic politics in the period from 1991 to 2013 were marked by divisions that emerged during the parliamentary and presidential elections of 1994 and continued to dominate elections down to 2014, when the Euromaidan revolution set in motion a political and international crisis, leading to Russian annexation of Crimea and a civil war in southeastern Ukraine.[1] The core features of the divided electoral map during those twenty years was a solid west, formed by territories which had been part of the Habsburg Empire and then Interwar Poland and Romania. Here Ukrainian nationalism took on a particularly anti-Russian character, and western Ukraine was anxious to integrate itself into central Europe. Central Ukraine reflected the values of Kyiv and was concerned with holding the country together and balancing the pull of east and west. Eastern and southern Ukraine had large Russophone and Russophile populations where ethnicity and economics have combined to support closer ties with Russia. Under Putin, Russia's economic recovery brought renewed ties to Russia and re-enforced ethnic and economic ties. Down to 2013, western Ukraine could be counted on to favour candidates sceptical of closer ties with Russia, the centre acting as a region dominated by pragmatism and shifting loyalties and the east and south Ukraine supporting parties and candidates favouring closer ties to Russia.

Zbigniew Brzezinski[2] argued that both Ukraine and Russia were playing by the rules of the game laid down at the end of the Cold War, when both states were striving to be part of the emergent Western-dominated, Euro-Atlantic-centric world order. Instability in Ukraine was nothing new, nor were Ukrainian–Russian tensions. They had confrontations in the past over naval bases in Crimea, over gas prices and the status of the Russian minority in Ukraine's east and south. Ukraine had a revolution at the end of February 2014, which overthrew a pro-Moscow government, but this also was nothing new. Just a decade earlier we had all witnessed Ukraine's first colour revolution (orange) between November 2004 and January 2005, which brought Viktor Yushchenko to power, when crowds protested that the presidential elections had been rigged to favour Viktor Yanukovich, who was seen as pro-Russian. Yushchenko came to power by promising to change Ukraine's orientation from east to west and to rid Ukraine of both Russian influence and governmental corruption.

But not much really changed; state corruption had gotten worse, and Russian influence in Kyiv remained a dominant political fact of life (witness Yanukovich's election as President in 2010). The regional, ethnic, and socio-economic divisions that had shaped post-Cold War Ukraine still seemed to apply (see Lieven 1999). The attraction to Putin's Russia was another matter, precisely because the Russian national economy had recovered after 1999. By 2013, per capita GDP in Russia was about $14,500 versus $4,000 in the Ukraine (World Bank undated). Whereas western Ukraine was attracted to central Europe, tsarist and Soviet industrialization had made the east, and like "rust belts" elsewhere, it could find no easy way to become part of a post-industrial, global order.

This time, however, the game involved another player, the European Union, which in 2012 had offered Ukraine an Associate Agreement. That Agreement was intended to bring about structural reforms of the Ukrainian economy to make it more compatible with the European Union and enhance economic stability. From a Russian perspective this associate agreement was a means of foreclosing Ukrainian membership in Putin's own project for a Eurasian Economic Union. It also contained provisions calling for closer cooperation with EU members in the areas of defence and security policy (EEAS undated). Yanukovich did not say no to a deal with the EU at some future point and hoped that he could manoeuvre Ukraine into being an associate of the EU and still a partner with Moscow. Some speculated that Yanukovich's backpedalling was the result of pressure from President Vladimir Putin to join Russia's Eurasian Economic Union, which Russia had presented as a first step towards a regional reorientation to an emerging Asian-centric economic order. Putin responded by saying that it was the EU that was engaged in "blackmailing and pressur[ing]" Kyiv in the form of mass demonstrations (RT 2013).

Putin now viewed Ukraine as a battleground between two competing and increasingly incompatible economic orders. One was seeking to exclude Russia by capturing Ukraine, and the other, a Eurasian order, based on Russia's re orientation towards an Asian-Pacific world, would dominate the 21st century Russia's membership depended on the maintenance and strengthening of it strategic partnership with the People's Republic of China. Putin wanted Ukraine to be inside that new order. Western critics tended to see Putin's Eurasian Economic Union as a way to re-create the Soviet Union, but it was something quite different from that. If Peter the Great had clawed open a window on a dynamic Europe, Putin wanted to take a relatively weak Russia in the Far East and make it a key player in Asian economic order. Putin was not about to give up on his Eurasian project.[3] And Ukraine was supposed to be part of it.

Indeed, Yanukovych's first foreign visit after the initial Maidan demonstrations was not to Moscow but to Beijing in early December 2013. Yanukovych was well received in the PRC with an assurance of Chinese economic assistance, signalling Beijing's Eurasian focus on the Ukrainian crisis. China offered Ukraine loans and credits worth an estimated $8 billion and then added a nuclear guarantee in case of an attack by a nuclear-armed state (LB.Ua 2013; Evropaiskaia pravda 2013; Conroy 2014). Only after the visit to Beijing did Yanukovich go to Moscow and get loans and credits worth $15 billion and a 30 per cent reduction in gas prices from Putin's government (Komsomol'skaia pravda 2013). Putin assumed that he had raised the EU out of the game and that the crisis in Kyiv would simply disappear over time.

The initial crisis facing Yanukovich looked very much like that of 2004–2005 aiming at redirecting the Ukrainian economy and society to the West. The European Union had for the preceding quarter century looked like a real engine of the global economy and all the states which had emerged from the Soviet bloc saw access to the European Union as the surest step towards ensuring a civil society, a market economy, and a stable currency. In the immediate aftermath of the Cold War, when security questions were econdary matters, except for the Balkans, the European Union held out the brightest future for the states of central and eastern Europe. Now by 2013 the economic lustre of the European Union had faded somewhat in the aftermath of the Great Recession of 2008 and the serious debt problems of a number of EU member states. But this was not the case for Ukraine's struggling middle class, which saw access to the West as the only hope against a corrupt state, oligarchic economy, and persistent Russian leverage. The question was did Euromaidan ask for concessions from the sitting government or for its removal by violent means? If the latter, how would Russia react?

By late February 2014, after three months of increasingly violent demonstrations in Maidan Square, the revolutionary situation reached its culmination. It was evident that those in power had lost their credibility in Kyiv but retained the capacity to use violence to hold on to power. And those out of power were only just deciding that they could use violence to bring about a transfer of power. In this context the European Union sent three foreign ministers to negotiate an agreement between the Yanukovich government and its political opposition. The French, German and Polish Foreign Ministers announced their visit on 19 February, and by 21 February they had negotiated a deal between the Yanukovich Government and the opposition politicians, which was signed on that day. But by this stage the opposition politicians from the *Rada* no longer had control of the demonstrators and, before the ink was dry on the agreement for a gradual transfer of power, the Yanukovich government had collapsed an President Yanukovich had fled Kyiv.

The critical event was the rising tide of violence between government securit forces and demonstrators, who were armed. Those events remain murky wit the emergence of two narratives: one depicting Maidan as a people's revolutio against tyranny and corruption, and another claiming that proto-fascist elemen manipulated violence to their own ends to sabotage the EU-brokered agreemer and set in motion a revolution, which was internally and internationally ant Russian. One key factor in the emergence of these opposing narratives was th leak of a private phone conversation between the Estonian Foreign Ministe Urmas Paet, and Baroness Katherine Ashton, the EU High Representative fc Foreign Affairs, and Security Policy Republic of Estonia (Ministry of Foreig Affairs 2014).[4] Events in Odessa on 2 May, especially the burning of the Hous of Trade Unions and the massacre of Pro-Federalist demonstrators inside, raise similar issues (Johnson's Russia List 2014). By that point, however, both prc Maidan and pro-Russian media had each created their own exclusive narratives c good and evil, of Fascists vs. Putinism.

Putin's Russia and the European Union: from partner to enemy

The Euromaidan Revolution brought a fundamental shift in Russian polic towards the Ukraine and the European Union. Down to the Great Recession o 2008 the Russian Federation had emphasized the development of its relations wit the European Union as a positive measure of Russia's status as a European powe Russia's relations with the EU had developed from the signing of the Partnershi and Cooperation Agreement in 1994 to the shaping of the Four Common Space at the EU–Russia St. Petersburg summit in 2003 to address a wide range of share interests on the basis of common values,[5] and the establishment of biannua summits and numerous mechanisms for cooperation such as the Permanen Partnership Councils (PPCs). These PPCs have met as often as deemed necessar at the ministerial level, and have been the main mechanism for the functioning o the relationship across numerous areas of cooperation, including foreign policy justice and home affairs, energy, transport, agriculture, and culture. In 2005, th EU and Russia agreed on road maps, which laid out specific objectives and sough to put the Common Spaces into effect.[6] But the European Union, like most Euro Atlantic governments, saw Russia through a particular prism and language. Russi after the Cold War was supposed to transition to a normal state which would shar the values of the Euro-Atlantic Community, whose very institutions accepted limits on national sovereignty to achieve larger community on these shared value of democracy, civil society, and market economies facilitating global trade. Thi vision was articulated by Francis Fukuyama:

> I believe that the European Union more accurately reflects what the worl
> will look like at the end of history than the contemporary United States

The EU's attempt to transcend sovereignty and traditional power politics by establishing a transnational rule of law is much more in line with a 'post-historical' world than the Americans' continuing belief in God, national sovereignty, and their military.

(Fukiyama 2007)

Writing one year before the onset of the Great Recession, he had caught the European Union at the moment when it seemed to be the viable alternative to a militarized United States and emerging authoritarian forms of capitalism. Europe was increasingly demilitarized and it seemed to have far better relations with Russia than the United States. Both Presidents Medvedev and Putin also emphasized bilateral relations with key EU members accepting the mutual dependence that came from energy exports. Bringing Russia out of a decade of economic crisis (1989–1999), Putin emphasized integration into global energy markets as the key path to the economic and political recovery of Russia (Goldman 2008).

After 2008 and the onset of the Great Recession, the Russian elite was not so sure that this vision fit Russia's future. From his third election as president Vladimir Putin had emphasized that Russia's peace and stability depended upon a strong centralized state to "manage democracy". Russia could aspire to a place in the global economy, but that place would be defined by her national interests rather than shared values. After 2008, Russian commentators spoke of the "renationalization" of world politics. Sergei Karaganov called this a positive development because it fit the Russian approach to international relations, based as it was upon "balance of power diplomacy with their modernist amendments", by which Karaganov was referring to strategic stability based upon nuclear deterrence. The European Union, especially its strongest members, France and Germany, had a bad case of following Brussels's bureaucrats when they should have been leading. The continuing deep economic crisis within the EU was creating a deeper instability. "A situation is developing where the island of stability, Europe, is almost becoming a factor of unpredictability" (Karaganov 2011).

Putin has tended to emphasize bilateral relations with European states and played down ties to Brussels. In the period just prior to the February Revolution, Moscow had good evidence from leaked telephone conversations between US Assistant Secretary of State for the European and Eurasian Affairs, Victoria Nuland, and the US Ambassador to Ukraine, Geoffrey Pyatt, in which Nuland expressed her frustration with getting the EU on board with a US solution to the crisis in Ukraine (Taylor and Tharoor 2014). Nuland anticipated that Putin would respond by seeking to undermine support among various European governments to the American initiative. Events in Ukraine did underscore the wisdom of that appreciation of Moscow's policy. The High Representative of the Union for Foreign Affairs and Security Policy, Baroness Katherine Ashton, had a prominent role in the events leading up to the Maidan Revolution, and since then has been a steady voice in support of the Maidan government (Truth-Out 2014). On her visit to Kyiv after the revolution Ashton gave every indication of the European Union's support for the new government as well as the state's territorial integrity and national sovereignty, and promised to work toward long-term solutions to Ukraine's problems (Liga Novosti 2014). On 27 March 2014, she gave the keynote address at the European Defence Agency's Annual Conference, in which she emphasized Europe's commitment to support the new government in Ukraine and stressed the importance of European defence cooperation in the light of new threats and budget constraints. But the pledges did not translate into actual military assistance to Ukraine by the members of the European Union.

In early March Pro-Russian protestors had risen and seized administrative buildings in Luhansk and Donetsk regions of east Ukraine. Support from Russia was widely debated in the press with much talk about "little green men" who were not so polite as those in Crimea had been. There were, however, locals who made up most of the protesters. Kyiv dismissed these locals as Ukrainophobic parasites, drunks, and drug addicts (Kyiv Post 2014a). The Ukrainian government in early April declared that it would launch an anti-terrorist operation (ATO) against the Pro-Russian forces. The EU responded by joining the United States and Canada in a very narrow set of sanctions, suspending talks on military matters, space investment, and visa requirements and imposing restrictions on travel to prevent Russian and Crimean officials and politicians travelling to Canada, the United States, and the European Union (European Union 2014a). The United States and the European Union coordinated the imposition of a second round of sanctions against individuals and companies on 28 April. The EU explained that its sanctions were not punitive but designed to bring about a change in Russian policy and to ensure the territorial integrity of Ukraine and stated that it would make every effort to reduce the sanctions' impact on the civilian population. In May after plebiscites the separatist oblasts declared their independence as the Lugansk People's Republic and Donetsk People's Republic. They were not, however, recognized as independent states by Russia.

At this juncture, the Western media and political leaders needed a term to describe what they thought had happened in Crimea and was happening in eastern Ukraine. The answer was, "hybrid warfare". Writing on hybrid warfare Nadia Schadlow assumed Russia had just such a capability. As Sherr observed "in the hands of Russia hybrid warfare could 'cripple a state before that state even realizes the conflict had begun,' and yet it manages to 'slip under NATO' threshold of perception and reaction" (Schadlow 2015).[7] Western observers have fallen into a familiar parlance for describing Russia's annexation of Crimea an subsequent invasion of eastern Ukraine. Frequently termed Russia's "hybrid war" against Ukraine, it is seen by the West as a threatening precedent – even likely model – for future conflicts on Russia's periphery (Kofman and Rojansk 2015). Both NATO and the EU continued their vocal support for Kyiv's ATO as means to restore Ukraine's territorial integrity and worried about further Russian military intervention. As the ATO progressed in its advance into eastern Ukraine Russian covert military assistance increased in quality and quantity. The ATO began to make use of air power to attack the separatists, and Moscow answered by providing manpads and then more robust air defence systems, while at the same time denying any involvement. Dmitri Trenin frankly described Russia policy there as supporting the separatists while seeking to maintain "plausible deniability" and trying to create and enlarge the gap between the US sanction policy and that of the EU. Judging by the response in the Western media, Trenin believed that Putin's policy now faced serious risks of failure (Trenin 2014). His policies were now being held responsible for the loss of life in eastern Ukraine. As Michael Ignatieff wrote:

> It no longer matters whether the charge against President Putin is direct incitement of those who shot down the plane or reckless endangerment by supplying them with weaponry. By reaffirming his support for secession, he has made his choices, and it is up to Western leaders to make theirs. What matters now is to be very clear, so that political responsibility is fixed where it belongs, so that actions have consequences, so that security guarantees are given to the vulnerable allies on Russia's borders and that these guarantees are believed.
>
> (Ignatieff 2014: 30)

Between 25 and 30 July the EU extended its second round of sanctions against Russia to additional individuals and enterprises. On 31 July the EU announced a new round of sanctions against Russia's financial sector, energy sector, defence industries, and additional individuals and entities (European Union 2014b). Over the following months other governments approved sanctions against Russia. At the same time, the focus of analysis of the crisis began to narrow to Putin and Putinism. Strobe Talbott III argued that the threat of Putinism had been there from the day of his rise to power in 2000. Talbott, a well-recognized expert on Russia and the Soviet Union and former Deputy Secretary of State, identified Putinism with those who sought to preserve and later to restore the Soviet Union by any means available (Talbott 2014). The success of Putinism will depend a great deal on the success of Putin and Russia under him. If he triumphs in Ukraine, turning it into a basket case that eventually comes begging to Moscow, he will look like a winner. If, on the other hand, Ukraine succeeds outside of Russia's orbit and the Russian economy continues to weaken, Putin might find himself presiding over a globally isolated Siberian petro-state (Talbott 2014).

Putin's continued silence about the heavy involvement of Russian regular forces in the counter-offensive to ATO might have strengthened his hand in eastern Ukraine and even Kyiv, even as it increased the level of distrust between Western leaders and Putin. However, there was a real sense of doubt among those leaders as to what to do under the new circumstances. The unexpected defeat of the ATO's forces encircled at Ivolaisk in late August was complete and created a crisis in the military leadership and in the government in Kyiv. On 26 August, 2014 Baroness Ashton joined Karel De Gucht, EU Commissioner for Trade, and Günther Hermann Oettinger, EU Commissioner for Energy, to attend the talks in Minsk where President Aleksandr Lukashenko of Belarus, President Nursultan Nazarbaev of Kazakhstan, and President Vladimir Putin met with President Petro Poroshenko of Ukraine. The bilateral meeting between Putin and Poroshenko was a first step toward some kind of negotiations to try to end the fighting in the east. At the same time, Dmitri Peskov, Putin's Press Secretary, mentioned Ukraine's Association Agreement with the EU as an important topic for bilateral conversations (RT 2014).

The subsequent EU Summit in Brussels and the NATO summit in Wales both addressed the crisis in Ukraine but did not fundamentally change policy. In appointing new leadership for the EU there seemed to be a desire to balance western and eastern European views of the crisis. Donald Tusk, the Prime Minister of Poland, was named the new EU President and Federica Mogherini, the Italian Foreign Minister, was appointed High Representative of the Union for Foreign Affairs and Security Policy, replacing Ashton (BBC 2014a). Tusk brings to his new post all the concerns of NATO's eastern members about Russia's efforts to intimidate the Ukraine by economic, political, and military means. Mogherini immediately took the opportunity to make NATO the chief provider of security in eastern Europe by emphasizing the need for the alliance to guarantee that Article Five is worth more than the paper it is written upon. She also stated that the EU would shortly address further sanctions against Russia (BBC 2014b). To date, the EU sanction regime remains intact. NATO has proven more adept at re-assuring its new Baltic members that Article V still does exist and applies to them.

In the meantime, Putin responded to the EU and NATO summits by presenting a seven-point peace plan to end the conflict in eastern Ukraine, which involved an agreement between Kyiv and the separatists with a ceasefire monitored by the OSCE. Unveiling the plan in Mongolia during a state visit, Putin asserted: "I believe that a final agreement between the authorities of Kiev and southeastern Ukraine can be reached and cemented during a meeting of the Contact Group on September 5" (Jones and Soldatkin 2014). Western leaders were sceptical about the proposal and saw it as an attempt to influence the EU and NATO Summits. However, the real impact came from Ukraine's agreement on a ceasefire with the separatists (Walker 2014). The EU did approve another round of sanctions against Russia but then decided to delay their introduction to see if the cease-fire would hold (Smith 2014). Since then, the ceasefire has held but with major outbreaks of artillery fire and combat in various eastern regions. On 16 September 2014, President Poroshenko signed the Ukraine–EU Association Agreement into law (Kyiv Post 2014b). However, a last minute agreement between the Ukraine and the EU had a key measure in the agreement – implementation of part of the free trade agreement – delayed from taking effect for over a year in order to assuage Russian concerns. As a result of that delay Deputy Foreign Minister of Ukraine Danilo Lubkivsky, handed in his resignation (Focus News Agency 2014). Steve Pifer commented in his trip report from a visit to Kyiv in mid-September that while the Association Agreement was very popular in Kyiv, the delay had caught everyone by surprise. He also noted that NATO had gained in popularity in Kyiv and was considered in case of a Russian invasion the only means to defend Ukraine. Prime Minister Arseniy Yatsenyuk stated that NATO was not, however, ready to accept Ukraine within the alliance (Pifer 2014).

Minsk I did not lead to an end to fighting in Lugansk and Donetsk. Ukrainians took renewed confidence in the stubborn defence of Donetsk airport. Fighting continued into February 2015. At this juncture the Normandy Quartet, composed of Germany, France, Ukraine, and Russia, agreed to a second round of negotiations in Minsk with the goal of de-escalating the fighting in eastern Ukraine. Russia assumed the role of representing the interests of its allies, the separatist forces of the Lugansk People's Republic, and the Donetsk People's Republic. On 12 February the leaders of the two republics, Aleksandr Zakharchenko and Igor Plotnitskii, arrived in Minsk. On that day the Quartet signed a 13-point agreement intended to bring about a de-escalation of the fighting, create a buffer zone between the opposing forces, and to re-deploy a heavy weapons system to ensure that the combatants would not be able to quickly mount large-scale combat operations. The OSCE forces already deployed were expected to monitor the execution of the agreement by the two sides (BBC 2015).

In reaction to the Ukrainian crisis, while there has been a clear set of actions to strengthen the defences of NATO's Baltic members, little has been done to aid Ukraine in its defence. There are those in Washington who see the lack of action by the Obama administration as evidence of a lack of support for Ukraine and see such inaction as a death sentence for the Euromaidan Revolution (Diehl 2015). But the fear of the Russian general offensive may be a deep misreading of Russian policy where the objective is to undermine the legitimacy of the Euromaidan state and count upon economic and social pressures to weaken the government to the point where its successor will see a Eurasian future as a brighter prospect than a European Union in crisis and a NATO bent on keeping Ukraine at arm's length.

Conclusion: is the Ukrainian crisis a European or a Eurasian question?

The European Union had a major, although hardly sole, role in unleashing the current crisis in Ukraine. Its association agreement served to motivate the crowds in Maidan and moved the opposition politicians to support the overthrow of the elected president of Ukraine. The EU, however, did not have any effective instruments to counter Russia's occupation and then annexation of Crimea or to end the separatists fighting in the east or to block Russian military support. Both the EU and NATO have stressed the role of sanctions in isolating Russia, but that vision depends on seeing the crisis as a strictly European one and assumes the ability of the EU and NATO to organize a unified European bloc.

Putin's answer to this view of the crisis is to suggest that it is a Eurasian one. On 12 September 2014 Putin flew into Dushanbe, Tajikistan, for bilateral conversations with Xi Jinping before the opening of the Shanghai Cooperation Organization (SCO) Summit there. In the bilateral Sino-Russian talks Putin stated that Russia "attaches importance to and appreciates China's stances and proposals on the Ukraine issue" and that he values the exchanges of opinion with China on the situation in Ukraine. Xi Jinping, for his part meanwhile, affirmed China's call for a political solution, calling for Ukraine "to launch inclusive dialogues at an early date" (Tiezzi 2014). At the summit itself Russia and China agreed to support the expansion of the SCO to include other Eurasian states (Weitz 2014). Richard Weitz saw several factors driving this increased level of cooperation: the instability associated with the Arab Spring, the NATO draw-down in Afghanistan, the crisis in Ukraine, and China's increasing threat from indigenous terrorism in China. One could add Chinese concerns over tensions in the South China Sea, where the United States and its allies are seen as hostile to the PRC's territorial claims.

NATO's response at its summit in Wales seemed to confirm Putin's understanding of the crisis. NATO spoke of support for Ukraine but put its major efforts into creating a 4,000-person Rapid Reaction Force to protect its Baltic members from the Russian Threat (MacAskill 2014). The European world may be the land of Venus, but Eurasia remains the land of Mars. According to the former Ukrainian Minister of Defence, General Valery Heletej, the NATO summit had led to some states agreeing to transfer combat arms to Ukraine, but the states were not named. However, defence officials in Italy, Poland, and Norway denied that they had any plans to transfer any weapons to Ukraine (BBC 2014c). Ten months after the NATO Summit in Wales, military assistance to Ukraine from NATO members has been minimal. The US Congress did vote funding for "lethal defence weapon systems", though little has arrived. Other NATO members offered token military aid.

Russian's relations with the European Union have been badly damaged. The supposed leverage, which Gazprom was to provide Moscow in its dealings with western Europe, are gone with the sanctions and declining energy prices. Russia has re-directed its energy "soft power" towards Eurasia and its strategic partner, the People's Republic of China. The expansion of the EU is not so obviously a good after 2008, while Europe's inability to respond decisively to both domestic and non-domestic crises has been vividly displayed in the last eight years. Having thoughtlessly alienated Russia, the EU now finds itself incapable of responding effectively to Russia's annexation of the Crimea or its support of Ukrainian separatists. Having played the sanction card to little effect, Europe has run out of options for influencing events in the Ukraine. Europe's internal problems have contributed to its weakness, but the larger issue is the identity of Europe itself. Where does Europe end and Asia begin? Does Europe really want Russia to be a non-European country? Because the 2008 crisis has so severely divided Europe, the EU appears incapable of answering with a single voice these pressing questions about its relations to Russia.

Notes

1 Regarding the emergence of this pattern see Kipp and Connor (1994).
2 See Brzezinski (2014). Brzezinski continues to see "Finlandization" as a possible solution to the Ukrainian crisis. In this regard, he is proposing to provide Ukraine with defensive weapons to protect its cities and to reach an accommodation where Ukraine would be sovereign but neutral: "Ukraine should have the right to freely choose their political identity and more contact with Europe. At the same time it is necessary to

assure Russia that Ukraine will not be accepted into NATO. This is the formula of the solution (to the conflict)." See UNIAN (2015).

Western analysts for a long time have criticized the Soviet and now Russian tendency to over-develop marginal territories with limited carrying capacity. This was particularly true of the USSR's far north in connection with extractive industries and defence complexes (see Kipp 1999). On Putin's current plans for Eastern Siberia and the Russian Far East see Gaddy (2013).

For the evidence of shots being fired from the Dnepro Hotel see the April 10th broadcast of German television's ARD's Monitor programme, which provided an in-depth report on its own investigation into the shootings in Kyiv on February 20. Video report, beginning at 10:50: www.wdr.de/tv/monitor//sendungen/2014/0410/maidan. php5 (accessed 12 April 2014).

The Common Spaces were intended to intensify cooperation between the EU and Russia and include: the Common Economic Space, the Common Space for Freedom, Security and Justice, the Common Space of External Security, and the Common Space of Research and Education, including cultural issues. See www.eeas.europa.eu/russia/common_spaces.

The road maps are available at www.eeas.europa.eu/russia/docs/roadmap_economic_en.pdf.

On Sherr's ideas on the Russian application of hard and soft power see Sherr (2013: 117–129). He argued that Putin's system was self-defeating because it tends to isolate Russia; Sherr reflects a Euro-Atlantic bias in its assessment.

References

BBC. 2014a. "Italy's Mogherini and Poland's Tusk Get Top EU Jobs." 3 September. Available at www.bbc.com/news/world-europe-28989875 (accessed 4 September 2014).

BBC. 2014b. "EU's Mogherini Calls for NATO Muscle in Eastern Europe." 2 September. Available at www.bbc.com/news/world-europe-29030736 (accessed 4 September 2014).

BBC. 2014c. "NATO Members Start Arms Deliveries to Ukraine." 14 September. Available at www.bbc.com/news/world-europe-29198497 (accessed 14 September 2014).

BBC. 2015. "Ukraine Ceasefire: New Minsk Agreement Key Points." 12 February. Available at www.bbc.com/news/world-europe-31436513 (accessed 13 February 2015).

Brzezinski, Z. 2014. "Russia Needs a Finland Option for Ukraine." *Financial Times* (23 February). Available at www.ft.com/intl/cms/s/0/7f722496-9c86-11e3-b535-00144feab7de.html#axzz3Bol4y9KF (accessed 26 February 2014).

Conroy, C. 2014. "China's Nuclear Parasol." *The Diplomat* (26 January 2014). Available at http://thediplomat.com/2014/01/chinas-nuclear-parasol (accessed 5 February 2014).

Diehl, J. 2015. "Will We Let Ukraine Die?" *The Washington Post* (5 July). https://www.washingtonpost.com/opinions/the-dangerous-neglect-of-ukraine/2015/07/05/37d08050-20cf-11e5-84d5-eb37ee8eaa61_story.html (accessed 15 July 2015)

EEAS. Undated. "EU–Ukraine Association Agreement – The Complete Texts." Available at http://eeas.europa.eu/ukraine/assoagreement/assoagreement-2013_en.htm (accessed 10 May 2014).

European Union. 2014a. "Concerning Restrictive Measures in Respect of Actions Undermining or Threatening the Territorial Integrity, Sovereignty, and Independence of Ukraine." Council Decision 2014/145/CFSP of 17 March. Available at http://eur-lex.europa.eu/LexUriServ/LexUriServ.do?uri=OJ:L:2014:078:0016:0021:EN:PDF (accessed 10 August 2014).

European Union. 2014b. "Concerning Restrictive Measures in View of Russia's Actions Destabilizing the Situation in Ukraine." Council Regulation (EU) 833/2014 of 31 July. Available at http://eur-lex.europa.eu/legal-content/EN/TXT/?uri=uriserv:OJ .L_.2014.229.01.0001.01.ENG.

Evropaiskaia pravda. 2013. "Kitai poobeshchal Yanukovichu iadernuiu zashchitu Ukrainy-СМИ." *Evropaiskaia pravda* (13 December). Available at www.pravda.com.ua/rus/ news/2013/12/13/7006647 (accessed 10 May 2014).

Focus News Agency. 2014. "Ukraine Deputy Foreign Minister Resigns." Focus News Agency (13 September). Available at www.focus-fen.net/news/2014/09/13/348433/ ukraine-deputy-foreign-minister-resigns.html (accessed on 17 September 2014).

Fukiyama, F. 2007. "The History at the End of History." *The Guardian* (3 April). Available at www.theguardian.com/commentisfree/2007/apr/03/thehistoryattheendofhis (accessed 10 August 2014).

Gaddy, C. G. 2013. "Russia's Development of Siberia: What is to be Done?" June. Available at www.theasanforum.org/russo-chinese-relations-in-strategic-perspective (accessed 10 August 2014).

Goldman, M. I. 2008. *Petrostate: Putin, Power and the New Russia*. Oxford: Oxford University Press.

Ignatieff, M. 2014. "The New World Disorder." *The New York Review of Books* 61(14) (25 September). Available at www.nybooks.com/articles/2014/09/25/new-world-disorder.

Johnson's Russia List. 2014. "Re: Pictures of the Odessa Massacre." 27 August. Available at http://ersieesist.livejournal.com/813.htm (accessed 27 August 2014).

Jones, G. and V. Soldatkin 2014. "Putin Unveils Ukraine Ceasefire Plan, France Halt Warship." 3 September. Available at www.reuters.com/article/2014/09/03/us-ukraine-crisis-idUSKBN0GX21720140903.

Karaganov, S. 2011. "The World in More Chaos." *Rossiiskaya Gazeta* (2 September) http://eng.globalaffairs.ru/pubcol/A-revolutionary-chaos-of-the-new-world-1541 (accessed 20 September 2015).

Kipp, J. W. 1999. "Russia's Northwest Strategic Direction." *Military Review* 4 (July August): 52–65.

Kipp, J. W. and W. M. Connor. 1994. *The Ukrainian and Belarusian Presidential Elections Assessment and Implications*. August. Fort Leavenworth, KS: The Foreign Military Studies Office.

Kofman, M. and M. Rojansky 2015. "A Closer Look at Russia's 'Hybrid War'. *Kennan Cable* 7(l) (April). Available at www.wilsoncenter.org/sites/default/files/ KENNAN%20CABLE-ROJANSKY%20KOFMAN.pdf.

Komsomol'skaia pravda. 2013. "Putin i Yanukovich dogovorilis' o snizhenii tseny na gaz *Komsomol'skaia pravda* (17 December). Available at www.kp.ru/daily/26172/306191

Kyiv Post. 2014a. "Dmitry Tymchuk's Military Blog: Rebels No Longer Hide The Russian Citizenship." *Kyiv Post* (13 August). Available at www.kyivpost.com opinion/op-ed/dmitry-tymchuks-military-blog-rebels-no-longer-hide-their-russia citizenship-360386.html (accessed 20 August 2014).

Kyiv Post. 2014b. "Poroshenko Signs Law Ratifying EU–Ukraine Association Agreement *Kyiv Post* (16 September). Available at www.kyivpost.com/content/ukrain poroshenko-signs-law-ratifying-eu-ukraine-association-agreement-in-parliamen session-hall-364820.html (accessed 17 September 2014).

LB.Ua. 2013. "Yanukovich popisal v Kitae dogovory na $8 mlrd." *LB.Ua* (5 December). Available at http://economics.lb.ua/state/2013/12/05/244512_yanukovich_podpisal_kitae_dogovori.html (accessed 10 May 2014).

Lieven, A. 1999. *Ukraine and Russia: A Fraternal Rivalry*. Washington, DC: USIP Books.

Liga Novosti. 2014. "Verkhovnyi predstavitel' ES Ketrin Ashton segodnia priedet v Kiev." *Liga Novosti* (24 February). Available at http://news.liga.net/news/politics/987932-verkhovnyy_predstavitel_es_ketrin_eshton_segodnya_priedet_v_kiev.htm (accessed 20 August 2014).

MacAskill, E. 2014. "NATO to Announce 4,000-Strong Rapid Reaction Force to Counter Russian threat." *The Guardian* (5 September). Available at www.theguardian.com/world/2014/sep/05/nato-4000-rapid-reaction-force-baltics-russia (accessed 7 September 2014).

Ministry of Foreign Affairs. 2014. "On the Telephone Conversation between Foreign Minister Paet and EU High Representative for Foreign Affairs Catherine Ashton." 6 March. Available at www.vm.ee/?q=en/node/19353 (accessed 6 March 2014).

Pifer, S. 2014. "Trip Report: Mid-September Impressions from Kyiv." Brookings Foreign Policy Trip Report no. 60 (15 September). Available at www.brookings.edu/blogs/up-front/posts/2014/09/15-trip-report-impression-kyiv-Pifer?utm_campaign=Brookings+Brief&utm_source=hs_email&utm_medium=email&utm_content=14152523&_hsenc=p2ANqtz-4h4WumhET5_4yq9aaVyLReZbqgq2gd3CdLJD9jWAHCyxDwT5ufU6juhZ4_AjEwtgVO7GHLt25_irey2OziT2mxPlAQg&_hsmi=14152523 (accessed 1 October 2015).

RT. 2013. "Putin: EU Blackmailing Ukraine Over Halt in Trade Deal." *RT* (22 November). Available at http://rt.com/news/putin-eu-ukraine-blackmail-151 (accessed 20 May 2014).

RT. 2014. "Russian and Ukrainian Leaders Meet for Face-to-Face Talks in Belarus – Kremlin." *RT* (25 August). Available at http://rt.com/news/182892-ukraine-russia-peace-plan (accessed 27 August 2014).

Schadlow, N. 2015. "The Problem with Hybrid Warfare." *War on the Rocks* (2 April). Available at http://warontherocks.com/2015/04/the-problem-with-hybrid-warfare (accessed 5 April 2015).

Sherr, J. 2013. *Hard Diplomacy and Soft Power: Russia's Influence Abroad*. London: Chatham House.

Smith, G. 2014. "EU Delays New Sanctions against Russia, Eyeing Shaky Ceasefire." *Fortune* (9 September). Available at http://fortune.com/2014/09/09/e-u-delays-new-sanctions-against-russia-eyeing-shaky-ceasefire (accessed 10 September 2014).

Talbott, S. 2014. "The Making of Vladimir Putin." *Politico Magazine* (19 August). Available at www.politico.com/magazine/story/2014/08/putin-the-backstory-110151.html#.VBmz1PldXw0 (accessed 20 August 2014).

Taylor, A. and I. Tharoor. 2014. "The Crisis in Ukraine, as Told by Leaked Phone Calls." *Washington Post* (3 September). Available at www.washingtonpost.com/blogs/worldviews/wp/2014/09/03/the-crisis-in-ukraine-as-told-by-leaked-phone-calls (accessed 5 September 2014).

Tiezzi, S. 2014. "Xi Jinping, Vladimir Putin Meet Ahead of SCO Summit." *The Diplomat* (12 September). Available at http://thediplomat.com/2014/09/xi-jinping-vladimir-putin-meet-ahead-of-sco-summit (accessed 13 September 2014).

Trenin, D. 2014. "Will MH17 Air Crash Damage Russia's Putin?" 22 July. Available at www.bbc.com/news/world-europe-28421196.

Truth-Out. 2014. "A Coup or a Revolution? Ukraine Seeks Arrest of Ousted President Following Deadly Street Protests." 24 February. Available at http://truth-out.org/news/item/22082-a-coup-or-a-revolution-ukraine-seeks-arrest-of-ousted-president-following-deadly-street-protests

UNIAN. 2015. "Bzhezinskii predlagaet razreshit' Ukrainskii krizis po obraztsu Finliandii." 30 June. www.unian.net/politics/1095001-bjezinskiy-predlagaet-razreshit-ukrainskiy-krizis-po-obraztsu-finlyandii.html (accessed 1 July 2015).

Walker, S. 2014. "Ukraine Ceasefire Holds So Far as Poroshenko Orders Halt at Dusk." *The Guardian* (5 September). Available at www.theguardian.com/world/2014/sep/05/ukraine-ceasefire-holds-but-leaders-sceptical.

Weitz, R. 2014. "Responding to Crises, SCO Finally Embraces Expansion." *World Politics Review* (16 September). Available at www.worldpoliticsreview.com/articles/14065/responding-to-crises-sco-finally-embraces-expansion (accessed 17 September 2014).

World Bank. Undated. "GDP Per Capita (Current US$)." Available at http://data.worldbank.org/indicator/NY.GDP.PCAP.CD (accessed 20 April 2015).

Index

For Product Safety Concerns and Information please contact our EU
representative GPSR@taylorandfrancis.com
Taylor & Francis Verlag GmbH, Kaufingerstraße 24, 80331 München, Germany

www.ingramcontent.com/pod-product-compliance
Ingram Content Group UK Ltd.
Pitfield, Milton Keynes, MK11 3LW, UK
UKHW021012180425
457613UK00020B/905